slow wine

A YEAR IN THE LIFE
OF ITALY'S VINEYARDS
AND WINES

Slow Food® Editore

slow wine 2014

A YEAR IN THE LIFE OF ITALY'S VINEYARDS AND WINES

Editors: Giancarlo Gariglio, Fabio Giavedoni

Deputy editors: Paolo Camozzi, Jonathan Gebser, Davide Panzieri, Fabio Pracchia

Editorial assistants: Eliana Bruno, Elisabeth Sievers

Chief contributors: Francesco Abate, Davide Acerra, Richard Baudains, Alessia Benini, Francesca Bidasio degli Imberti, Gian Paolo Ciancabilla, Savio Del Bianco, Alessandra Etzo, Andrea Fontana, Stefano Ferrari, Fausto Ferroni, Vito Lacerenza, Maria Grazia Melegari, Francesco Muci, Luciano Pignataro, Francesco Quercetti, Diego Soracco, Fabio Turchetti, Simone Zoli

Contributors: Marina Alaimo, Andrea Aldrighetti, Alberto Alfano, Francesco Anastasi, Adriano Anglani, Duccio Armenio, Tommaso Aronov, Stefano Asaro, Artemio Assiri, Cecilia Auxilia, Bruno Bacci, Emidio Bachetti, Antonio Balassone, Alessandro Barletta, Gabriele Bartalena, Salvatore Basta, Paolo Battimelli, Claudia Beccato, Marco Bechi, Annarita Beltrame, Nino Bentivegna, Anna Berghella, Lorenzo Berlendis, Margherita Bisoglio, Carla Bocchio, Federica Bolla, Ivan Bon, Giulia Bonetti, Francesco Bonini, Simona Bonsignore, Valerio Borgianelli Spina, Paolo Bortolazzi, Nicola Bove, Marco Braganti, Filippo Bregonzio, Massimo Brucato, Ilaria Bruzzesi, Sara Cabrele, Marco Cagnetta, Marco Callegari, Tommaso Calosci, Mara Campo, Alberto Capasso, Giorgio Cariaggi, Luca Carletto, Giulio Carli, Pasquale Carlo, Sara Carnati, Nadia Castellaccio, Carlo Catani, Alessandro Cesca, Felix Chamorro, Roberto Checchetto, Valter Chiabolotti, Marco Cipolla, Carlo Cleri, Maria Cobo, Pierluigi Cocchini, Enzo Codogno, Filippo Colombo, Lorenzo Colombo, Francesco Costa, Corinne Cremonini, Giovanni Cucchiara, Barbara D'Agapiti, Mario D'Alesio, Silvana Dal Maso, Silvia Dal Molin, Marco Dell'Era, Annamaria D'Eusanio, Marcella De Vita, Emanuele De Vittoris, Massimo Di Cintio, Gianni Di Mattia, Serena Di Nucci, Giulio Di Sabato, Livio Di Sante, Anete Dinne, Sonia Donati, Florian Ehn, Peter Engelmayer, Alberto Farinasso, Luigi Fenoglio, Lapo Ferrini, Piero Fiorentini, Alessandro Foggi, Mario Freda, Fabio Fusina, Andrea Gaggero, Sonia Gambino, Valerie Ganio Vecchiolino, Pietro Garibbo, Roberto Gazzola, Francesco Ghiglione, Mariasole Giannelli, Federico Giovannone, Francesca Gori, Danilo Gramegna, Davide Grimaldi, Ivana Guantiero, Mauro Guastapaglia, Matteo Guidorizzi, Shota Hayashi, Susan Hedblad, Karin Huber, Sandra Ianni, Marcello Ingrassia, Francesco Paolo Lauriola, Gianpiero Laviano, Cristiana Locci, Silvio Magni, Carmelo Maiorca, Alessandro Manna, Michele Marangio, Sara Marte, Franco Martino, Mino Martucci, Mirco Masera, Daniele Massa, Patrizio Mastrocola, Giulia Mattalia, Silvano Mattedi, Lorenzo Marziali, Pierluca Masciocchi Monica Mastino, Giacomo Mazzavillani, Tommaso Mazzocca, Paolo Mazzola, Marco Meistro, Lanfranco Meritotti, Teresa Mincione, Andrea Montanaro, Franco Motta, Gaia Muci, Pierfrancesco Multari, Nicola Nebbia, Giovanni Norese, Gabriel Olivieri, Carmen Ordiz, Elisa Padoin, Edoardo Paggi, Paolo Palazzini, Maria

Josè Parra, Daniele Parri, Elena Pasero, Carlotta Passuello, Giovanni Pastorino, Marco Peluso, Gianluca Pepe, Anna Perini, Peppino Placentino, Giorgio Picco, Adriana Pieroni, David Pieroni, Myriam Pinkas, Monica Piscitelli, Alessandra Piubello, Giuseppe Pollio, Antonio Previdi, Salvatore Pulimeno, Enrico Radicchi, Giancarlo Rafele, Lara Rocchietti, Giancarlo Rolandi, Claudio Romano, Stefano Ronconi, Adriano Rossi, Francesco Rossi, Andrea Russo, Giancarlo Russo, Susan Russo, Anna Sacchetto, Alice Saglia, Luisa Sala, Alessandra Saponara, Flora Saponari, Fabrizio Scarpato, Maria Teresa Scarpato, Marco Schiavello, Isabelle Schoebi, Gregorio Sergi, Eugenio Signoroni, Maurizio Silvestri, Benedetto Squicciarini, Maurizio Stagnitto, Enrico Tacchi, Riccardo Taliano, Giada Talpo, Salvatore Taronno, Camilla Tomao, Stefano Tonanni, Franco Utili, Maurizio Valeriani, Andrea Vannelli, Federico Varazi, Valentina Vercelli, Laura Vescul, Riccardo Vendrame, Irene Vianello, Alessandra Virno, Massimo Volpari, Andrea Zucchetti, Chiara Zucchetti

Italian editing: Tiziano Gaia, Bianca Minerdo

Adaptations: John Irving

Art director: Fabio Cremonesi

Information systems, automation and graphics: Maurizio Burdese

Maps: Touring Editore

Printed November 2013
by Stamperia Artistica Nazionale spa Trofarello (Turin) ITALY

Slow Food® Editore srl
Via della Mendicità Istruita, 45 - 12042 Bra (Cn)
Tel. 0172 419611 - Fax 0172 411218

Website: www.slowine.it - www.slowfood.it

Editor in chief: Marco Bolasco

Managing editor: Olivia Reviglio

ISBN 978-888499-347-2

Contents

Introduction

"The Great Beauty" — the title of the recent Paolo Sorrentino movie aptly describes our work over the last year, spent on the spectacular set of the vineyards and wine-growing districts of Italy, a set on which the cameras never stop rolling. Yes, Great Beauty: there's a reason why Dante described Italy as "*il Bel Paese*", the Beautiful Country, and it's a reason — a value, a sentiment — that we need to recover and establish as the point of departure for a new and necessary Renaissance. Travel down any of the many roads that skirt the vine rows of Italy and you'll understand our words and the hopes they enfold. It's often said that winemakers are the stewards of the landscape, one of our main attractions for tourists, foreign investors and young people in pursuit of a possible future. With our labels set to conquer overseas markets, the time has come for the Italian wine industry to play its trump card, as this new edition of the guide feels obliged to point out.

No other country can boast such a high average standard of winemaking. True, France, our main competitor on every market on the planet, has high, some might say unscalable peaks of quality, but also prices to match, prices unaffordable for the majority, more consonant with luxury goods than with wine as we understand it — and consume it. Our tastings draw a picture of a wine industry that's never been so healthy and our most prestigious denominations have shoulders broad enough to take on the most celebrated wines of other producer nations in an even contest. Despite the warm 2009, Barolo deserves a round of applause and, after recovering from the salutary shock of the scandal that hit the DOCG a few years ago, Brunello is back on top form too. As are Barbaresco, simply perfect in 2010, and Chianti Classico, a goldmine of fantastic wines. Arguably the best reason for celebrating lies elsewhere, away from the two giants, Piedmont and Tuscany. For today there are a myriad of different terroirs with as many native grape varieties. A few concrete examples? Well, the Southern Italian regions are no longer the Cinderellas of our wine industry and Alto Adige, Friuli, Marche and Campania, where Fiano is projected towards the wine stratosphere, are producing great cellarable whites all the time. And what about the great reds of Veneto and Central Italy? With so many strings in our bow, we have the wherewithal to conquer important markets like America and the rest of Europe, and emerging ones too. Provided, that is, we raise the profile of our quality intelligently and tell the world about our excellence with one voice.

Now in its fourth edition (four years, the minimum age for a red wine to be called "*grande*", great!), *Slow Wine* now has a precise identity of its own based on the Slow Food philosophy of "good, clean and fair". Its modern definition of quality no longer considers only organoleptic pleasure but observes Italian winemaking through a different lens, taking note of values such as eco-sustainability, the extent to which winemakers are *en rapport* with their land and, of course, beauty. Great Beauty — enjoy the movie.

Giancarlo Gariglio and Fabio Giavedoni

How to read the guide

Winery:

⊚⋎ snail
symbol awarded to a winery that we particularly like for the way
it interprets Slow Food values (sensory perceptions, territory,
environment, identity) and also offers good value for money.

▐ bottle
symbol awarded to wineries whose bottles presented excellent
average quality at our tastings.

€ coin
symbol awarded to wineries whose bottles are good value for
money.

Wines:

slow wine SLOW WINE
bottles of outstanding sensory quality, capable of condensing in the
glass territory-related values such as history and identity, as well as
offering good value for money.

Great Wine
the finest bottles from the sensory point of view.

Everyday Wine
bottles that offer excellent value for money with a retail price of
€10 or under.

Welcome:

🍲 pot
A cellar which, either on the premises or in the immediate vicinity,
offers food and refreshments.

🔑 key
A cellar which, either on the premises or in the immediate vicinity,
offers hospitality.

Promotion:

10% discount
this symbol denotes wineries that offer a 10% discount on purchases
to customers who present a copy of *Slow Wine* 2014. The promotion
is valid for one year from January 2014 to January 2015.

ha
hectares of land, owned or leased, managed and cultivated directly by the winery.

bt
total number of bottles produced by the winery.

○ white wine

◉ rosé wine

● red wine

General abbreviations:
Cl. ....Classico (Classic)
Et. ....Etichetta (Label)
M. ....Method
        (e.g., M. Cl. = Metodo Classico/Classic Method)
P.R. ....Peduncolo Rosso (Red Bunchstem)
Rip. ....Ripasso
Ris. ....Riserva (Reserve)
Sel. ....Selezione (Selection)
Sup. ......Superiore (Superior)
V.T. ....Vendemmia Tardiva (Late Harvest)

Geographical abbreviations
(names of DOCs and DOCGs):
A.A. ....Alto Adige
C.B. ....Colli Bolognesi
COF ......Colli Orientali del Friuli
C.P. ....Colli Piacentini
O.P. ....Oltrepò Pavese

FERTILIZERS
PLANT PROTECTION
WEED CONTROL
YEASTS
GRAPES
CERTIFICATION

The data in the box on viticultural and enological practices were supplied directly by the wineries during our visits.

Glossary

FERTILIZERS

Organic-minerals
Obtained from the blending or reaction of one or more organic fertilizers with one or more parts of simple mineral fertilizer or compound, organo-minerals are halfway between organic fertilizers, with respect to which they have more nutritional elements, and mineral fertilizers, with respect to which they are more efficient. Nitrogen and phosphorus must come at least in part from organic fertilizers, while potassium and the remaining parts of nitrogen and phosphorus must derive from the mineral part.

Minerals
Fertilizers obtained from mineral compounds. Most of these products are made by the extractive and chemical industries, hence mineral fertilizers are largely known as chemical fertilizers. Since they do not contain carbon, they are defined by their principal component. Hence, phosphorus, nitrogen, potassium fertilizers and so on.

Manure
Manure is fundamental in any type of agriculture. It is an organic fertilizer which permits improvements to the physical and chemical characteristics of the soil. From the physical point of view, it acts as a soil improver, enriching the mechanical properties of the soil. From the chemical point of view, it provides precious substances for the fertility of the soil. The characteristics of a manure vary according to the animal it comes from.

Compost
Compost is made from the decomposition of a mixture of organic substances, residues from pruning, left-over food, manure and sewage. Fundamental agents are oxygen and the balance between the chemical agents present in the matter as it transforms. The action of micro and macro-organisms takes place in special conditions and tends to form a dark, damp mass of matter that is valuable for agriculture. Its use with the addition of organic substance improves the structure of the soil and the availability of nutritional elements. As an organic activator, compost also improves the biodiversity of micro-flora in the soil.

Biodynamic preparations
Agricultural actions designed to improve the physical and chemical peculiarities of the soil and vegetation in biodynamic vineyard management. There are basically two types of preparation: sprays and composts, both used in precisely defined quantities. The two main sprays are: 500, or horn manure, which develops the humus in the soil, and 501, or horn silica, which aids photosynthesis. Compost preparations are used to enrich the organic substances to be spread over the soil. Compost made with precisely defined vegetable and animal elements is a precious fertilizer.

Green manure
An agronomic practice whereby specific crops are ploughed under the soil to maintain and improve its fertility. Its many results include: increase in the amount of organic matter in the soil; suppression of soil erosion; preservation of the soil's nitrogen component. Especially important are leguminous green manures, which fix atmospheric nitrogen into the soil.

PLANT PROTECTION

Used to protect plants from the attack of parasites and pathogens, to control the development of weeds and ensure high quality standards for agricultural produce. They may be natural or synthetic and may be marketed only in sealed, tamper-proof wrappers or packages with labels authorized by the Italian Health Ministry bearing the name of the commercial formula and trademark, if any. Other compulsory information includes the primary activity or action performed by the active substance, denominated according to ISO classification, on the target (insecticide, fungicide, weed killer) and the type of formulation (dilutable, powder, emulsionable) with which the product is presented.

Chemicals
This group comprises all products made synthetically.

Copper and sulphur
The most common fungicides, copper against downy mildew, sulphur against powdery mildew. Sulphur presents risks of phytotoxicity in young shoots, especially with high summer temperatures. It may interfere with the fermentation process, especially in the case of early-ripening white grapes. The prolonged use of copper determines a sizeable increase in its levels in the soil, creating ecotoxicological problems for the environment.

Organics
Organic substances, such as milk, infusions and tisanes, are used in organic and biodynamic farming. Their action must be coordinated with a series of other interventions, mostly preventive, disciplined by the agricultural management system adopted.

WEED CONTROL

Weed control is an integral part of vineyard soil management and is designed to prevent weeds from entering into competition with the vine and jeopardizing its development. Chemical weeding is carried out with synthetic products which act by contact (on the visible part of the plant), by transfer (systemic products which attack root and plant) or by residual action (over time they prevent the seed from germinating). Although it damages organic substances in the soil, chemical weeding is now becoming simpler and more effective, safer for the plant and more respectful of the environment. Mechanical weeding uses mechanical actions, such as mowing, to remove weeds. This practice ensures total respect for the environment and is part of organic and biodynamic vineyard management.

YEASTS

Yeasts are responsible for fermentation, the process by which sugar in must is transformed into alcohol (ethanol) and carbon dioxide. Yeasts, known as native or wild or ambient yeasts, are to be found in the bloom of the skins of grapes. Improvements in cellar techniques have made it possible to select strains of yeast capable of responding to the special needs of each producer or to aid native yeasts if they encounter obstacles in this delicate and fundamental phase in the vinification process. On the basis of these requirements, each producer may choose to carry on the fermentation with native yeasts, hence only those of his or her own grapes, or with selected yeasts, when fermentation is performed with yeast strains brought in from the outside. Activating yeasts also exist. These are used with particularly lazy musts or in the case of a stuck fermentation.

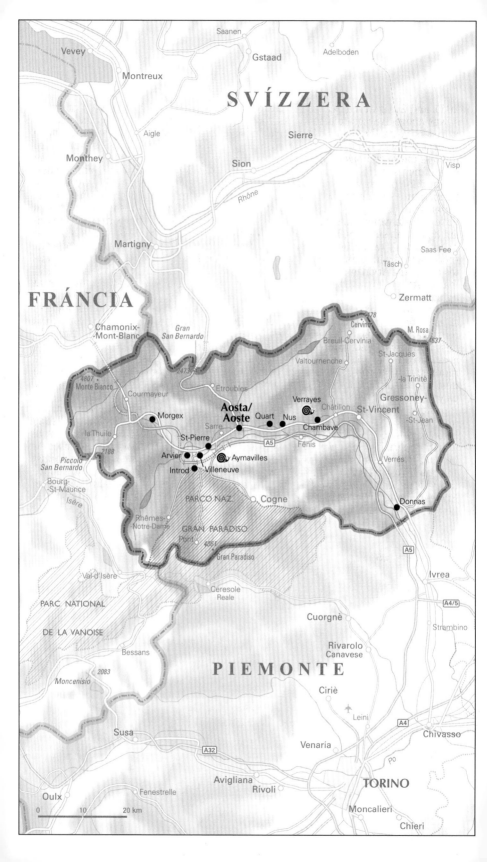

VALLE D'AOSTA

2011 and 2012 weren't easy growing years for the region. Unlike in the past, when it was above-average rainfall or low temperatures that damaged the grape harvest, in recent years the banes of winemakers have been heat and drought. Contrary to what one might think, the Valle d'Aosta experiences very dry, rainless summers, so rainless the region has a high-tech artificial back-up irrigation system at the ready in case of necessity. If, as happened in 2011 and 2012, conditions become extreme and the heat is oppressive, the white grapes especially fail to ripen optimally. Day-to-night temperature swings are also essential to enrich the aromas and flavors of white wines. Unfortunately, the two vintages in question weren't ideal from this point of view, though Valle d'Aosta winemakers made the best of a bad job in both the vineyards and the cellar. It is worth stressing how the quality potential of the region's white wines is unique nationwide. It would be hard in other areas of Italy to taste wines more agreeable, more packed with personality than the valley's Chardonnays, Pinot Grigios, dry Moscatos and Petite Arvines. The grape used to make the latter, a native of the Swiss Vallese, has all it takes to be a success on the market: namely salinity, very rich aromas, great aging potential, pungent acidity and, in some cases, even a hint of sweetness from the high alcohol content. Our impression was that red wines had been slightly less affected by the detrimental conditions, indeed red varieties such as petit rouge, the most planted grape in the valley, drew advantage and acquired greater strength, richness and flavor. Also grabbing the spotlight was the fumin grape, potentially a huge a resource for the region. The typology's only drawback, as far as we can see at the moment, is that enologists are unfamiliar with it and still have yet to figure out the best way to turn it into monovarietal wines. Some know how to do the job, however, as you will read below.

A positive piece of news is the increase in the number of wineries that already practice organics or have applied for certification. In the past, the Valle d'Aosta never really stood out for eco-friendly agricultural practices, especially with regard to weed control which, especially which following the example of neighboring Switzerland, used to be total. Now, thanks to the work of a few technicians, among whom the agronomist Fabrizio Prosperi, and to the fact that low rainfall will help winegrowers to reduce their use of plant protection products, the situation is changing. Cooperative dell'Enfer, Ermes Pavese, Grosjean, Cave di Morgex (on some plots), Les Granges, La Vrille and Les Crêtes —these are some of the wineries that are moving in this direction.

snails ◉꙳

16 LES CRÊTES
17 LA VRILLE

bottles ▮

17 ANSELMET

AYMAVILLES (AO)

Les Crêtes

Località Villetos, 50
tel. 0165 902274
www.lescretes.it
info@lescretes.it

25 ha - 220,000 bt

66 A winery, Les Crêtes, and a winemaker, Costantino Charrère, who have written the recent history of Valle d'Aosta viticulture and, thanks to Charrère's work as president of FIVI, the Italian Federation of Independent Winemakers, of the Italian productive system. All this based in a small region of marginal enology. 99

PEOPLE - A lot of work has been done at Les Crêtes, with the addition of a new wing to the cellar and a spectacular tasting room.

VINEYARDS - The efforts of Costantino and his daughters Elena and Eleonora are focusing above all on work in the vineyard, which they are making cleaner by experimenting with organic and biodynamic techniques. Helping them is their friend Saverio Petrilli. The panettone-shaped hill of Coteau La Tour is greener and more spectacular than ever, increasingly the symbol of a region that is making giant leaps forward in quality and sustainability.

WINES - The range submitted moved at two speeds, the young wines on top form, the wood-aged ones struggling to digest the sweet spices. The magnificent **Valle d'Aosta Chardonnay 2012** (O 30,000 bt) combines classic notes of grapefruit and pineapple with great tanginess and oozes juice. **Valle d'Aosta Petite Arvine 2012** (O 16,000 bt) was in good shape too with inviting, palate-prolonging acidity. The fruity, pleasing **Valle d'Aosta Torrette 2012** (● 30,000 bt) is a house classic. Of the more ambitious wines, the one that impressed us most was **Valle d'Aosta Syrah Coteau La Tour 2011** (● 10,000 bt). **Valle d'Aosta Fumin 2010** (● 16,000 bt) is on the clenched side and **Valle d'Aosta Chardonnay Cuvée Bois 2011** (O 18.000 bt) will have to be waited for.

QUART (AO)

Grosjean

Frazione Olligan, 1
tel. 0165 775791
www.grosjean.vievini.it
grosjean@vievini.it

10 ha - 105,000 bt

PEOPLE - This guide often tells the stories of farming families, but rarely of "tribes" like the Grosjeans: five brothers and their respective children and spouses, all of whom contribute to the present and future of the cellar and the farm. Like every self-respecting tribe they have a chief: elder brother Vincent Grosjean, a man who has done a lot for winemaking in the valley.

VINEYARDS - The Grosjeans' is one of the few wineries in the region to be certified organic. The recognition is the end-result of a virtuous process begun many years ago and concluded in 2012. The parcels planted with vines are very beautiful, especially Rovettaz, a veritable cru of five hectares on a single plot. To achieve an area of this size the Grosjean had to draw up as many as 22 notary deeds.

WINES - The range submitted last year was outstanding. **Valle d'Aosta Muscat Petit Grain 2012** (O 1,500 bt) is pleasantly varietal. **Valle d'Aosta Torrette 2012** (● 18,000 bt) is fresh and blossomy. **Valle d'Aosta Cornalin Vigna Rovettaz 2011** (● 4,000 bt) is fuller-bodied and richer. **Valle d'Aosta Gamay 2012** (● 12,000 bt) is scented and subtle, by no means devoid of originality. The partly oak-aged **Valle d'Aosta Petite Arvine Vigna Rovettaz 2011** (O 11,000 bt) is minerally with notes of hazelnut.

> **vino slow** VALLE D'AOSTA FUMIN VIGNA ROVETTAZ **2010** (● 4,000 bt) A very complex, rich nose with hints of leather and sweet spices and an exuberant, juicy palate with just the right degree of acidity. Notably terroir-dedicated, this is a wine built to last.

FERTILIZERS natural manure
PLANT PROTECTION chemical, copper and sulphur
WEED CONTROL chemical, mechanical
YEASTS selected
GRAPES 30% bought in
CERTIFICATION none

FERTILIZERS natural manure
PLANT PROTECTION copper and sulphur
WEED CONTROL mechanical
YEASTS native
GRAPES 8% bought in
CERTIFICATION organic

La Vrille

Hameau du Grandzon, 1
tel. 0166 543018
www.lavrille-agritourisme.com
lavrille@gmail.com

1.5 ha - 12,000 bt

66 A place with slowness in its soul. This year, besides receiving the Snail symbol in our guide, it also gets one in the Osterie d'Italia guide. Which gives some idea of how much attention it attaches to excellence, environment and agriculture. 99

PEOPLE - Hervé Deguillame and his wife Luciana Neyroz have given life to an oasis of well-being, a model wine cellar, an excellent osteria and a comfortable guesthouse. All in less than ten years.

VINEYARDS - To his credit, Hervé is making prodigious efforts to keep the use of chemicals down to a minimum. The vineyards are all close to the house-cum-cellar and some grow very old vines, especially of gamay grapes. The cow's manure used is supplied by a friend who's a livestock breeder and, given the lack of rainfall in summer, some plantings are fitted with irrigation systems.

WINES - The range submitted was first-rate as always. Though no wine stood head and shoulders above the rest, the general standard was very high. **Valle d'Aosta Chambave Muscat Flétri 2011** (○ 1,000 bt) is a passito perfectly poised between sweetness and acidity with very rich, complex aromas. The dry version **Valle d'Aosta Chambave Muscat 2011** (○ 3,300) is mineral and tangy. **Valle d'Aosta Gamay 2011** (● 700 bt) is very spicy and, in its own way, complex. **Valle d'Aosta Fumin 2010** (● 2,600 bt) is full-bodied and husky with a deep-reaching fruity finish (some of the grapes used are left in crates for extra ripening). **Valle d'Aosta Chambave 2010** (● petit rouge, fumin, cornalin; 2,000 bt) is enjoyable with delicious acidity.

FERTILIZERS natural manure
PLANT PROTECTION copper and sulphur
WEED CONTROL mechanical
YEASTS selected
GRAPES 100% estate-grown
CERTIFICATION none

Anselmet

8.5 ha - 70,000 bt · **10% discount**

PEOPLE - Giorgio Anselmet has grown continuously and consistently in recent years. After building a new modern cellar, he is better equipped to manage every phase of production (especially oak-aging) and the quality of his wines is improving all the time. His family members — from his wife Bruna Cavagnet and son Henry to his father Renato, who established the winery in the 1970s — all help and support him in his work.

VINEYARDS - Many small plots with different characteristics and positions combine to form a precious mosaic of vineyards that Giorgio follows with passion. His agricultural approach isn't organic; we'd define it more as artisan and old-fashioned, the fruit of the experience he picked up first at the Institut Agricole in Aosta, then at La Crotta di Vegneron in Chambave. Worth of a special mention is the spectacular Saint-Pierre vineyard, buttressed by very steep dry stone walls.

WINES - The Anselmets produce a mind-boggling 18 labels, but only 70,000 bottles! Their Burgundy-style approach extends to a measured use of wood. We were bowled over by **Valle d'Aosta Chardonnay 2012** (○ 1,300 bt), which is rich, carefully crafted and fruity to the right degree. **Valle d'Aosta Chardonnay Élevé en Fût de Chêne 2012** (○ 4,500 bt) is more buttery, rich and spicy. **Valle d'Aosta Petite Arvine 2012** (○ 1,300 bt) is the result of an exemplary use of barriques and has a razor-sharp palate. Our favorite red was **Valle d'Aosta Syrah Henry Élevé en Fût de Chêne 2011** (● 2,000 bt), which has nuances of black pepper and strawberry. **Valle d'Aosta Pinot Noir Élevé en Fût de Chêne 2011** (● 2,200 bt) is a tad alcoholic. **Valle d'Aosta Fumin 2011** (● 2,200 bt) will grow in the fullness of time.

FERTILIZERS manure pellets
PLANT PROTECTION chemical, copper and sulphur
WEED CONTROL chemical, mechanical
YEASTS selected
GRAPES 15% bought in
CERTIFICATION none

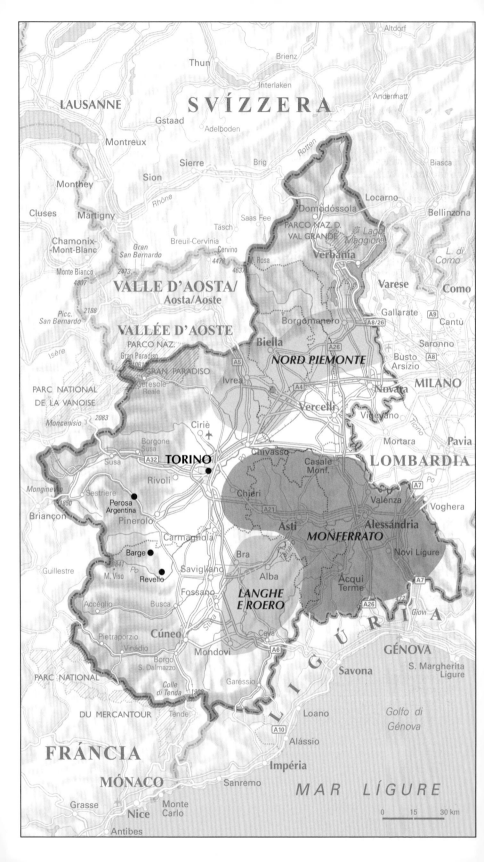

PIEDMONT

This year we had the chance to taste the 2009 Barolos, a vintage presented almost as a repeat of 2007, hence of warm, not particularly dynamic wines. But our tastings suggested otherwise. Since the scorching 2003 vintage, many producers have learned to manage warm growing years well, often, though not always, turning out excellently racy wines, well supported by natural acidity. Our compliments go, therefore, to the many winemakers who came up with wines of an indisputably high standard. The 2010 Barbarescos, instead, were the product of a vintage of great depth, pretty much perfect for the nebbiolo grape, and naturally included wines of notable quality. 2011 was positive for Barbera in the Asti and Alba areas, whereas 2012 was slightly disappointing for Gavi, less racy than the previous year. Arneis from Roero, finally, appeared to be in good form.
Sales difficulties persist unfortunately, in some areas more than others, and local and national markets are at a standstill due to failures to make payments and deferred purchases. Overseas markets, though, seem to be recovering and this is obviously a source of satisfaction.

snails 🐌

21	LE PIANE
21	ANTICHI VIGNETI DI CANTALUPO
25	SERAFINO RIVELLA
26	ROAGNA - I PAGLIERI
27	GIACOMO BREZZA & FIGLI
29	GIUSEPPE RINALDI
29	G.D. VAJRA
30	CASCINA CA' ROSSA
32	BROVIA
32	CAVALLOTTO FRATELLI
34	CASCINA CORTE
34	PECCHENINO
35	ANNA MARIA ABBONA
36	ELIO ALTARE - CASCINA NUOVA
38	CONTERNO FANTINO
40	ELIO GRASSO
41	PIERO BUSSO
42	SOTTIMANO
43	ELVIO COGNO
43	HILBERG - PASQUERO
46	CA' DEL BAIO
46	FIORENZO NADA
47	ALESSANDRIA FRATELLI
49	DACAPO
51	IULI
52	LUIGI SPERTINO
53	VIGNETI MASSA
54	CARUSSIN
55	CASTELLO DI TASSAROLO

bottles ▮

24	GAJA
25	MARCHESI DI GRÉSY
26	BORGOGNO & FIGLI
28	E. PIRA & FIGLI CHIARA BOSCHIS
28	BARTOLO MASCARELLO
30	MATTEO CORREGGIA
31	MALVIRÀ
31	MONCHIERO CARBONE
33	VIETTI
33	MARZIANO ABBONA
35	LA SPINETTA
37	CORDERO DI MONTEZEMOLO MONFALLETTO
38	GIUSEPPE MASCARELLO E FIGLIO
39	GIACOMO CONTERNO
42	CASTELLO DI NEIVE
44	CASA DI E. MIRAFIORE
45	GIOVANNI ROSSO
54	MARCHESI ALFIERI
55	LA COLOMBERA

coins €

23	MARCO E VITTORIO ADRIANO
23	GIGI BIANCO
24	GIUSEPPE CORTESE
36	BRANDINI
39	GIACOMO FENOCCHIO
40	GIOVANNI ALMONDO
41	ANGELO NEGRO & FIGLI
44	MOSSIO FRATELLI
49	PAOLO AVEZZA
51	L'ARMANGIA
53	LA GIRONDA

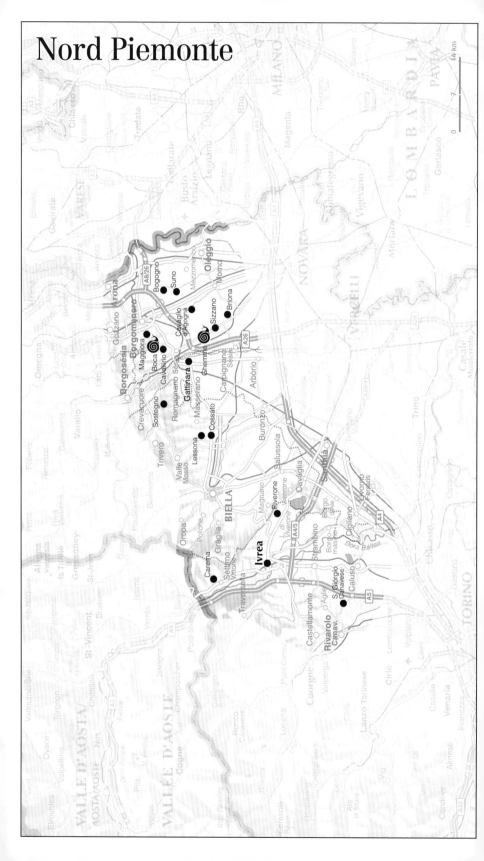

Nord Piemonte

BOCA (NO)

Le Piane

Località Le Piane
tel. 348 3354185
www.bocapiane.com
info@bocapiane.com

8 ha - 45,000 bt

66 Anyone can become a winemaker provided they have passion, intelligence and sensitivity. This is Christoph Künzli's recipe anyway, and it has worked for him. Born in Switzerland and a great Boca fan, judging by the results he achieves in the vineyard and in the bottle he is now a model winemaker. 99

PEOPLE - Künzli has a talented team behind him, led by wine lovers like himself, such as Nicola Del Boca and Sergej in cellar.

VINEYARDS - The team already own more than 20 vineyards and continue to be charged with the management of those of local farmers. Most of them are old and trained with the difficult, all-manual maggiorina training system. The fact is that Christoph and Nicola are great believers in the potential of this old local system and are about to replant a vineyard to test a new take on it. The overall agronomic management is amazingly shrewd and rational.

WINES - In the cellar Christoph listens to what his collaborators have to say. He is always ready to change direction according to a wine's evolution in the barrel and has learnt how to coax the best out of his grape varieties. Croatina and vespolina, for example, are becoming increasingly expressive. **La Maggiorina 2012 (●** croatina, vespolina, uva rara, nebbiolo; 15,000 bt) is a beautifully interpreted red wine with a bouquet of crisp fruit and blossom and a juicy palate with just the right sinew. **Boca 2009 (●** nebbiolo, vespolina; 13,000 bt) offers riper fruit and almost Langa-style body, extracts and tannins, all with a characteristically elegant pitch — a Great Wine. Piane 2010 wasn't produced, merging with two barrels of Boca 2010 into the new **Mimmo 2010 (●** nebbiolo, croatina, vespolina; 12,000 bt) delicate and more approachable.

FERTILIZERS natural manure, green manure, humus
PLANT PROTECTION chemical, copper and sulphur, organic
WEED CONTROL mechanical
YEASTS native
GRAPES 10% bought in
CERTIFICATION none

GHEMME (NO)

Antichi Vigneti di Cantalupo

Via Michelangelo Buonarroti, 5
tel. 0163 840041
www.cantalupo.net
info@cantalupo.net

33 ha - 180,000 bt

66 Alberto Arlunno is the stalwart defender of a whole denomination and one of the ablest interpreters of these northern nebbiolos. A dead cert and an example to follow. 99

PEOPLE - Every year we add a new bit to our knowledge of history and geology when we sit down and chat with Alberto Arlunno. Now we've discovered that it was the monks of Cluny who started growing wine in the area and the super volcano of the Valsesia that shaped the land with the orogenesis of the Alps.

VINEYARDS - Many of the vineyards are rimmed by woodland. They are situated on the first and second hills of Ghemme, many in the best crus, Carelle, Breclemae and Locche. The hills are low with acid pH, morainic, hence with clay soil scattered with pebbles (detritus, as Alberto explains, of both African and European origin).

WINES - Thanks to the usual consultancy of Donato Lanati, the nebbiolos were again impressive. The Ghemmes are all 100 per cent nebbiolo. **Ghemme Collis Breclemae 2005 (●** 10,000 bt) appeared after a long wait: it's a magnificent wine with a deep, complex, elegant bouquet and a palate packed with energy, acidity and plenty of grip. **Colline Novaresi Abate di Cluny 2007 (●** nebbiolo; 10,000 bt) is a new wine made with grapes earmarked for Ghemme, the fruit of ten days of beautifully judged overripening; devoid of cooked notes, it releases sumptuous, mature fragrances segued by assertive, well-knit tannins. **Colline Novaresi Nebbiolo Agamium 2008 (●** 11,000 bt) is stylish and deep.

> **vino slow** **GHEMME 2007 (●** 15,000 bt) The young, intense, complex aromas are still redolent of fruit and the mid-palate is meaty and full-bodied. Flavorful, rich and concentrated — North Piedmont in a glass.

FERTILIZERS organic-mineral, natural manure
PLANT PROTECTION chemical, copper and sulphur
WEED CONTROL chemical, mechanical
YEASTS selected
GRAPES 10% bought in
CERTIFICATION none

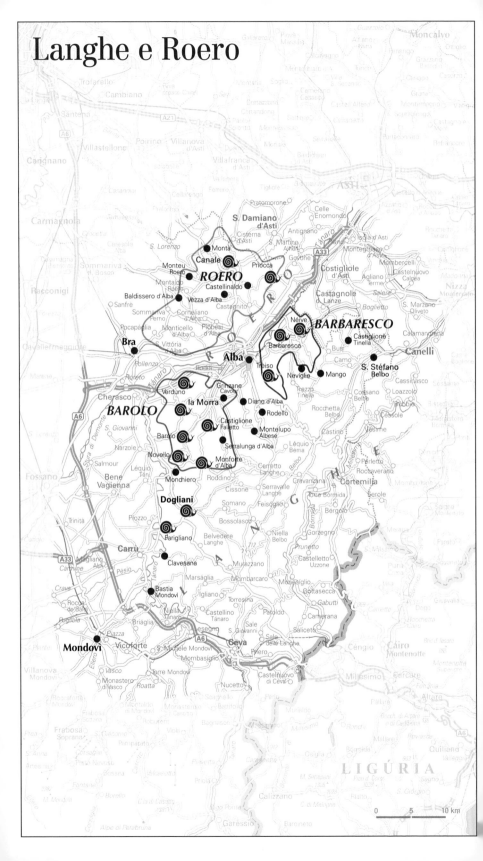

Langhe e Roero

ALBA (CN)

Marco e Vittorio Adriano €

Frazione San Rocco Seno d'Elvio, 13 A
tel. 0173 362294
www.adrianovini.it
info@adrianovini.it

22 ha - 130,000 bt | **10% discount**

PEOPLE - The team of Marco and Vittorio Adriano and their wives Luciana and Maria Grazia run this winery, which has always adopted differentiated farming. Besides growing vines it used to breed livestock, now it also produces hazelnuts. The cellar, which now has a new tasting room, houses a small museum of agricultural utensils.

VINEYARDS - The Basarin vineyard, near the wine cellar, is on a steep slope, a fact that ensures good drainage but doesn't facilitate operations. The wines born in this soil are all endowed with finesse and classic, nuanced aromas. The other Barbaresco has the dialect name of the village on the outskirts of Alba where it is made. Alongside the cellar is a lovely barbera vineyard with very old vines. The good news this year is that the company has decided to discontinue chemical weed control below the vines.

WINES - Blossomy but well-structured, **Barbaresco Basarin Ris. 2008** (● 5,000 bt) reflects a truly great vintage. Albeit still slightly undeveloped, **Barbaresco Sanadaive 2010** (● 12,000 bt) has solid structure and a fair amount of juice. Earthy and full of verve, **Barbera d'Alba Sup. 2011** (● 10,000 bt) offers morello cherry on the nose and palate and a lingering finish. **Dolcetto d'Alba 2012** (● 20,000 bt) is approachable, easy and quaffable. **Langhe Sauvignon Basaricò 2012** (○ 13,000 bt) is aromatic but not excessively so, with measured, enjoyably delicate fruity notes and a no-nonsense, lean palate.

vino slow BARBARESCO BASARIN 2010 (● 20,000 bt) Notes of violet and rose, deep, supple, with a long finish — a wine of great complexity at a more than reasonable price.

FERTILIZERS manure pellets
PLANT PROTECTION chemical, copper and sulphur
WEED CONTROL mechanical
YEASTS selected
GRAPES 100% estate-grown
CERTIFICATION none

BARBARESCO (CN)

Gigi Bianco €

Via Torino, 63
tel. 0173 635137
www.gigibianco.it
aziendagigibianco@libero.it

2.4 ha - 18,000 bt

PEOPLE - The dream cellar for any wine tourist, situated right under one of the best loved symbols of the Langa hills, the tower of Barbaresco, which for centuries has watched over the River Tanaro as it winds and wriggles down the valley below. The place is run by Maria Vittoria, her daughter Susanna and Susanna's partner Salvatore Angelica. Production is limited and sales are mostly direct.

VINEYARDS - It was Susanna who took us round the fantastic Ovello vineyard, set in a perfect position in a sunny hollow, rightly regarded as one of the most attractive in the whole denomination. The Biancos own a broad strip of land here, conspicuous for the lack of chemical weed control and painstaking care for the vines. Another good growing vineyard is Pora, smaller but just as well positioned.

WINES - The Biancos produce value-for-money, soundly traditional, strongly terroir-dedicated wines. The cream of the crop, **Barbaresco Ovello 2010** (● 6,000 bt) has stiff tannins, which will settle with bottle-aging. Both **Langhe Nebbiolo 2009** (● 2,000 bt) and **Langhe Nebbiolo 2011** (● 1,500 bt) are excellent labels: albeit produced from warm growing years, they are both very delicate and harmonious, a joy to drink. If you're looking for a fruity, flavorful wine, **Dolcetto d'Alba 2012** (● 1,800 bt) is the one for you.

vino slow BARBARESCO PORA 2010 (● 2,600 bt) A nose of violets, well-gauged tannins, juice and an aftertaste of wild strawberries — a perfect nebbiolo with all the the massive complexity of the terroir.

FERTILIZERS none
PLANT PROTECTION chemical, copper and sulphur
WEED CONTROL mechanical
YEASTS native
GRAPES 100% estate-grown
CERTIFICATION none

Giuseppe Cortese €

Strada Rabajà, 80
tel. 0173 635131
www.cortesegiuseppe.it
info@cortesegiuseppe.it

Gaja

Via Torino, 36
tel. 0173 635158

---

8 ha - 50,000 bt

PEOPLE - The company anyone would love to own: small, well-run with typical non-nonsense Piedmontese common sense. Established in 1971 by Giuseppe and his dad Giacomo Cortese, it's now run by Giuseppe's children: Piercarlo, in charge of the cellar, and Tiziana, in charge of sales. Giuseppe himself, born in 1941, still works untiringly in the vineyards and his son-in-law Gabriele collaborates with his wife on public relations.

VINEYARDS - The vineyards, two blocks of four hectares each, are situated in the Rabajà cru, where the cellar also stands, and the adjacent Trifolera cru. In the first, which has a south- and southwest facing location, grow nebbiolo vines planted 40 to 60 years ago and the oldest vines whose grapes go into the Riserva, which border with Camp Gros di Martinenga. The second, which has a variety of different locations, is given over to dolcetto, barbera and nebbiolo (for Langhe Nebbiolo), while the chardonnay grapes are further north.

WINES - The exceptional **Barbaresco Rabajà Ris. 2006** (● 5,500 bt) has been released after seven years of aging — 40 months in barrel and 36 in bottle! Its nose has notes of tar, fur and wood, the palate is tannic, concentrated and long. **Langhe Nebbiolo 2011** (● 10,000 bt) has aromas of tobacco and a delicate, fruity palate. Neither **Barbera d'Alba Morassina 2011** (● 6,000 bt), the only wine aged in (pre-used) barriques, nor **Dolcetto d'Alba 2012** (● 8,000 bt) disappoints. **Langhe Chardonnay 2012** (○ 3,000 bt) is a pleasing tipple.

---

vino slow **BARBARESCO RABAJÀ 2010** (● 17,000 bt) Piercarlo won't be releasing the 2010 Riserva del 2010, so this Barbaresco contains all the best grapes — and you can tell. Cleanness, drinkabiity, complexity, elegance and harmony — the essence of the Langa hills distilled in a glass.

FERTILIZERS none
PLANT PROTECTION chemical, copper and sulphur
WEED CONTROL chemical, mechanical
YEASTS selected
GRAPES 100% estate-grown
CERTIFICATION none

---

100 ha - 350,000 bt

PEOPLE - This the fourth year in the row that we have visited the Gaja family's cellar in the springtime. This time it was Rossana, the great Angelo's daughter, who took us round. Through the years we have noted a whole host of positive changes, the like of which are hard to fine elsewhere in Italy. Not much is said about it, but the precision and artisan care that have given the winery world fame are now backed by great attention to eco-sustainability.

VINEYARDS - The imperative chez maison Gaja is creating the conditions for the vines to grow well. Elimination of chemical weed control, the massive use of humus piles, the sowing of grasses and legumes between the vine rows, gender confusion and soft pruning — we don't know whether these choices have been made for the environment or to improve the grapes. Whatever, we appreciated them a lot. Chapeau!

WINES - A stellar range as always. Nothing has changed in the cellar for the Langhe wines: meaning 12 months' aging in wood casks and 12 months in wood barrels with a blend of 95 per cent nebbiolo and 5 per cent barbera. The magnificent **Barbaresco 2010** (● 50,000 bt), has scents of violet well fused with spices. On the palate the tannins are robust but well supported by juice and acidity — this year's Great Wine for the cellar! The celebrated **Langhe Nebbiolo Sorì San Lorenzo 2010** (● 15,000) is made with grapes from the Masué vineyard's Secondine cru. In the Roncagliette sub-denomination, we find **Langhe Nebbiolo Costa Russi 2010** (● 15,000 bt) and **Langhe Nebbiolo Sorì Tildin 2010** (● 15,000 bt). The two "Barolos" are the products of a warm vintage but are hugely impressive nonetheless. **Langhe Nebbiolo Conteisa 2009** (● 15,000 bt) is harmonious and soft, **Langhe Nebbiolo Sperss 2009** (● 24,000 bt) is more tannic and long-lasting.

FERTILIZERS natural manure, compost
PLANT PROTECTION copper and sulphur
WEED CONTROL mechanical
YEASTS native
GRAPES 100% estate-grown
CERTIFICATION none

Marchesi di Grésy

Strada della Stazione, 21
tel. 0173 635221
www.marchesidigresy.com
wine@marchesidigresy.com

35 ha - 200,000 bt

PEOPLE - Marchesi di Grésy, in the Barbaresco zone, is exemplary for the consistently high quality of its wines. It's also a focus for lovers of the great reds of the Langhe hills. Year by year, in fact, its stylistically impeccable wines, are a faithful mirror of the terroir of their birth. The company is run by Alberto di Grésy and produces classic Piedmontese reds and top-notch whites.

VINEYARDS - Di Grésy is made up of four different estates, two in the Langa hills, at Barbaresco and Treiso, and two at Cassine in the Monferrato district at La Serra and Monte Colombo, where the Barbera and Moscato d'Asti are produced. The view of Martinenga at Barbaresco takes the breath away. A magnificently positioned hollow, well-drained with good air circulation, it seems specially created to regale us with great wines. The agronomist is Matteo Sasso.

WINES - Refreshing, deep, nuanced, precise and terroir-dedicated, **Barbaresco Camp Gros 2009** (● 2,700 bt) appears not to have suffered the warm growing year – a Great Wine. **Barbaresco Gaiun 2009** (● 2,700 bt) has magnificent blossomy fragrances and fruity flesh, buttressed by close-knit, well-defined, sweet, mature tannins. The palate of **Barbaresco Martinenga 2010** (● 13,300 bt) is so captivating it masks the energy that bubbles under its surface, while the superb finish is juicy and long. **Dolcetto d'Alba Monte Aribaldo 2012** (● 23,000 bt) is nice and typical and shows what a good growing area Treiso is for this particular grape. **Langhe Sauvignon 2012** (○ 18,000 bt) is as good as ever, unobtrusively varietal with a delicious finish. **Langhe Chardonnay 2012** (○ 4,000 bt) oozes verve and works well.

FERTILIZERS organic-mineral
PLANT PROTECTION chemical, copper and sulphur
WEED CONTROL chemical, mechanical
YEASTS selected
GRAPES 100% estate-grown
CERTIFICATION none

Serafino Rivella

Località Montestefano, 6
tel. 0173 635182

2 ha - 11,000 bt

❝ Low stats but high standards when it comes to farm management and wine quality — this, in a nutshell, is the winery of Teobaldo Rivella. Go and visit it; you'll be won over. ❞

PEOPLE - As we chatted, Teobaldo Rivella explained that, "The winery is still registered under my father Serafino's name. He used to make wine too but without bottling it. He would sell some of the grapes and demijohns of wine to customers in Turin and surrounds. I began bottling in 1967 and my wife [Maria Musso, editor's note] was already there to help me".

VINEYARDS - Our conversation continued among the vine rows of Montestefano. A single two-hectare vineyard wraps round the hillside in a south and southwest-facing location, the best of all. "The nebbiolos were never grown at he bottom or the top. The dolcettos are at the top and, like the nebbiolos, date from 1963. Speaking of nebbiolo, here we also have the lampia and michet clones. Once we also had rosé, but it had a poor yield and color, so my father stopped planting it".

WINES - Teobaldo was still talking when we got to the cellar. "It was always my idea to make good local wine. I hope I've succeeded," he says. Well, he has. He vinifies nebbiolo in 25-hectoliter wood barrels with spontaneous fermentations of at least three weeks with classic pumpovers and manual punching-down and without temperature control. The outcome is cut-glass wines that mirror the vintage and the soil. **Dolcetto d'Alba 2012** (● 3,000 bt) is fruity and quaffable.

vino slow **BARBARESCO MONTESTEFANO 2009** (● 8,500 bt) Barrel-aging for about 30 months forges this wine's identity. Midway between a drinkable 2007 and a more austere, classic 2008, it's soft with plenty of young tannins and a fuller body.

FERTILIZERS manure pellets, natural manure
PLANT PROTECTION copper and sulphur
WEED CONTROL mechanical
YEASTS native
GRAPES 100% estate-grown
CERTIFICATION none

BARBARESCO (CN)

Roagna - I Paglieri

Località Paglieri, 9
tel. 0173 635109
www.roagna.com
info@roagna.com

12 ha - 60,000 bt

66 When one puts nature before oneself, one is at its disposal without any wish to dominate it. On the contrary, one supports it and coaxes the best out of it. When all this leads to exceptional results, it's possible to speak of the success of an alliance between human beings and the environment. This is what father and son Alfredo and Luca Roagna have done and are doing. 99

PEOPLE - The winery now has a new cellar. It boasts eight hectares of vines in Barbaresco and four in Castiglione Falletto.

VINEYARDS - The Roagnas' properties have prestigious names: Asili, Montefico and Pajé in Barbaresco, eight hectares which also include a little dolcetto, and the monopole Pira in Castiglione Falletto. All the vineyards stand in grass with no mowing or shredding. Chemicals in any form are strictly banned and obsessive care is devoted to pruning and the preservation of old vines. The vine rows are a feast for the eyes.

WINES - A breathtaking array of Barbarescos and Barolos of quality and depth snare the various terroirs in the glass. The overwhelming **Barbaresco Crichet Pajé 2004** (● 1,640 bt) is still very young, but its goodness and harmony are amazing. On a par yet even younger are **Barbaresco Asili Vecchie Vigne 2008** (● 1,300 bt) and **Barbaresco Pajé Vecchie Vigne 2008** (● 1,200 bt): the first combines style and energy, the second is more decadent and irresistibly seductive. **Barbaresco Montefico Vecchie Vigne 2008** (● 1,200 bt) dances gracefully across the palate before becoming strongly assertive. The blossomy **Barbaresco Pajé 2008** (● 8,000 bt) is more direct. The gutsy **Barolo La Pira 2008** (● 15,000 bt) still needs time to develop.

FERTILIZERS none
PLANT PROTECTION copper and sulphur
WEED CONTROL mechanical
YEASTS native
GRAPES 100% estate-grown
CERTIFICATION none

BAROLO (CN)

Borgogno & Figli

Via Gioberti, 1
tel. 0173 56108
www.borgogno.com
info@borgogno.com

17 ha - 130,000 bt   **10% discount**

PEOPLE - Since they bought it in 2008, the Farinetti family have revolutionized this historic Langa cellar. First they restored the façade to its former splendor, then they set to work on the vineyard, shrewdly eliminating weed control and, thanks to the insistence of the youthful Andrea, who has controlled the operation from the outset, re-introducing cement vats.

VINEYARDS - Liste, Fossati and Cannubi are the three crus that agronomist Alberto Grasso manages with bravura and skill. His aim is to prolong the life of the vines by using as few chemicals as possible. Hence the elimination of weedkillers and chemical fertilizers. A series of weather stations help to contain damage. The Liste vineyard, planted in 1947, is still cultivated with great care and attention.

WINES - This is the first year in which grapes from the three crus have been vinified separately, and we have to say that the range of wines submitted was of a very high standard indeed. Top step of the podium goes to **Barolo Liste 2008** (● 6,000 bt), which combines a complex nose of red berries with an almost creamy palate of low-profile tannins and a perfect finish — a Great Wine. Slightly less rigid, **Barolo Cannubi 2008** (● 6,000 bt) comes from a cru that gives more fragrance and a tad less austerity. Refreshing and tannic, **Barolo Fossati 2008** (● 6,000 bt) is made with grapes from a high-altitude vineyard. One of the house specialties, **Barolo 2008** (● 22,000 bt), is as complex and enjoyable as ever. The very traditional **Barbera d'Alba Sup. 2011** (● 12,000 bt) is a pleasure to drink. **Langhe Nebbiolo No Name 2009** (● 18,000 bt) is a Barolo in miniature, hence a bargain buy.

FERTILIZERS natural manure
PLANT PROTECTION chemical, copper and sulphur
WEED CONTROL mechanical
YEASTS native
GRAPES 100% estate-grown
CERTIFICATION none

BAROLO (CN)

Giacomo Brezza & Figli 🐌

Via Lomondo, 4
tel. 0173 560921
www.brezza.it
brezza@brezza.it
🍲 🚜⁰

BAROLO (CN)

Damilano

Via Roma, 31
tel. 0173 56105
www.cantinedamilano.it
info@damilanog.com
🍲

---

16 ha - 80,000 bt   **10% discount**

73 ha - 440,000 bt

❝ Thanks to experience abroad and uncommon farming sensitivity, Enzo Brezza interprets the vineyards he manages with great bravura, treating us to sincere wines with a conspicuous sense of place. ❞

PEOPLE - The cellar is in the middle of town with an adjoining typical Piedmontese restaurant and hotel.

VINEYARDS - The vineyards are managed impeccably, organic cultivation cleverly supplemented by centuries of peasant guile. Not that there's any lack of innovative technologies such as quads, which are lighter than caterpillars and thus solve the problem of soil compression. The Brezzas have the fortune to manage some of the finest Barolo crus, such as the celebrated Cannubi and Sarmassa, and do so with commendable competence.

WINES - Enzo's style is to privilege large wood barrels and could be defined traditional. What impresses us most about his wines is the purity of the fruit and tremendous drinkability. **Barolo Bricco Sarmassa 2009** (● 6,400 bt) is violet-scented with lots of flavor and very enjoyable tannins. **Barolo Sarmassa 2009** (● 8,200 bt) is a smidgeon less potent but has a comparable suite of aromas. The less important wines are fantastic: the magnificent **Langhe Nebbiolo 2012** (● 8,000 bt) has welcome fleshiness; aged for a year in large wood barrels, the robust **Barbera d'Alba Sup. 2011** (● 16,000 bt) has acidity and tanginess, while **Nebbiolo d'Alba Santa Rosalia 2011** (● 8,000 bt) is stylish and complex.

| vino slow | **BAROLO CANNUBI 2009** (● 8,400 bt) Enzo told us that, as in all the previous warm growing years, the cru had suffered somewhat but,as far as we were concerned, it was splendid and unique — land-rooted, subtle and very flavorful indeed. |

PEOPLE - Since the fourth generation of the Damilano family joined the company in 1997, many things have changed — for the better. Most importantly, investments have been made in the buying and renting of vineyards. Secondly, the quality of the wines — now at the top of their respective denominations — has improved a lot with the backing of technician Beppe Caviola. Finally, thanks to Paolo Damilano, in autumn 2013 Michelin star-chef Massimo Camia opened a restaurant in the cellar.

VINEYARDS - The Damilanos have banked a lot on the Cannubi cru, where they now own and rent ten out of a total 15 hectares! The agronomic management is in the firm hands of Gian Piero Romana, who adopts conventional viticultural methods while respecting the vineyards' different climates and soils. Other crus are Liste, Brunate and Cerequio.

WINES - There are other new developments other than the ones already mentioned. Work is under way, for example, on a Cannubi Riserva, which will be released next year with the 2006 vintage. The release of Liste 2009 has also been postponed to 2014. The best of the bunch for pleasantness and character this year is the warm, muscular **Barolo Lecinquevigne 2009** (● 68,000 bt). It's a Great Wine: for once the underdog has come out on top. We were very impressed by **Barolo Cannubi 2009** (● 49,000 bt) with its aromas of violet and rose and deep, soft palate. We also thoroughly recommend the enjoyable **Langhe Nebbiolo Marghe 2011** (● 70,000 bt), which ages for ten months on second- and third-use barriques. **Barbera d'Alba Lablù 2011** (● 20,000 bt) is aged for 16 months in second-use barriques and is redolent of strawberries and cherries. **Dolcetto d'Alba 2012** (● 20.000 bt) is fragrant and juicy.

FERTILIZERS natural manure
PLANT PROTECTION copper and sulphur
WEED CONTROL mechanical
YEASTS native
GRAPES 100% estate-grown
CERTIFICATION converting to organics

FERTILIZERS manure pellets
PLANT PROTECTION chemical, copper and sulphur
WEED CONTROL chemical, mechanical
YEASTS selected, native
GRAPES 5% bought in
CERTIFICATION none

E. Pira & Figli - Chiara Boschis

Via Vittorio Veneto,1
tel. 0173 56247
www.pira-chiaraboschis.com
info@pira-chiaraboschis.com

10.5 ha - 35,000 bt | **10% discount**

PEOPLE - Chiara Boschis is a solar, friendly person and you could talk to her about wine for hours and hours. Never content and always on the lookout for new challenges, she is accompanied on her adventure by her brother Giorgio. Their small winery in the center of Barolo reflects Chiara's personality. We warmly recommend you pay her a visit if she's at home.

VINEYARDS - Chiara decided to go organic out of conviction and common sense, not to follow fashion, and now she has received official certification. The idea was the logical conclusion of years of vineyard management based on respect for the land. Now organic methods are an extra that add value to her vineyards, which are situated in some of the most important Barolo crus, such as Cannubi, Ravera, Mosconi and Gabutti.

WINES - Chiara has seen many a grape harvest and isn't lacking in experience, while Giorgio's enthusiastic contribution is also fundamental. This year the range of wines they submitted was of the highest standard. The candid, impeccable Barolos speak the language of their respective crus of origin. The exemplary **Barolo Cannubi 2009** (● 3,800 bt) is delicate, packed with energy, classic in style, juicy and penetrating, a Great Wine with all the majesty one of the great Langa crus. Also very good indeed is **Barolo Mosconi 2009** (● 5,900 bt), made with grapes from young vineyards: already deep and rich, it's braced by vibrant acidity. **Barolo Via Nuova 2009** (● 7,000 bt) is immediate, enhanced by smoky notes and good tannins. **Langhe Nebbiolo 2011** (● 3,200 bt) is very enjoyable and fresh, while **Barbera d'Alba Sup. 2011** (● 5,000 bt) is typical.

Bartolo Mascarello

Via Roma, 15
tel. 0173 56125

5.5 ha - 33,000 bt

PEOPLE - If Maria Teresa Mascarello, the owner and guiding spirit of this legendary Barolo cellar, belonged to an endangered species, it would be our overriding duty to protect her and save her from the siege of ephemeral fashion and manipulated wines. Luckily she doesn't and other producers like her continue to wield the banner of an intelligent tradition capable of renewing itself without betraying the spirit of the past.

VINEYARDS - The vineyards, some of which, San Lorenzo especially, very old, are mostly at Barolo, though there's also one in the commune of La Morra. The work in the country is carried out with great attention to sustainability. No chemical weedkillers and systemic products are used any more, and great care is dedicated to the fertility of the soil, while, due to climate change, bunches are never overcut. It's a choice we agree with.

WINES - Barolo 2009 (● 19,000 bt) has nuanced aromas with hints of blossom and crisp fruit, while on the palate it has depth, roundness, verve and length. In short, it's a Great Wine. **Langhe Nebbiolo 2011** (● 2,500 bt) is spicy with encores of violet and wild strawberry. The traditionally crafted **Barbera d'Alba 2011** (● 5,500 bt) places the onus on succulence as opposed to concentration and we liked it a lot. **Dolcetto d'Alba 2012** (● 5,500 bt) is a faithful mirror of the terroir, tannic with good expansion. **Langhe Freisa 2011** (● 2,000 bt) is a very typical, very distinctive wine, the product of a grape sadly forgotten by the majority of Langa winemakers. It's a pity because the Mascarello version is beautifully scented, savory and stylish.

FERTILIZERS natural manure, green manure
PLANT PROTECTION copper and sulphur, organic
WEED CONTROL mechanical
YEASTS selected
GRAPES 100% estate-grown
CERTIFICATION organic

FERTILIZERS organic-mineral
PLANT PROTECTION copper and sulphur
WEED CONTROL mechanical
YEASTS selected
GRAPES 100% estate-grown
CERTIFICATION none

BAROLO (CN)

Giuseppe Rinaldi

Via Monforte, 3
tel. 0173 56156

BAROLO (CN)

G.D. Vajra

Via delle Viole, 25
tel. 0173 56257
www.gdvajra.it
info@gdvajra.it

6.5 ha - 38,000 bt

❝ Sense of place, tradition, respect for the environment, great wines at honest price — given the name the cellar has made for itself. ❞

PEOPLE - We were taken round by Marta Rinaldi who, with enthusiasm and savoir-faire, is helping her father Beppe to run this, a historic Barolo cellar projected towards ambitious goals with a sustainable modern vision.

VINEYARDS - The vine rows that encircle the house-cum-cellar are part of the Le Coste cru. We walked round them with Marta, who explained the Rinaldi agronomic philosophy along the way: few interventions but plenty of controls with an eye on the weather as opposed to the calendar and constant monitoring of the vines. Weed control is non-existent and no chemicals are used to boost the vigor of the vines. Cannubi San Lorenzo, Brunate and Ravera are the other celebrated vineyards cultivated by the winery.

WINES - In the cellar they use traditional natural vinication methods. The result is a series of labels that faithfully reproduce their terroir and grapes of origin. As always our favorite is **Barolo Brunate-Le Coste 2009** (● 10,000 bt) which has a very open nose with outspoken acidity and undertones of meadow violets. Slightly less focused is **Barolo Cannubi San Lorenzo-Ravera 2009** (● 6,000 bt) whose juicy palate is refreshed by lingering acidity. **Langhe Nebbiolo 2011** (● 7,000 bt) is a junior Barolo that ages 18 months in wood barrels. **Barbera d'Alba 2012** (● 8,000 bt) is very young and enjoyable. We've often remarked that the best Piedmontese Ruché is made in Barolo and **Rosae 2012** (● 2,500 bt), with its inebriating scents, verve and notable complexity, suggests we aren't wrong.

FERTILIZERS natural manure
PLANT PROTECTION copper and sulphur
WEED CONTROL mechanical
YEASTS native
GRAPES 100% estate-grown
CERTIFICATION none

60 ha - 350,000 bt

❝ Classic, deep, at once land-rooted and approachable, the cellar's wines are a perfect reflection of the Vajras' philosophy of life. ❞

PEOPLE - We have known Aldo Vaira and his family, wife Milena and children Francesca, Giuseppe and Isidoro, all motivated and earnest about their work, for years. In all that time we have always displayed extraordinary scrupulousness, meticulousness and transparency.

VINEYARDS - The vineyards are as neat and tidy as gardens. Not only the magnificent Bricco delle Viole, but also all the others, including the new ones at Serralunga, Cerretta first and foremost. Total care and attention are dedicated to the growth cycle, from pruning to foliage management, with maximum respect for the environment. No chemicals are used, save for a modicum of weed control under the vine rows in particularly steep areas in the least favorable growing years.

WINES - Excellent as ever, the monovarietal, land-rooted **Langhe Riesling 2012** (○ 12,500 bt) is racy and highly-strung. Barolo Albe 2009 (● 50,000 bt) has clear-cut blossomy notes with a full-bodied, racy, dynamic palate and a refreshing finish. **Barolo Baudana Cerretta 2008** (● 4,000 bt) smacks of leather and ripe fruit with a palate that displays power and warmth, spaciousness and maturity. **Barolo Bricco delle Viole 2009** (● 16,000 bt) has a nose of nicely ripe fruit and a palate with just the right amount of body and enough acidity that ushers in a grand finale of flavor and leisurely length — a Great Wine. **Langhe Freisa Kyè 2010** (● 7,000 bt) is a quaffable wine with distinct fruity, spicy fragrances. **Dolcetto d'Alba Coste & Fossati 2011** (● 10,000 bt) is solid with plenty of ripe fruit.

FERTILIZERS natural manure, green manure
PLANT PROTECTION copper and sulphur
WEED CONTROL chemical, mechanical
YEASTS selected
GRAPES 100% estate-grown
CERTIFICATION none

CANALE (CN)

Cascina Ca' Rossa

Località Cascina Ca' Rossa, 56
tel. 0173 98348
www.cascinacarossa.com
angelo.ferrio@gmail.com

CANALE (CN)

Matteo Correggia

Località Garbinetto
Case Sparse, 124
tel. 0173 978009
www.matteocorreggia.com
cantina@matteocorreggia.com

---

15 ha - 70,000 bt

66 Clean, stylish wines, full of fruit and finesse, which respect the soil (the cellar was certified organic in June 2012) and the terroir of the Roero. 99

PEOPLE - The soul of the winery is the untiring, generous Angelo Ferrio, whose contagious good spirits and cheerfulness infect all around him. As of this year, he has a new helper in his son Stefano, fresh from a six-year enology course in Alba.

VINEYARDS - The vine rows are in the best positions in the Roero district. Mompissano, a south-facing hillside of one and a half hectares of immaculately tended nebbiolo vines growing on limestone, is a jewel of a vineyard; here most operations are performed by hand and topping is strictly forbidden. Mulassa, the barbera vineyard, is on the same hill. Audinaggio, a 60-year-old two-hectare vineyard with sandy soil, is near the village of Vezza, and in Santo Stefano Roero a new three-hectare property has been planted with nebbiolo and arneis.

WINES - The most important vineyards produce the three (non-filtered) flagship red wines, which are normally fermented for 25-30 days with native yeasts. **Roero Mompissano Ris. 2010** (● 6,000 bt), which ages for 30 months in 25-hectoliter caks has structure and finesse. The wonderful 2011 vintage gives us the grapey, stylish **Roero Audinaggio 2011** (● 4,000 bt) and, more enjoyable still, **Barbera d'Alba Mulassa 2011** (● 4,000 bt), aged in large barrels. Want to know a secret? Expect a great Mompissano from this vintage! The simplest wines are characterized by drinkability and fruit: with its blossomy nose and fruity finish, Roero Arneis 2012 (○ 24,000 bt), is a classic in its category, an excellent Everyday Wine. **Barbera d'Alba 2012** (● 12,000 bt) is even-textured, warm and alluring, **Langhe Nebbiolo 2011** (● 20,000 bt) is pleasantly grapey.

---

20 ha - 135,000 bt

PEOPLE - We are delighted to announce that Giovanni Correggia has now taken his place in the company. He's the son of the late Matteo and Ornella Costa, who has kept this wonderful winery on its feet over the last ten years since her husband's premature death. Giovanni appears to be geed up for the job and raring to go. He has the good fortune to be flanked by another "seasoned youngster", enologist Luca Rostagno.

VINEYARDS - Matteo Correggia selected some of the most important vineyards in the Roero hills personally and cultivated them with much care. He soon made them famous the world over and the first crus are now household names: Marun, near the cellar, where the barbera grapes grow, and Ròche d'Ampsèj, also in Canale but at a higher altitude, where the grapes for the magnificent Roero, described below, are grown.

WINES - We are happy to note that the cellar has made a cannier use of oak over the last few years. The wines are so fresh they reveal traces of their individual terroirs from a very early age. We really enjoyed **Roero Val dei Preti 2011** (● 10,700 bt), subtler than its elder brother but very typical. **Barbera d'Alba Marun 2011** (● 11,200 bt) is as burly and explosive as ever. **Barbera d'Alba 2011** (● 23,000 bt) is crisp and quaffable. The enjoyable **Roero 2011** (● 24,000 bt) is tinged with violet and strawberry. **Roero Arneis 2012** (○ 45,000 bt) is fragrant and tangy.

> **vino slow** ROERO RÒCHE D'AMPSÈJ RIS. 2009 The full-bodied palate is bolstered by complex varietal aromas and refreshing acidity. The label that introduced the Roero district to the world has made a magnificent comeback.

FERTILIZERS natural manure, compost	FERTILIZERS green manure
PLANT PROTECTION copper and sulphur	PLANT PROTECTION chemical, copper and sulphur
WEED CONTROL mechanical	WEED CONTROL chemical, mechanical
YEASTS selected	YEASTS selected
GRAPES 100% estate-grown	GRAPES 100% estate-grown
CERTIFICATION organic	CERTIFICATION none

CANALE (CN)

Malvirà

Località Canova
Case Sparse, 144
tel. 0173 978145
www.malvira.com
malvira@malvira.com

42 ha - 300,000 bt — **10% discount**

PEOPLE - For sales volumes and historical background, Malvirà is arguably the most important quality wine company in the Roero Arneis production zone. The company has always been family-run: Massimo and Roberto's father and his father before him were winemakers, as will be Roberto's son Giacomo, a graduate in enology, who is now taking charge of the cellar and foreign sales.

VINEYARDS - The vineyards are managed by Massimo in accordance with the criteria of eco-sustainability. Care for the landscape is fundamental for the Damonte brothers, among the leading promoters of the Roero district. An example of their contribution is their restoration of Villa Tiboldi, surrounded by the 18-hectare arneis and nebbiolo Trinità Renesio cru, cited in the Canale land register of 1750, which anticipated the zoning system Malvirà hopes to see introduced in the future.

WINES - If you can find bottles of the Arneis 2008 crus, now is the time to uncork them. Which is a testimony to the longevity this grape — a lover of sandy soil, which gives it aroma and finesse — is capable of. These are precisely the characteristics of **Roero Arneis Trinità 2011** (O 20,000 bt), for example, whose alter ego, **Roero Arneis Renesio 2011** (O 20,000 bt), made with grapes grown on silty limestone soil, is rounded and broad on the palate. The excellent, complex **Roero Arneis Saglietto 2011** (O 13,000 bt), 50 per of the grapes for which ferment in new barrels, is more complex. The red we were most fond of was **Roero Renesio Ris. 2009** (● 9,300 bt), blossomy and earthy with a long, full-flavored finish.

> **vino slow** **ROERO TRINITÀ RIS. 2009** (● 20,000 bt) Soft, supremely scented, stylish, subtle, sapid … On top of which, this is the first wine in the Roero district to self-certify its vineyard of origin and the traceability of its grapes on the label.

FERTILIZERS natural manure, humus
PLANT PROTECTION chemical, copper and sulphur
WEED CONTROL chemical, mechanical
YEASTS selected, native
GRAPES 100% estate-grown
CERTIFICATION none

CANALE (CN)

Monchiero Carbone

Via Santo Stefano Roero, 2
tel. 0173 95568
www.monchierocarbone.com
info@monchierocarbone.com

21 ha - 180,000 bt

PEOPLE - The good humor and optimism of Francesco Monchiero and his wife Lucrezia Scarsi are contagious. Together, assisted by Francesco's mother Luciana Carbone, they run this successful Roero winery with passion and energy. Their wines are the Roero, classics, with Arneis, Francesco's favorite, ruling the roost. The reds, Roero and Barbera, are interpreted in a modern key.

VINEYARDS - The Roero district owes its charm to the diversity of its soil. Clay and/or limestone produce deep, well-structured reds, sandier terrain gives life to scented, nicely mineral whites. Another distinctive feature of the area are the often extreme gradients, of the vineyards — hence excellent drainage. Here the viticulture is conventional but with limited recourse to chemicals.

WINES - The company submitted a good range of wines as usual. Of the two Arneis labels, Roero Arneis Recit 2012 (O 70,000 bt) has a very typical fruity nose and a beautifully fresh palate, which is why we crowned it as an Everyday Wine, while **Roero Arneis Cecu d'la Biunda 2012** (O 22,000 bt) is very aromatic with notes of grass and a textured, fleshy palate. **Barbera d'Alba Monbirone 2011** (● 10,000 bt) has a bouquet of fruit and sweet spices and a full-bodied, fleshy, very juicy palate. The well-crafted **Langhe Nebbiolo Regret 2011** (● 25,000 bt) is an enjoyable tipple. The aromas of **Roero Srü 2010** (● 8,000 bt) are well-defined, the palate full of fruit with a lingering finish. **Roero Printi 2009** (● 6,000 bt) has a spacious nose redolent of ripe fruit and a palate of solid structure and juicy flesh with a super zippy finish.

FERTILIZERS natural manure
PLANT PROTECTION chemical, copper and sulphur
WEED CONTROL chemical, mechanical
YEASTS selected
GRAPES 15% bought in
CERTIFICATION none

Brovia

Frazione Garbelletto
Via Alba-Barolo, 54
tel. 0173 62852
www.brovia.net
info@brovia.net

16.5 ha - 60,000 bt

66 Brovia is a cellar which strives incessantly to give its wines a sense of place and pure expressiveness. Precise and clear-cut, they combine complexity and elegance. 99

PEOPLE - The Brovia family have been making Barolo for a century and a half. Set up in 1863, the cellar is run by sisters Cristina and Elena. The former is a wine lab technician who works in the vineyards, the latter an agronomist who works in the cellar. At the ripe old age of 86, their father Giacinto still plays an active part in the running of the business, and Elena's husband Alex Sanchez, from Barcellona, oversees sales and logistics.

VINEYARDS - The 10-hectare south- and southeast-facing Ca' Mia di Serralunga property in the Brea cru, given over mainly to nebbiolo grapes, is particularly attractive. It comprises the 1955 vineyards that produce the grapes for the wine of the same name. The other properties — whose grapes are vinified separately for the single crus — are in Villero, Rocche and Garbelletto Superiore in Castiglione Falletto. The winery went organic three years ago and respects the life cycle of the vine with prudent pruning.

WINES - Only grapes from old vines are used in the four crus. Fermentations are spontaneous and are performed in 100-hectoliter cement vats for about three weeks. The wines are aged in large barrels. Rose, wood and tobacco lift the finesse of **Barolo Rocche 2009 (●** 5,000 bt), a Great Wine. **Barolo Ca' Mia 2009 (●** 5,000 bt) combines power, complexity, and lightness in an enviable palate, a copybook wine. **Barolo Villero 2009 (●** 5,000 bt) is masculine with assertive tannins. **Barolo Garblèt Suè 2009 (●** 3,500 bt) is tannic, fruity and meaty. The great **Barolo Ris. 150° Anniversario Rocche Villero 2005 (●** 1,700 magnum) was released to celebrate the winery's 150th anniversary.

FERTILIZERS natural manure, green manure	
PLANT PROTECTION copper and sulphur, organic	
WEED CONTROL mechanical	
YEASTS native	
GRAPES 8% bought in	
CERTIFICATION converting to organics	

Cavallotto Fratelli

Località Bricco Boschis
Strada Alba-Monforte, 40
tel. 0173 62814
www.cavallotto.com
info@cavallotto.com

23 ha - 100,000 bt

66 The winery is run by two brothers and a sister, Alfio, Giuseppe and Laura, who have introduced a number of innovations, especially with regard to vineyard management which is now, de facto, organic. The style of their wines is the quintessence of tradition. 99

PEOPLE - It's a long story — that's how the tale of the Cavallottos might begin. The family have lived in the pretty Bricco Boschis valley for so long they are now part of the landscape.

VINEYARDS - The natural amphitheater that surrounds Bricco Boschis is ideal for winemaking. One only has to see the place to realize that only great wines of unmatchable finesse and depth can come out of it. Good air circulation, abundant sand in the soil, old vineyards, cover cropping and the dropping of chemicals are the factors essential to the growing of healthy, clean, adequately concentrated grapes.

WINES - Barolo Bricco Boschis 2009 (● 28,000 bt) has very lively fruit on the nose and a well-structured, succulent palate; given time, it will grow to become magnificent. **Barolo Bricco Boschis Vigna San Giuseppe Ris. 2007 (●** 6,600 bt) has a bouquet of ripe fruit and a palate packed with energy and flesh, which leads into a lingering blossomy finish. On the nose **Barolo Vignolo Ris. 2007 (●** 3,300) exudes all the ripe fruit typical of warm growing years, on the palate it is spacious with a strong initial impact that holds back a little on the finish — the errors of youth! **Langhe Nebbiolo 2011 (●** 15,000 bt) is fresh and typical. **Barbera d'Alba Vigna del Cuculo 2010 (●** 15,000 bt) is racy and high-spirited with nice fruit and refreshing acidity. **Langhe Freisa 2011 (●** 4,000 bt) is solid and juicy.

FERTILIZERS green manure	
PLANT PROTECTION copper and sulphur	
WEED CONTROL mechanical	
YEASTS native	
GRAPES 100% estate-grown	
CERTIFICATION none	

CASTIGLIONE FALLETTO (CN)

Vietti

Piazza Vittorio Veneto, 5
tel. 0173 62825
www.vietti.com
info@vietti.com

37 ha - 250,000 bt **10% discount**

PEOPLE - Rigor, style and local character are the distinctive features of this pearl of Langa winemaking. Luca Currado and Mario Cordero, the brains behind this solid winery, are assisted by a top-level team that helps raise its bar of quality year by year. The cellar is situated in the old center of Castiglione and is worth a visit partly for its modern architecture.

VINEYARDS - The winery boasts an immense area of land planted with vines, including some of the most prestigious vineyards in the area. In fact, Mario and Luca, who work with the precious consultancy of Gian Piero Romana, own parcels in the Lazzarito, Brunate, Rocche, Villero and Scarrone crus. A few years ago they also acquired the La Crena vineyard at Agliano Terme. Trials with organic viticulture are well under way.

WINES - Vietti's are reliable wines. From the first to the last, their style is characterized by extreme cleanness, precision, balance and land-rootedness. **Barolo Villero Ris. 2006** (● 3,400 bt) has crystalline class with a very rich, nuanced nose and wonderful harmony: it's a Great Wine. This year's range includes a masterful **Barolo Lazzarito 2009** (● 6,100 bt), delicate and earthy, an emblem of classicism Langa-style. On a par is **Barolo Rocche 2009** (● 3,800 bt), characterized by balsamic texture and length. **Barolo Brunate 2009** (● 3,800 bt) is more open, a sign of the warm growing year. The Barbera range was most impressive: the cream of the crop was **Barbera d'Asti Sup. Nizza La Crena 2010** (● 6,500 bt), a juicy and typical expression of the Nizza-subzone. **Barbera d'Alba Vigna Vecchia Scarrone 2011** (● 3,500 bt) is fruity and well structured.

FERTILIZERS organic-mineral, manure pellets, natural manure, compost, green manure
PLANT PROTECTION chemical, copper and sulphur
WEED CONTROL mechanical
YEASTS selected
GRAPES 100% estate-grown
CERTIFICATION none

DOGLIANI (CN)

Marziano Abbona

Borgata San Luigi, 40
tel. 0173 721317
www.abbona.com
abbona@abbona.com

45 ha - 270,000 bt

PEOPLE - Meeting people like Marziano Abbona is not only enjoyable, it's also a way of discovering the genuine, hospitable spirit of the Langa hills. Now with more than a few grape harvests under his belt, Marziano has built himself a precise identity as a talented interpreter first of the Dogliani zone, where he was born, then that of Barolo. He runs his winery with the support of his wife and two daughters.

VINEYARDS - Marziano is quick-witted and misses nothing that might serve to promote and defend his territory. One example is his fantastic orchard, where he grows many old Piedmontese fruit varieties. This may be irrelevant for enological purposes, but it does reveal Marziano's sensibility as a farmer. Despite the vast area of its vineyards, the cellar has always adopted a reasoned approach and chemical weedkillers are banned.

WINES - The range submitted by the cellar team — namely Marziano and his mate Beppe Caviola — impressed again this year. **Barolo Terlo Ravera 2009** (● 14,000 bt) and **Barolo Pressenda 2009** (● 19,000 bt), for example, are both excellent versions of the wine with a style that banks on classicism, richness of fruit and balsamic tones. The first is more ethereal and caressing, the second fresh and tannic. The deep, juicy **Nebbiolo d'Alba Bricco Barone 2011** (● 18,000 bt) works to a similar register. **Dogliani San Luigi 2012** (● 80,000 bt) is reliable, **Langhe Bianco Cinerino 2012** (O viognier; 14,000 bt) mesmerizing.

vino slow **Dogliani Papà Celso 2011** (● 48,000 bt) An appointment not to be missed with the terroir. Even in a warm growing year, it showed character and finesse — a really effective wine.

FERTILIZERS natural manure
PLANT PROTECTION copper and sulphur
WEED CONTROL mechanical
YEASTS native
GRAPES 100% estate-grown
CERTIFICATION none

DOGLIANI (CN)

Cascina Corte

Borgata Valdiberti, 33
tel. 0173 743539
www.cascinacorte.it
info@cascinacorte.it

5.5 ha - 26,000 bt   **10% discount**

66 Approachable, natural wines produced in complete harmony with the environment and sold at very reasonable prices. 99

PEOPLE - Sandro Barosi is a humorous, unassuming guy who's always ready to listen to the advice of others, even though he has acquired a lot of winemaking experience himself. Go to meet him, take a walk through his vineyards and taste his wines in his company. You'll find the experience interesting and the wines delicious.

VINEYARDS - How many times have we heard the objection that it's impossible to go organic because vine diseases would destroy everything? Somebody must have forgotten to tell peronospora seeing how this year Cascina Corte and many other organic and biodynamic wineries were left untouched by the infection which preferred to eat up chemically treated wines.

WINES - Dogliani Sup. Pirochetta Vecchie Vigne 2011 (● 6,000 bt) stands out for its acid freshness and verve on the palate, which it rounds off with notes of fruit and grass. Dogliani 2012 (● 8,000 bt) offers the nose concentrated, intact fruit and fruity flesh and inviting juiciness on the palate: it's an excellent Everyday Wine. **Langhe Nebbiolo 2011** (● 4,500 bt), which displays commendable solidity and a typical inviting florality, is still very young and will improve in the bottle. **Langhe Barbera 2011** (● 6,000 bt) has classic fragrances of cherry and plum accompanied by a touch of lively acidity. The red **Barnedol** (● barbera, nebbiolo, dolcetto; 2,000 bt), a 2011-2012 assemblage, combines solid tannins with a certain juiciness.

FERTILIZERS natural manure
PLANT PROTECTION copper and sulphur
WEED CONTROL mechanical
YEASTS native
GRAPES 100% estate-grown
CERTIFICATION organic

DOGLIANI (CN)

Pecchenino

Borgata Valdiberti, 59
tel. 0173 70686
www.pecchenino.com
pecchenino@pecchenino.it

25 ha - 120,000 bt

66 Many regard this winery as a beacon for the Dogliani district, a fact that is enough on its own to make brothers Orlando and Attilio Pecchenino the ambassadors of a terroir and a wine that they interpret with genius and precision. 99

PEOPLE - Stars in Dogliani, the Pecchenino are now beginning to shine in the Barolo firmament. They have also invested heftily in the restructuring of their beautiful farmhouse.

VINEYARDS - One sees how much the brothers are in earnest visiting their vineyards, close by the cellar. We were taken round by Orlando, who showed us how sustainability is more than just abstraction, preconception, paper work and red tape. The two brothers apply the "farmer's" management model handed down to them by their father, a model they have enhanced with knowledge, observation, testing and ongoing discussion.

WINES - Once more this year all the labels submitted proved impressive. Dogliani comes in three versions and highlights the precise style of the Pecchenino brothers. The succulent, quaffable **Dogliani San Luigi 2012** (● 65,000 bt), the simplest of the trio is top-notch. **Dogliani Sup. Bricco Botti 2010** (● 5,500 bt), an interpretation aged on wood that demonstrates the versatility of the grape, is also very good. From the Monforte vineyards come **Barolo Le Coste 2009** (● 6,500 bt) and **Barolo San Giuseppe 2009** (● 6,800 bt;), the first deep and full of grip, the second fruity and potent, both excellent.

vino slow DOGLIANI SUP. SIRÌ D'JERMU 2011 (● 23,000 bt) An icon of the terroir. Its compact, balsamic, deep taste profile makes it a flagship for the entire DOCG.

FERTILIZERS organic-mineral, compost, green manure, humus
PLANT PROTECTION copper and sulphur
WEED CONTROL mechanical
YEASTS selected
GRAPES 100% estate-grown
CERTIFICATION none

FARIGLIANO (CN)

Anna Maria Abbona

Frazione Moncucco, 21
tel. 0173 797228
www.annamariabbona.it
info@annamariabbona.it

12 ha - 75,000 bt

66 Land-rooted labels, country common sense, honest prices, memorable wines — a life project that has developed into a top-level winery. 99

PEOPLE - The Abbona family treated us to a big surprise this year with their decision to manage a new vineyard in Monforte and produce Barolo there. When we made our visit, Anna Maria Abbona's husband Franco Schellino was busy trench-plowing the soil.

VINEYARDS - The isolated Moncucco district is set in a beautiful landscape. The vineyards are managed with great respect for the environment and some of them are very old: Maioli dates from 1935, San Bernardo from 1943. One factor which influences the wines considerably is the altitude of the plantings, from 490 meters to 570. This is one of the reasons why the winery has gambled, among other grapes, on riesling and nascetta.

WINES - A range of consistently high quality at very reasonable prices. **Langhe Dolcetto 2012** (● 14,000 bt) is fresh, flavorful, clean-tasting, by no means banal. It's hard to find a better wine in this typology — and at this price! The maison's bestseller is Dogliani Sorì dij But 2012 (● 25,000 bt), a hymn to the fragrance and vinosity of the dolcetto grape with the flesh and juice of a cherry just plucked from the tree — a perfect Everyday Wine. **Dogliani Maioli 2011** (● 7,000 bt), made with grapes from an older vineyard, is longer and more complex. The rich, muscular **Dogliani San Bernardo 2010** (● 4,000 bt) is the fruit of brief drying of the grapes and aging for 18 months and more in wood barrels. **Langhe Nebbiolo 2010** (● 7,000 bt) is spicy and highly scented. The blossomy **Langhe Bianco Netta 2012** (○ nascetta; 1.500 bt) is aged exclusively in steel vats.

GRINZANE CAVOUR (CN)

La Spinetta

Località Campé
Via Carzello, 1
tel. 0141 877396
www.la-spinetta.com
info@la-spinetta.com

100 ha - 450,000 bt

PEOPLE - La Spinetta is a name that shines on the Piedmontese wine scene. With the sheer quantity and superlative quality of the typologies it produces, it has won international accolades and popularity. The brains behind the glory are the Rivetti brothers, captained by the talented Giorgio. Theirs is a family of true wine entrepreneurs, firmly tied to the land.

VINEYARDS - The company owns a complex mosaic of vineyards from the Langa hills to the province of Asti. Albeit historic moscato growers and producers, the Rivettis became able interpreters of Barbaresco and Barolo after shrewdly buying a series of fantastic vineyards: Gallina, Starderi, Valeirano and Bordini, plus the lesser Garetti and Campé, are just some of their crus. The barbera vineyard in the Bionzo district is a sight to behold.

WINES - Distinctive and original, La Spinetta speaks the plain language of enological perfection. Giorgio looks for power and ripeness in the fruit, buttressed by high concentration and proper use of wood. Years on, the wines project the company's full potential. **Barbaresco Valeirano 2010** (● 7,000 bt) has ripe fruit and stand-out tannins. The succulent **Barbaresco Starderi 2010** (● 14,000 bt) is more approachable, while **Barbaresco Gallina 2010** (● 10,000 bt) is deep, rich and pervasive. **Barbaresco Bordini 2009** (● 10,000 bt) is still on the stiff side. The two reserves are also noteworthy: the extraordinary, much-aged **Barolo Campé Ris.** 2004 (● 1,000 magnum) is a Great Wine. **Barbaresco Valeirano Ris. 2004** (● 700 magnum) is enfolding and well-rounded.

FERTILIZERS none
PLANT PROTECTION chemical, copper and sulphur
WEED CONTROL chemical, mechanical
YEASTS selected
GRAPES 100% estate-grown
CERTIFICATION none

FERTILIZERS green manure, humus
PLANT PROTECTION chemical, copper and sulphur
WEED CONTROL mechanical
YEASTS selected
GRAPES 100% estate-grown
CERTIFICATION none

Elio Altare - Cascina Nuova 🐌

Frazione Annunziata, 51
tel. 0173 50835
www.elioaltare.com
elioaltare@elioaltare.com

10.5 ha - 60,000 bt

66 After "writing the history" of Barolo in the last 30 years, this winery is approaching the future with new momentum and energy. 99

PEOPLE - The cellar, now a star in the international wine firmament and rightly so, is run by a close-knit team. At least formally, Elio Altare has handed over the reins to his daughter Silvia, whose collaborators are her partner Massimo Marengo and the trusty Tesu Cyo.

VINEYARDS - The vineyards are as well kept as the family garden. This is not to say that they are all neat and perfect, but rather that every single vine is regarded as a single individual. This is one of the secrets of the longevity of Altare's wines. The Arborina cru, for example, was planted in 1948 and is still in full production. Another secret is the decision, taken some time ago, to ban all chemical fertilizers and burndown weed control products from the vineyards.

WINES - Altare's Barolos age wonderfully well as we found out on our visit, during which we were lucky enough to taste the 1991 and 1992, both in scintillating form despite being the fruits of damp, poor growing years. We were totally won over by **Langhe Rosso Larigi 2011** (● barbera; 2,300 bt), fruity and acid to the right degree, complex and rich. No less impressive is **Barolo Bricco Cerretta 2007** (● 6,000 bt), deep, powerful and harmonious with a long, lingering finish. Both **Barolo 2009** (● 12,000 bt) and **Barolo Arborina 2009** (● 8,000 bt) have slightly stiff tannins and need more time in the bottle. **Langhe Rosso Arborina 2011** (● nebbiolo; 2,300 bt) and **Langhe Rosso La Villa 2011** (● nebbiolo, barbera; 2,300 bt) are both beautifully crafted and stylistically impeccable.

Brandini €

Frazione Brandini, 16
tel. 0173 50266
www.agricolabrandini.it
info@agricolabrandini.it

7 ha - 60,000 bt

PEOPLE - The big news at Brandini's is that owner Carlo Cavagnero has sold off all his shares to the businessmen who control Eataly and who were his partners for some time. The youthful Danila Chiotti has thus been hired to oversee the vineyards and the cellar. She will be assisted in the task by consultants of the caliber of agronomist Alberto Grasso and enologist Beppe Caviola.

VINEYARDS - Brandini was one of the first wineries in the Langa hills to successfully adopt organic agriculture. This farsighted choice has raised the profile of a corner of La Morra still underrated by nebbiolo lovers. Visiting the Brandini vineyards and walking among the vine rows is a fantastic experience during which you see insects and birds and many, many flowers, a reminder of how it's possible for viticulture to integrate with the environment.

WINES - The range of wines submitted was good, especially considering their truly competitive pricing. To begin with, the excellent Everyday Wine, Langhe Rosso 2012 (● nebbiolo, barbera; 4,000 bt), which combines the fragrant elegance of the nebbiolo grape with the journeyman huskiness of barbera. **Barolo Brandini 2009** (● 8,000 bt) has complex aromas with undertones of violet and cherry. **Barolo 2009** (● 25,000 bt) is excellent value for money. The two Vino Libero labels impressed: **Barbera d'Alba Sup. Rocche del Santo 2011** (● 8,000 bt) is aged in barrels, **Langhe Nebbiolo Filari Corti 2011** (● 8,000 bt) is a textbook wine in the precise way it captures the aromas of the grape. **Dolcetto d'Alba San'Anna 2012** (● 8,000 bt) is highly scented.

FERTILIZERS natural manure	FERTILIZERS manure pellets
PLANT PROTECTION copper and sulphur	PLANT PROTECTION copper and sulphur
WEED CONTROL mechanical	WEED CONTROL mechanical
YEASTS native	YEASTS native
GRAPES 100% estate-grown	GRAPES 100% estate-grown
CERTIFICATION none	CERTIFICATION organic

LA MORRA (CN)
Cordero di Montezemolo ▮
Monfalletto
Frazione Annunziata, 67 Bis
tel. 0173 50344
www.corderodimontezemolo.it
info@corderodimontezemolo.com
⌐o

35 ha - 240,000 bt

PEOPLE - Be sure to phone ahead and fix an appointment, if you want to visit this Langa jewel. When you walk into the cellar at Annunziata di La Morra, don't expect a stuffy, formal reception. On the contrary, here you'll receive a warm welcome from Alberto, a young member, like his sister Elena, of the new generation of Corderos. He'll then take you on a journey to discover the world of Barolo.

VINEYARDS - The Corderos are among the few to concentrate their vineyards round their farmhouse. This is very good growing land and the vines grow in the shade of a magnificent Lebanese cedar, the symbol of the winery and of the local area. The lovely vineyard at Castiglione Falletto is part of the Villero cru and produces the grapes for Enrico VI, the top wine in the range.

WINES - The wines capture the essence of the Langa hills. Their common traits are purity and limpidness, elegance and approachability, qualities typical of all Annunziata Barolos. In **Barolo Monfalletto 2009** (● 45,000 bt) the sweetness of the fruit is enhanced by pronounced spicy nuances, the tannins are deft and drinkability is exceptional. **Barolo Bricco Gattera 2009** (● 5,500 bt), which has notes of mint and undergrowth, is a little clinched, likely due to its youthfulness. **Barolo Enrico VI 2009** (● 9,000 bt) is open and very fruity with hefty alcohol and a forceful toasted finish. The winery also produces an excellent classic, juicy **Barbera d'Alba Funtanì 2010** (● 9,400 bt). As well-crafted as ever, **Langhe Chardonnay Elioro 2011** (○ 5,500 bt) is an ambitious white that banks on bottle-aging.

LA MORRA (CN)
Osvaldo Viberti
Frazione Santa Maria
Borgata Serra dei Turchi, 95
tel. 0173 50374
www.vibertiosvaldo.it
osvaldo.viberti@alice.it - viberti.osvaldo@libero.it

10 ha - 30,000 bt

PEOPLE - The new cellar at Osvaldo Viberti's winery is almost ready and will be operational for the next harvest. An extra half a hectare of vineyard has also been acquired at Serralunga. Osvaldo's wife Carla is a great help in the vineyards, while enologist Sergio Molino collaborates in the wine cellar. Of the company's production, almost 90 per cent is sold abroad, while the rest ends up in the local catering trade or on sales directly at the cellar.

VINEYARDS - The main vineyards are at Serra dei Turchi, with an hectare given over to nebbiolo, and at Meriame di Serralunga, with three hectares given over to barbera an two to nebbiolo. This year the winery began to produce Nascetta, from an old, almost extinct grape variety native to Novello. Treatments in the vineyard are conventional and mostly pre-used large barrels and barriques are adopted in the cellar.

WINES - **Barolo Serra dei Turchi 2009** (● 3,000 bt) has ripe fruit and spices and a long, lingering potent palate. **Barolo 2009** (● 7,000 bt) is floral and fruity, well-balanced with non-aggressive tannins. **Nebbiolo d'Alba 2011** (● 2,500 bt), which ages six months in second-use mid-sized casks, is fresh and fruity, full-flavored and pleasing in the glass. **Barbera d'Alba Sup. Mancine 2011** (● 3,000 bt) releases complexity and balance, notes of toastiness and plenty of length. On its debut, **Langhe Nascetta 2012** (○ 2,000 bt) is blossomy and mineral.

| vino slow | **BAROLO SERRALUNGA 2009** (● 2,500 bt) An austere, complex wine with tannins well to the fore and a grand finale of fruit enriching its flavor in the glass. A typical and excellent example of nebbiolo di Serralunga. |

FERTILIZERS organic-mineral, natural manure, compost
PLANT PROTECTION copper and sulphur, organic
WEED CONTROL mechanical
YEASTS selected
GRAPES 100% estate-grown
CERTIFICATION none

FERTILIZERS organic-mineral
PLANT PROTECTION chemical, copper and sulphur
WEED CONTROL chemical, mechanical
YEASTS selected
GRAPES 100% estate-grown
CERTIFICATION none

Giuseppe Mascarello e Figlio

Strada del Grosso, 1
tel. 0173 792126
www.mascarello1881.com
mauromascarello@mascarello1881.com

12.5 ha - 60,000 bt

PEOPLE - We were lucky enough to taste a Barolo Monprivato 1970, the first vintage of the cru to be produced by Mauro Mascarello, now at the helm of this legendary winery. On that occasion, Mauro told us all about his wine and his career. 1970 was so sublime, he says, it's still impressed in his memory. At his side work his wife Maria Teresa and his kids Giuseppe and Elena.

VINEYARDS - At Monprivato, the Mascarello's six-hectar monopole, the soil is particularly rich in active limestone, which gives the wines great longevity. It faces southwest and has good air circulation. The average age of the vines is high and the hectare which gives life to Ca' d'Morissio was replanted 25 years ago. The other vineyards are at Santo Stefano di Perno (six hectares), at Monforte and in the magnificent Villero at Castiglione Falletto.

WINES - We were overwhelmed again by **Barolo Monprivato**, this year in its 2008 version (● 17,500 bt), reticent a first, then blossoming out with hints of soil and leather; racy and juicy, leisurely and deep, on the palate it shows extraordinary verve. Nuanced, savory and mineral, **Barolo Villero 2008** (● 2,400 bt) has a wonderfully lively, compact palate; it's a Great Wine. **Barolo Santo Stefano di Perno 2008** (● 2,400 bt) is almost on a par for depth of mouthfeel, assertiveness and length. **Dolcetto d'Alba Bricco Mirasole 2011** (● 4,500 bt) has close-focused, vivacious fruit on the nose and an enchantingly fresh and lively palate. **Dolcetto d'Alba Vigna Santo Stefano di Perno 2011** (● 6,000) has less structure and density, mature tannins and a characteristically almondy finish. **Langhe Freisa Toetto 2007** (● 3,500 bt) is good, typical and classic.

FERTILIZERS natural manure
PLANT PROTECTION chemical, copper and sulphur
WEED CONTROL chemical, mechanical
YEASTS selected
GRAPES 100% estate-grown
CERTIFICATION none

Conterno Fantino

Via Ginestra, 1
tel. 0173 78204
www.conternofantino.it
info@conternofantino.it

26 ha - 140,000 bt

❝ This year we are delighted to announce that the vineyards of this magnificent winery in Monforte have received organic certification. Thirty years on from its first bottling, the business continues to hold high its standards of quality in terms of quality, professionalism, commitment and care for the environment, with the use of geothermic and photovoltaic energy. ❞

PEOPLE - The wines of Claudio Conterno, who works in the vineyards, and Guido Fantino, who works in the cellar with his son Fabio, are excellent, land-rooted and deep.

VINEYARDS - Gian Piero Romana has been helping Claudio Conterno to oversee the vineyards for 20 years now. All the parcels are managed using organic methods and impeccably kept, from pruning to foliage treatment, anything but secondary in years that are increasingly warm. The names of the crus speak for themselves: Ginestra, Mosconi and so on, all celebrated vineyards from which the winery draws magnificent, perfectly ripe and healthy fruit.

WINES - **Barolo Mosconi 2009** (● 5,200 bt) is made with the grapes from a vineyard of which the cellar is expecting great things. Racy and full of verve, it has juicy flesh braced by precise, close-knit, non-invasive tannins — a Great Wine. **Barolo Vigna del Gris 2009** (● 6,500 bt) still shows the signs of aging and has a palate of juicy, sweet flesh. **Barolo Sorì Ginestra 2009** (● 14,900 bt) has delicate blossomy notes on the nose and, on the palate, masks the power typical of Ginestra wines with amazing suppleness and drinkability. **Langhe Nebbiolo Ginestrino 2011** (● 31,000 bt) is good, while **Langhe Rosso Monprà 2010** (● barbera, nebbiolo, cabernet sauvignon; 8,600 bt) has enticing, fruity flesh with structure to match. **Barbera d'Alba Vignota 2011** (● 12,000 bt) has great vivacity.

FERTILIZERS compost, green manure
PLANT PROTECTION copper and sulphur
WEED CONTROL mechanical
YEASTS native
GRAPES 100% estate-grown
CERTIFICATION organic

Giacomo Conterno

Località Ornati, 2
tel. 0173 78221
www.conterno.it

Giacomo Fenocchio €

Località Bussia, 72
tel. 0173 78675
www.giacomofenocchio.com
claudio@giacomofenocchio.com

---

17 ha - 60,000 bt

PEOPLE - When we think about the great Langa wineries and their generational turnovers, we always have a sneaking fear that some of the magical mechanisms that have helped create mythical labels are about to break. In 2004, when Giovanni Conterno died, the general opinion was that his son Roberto would rise to the occasion. Ten years on we can confirm that all the rosiest expectations have been lived up to.

VINEYARDS - Great wines can only be born in great vineyards. That may sound like a platitude but it's a fact worth remembering occasionally. In 1974 Giovanni Conterno bought Cascina Francia and since then the aura of his labels grew and grew. So much so that Monfortino became the Barolo par excellence. In 2008 Roberto bought three hectares of land in another gorgeous Serralunga cru at Cerretta, where a new Barolo will see the light soon.

WINES - This is the year of Monfortino, inevitably so given the magnificent 2006 vintage. The nose of **Barolo Monfortino Ris. 2006** (● 10,000 bt), tinged with violets and wild strawberries, couldn't be more classical, while the palate is full of flavor with the right degree of acidity and depth. It's a Great Wine that helps lift the fame of the Langa hills. **Barolo Cascina Francia 2009** (● 18,000) is also aged in wood barrels and macerated the traditional way. Hence the deliciously sweet fruit and powerful, beefy tannins which recall the wine's birthplace, Serralunga. **Barbera d'Alba Cerretta 2011** (● 4,000 bt), which has forthright, precise acidity, and **Barbera d'Alba Cascina Francia 2011** (● 18,000 bt), which is sweeter and more rounded, are both top-notch.

---

15 ha - 90,000 bt **10% discount**

PEOPLE - Claudio Fenocchio, a member of the fifth generation of a family of Bussia winegrowers, runs this splendid winery professionally and coherently; the place is one of the most reliable for anyone in search of the pure, classic soul of Barolo. Not that this personable, smiling vigneron is a stubborn follower of obsolete methods. He is, rather, a curious experimenter, always keen to learn and improve. The big news this year was the inauguration of "Terroir-ist", a point-of-sale in Castiglione Falletto, where it's also possible to taste other local products.

VINEYARDS - The company boasts top-notch vineyards: Bussia at Monforte and Villero at Castiglione have similar altitudes and soils, classic Langa clayey-calcareous marls, and produce wines of remarkable structure. At Cannubi, lower down, the soil is still marly but with a higher percentage of sand. All the vineyards produce wines of great florality, most evident in the classic vintages.

WINES - **Barolo Villero 2009** (● 5,000 bt) is distinguished by integrity, density and earthy energy. The excellent **Barolo Bussia 2009** (● 15,000 bt), is more open and expansive, less austere than usual. **Barolo Bussia Ris. 2007** (● 5,000 bt) is generous, warm and very complex on the nose with a palate marked by amazing contrasts of texture, sweet fruit and deftness. **Barbera d'Alba Sup. 2011** (● 15,000 bt) is delicious, **Langhe Nebbiolo 2011** (● 5,000 bt) as reliable as ever.

vino slow | **BAROLO CANNUBI 2009** (● 3,000 bt) A refined interpretation of a great vineyard, with subtle, inebriating floral and ethereal fragrances, a wine that glides over the palate with grace and style. The tannins are close-knit but sweet, the palate very long indeed.

FERTILIZERS natural manure
PLANT PROTECTION copper and sulphur
WEED CONTROL mechanical
YEASTS selected
GRAPES 100% estate-grown
CERTIFICATION none

FERTILIZERS humus
PLANT PROTECTION chemical, copper and sulphur
WEED CONTROL chemical, mechanical
YEASTS selected
GRAPES 100% estate-grown
CERTIFICATION none

Elio Grasso

Località Ginestra, 40
tel. 0173 78491
www.eliograsso.it
info@eliograsso.it

18 ha - 90,000 bt

❝ The Snail symbol we have awarded Elio Grasso is a well-deserved and due recognition for a man who, with decision, character, humility and the spirit of a farmer, invested everything in a return to the land in years when work was hard and rewards were few and far between. His is a model of "liberation" that defines the identity of the Langa hills today. ❞

PEOPLE - Elio is helped by his wife Marina and his brilliant son Gianluca, and together they form an effective family team.

VINEYARDS - It's hard not to fall into rhetoric when describing this winery's work. Concepts such as vocation, quality, sustainability and manuality are foundations on which Elio has built his identity. The Ginestra cru, which encompasses various parcels of land, including Gavarini and Runcot, is the vineyard in which the cellar's property is distributed. A large swath of woodland is proof that the Grassos aren't monoculture minded.

WINES - Elio and Gianluca's wines are crystalline and exciting. Their message is loud and clear: obsessive attention to every detail. **Barolo Ginestra Casa Maté 2009** (● 9,200 bt) is a complex, deep, earthy wine that lingers vibrantly on the palate. **Barolo Gavarini Chiniera 2009** (● 9,200 bt) displays greater density but is also more approachable with a supple finish. This is the year of **Barolo Runcot Ris. 2007** (● 8,000 bt), made with grapes from the vineyard of the same name just down from the cellar. The impressive result of over 30 years of aging in barriques, it reveals Gianluca's skill with wood. The other bottles in the range, such as **Langhe Nebbiolo Gavarini 2012** (● 18,000 bt) and **Barbera d'Alba Vigna Martina 2010** (● 18,400 bt) are as reliable as ever.

FERTILIZERS natural manure
PLANT PROTECTION copper and sulphur, organic
WEED CONTROL mechanical
YEASTS selected
GRAPES 100% estate-grown
CERTIFICATION none

Giovanni Almondo €

Via San Rocco, 26
tel. 0173 975256
www.giovannialmondo.com
almondo@giovannialmondo.com

15 ha - 80,000 bt

PEOPLE - This solid family company, a shining beacon in the Roero district, took shape in the early 1980s when Domenico Almondo directed production towards specialized quality viticulture. Today Almondo is famous notably for his Arneis, but his passion for minerally white wines has also brought about an excellent Riesling, and with the arrival on the scene of his sons Stefano and Federico, a graduate in viticulture and enology, the reds are achieving very high standards too.

VINEYARDS - The vineyards are in two different zones near Montà d'Alba. The first, north of the village, has very sandy soil, up to 80 per cent, on the very steep Burigot plot, slightly less in the Bricco delle Ciliegie plot. Southwards, on the boundary with Canale and Santo Stefano, the geological formation of the soil, sandy of marine origin, is older but also firmer with a higher percentage of silt and fossils. This is where the magnificent natural amphitheater of Bric Valdiana is situated.

WINES - The excellent **Roero Arneis Vigne Sparse 2012** (○ 38,000 bt) has precise, classic fruity, floral notes. Also excellent is **Langhe Riesling Sassi e Sabbia 2012** (○ 2,400 bt), taut and gutsy, still youthful. The most stylish, typical red is **Roero 2011** (5.500 bt), which is aged in large barrels. **Roero Bric Valdiana 2010** (● 3,800 bt), aged in barriques, has solid texture and a spicy finish. **Barbera d'Alba Valbianchera 2011** (● 3,000 bt), made with grapes from 80-year-old vineyards, is deep, concentrated and juicy.

vino slow ROERO ARNEIS BRICCO DELLE CILIEGIE 2012 (○ 40,000 bt) A partially barrel-fermented wine of huge character with a vibrant, full-flavored palate. A historic terroir-dedicated label with outstanding aromas.

FERTILIZERS organic-mineral, natural manure
PLANT PROTECTION chemical, copper and sulphur
WEED CONTROL mechanical
YEASTS selected
GRAPES 100% estate-grown
CERTIFICATION none

Angelo Negro & Figli €

Frazione Sant'Anna, 1
tel. 0173 90252
www.negroangelo.it
negro@negroangelo.it

Piero Busso

Via Albesani, 8
tel. 0173 67156
www.bussopiero.com
bussopiero@bussopiero.com

---

54 ha - 300,000 bt

PEOPLE - The winery of the Negro family — Giovanni, his wife Maria Elisa and their children Angelo, Emanuela, Giuseppe and Gabriele — is important not only for being firmly rooted in the Roero district, where it has existed for centuries, but also for its size, which allows it to make its vines known all over the world. The secret of its success is meticulous work at every stage in the production chain from clone selection onwards.

VINEYARDS - The company has vineyards in Monteu Roero, Canale, Santo Stefano Roero and Montaldo Roero, as well as a small four-hectare plot at Basarin di Neive, birthplace of the two Barbarescos. The utmost attention is devoted to the agronomic work, which is conducted with maximum respect for the environment: hence weed control only where steep gradients make it unavoidable, fertilization with natural manure, tests with organic methods in some vineyards and treatments with copper and sulphur only.

WINES - Roero Arneis Perdaudin 2012 (○ 20,000 bt) shines for freshness and zest. **Barbera d'Alba Nicolon 2011** (● 14,000 bt) has good texture, a nose of fresh fruit and a lively after-aroma of cherry. **Roero Sudisfà 2010** (● 6,500 bt) has delicate fruit on the nose and perfect texture with solid but never obtrusive tannins and a spick-and-span finish. Also excellent is **Roero San Bernardo 2010** (● 6,500 bt), which has structure with flesh to match, close-knit tannins and the ripe fruit typical of the Roero. **Barbaresco Cascinotta 2009** (● 8,000 bt) is made with grapes from young vineyards near the village of Neive. Eminently quaffable with clear-cut blossomy aromas, it is approachable and even.

> **vino slow** **ROERO PRACHIOSSO 2010** (● 6,000 bt) Magnificent for drinkability and typicality, juiciness and harmony, a great and unmissable wine that smacks of the terroir.

FERTILIZERS natural manure, green manure, humus
PLANT PROTECTION copper and sulphur
WEED CONTROL chemical, mechanical
YEASTS selected
GRAPES 100% estate-grown
CERTIFICATION none

---

10 ha - 45,000 bt

❝ Sustainable, painstaking farming built on sound traditional foundations for modern terroir-dedicated wines that age magnificently. **❞**

PEOPLE - We were taken on our tour of the winery by Pier Guido, a member of the new generation of Bussos. This is a strictly family concern with an open vision towards the future of winemaking.

VINEYARDS - The vineyards are impeccably kept with rare agricultural sensitivity. The Bussos don't advertise their natural management but in practice they apply it. Chemical weedkillers and systemic fungicides are banned even in the steepest, hard-to-manage vineyards such as Santo Stefanetto. Old michet vines are still cultivated to exalt the clonal biodiversity of the grape.

WINES - The range submitted was very impressive indeed, especially the Barbaresco, full of freshness and ageability. The excellent **Barbaresco San Stunet 2010** (● 6,000 bt) combines still slightly edgy tannins with satisfyingly sweet fruit. **Barbaresco Gallina 2010** (● 1,000 bt) shows the effects of prolonged aging in wood casks and will take a few more months to relax. The reasonably priced **Barbaresco Mondino 2010** (● 5,000 bt) is simpler but very enjoyable. The inebriatingly scented and succulent **Barbera d'Alba Majano 2011** (● 6,500 bt) spends half its aging period in wood barrels. Last but not least, the stylish **Langhe Nebbiolo 2011** (● 4,500 bt) captures a strong sense of place.

> **vino slow** **BARBARESCO ALBESANI BORGESE 2010** (● 5,000 bt) A well-gauged nebbiolo with plenty of backbone. Its character, richness and power are fleshed out by vibrant acidity and energy.

FERTILIZERS natural manure
PLANT PROTECTION copper and sulphur
WEED CONTROL mechanical
YEASTS native
GRAPES 100% estate-grown
CERTIFICATION none

Castello di Neive

Via Castelborgo, 1
tel. 0173 67171
www.castellodineive.it
info@castellodineive.it

Sottimano

Località Cottà, 21
tel. 0173 635186
www.sottimano.it
info@sottimano.it

---

26 ha - 160,000 bt | **10% discount**

PEOPLE - The big news this year is that the company, housed in Neive's magnificent castle, now has an efficient new cellar, and from the 2012 harvest all vinification work will be performed in it. The new facility has made it possible to carry out an experiment that would appear to have been a great success: namely a Barbera produced without sulphite. A combination of tradition and innovation courtesy of Italo Stupino and his right-hand man Claudio Roggero.

VINEYARDS - The scientific approach imposed by Italo Stupino in collaboration with Turin University seeks to progressively reduce the use of synthetic chemicals in the vineyards. The first results are already visible. The company crus have world famous names, like Santo Stefano, virtually a monopole, and Gallina, and others maybe less resounding but top-notch just the same, like Basarin and Messoirano. A great deal of care and attention is dedicated to the foliage-fruit ratio.

WINES - Barbaresco Santo Stefano 2010 (● 15,000 bt) is supremely stylish on both nose and palate with tannins of great finesse, irresistible verve and above-average length. **Barbaresco Gallina 2010** (● 3,000 bt) has a temptingly nuanced nose, a delicately succulent palate and a finish of violets and liquorice. It's a Great Wine. There is no such thing as perfection, but **Barbera d'Alba Santo Stefano 2010** (● 10,000 bt) comes tantalizingy close with fantastic typicality, juiciness and mouthfeel. **Barbera d'Alba Sulphites Free 2012** (● 1,000 bt) brims over with lively, intact fruit and delicious fruity flesh. **Dolcetto d'Alba Messoirano 2012** (● 7,000 bt) displays well-gauged tannins and impeccable typicality. **Langhe Arneis 2012** (○ 36,000 bt) is at the top of its typology as always.

18 ha - 85,000 bt

❝ Perfection in all its forms, from grape to glass — the quintessence of Barbaresco. The Sottimano relate this and more in land-rooted, personal, "narrative" wines. The real thing and guaranteed to thrill. **❞**

PEOPLE - Father and son Andrea and Rino share the credit for this wonderful Langa winery, which they have gradually built up and always bound closely to their family identity. They are assisted in their task by Elena and Anna.

VINEYARDS - The crus that the Sottimano have acquired over the years now form an intricate mosaic. They are all relatively small parcels of land suited to family-scale agronomic management. The historic vineyards — Currà, Cottà, Fausoni and Pajoré — have been joined by others, such as the lovely one in the Basarin cru, given over, naturally enough, to nebbiolo. Rino and Andrea have always practiced healthy, pragmatic farming methods.

WINES - Barbaresco Cottà 2010 (● 10,000 bt) has sweet spices and leather on the nose with a prodigiously deep finish. **Barbaresco Fausoni 2010** (● 4,800 bt), made with grapes from another beautiful vineyard, has typically Langa character with an encore of dried flowers and violets. We weren't disappointed by racy and potent **Langhe Nebbiolo 2011** (● 22,000 bt), a well-judged wine from a warm vintage. **Barbera d'Alba Pairolero 2011** (● 12,000 bt) has nuances of cinnamon and vanilla, besides the classic notes of black cherry. **Dolcetto d'Alba Bric del Salto 2012** (● 22,000 bt) is flavorful and grapey.

vino slow **BARBARESCO PAJORÈ 2010** (● 5,000 bt) A nebbiolo of great structure and power, the fruit of modern vinification, interpreted with perspicacity and intelligence without excess. A cellarable wine that is sure to become hugely exciting with the passing of time.

FERTILIZERS none
PLANT PROTECTION chemical, copper and sulphur
WEED CONTROL chemical, mechanical
YEASTS selected
GRAPES 100% estate-grown
CERTIFICATION none

FERTILIZERS natural manure
PLANT PROTECTION chemical, copper and sulphur
WEED CONTROL mechanical
YEASTS native
GRAPES 100% estate-grown
CERTIFICATION none

NOVELLO (CN)

Elvio Cogno

Via Ravera, 2
tel. 0173 744006
www.elviocogno.com
elviocogno@elviocogno.com

PRIOCCA (CN)

Hilberg - Pasquero

Via Bricco Gatti, 16
tel. 0173 616197
www.hilberg-pasquero.com
hilberg@libero.it

11 ha - 68,000 bt   **10% discount**

❝ The first thing you notice when you get to Nadia Cogno and Valter Fissore's splendid 18th-century farm is the attention to detail: from the spick-and-span machinery to the order that reigns in the barrel stock. Then your gaze wanders to the surrounding vineyards and you take in the perfect harmony of the vine rows. ❞

PEOPLE - The secrets of their success are perfectionism and professionalism and passion. Daniele Gaia and Szymon Jachimowicz also play a fundamental part in the overall project.

VINEYARDS - Great care is reserved to the vineyards, which are situated round the hilltop on which the house-cum-wine cellar stands, all worked with commendable meticulousness. All the weed control is carried out with machinery that Valter has had specially designed. Ravera di Novello is a first-rate terroir that produces deep, classic wines, the differences in soil adding an array of nuances to the various Barolos.

WINES - Barolo Vigna Elena Ris. 2007 (● 3,300 bt) has a full, intense nose and a zippy plate with rock-solid tannins and a nice leisurely finish. **Barolo Ravera 2009 (●** 13,400 bt) begins with a bouquet of clear-cut ripe fruit and follows up with a palate of boisterous young tannins and a reasonably long finish. **Barolo Bricco Pernice 2008 (●** 3,300 bt) opens slowly with blossomy notes, hints of freshly mown grass and a whiff of wild strawberry, which lead into a muscular, succulent palate with a well-balanced long finish — a Great Wine. **Langhe Nascetta Anas-cëtta 2012 (○** 7,000 bt) has the acidity needed to support a rich full body. **Barbera d'Alba Bricco dei Merli 2011 (●** 10,000 bt) has exemplary acidity and bundles of fruit.

6 ha - 24,000 bt   **10% discount**

❝ Miclo and Annette let the land speak for itself. Their wines are genuine and sound, either filtered nor clarified, the fruit of spontaneous fermentations and a very sparse use of sulphur. ❞

PEOPLE - Wine has always had a place in the home of Michelangelo "Miclo" Pasquero. His grandfather and father Maggiorino used to make it and sell it in demijohns to customers in the city. When they died, between the late 1980s and early 1990s, the bottom fell through the market and Michelangelo and his wife Annette Hilberg, who he met on an agronomy course in Germany in 1982, decided to bottle their wine. Their first harvest was in 1994, the first label in 1997.

VINEYARDS - The winery's grapes grow nebbiolo and barbera (and a small amount of brachetto). The largest vineyards are Bricco Gatti, Monteforche and Bricco Stella, all round Priocca, and the soil of the three crus is clayey. The Monteforche vineyard, which produces the grapes for the Barbera Superiore, faces south, has limier soil and contains vines 55 years old. The Bricco Gatti vineyard, where the brachetto grapes and the barbera for the base wine are grown, faces east.

WINES - The soil at Priocca is devoid of sand, a feature typical of the Roero district which adds aroma and finesse to wines. Here the wines are well structured thanks to Miclo's deft use of wood casks. The juicy, fruity **Langhe Nebbiolo 2011 (●** 2,600 bt) makes for easy drinking. The full-bodied **Nebbiolo d'Alba 2011 (●** 4,500 bt) has a complex nose and refreshing palate with sweet, silky tannins. The deep, easy-termer **Barbera d'Alba Sup. 2011 (●** 4,000 bt) ages for 18-22 months in barriques and new mid-sized casks. **Barbera d'Alba 2012 (●** 8,000) is enjoyable, **Vareji 2012 (●** brachetto, barbera; 4,000) is refreshing.

FERTILIZERS natural manure, green manure
PLANT PROTECTION chemical, copper and sulphur
WEED CONTROL mechanical
YEASTS native
GRAPES 100% estate-grown
CERTIFICATION none

FERTILIZERS compost, biodynamic preparations, green manure
PLANT PROTECTION copper and sulphur
WEED CONTROL mechanical
YEASTS native
GRAPES 100% estate-grown
CERTIFICATION organic

RODELLO (CN)

Mossio Fratelli €

Via Montà, 12
tel. 0173 617149 - 338 4002835
www.mossio.com
mossio@mossio.com

10 ha - 50,000 bt | **10% discount**

PEOPLE - Remo and Valerio Mossio embody the rural, blunt, sincere yet affable side of the Langa hills. They are the leading players in a family winery open to all-comers which bases its identity on the glorification of Dolcetto d'Alba, a denomination unfairly regarded as secondary by many people. Besides being very good, their wines sell at a very honest price.

VINEYARDS - The winery's core business is the dolcetto grape. Which is why the Mossio reserve it the finest locations. Bricco Caramelli is a model vineyard, excellent for growing thanks to the coolness that comes from its altitude — almost 500 meters — and the breezes that blow down from the Alta Langa hills. Valerio and Remo also cultivate other traditional grapes such as nebbiolo and barbera.

WINES - The Mossios are unstoppable. Their eagerness to raise the profile of dolcetto makes them ask questions and carry out tests of every kind in the cellar. The result of their latest experiments is **Le Margherite 2010** (● 1.300 bt), a Dolcetto made with dried grapes of amazing freshness and a good degree of acidity. Moving on to the classics, **Dolcetto d'Alba Piano delli Perdoni 2012** (● 25,000) is as reliable as ever, typical, grapey and varietal with pleasant spiciness and outstanding drinkability. **Barbera d'Alba 2011** (● 5,000 bt) juggles with power and juice, while for its finesse and elegance **Langhe Nebbiolo 2009** (● 5,000 bt) is patently a Barolo manqué.

| vino slow | DOLCETTO D'ALBA BRICCO CARAMELLI 2012 (● 5,000 bt) Complexity, richness, harmony — these are the words that best describe this, a big red on sale at a small price. |

SERRALUNGA D'ALBA (CN)

Casa di E. Mirafiore

Via Alba, 15
tel. 0173 626117
www.mirafiore.it
info@mirafiore.it

20 ha - 100,000 bt

PEOPLE - The Casa di E. Mirafiore brand saw the light for the first time only a few years ago. Now it has been intelligently revived — seeing the prestige the place enjoyed at the turn of the last century — by the people who run Fontanafredda, part of the Eataly group. On the great Serralunga estate they have decided to vinify only grapes from the most prestigious crus and to interpret them super-traditionally.

VINEYARDS - The vineyards are masterfully managed by agronomist Alberto Grasso, who is replicating here the same methods already implemented for Borgogno, Brandini and Fontanafredda, in the vineyards the group owns there: meaning no weedkillers, non chemical fertilizers, no antibotrytis sprays. The grapes all come from celebrated good growing crus, such as Lazzarito and La Rosa at Serralunga and Paiagallo at Barolo.

WINES - Danilo Drocco, the enologist at Mirafiore and Fontanafredda is given virtually free rein. He has decided to try out old and traditional techniques with as little technology as possible. One result of his policy is **Barolo Lazzarito 2008** (● 20,000 bt), beefy as only great Serralunga can be and sure to last — a Great Wine. Down just a rung is the subtler, fruitier **Barolo Paiagallo 2008** (● 13,000 bt). The varietal **Langhe Nebbiolo 2010** (● 20,000 bt) is the product of a fantastic vintage and 40 days of maceration. **Dolcetto d'Alba 2012** (● 20,000 bt), aged for two months in large barrels to acquire complexity and softness, is vibrant and full-flavored. The label is part of the Vino Libero selection.

FERTILIZERS manure pellets, natural manure
PLANT PROTECTION copper and sulphur
WEED CONTROL chemical, mechanical
YEASTS native
GRAPES 100% estate-grown
CERTIFICATION none

FERTILIZERS manure pellets
PLANT PROTECTION chemical, copper and sulphur
WEED CONTROL mechanical
YEASTS native
GRAPES 100% estate-grown
CERTIFICATION none

Guido Porro

Via Alba, 1
tel. 0173 613306
www.guidoporro.com
guidoporro@guidoporro.com

8.5 ha - 30,000 bt

PEOPLE - The spotlights turned to this small family winery only recently. Yet it has been producing reliable classic Langa wines at very accessible prices for years now — as its numerous loyal customers will testify. Guido comes from the fourth generation of this family of winemakers. He's a blunt, quietly-spoken type who goes about his daily chores in an easy, laid-back manner. His wife Giovanna lends a helping hand a the company and his father, over 70, still makes an active contribution in the vineyard. The family also runs a pretty little agriturismo whose rooms look out over the splendid vineyards of Serralunga.

VINEYARDS - The farm overlooks the natural amphitheater of the Lazzarito cru, which comprises the Santa Caterina vineyard, only recently absorbed by the broader "additional geographical denomination". It grows the youngest vines, while Lazzairasco, lower down, boasts older plants and produces more austere nebbiolos. On our visit Guido showed us the replanting work on the small parcel he recently inherited in the majestic Vigna Rionda vineyard.

WINES - **Barolo Vigna Santa Caterina 2009** (● 4,000 bt) has blossomy spicy notes with a refreshing balsamic-minty streak and a lively, dynamic palate with wholesome, juicy tannins. **Barolo Seivì 2009** (● 4,000 bt) deftly captures a sense of the Serralunga terroir. **Nebbiolo d'Alba Camilu 2012** (● 2,600 bt) is more blossomy and racier. **Barbera d'Alba Vigna Santa Caterina 2012** (● 6,000 bt) is succulent, **Dolcetto d'Alba Vigna 'l Pari 2012** (● 4,500 bt) fragrant.

> **vino slow** **Barolo Vigna Lazzairasco 2009** (● 11,000 bt) Introverted and earthy, a wine of great classicism with solid, close-knit tannins on the finish.

FERTILIZERS manure pellets
PLANT PROTECTION copper and sulphur
WEED CONTROL chemical, mechanical
YEASTS native
GRAPES 100% estate-grown
CERTIFICATION none

Giovanni Rosso

Località Baudana, 6
tel. 0173 613142
www.giovannirosso.com
info@giovannirosso.com

18 ha - 100,000 bt

PEOPLE - Davide Rosso has regaled us with some of the most memorable Langa labels of the last few years. He's a confident, enterprising guy, always prepared to put himself on the line. As he did when he decided to sell the first Vigna Rionda vintage en primeur. Having acquired handy experience in Burgundy, he took over the reins of the company in 2001. This year he made his dream for a new, more spacious cellar come true.

VINEYARDS - Davide's vineyards are top-notch. The two flagship plots are La Serra, which is very steep with bleached white limestone soil, and Cerretta, where the soil is deeper and clayier. In 2010 Davide also inherited an hectare in the majestic Vigna Rionda vineyard. Broglio, Sorano, Meriame and other top crus grow the grapes for the masterful Barolo Serralunga. Despite the dizzy gradients, no chemical weedkillers are used and systemic products are only resorted to in cases of extreme necessity.

WINES - Fermentation in concrete vats and long aging in large wooden casks of french oak produce eloquent wines with a consistent sense of place. **Barolo La Serra 2009** (● 4.500 bt) has intact fruit with well-defined balsamic and blossomy notes and a solid, forthright palate with close-knit, juicy tannins. It was our favorite, for us a Great Wine. **Barolo Cerretta 2009** (● 7,000 bt) has warmer, more mature tones without reneging the austerity that is the hallmark of Serralunga. **Barolo Serralunga 2009** (● 50,000 bt) is wonderfully terroir-evocative. **Barolo Vigna Rionda Tommaso Canale 2009** (● 1,000 bt) has power, body and sweet pervasive tannins. The dense, fresh **Langhe Nebbiolo 2011** (● 20,000 bt) is more approachable. The crisp and juicy **Barbera d'Alba Donna Margherita 2011** (● 35,000 bt) is always a joy to drink.

FERTILIZERS natural manure
PLANT PROTECTION copper and sulphur
WEED CONTROL mechanical
YEASTS native
GRAPES 100% estate-grown
CERTIFICATION none

Ca' del Baio

Via Ferrere, 33
tel. 0173 638219
www.cadelbaio.com
cadelbaio@cadelbaio.com

20 ha - 100,000 bt

66 This cellar's wines, which consistently top the denomination for quality, are a faithful mirror of the terroir and sell at reasonable prices. 99

PEOPLE - A united family that works with passion and professionalism. Listen to Giulio Grasso and his wife Luciana, who run the company with their enthusiastic daughters Paola and Valentina, for a few minutes and you'll understand just how well they know the land and its history.

VINEYARDS - The valley in which the Grassos' cellar is situated is home to two crus, Valgrande, a monovarietal, and Marcarini, which enjoy excellent locations and a favorable microclimate. Two properties in vineyards of great prestige, Asili and Pora, are also to be found at Barbaresco. The second planting is very old and yields wines of notable structure. The viticulture is conventional with interventions limited to under-vine weed control and a negligible use of chemicals.

WINES - Barbaresco Pora 2009 (● 3,000 bt) is mature and powerful, full-bodied, fleshy and satisfying on the palate. **Barbaresco Valgrande 2010** (● 15,000 bt) has a lively note of peaches and a palate that combines energy and lightness with a racy, lingering, damp finish. **Langhe Nebbiolo Bric del Baio 2011** (● 13,000 bt), elegant on the nose with plenty of texture and structure, has a juicy, drinkable palate. **Dolcetto d'Alba Lodoli 2012** (● 20,000 bt) offers fruit on the nose and a fleshy, lively palate with an excellent racy finish. **Langhe Riesling 2011** (○ 3,500 bt) releases typical scents and ends on a slightly bitter note.

> **vino slow** BARBARESCO ASILI 2010 (● 12,000 bt) A wine in which the blossomy notes typical of the cru accompany nicely ripe fruit with lively, racy flesh on the palate.

FERTILIZERS	organic-mineral, manure pellets
PLANT PROTECTION	chemical, copper and sulphur
WEED CONTROL	chemical, mechanical
YEASTS	selected
GRAPES	100% estate-grown
CERTIFICATION	none

Fiorenzo Nada

Località Rombone
Via Ausario, 12-C
tel. 0173 638254
www.nada.it
nadafiorenzo@nada.it

7 ha - 45,000 bt

66 The bond that ties Bruno Nada to his native Treiso and the hills of the Langa district comes over in every gesture he makes and every word he utters. And in his magnificent terroir-dedicated wines. 99

PEOPLE - When we meet Bruno Nada, "refounder" and heart-and-soul of the company, we don't talk only about wine. On the contrary, sometimes we don't speak about it at all. Bruno's open mind and intellectual curiosity lead him to address the most various subjects.

VINEYARDS - Bruno Nada's vineyards are beautifully kept, growing in grass like gardens. Painstaking care and attention is paid to every job, from pruning through leaf removal to topping. In the valley below the cellar are the two Barbaresco crus: Rombone, where the soil is classic limestone, and Manzola, where there is also a sandy component. In the cooler corners of the first an old barbera vine yields the fruit for Seifile.

WINES - Barbaresco Rombone 2009 (● 4,000 bt) has a sumptuous structure with sweet, juicy tannins that gallops across the palate into a deliciously blossomy finish. **Langhe Nebbiolo 2011** (● 10,000 bt) has just the right juice and well-calibrated tannins. The very easy-drinking **Langhe Rosso Seifile 2009** (● barbera, nebbiolo; 3,000 bt) has notes of fruit and spice on the nose and a racy, succulent palate. **Barbera d'Alba 2011** (● 5,000 bt) and **Dolcetto d'Alba 2012** (● 10,000 bt) are exemplary for typicality, sense of place and craftsmanship.

> **vino slow** BARBARESCO MANZOLA 2009 (● 6,600 bt) Released a year late like Rombone, a racy, breezy red, fleshy and vivacious, fruity and floral with a long, lingering, harmonious finish.

FERTILIZERS	natural manure
PLANT PROTECTION	chemical, copper and sulphur
WEED CONTROL	mechanical
YEASTS	native
GRAPES	100% estate-grown
CERTIFICATION	none

Alessandria Fratelli

Via Beato Valfrè, 59
tel. 0172 470113
www.fratellialessandria.it
info@fratellialessandria.it

---

14 ha - 80,000 bt **10% discount**

66 Alessandria Fratelli stands out in Verduno for the classicism of its wine, invariably clean and deep, and for its high-level consistency. 99

PEOPLE - Step by step Vittore Alessandria, aided by father Gian Battista and uncle Alessandro, practices increasingly sustainable viticulture, banking on common sense and adapting to the situation intelligently.

VINEYARDS - In the vineyards they turf with a mixture of grasses to add vitality to the soil and avoid compression. At Verduno Alessandria has a plot of land in the Monvigliero district worthy of a grand cru, and another in the San Lorenzo district. Soil and microclimate differences explain the diversity among the wines born in these vineyards. Another splendid terroir is Gramolere di Monforte, which produces eminently cellarable wines that are more refined than potent.

WINES - The Barolos submitted deserve a round of applause. In this and many other cases, 2009 exceeded all expectations. With its lovely scents of freshly mown grass, the excellent, solid **Barolo 2009** (● 12,000 bt) is a wine for easy drinking. **Barolo Monvigliero 2009** (● 6,500 bt) enchants for the precision of its bouquet of dried flowers and for its palate, while remaining solid, stylish and juicy. **Barolo Gramolere 2009** (● 6,000 bt) has still undeveloped aromas but reveals a palate of great power and enviable length. **Verduno Pelaverga Speziale 2012** (● 14,000 bt) offers a bouquet of pepper and lots of juice on the palate. **Barbera d'Alba 2012** (● 6,000 bt) is typical and well-crafted.

| vino slow | BAROLO SAN LORENZO 2009 (● 4,500 bt) A typical wine of great finesse with well-defined aromas and a solid, lingering palate. The finish is magnificent with almost peppery notes that conjure up Verduno. |

FERTILIZERS mineral, manure pellets
PLANT PROTECTION chemical, copper and sulphur
WEED CONTROL mechanical
YEASTS native
GRAPES 100% estate-grown
CERTIFICATION none

Castello di Verduno

Via Umberto I, 9
tel. 0172 470284
www.castellodiverduno.com
cantina@castellodiverduno.com

---

10 ha - 60,000 bt

PEOPLE - The company run by Franco Bianco, his wife Gabriella Burlotto and daughter Marcella is much more than just a winery. Against the background of the castle of Verduno and its lovely grounds, it comprises a restaurant, a hotel and an agriturismo. It's a multifaceted place, but it's wine that occupies the place of honor. The style is classical, conventional and totally convincing. Special attention is reserved for the native pelaverga grape, vinified in a variety of ways.

VINEYARDS - The winery has good growing vineyards at Barbaresco (Rabajà and Faset) and Verduno (Massara and Monvigliero). The latter, in our opinion, is a grand cru and we can't fathom why critics don't laud it more. There are also very old barbera vineyards and a lot of land is also given over to pelaverga, an exclusive specialty of Verduno. The viticulture is virtuous and treatments are limited to a minimum.

WINES - **Barolo Massara 2008** (● 3,900 bt) is floral on the nose with a fleshy, well-structured palate and restorative freshness. Solid, never aggressive and remarkably long, **Barolo Monvigliero Ris. 2006** (● 2,000 bt) displays the energy and depth of a vintage that is sure to reward anyone willing to wait for it. **Barbaresco Faset 2009** (● 2,000 bt) has power, warmth and rich flesh with solid tannins. The fleshy, juicy **Barbera d'Alba Bricco del Cuculo 2011** (● 3,100 bt) is endowed with great freshness, hence great drinkability. The fascinating **Bellis Perennis 2012** (O pelaverga; 4,100 bt) is full of body and verve.

| vino slow | VERDUNO PELAVERGA BASADONE 2012 (● 15,800 bt) We were thrilled again by this red with its spicy notes and impeccably leisurely long palate. Dedicated to all those unfamiliar with it: what are you waiting for? |

FERTILIZERS none
PLANT PROTECTION organic
WEED CONTROL mechanical
YEASTS native
GRAPES 100% estate-grown
CERTIFICATION none

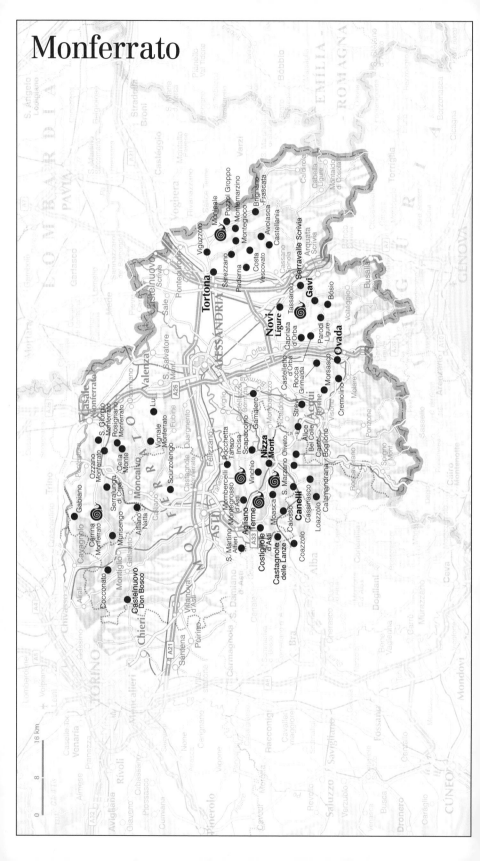

Monferrato

AGLIANO TERME (AT)

Dacapo

Strada Asti-Mare, 4
tel. 0141 964921
www.dacapo.it
info@dacapo.it

CANELLI (AT)

Paolo Avezza (€)

Regione Monforte, 62
tel. 0141 822296
www.paoloavezza.com
contatti@paoloavezza.com

7.5 ha - 50,000 bt

❝ That of Paolo Dania and Dino Riccomagno, the owners and managers of this Asti winery, has been some adventure. The distinguishing features of their work is care and respect for nature and local winemaking traditions. **❞**

PEOPLE - The novelty this year is the Grignolino, a classic that has now joined up with the other wines, old and new, that come out of the pretty 19th-century cellar, where the wooden casks are almost all pre-used.

VINEYARDS - Organic management brings with it extra risks, especially at the outset when the vines have to rebuild their natural defenses after years of being "drugged" by chemicals. Dino and Paolo have never been put off by attacks from vine diseases and have always carried on regardless; here weedkillers and chemicals are out, manual and mechanical work are in. The new grignolino vineyard is close by the cellar.

WINES - Barbera d'Asti Sup. Sanbastiàn 2011 (● 22,000 bt) claims the lion's share in terms of output. It has acid verve, succulence and all the hints of soil and fruit typical of the grape. It's an approachable wine, a thrill to drink. **Barbera d'Asti Sup. Nizza Vigna Dacapo 2010 (●** 7,500 bt) has an abundance of intense, fruity aromas and a concentrated, fleshy, racy, beautifully mature palate with a precise finish in which mineral aromas give an encore. **Ruché di Castagnole Monferrato Majoli 2012 (●** 7,000 bt) is spicy and dry, enjoyable with good supporting acidity. The beautifully second-fermented **M. Cl. Brut Rosé 2009 (☉** pinot nero, chardonnay; 4,000 bt) has plenty of fruit with a palate that manages to be at once light and dense. **Grignolino d'Asti 2012 (●** 1,000 bt) is typical, highly scented and a pleasure to drink.

---

7 ha - 22,000 bt   **10% discount**

PEOPLE - Paolo Avezza belongs to the third generation of a family of winemakers. He is helped by his parents Armando and Angioletta and his wife Gabriella. For years he sold his wine unbottled and, for a certain period, he even worked on commission. It was precisely coming into contact with other producers that he developed the urge to bottle his own wine, a dream that came true in 2002. Behind a friendly, smiling, witty façade, Paolo is a hard, determined worker, a thoroughbred barbera interpreter and an artisan spumantista.

VINEYARDS - Three hectares of land round the farm in the hills overlooking Canelli are planted with the classic local grapes — dolcetto, nebbiolo and moscato — supplemented in 1992 by numerous pinot nero and chardonnay clones for the Alta Langa project. The vineyards are managed traditionally but with eco-awareness. This year no weedkillers were used, despite the heavy spring rain. Since 2002 Paolo has rented four hectares of land just outside Nizza Monferrato, where he grows the grapes for the Nizza sotto la Muda selection

WINES - The steel-aged Barbera d'Asti 2012 (● 6,500 bt) was excellent once again this year; deservedly an Everyday Wine, it expresses the character of the grape with living, earthy, leafy fruit, a compact palate packed with verve and raciness and good acid contrast. **Barbera d'Asti Sup. Nizza sotto la Muda 2010 (●** 3,300 bt), which ages for a year in barriques of different ages, has delicate notes of spice and a stylish palate supported by fresh, tangy acidity. Fermented for 24 months on the yeasts, disgorged by hand and dosed with small amounts of passito di chardonnay, **Alta Langa M. Cl. Brut 2010 (○** pinot nero, chardonnay; 3,000 bt) is all freshness and fruity fragrance. **Moscato d'Asti La Commenda 2012 (○** 5,000 bt) is floral with a creamy palate.

FERTILIZERS green manure
PLANT PROTECTION copper and sulphur
WEED CONTROL mechanical
YEASTS selected
GRAPES 100% estate-grown
CERTIFICATION organic

FERTILIZERS manure pellets
PLANT PROTECTION chemical, copper and sulphur
WEED CONTROL chemical, mechanical
YEASTS selected
GRAPES 100% estate-grown
CERTIFICATION none

Cascina Barisél

Regione San Giovanni, 30
tel. 0141 824848
www.barisel.it
info@barisel.it

Contratto

Via Contratto, 56
tel. 0141 823349
www.contratto.it
info@contratto.it

4.5 ha - 30,000 bt   **10% discount**

PEOPLE - For a long time Franco Penna worked as an accountant, only making wine in his spare time. Then, about ten years ago, he decided to take the plunge, resigning from the firm he worked for and taking over his father Enrico's cellar. We can now say that he made the right choice. The wines he produces are forthright and enjoyable and perfectly reflect the land of their origin.

VINEYARDS - Franco cultivates the land with his father and brother Fiorenzo. The main vineyards are the ones that encircle their lovely, typically Piedmontese farmhouse. The grape they grow most is barbera, in an interesting vineyard with vines planted in 1948, from which the La Cappelletta selection is produced. Another large portion of the property is given over to moscato.

WINES - This year Franco Penna, who works in the cellar with enologist Lorenzo Quinterno as his consultant, submitted an excellent range of wines. The novelty was tantamount to an experiment that has worked: **Enrico Penna Brut** (O chardonnay, pinot nero; 600 bt): a very agreeable, very bubbly Metodo Classico. **Barbera d'Asti Sup. La Cappelletta 2010** (● 4,500 bt), barrique-aged for 18 months, is a potent, complex, long-living wine. The fresher and fruitier **Barbera d'Asti Sup. Listoria 2011** (● 6,000 bt) matures for 12 months in large barrels. The refreshing, easy-drinking Barbera d'Asti 2012 (● 4,500 bt) is a great Everyday Wine, perfect with everyday food. **Monferrato Bianco Foravia 2012** (O favorita; 2,000 bt) is simple without being banal, while the bestselling citrussy **Moscato d'Asti Canelli 2012** (O 13,000 bt) is very enjoyable.

---

25 ha - 265,000 bt

PEOPLE - It was easy to predict that Giorgio Rivetti, owner with his family of a number of successful brands such as La Spinetta and Casanova della Spinetta, wouldn't take long to restore this historic spumante company to its former glory. He bought it in 2011 and now its cellar— one of the finest in Italy, with historic aging tunnels reminiscent of the maisons of Champagne — is already an attraction for wine tourists once more.

VINEYARDS - One of the new owner's first moves was to rent enough vineyards to have plenty of good grapes, fundamental for excellent spumantes. Historically, Contratto used to buy in grapes from the Oltrepò zone and the Rivettas have continued this tradition with a 25-hectare vineyard at Montaldo Pavese, whose high altitude ensures slower ripening and acidity.

WINES - Our favorite was **M. Cl. Brut For England Blanc de Noir 2009** (O 32.000 bt), a monovarietal Pinot Nero, meaty, crisp, very acid and fresh; a great wine that goes well with main courses, not just as an aperitif nibbles. The base wine **M. Cl. Brut Millesimato 2009** (O pinot nero, chardonnay; 180,000 bt) is scented and enjoyable. To anyone who doesn't believe in such a thing as a very good Asti, we suggest they uncork a bottle of **Asti M. Cl. De Miranda 2010** (O 8,000 bt), a sweet spumante of rare finesse with a dry, racy finish. The inviting **M. Cl. Brut For England Rosé 2009** (◉ pinot nero; 20,000 bt) has a nose of strawberries and a full-bodied finish. **M. Cl. Pas Dosé Blanc de Blancs 2009** (O chardonnay; 12.000 bt) is mineral and iodine.

FERTILIZERS manure pellets
PLANT PROTECTION chemical, copper and sulphur
WEED CONTROL chemical, mechanical
YEASTS selected
GRAPES 20% bought in
CERTIFICATION none

FERTILIZERS organic-mineral, green manure
PLANT PROTECTION chemical, copper and sulphur
WEED CONTROL chemical, mechanical
YEASTS selected
GRAPES 30% bought in
CERTIFICATION none

CANELLI (AT)

L'Armangia

Regione San Giovanni, 122
tel. 0141 824947
www.armangia.it
armangiavini@libero.it

CERRINA MONFERRATO (AL)

Iuli

Via Centrale, 27
tel. 0142 946657
www.iuli.it
cavimon@iuli.it

---

10 ha - 95,000 bt   **10% discount**

PEOPLE - Ignazio Giovine, whose father Giuseppe was a respected wine merchant, has been in charge at Armangia since 1998. After studying enology, he decided not only to join the family business, but also to give it a facelift by buying and renting vineyards in different positions at different altitudes. Thanks to his passionate commitment, it is now is one of the most interesting wineries in the province of Asti.

VINEYARDS - Ignazio manages a large number of vineyards, where he likes to experiment and strike the right mix of different degrees of grape ripening. The most important barbera vineyards are at Moasca and Canelli, while the cru that gives life to Vignali is at San Marzano. To cope with climate change the company has decided to cultivate some non-south-facing vine rows to seek greater coolness and the aroma of fruit that is not overripe.

WINES - Armangia presented a first-rate range this year. **Barbera Sup. Nizza Vignali 2007** (● 2.000 bt) has very open, crisp fruit on the nose and an acid- and alcohol-rich palate. Ignazio Giovine proves once more that he knows how to interpret **Moscato d'Asti Canelli 2012** (○ 4,000 bt), whose sappy palate follows up enjoyably complex aromas. The young Barbera d'Asti Sopra Berruti 2012 (● 18,000 bt) is fresh and a joy to drink — an excellent Everyday Wine. The swish **Piemonte Chardonnay Pratorotondo 2011** (○ 5,000 bt) is aged in wood casks with long fermentations at low temperatures. **Piemonte Albarossa Macchiaferro 2010** (● 2,700 bt) is excellent.

> **vino slow** BARBERA D'ASTI SUP. NIZZA TITON 2010 (● 7,000 bt) This beautiful red, enhanced by laudable use of wood, is highly scented and fruity on the nose — excellent value for money.

---

17 ha - 50,000 bt

❝ Fabrizio Iuli and his partners believe in the potential of the wild Monferrato hills, forgotten by many; they practice impeccable organic production based on commonsense and farming knowledge; they like to exchange ideas with fellow winegrowers from every part of the world. This is how they see and make wine. **❞**

PEOPLE - Fabrizio's companions on the adventure he embarked on some years ago are his sister Cristina, his partner Summer Wolff and the Lerner brothers.

VINEYARDS - Here you won't find the monocultural landscape of other wine terroirs. Vines, hazelnut groves and, above all, woods (many of which grow over abandoned historic vineyards) live together to create a unique environment. The vines, much frequented by the local wildlife, are managed with scrupulous care using organic methods.

WINES - Fabrizio is a jack-of-all-trades. You'll find him in the front line at events and fairs promoting the identity of winemakers, but also back home at the farmhouse welcoming tourists and wine buffs and, of course, in the vineyard and the cellar where he oversees production personally. It's among the vats and the barrels that Fabrizio struts his stuff, confidently with a love of experimentation. This year's wines are as impressive as ever. Like **Monferrato Rosso Nino 2011** (● 3,500 bt), the successful result of the gamble to bank on pinot nero in the Monferrato district. It is typical, varietal, precise and, above all, firmly rooted in the terroir. A curiosity was the release of a batch of Barbera del Monferrato Barabba 2004 after long aging in magnums.

> **vino slow** BARBERA DEL MONFERRATO SUP. ROSSORE 2010 (● 8,000 bt) A lean fresh version with delicate nuances and vibrant acidity. The language it speaks is very different from that of the Barberas of the Asti and Tortona areas.

FERTILIZERS humus
PLANT PROTECTION chemical, copper and sulphur
WEED CONTROL chemical, mechanical
YEASTS selected
GRAPES 100% estate-grown
CERTIFICATION none

FERTILIZERS none
PLANT PROTECTION copper and sulphur
WEED CONTROL mechanical
YEASTS native
GRAPES 100% estate-grown
CERTIFICATION organic

Cascina La Ghersa

Regione Chiarina, 2
tel. 0141 856 012
www.laghersa.it
info@laghersa.it

Luigi Spertino

Strada Lea, 505
tel. 0141 959098
www.luigispertino.it
luigi.spertino@libero.it

23.5 ha - 150,000 bt   **10% discount**

PEOPLE - Massimo Pastura began managing this dynamic winery as a very young man, since when he has improved its quality and quantity. He has done so with the constant and invaluable help of his father Giulio, who unfortunately died last winter. We are confident that Massimo will continue the good work with customary tenacity and bravura.

VINEYARDS - La Ghersa manages a large number of plots, some its own, others rented, and buys a tiny percentage of its grapes from select outside suppliers. Besides its vineyards in the Asti area, at Moasca, Costigliole and Agliano, it also owns others round Tortona, which grow timorasso and croatina grapes. The feather in its cap is the Vignassa vineyard, which boasts vines almost 100 years old, all tended with the utmost care and attention.

WINES - Massimo Pastura is flanked in the cellar by consultant enologist Luca Caramellino. This year we were bowled over by the amazing **Barbera d'Asti Sup. Vignassa 2010** (● 5,000 bt), macerated for 45 days with the submerged-cap method. **Barbera d'Asti Piagè 2012** (● 55,000 bt) is as enjoyable, juicy and quaffable as ever. For **Barbera d'Asti Sup. Muascae 2010** (● 2,600 bt), some of the grapes are dried for four months. **Barbera d'Asti Sup. Camparò 2011** (● 40,000 bt) is aged in mid-sized casks and second-use barriques. **Colli Tortonesi Timorasso Timian 2011** (○ 2,500 bt) is floral, mineral, firm-structured and beautifully deep. **Colli Tortonesi Croatina Smentià 2011** (● 2.500 bt), whose grapes are cultivated at an altitude of 450 meters in the commune of Sarezzano, is a welcome novelty. It's a wine that's built to last.

9 ha - 38,000 bt   **10% discount**

66 Luigi's farming experience, Mauro's skill and will to work, perfectionism in all its forms — this is the Spertino model, the result, more than anything else, of respect for the land. 99

PEOPLE - The winery is run by Mauro under the expert and critical eye of his father Luigi. Anyone keen to discover the essence of wine craftsmanship in the province of Asti can't afford to miss the place.

VINEYARDS - Clambering among the vine rows of the over 60-year-old cortese vineyard is a dizzying experience. This breathtaking local landmark is so steep it's scary! The other vineyards are just as old and also necessitate hour upon hour of management work, in many cases manual only. The grignolino grapes come from Portacomaro, an important growing district for the variety.

WINES - Mauro possesses a lot of technical know-how. Before taking over his family's winery he worked as a production manager in a wine product company, an experience that has formed him and improved his qualifications. Spertino wines are traditional, the consequence of the generation clash between Mauro and Luigi. **Barbera d'Asti 2011** (● 15,000 bt) has earthy notes well braced by alcohol. The effective **Barbera d'Asti Sup. La Mandorla 2011** (● 3,000 bt), which reflects Mauro's passion for Amarone, is very stylish with a broad suite of aromas.

> **vino slow** **GRIGNOLINO D'ASTI 2012** (● 18,000 bt) An example of the purity and typicality of the grape. At the top of its category as ever, it is juicy and spicy with a long. leisurely finish.

FERTILIZERS organic-mineral, natural manure
PLANT PROTECTION chemical, copper and sulphur
WEED CONTROL mechanical
YEASTS selected
GRAPES 6% bought in
CERTIFICATION none

FERTILIZERS natural manure
PLANT PROTECTION copper and sulphur
WEED CONTROL mechanical
YEASTS native
GRAPES 100% estate-grown
CERTIFICATION none

Vigneti Massa

Piazza Capsoni, 10
tel. 0131 80302
vignetimassa@libero.it

La Gironda

Strada Bricco,12
tel. 0141 701013
www.lagironda.com
info@lagironda.com

---

23 ha - 110,000 bt

8.5 ha - 40,000 bt **10% discount**

❝ Formidable, volcanic, unstoppable, Walter Massa is the undisputed leader of the timorasso grape renaissance. A farmer, a winemaker and a great talker, he has allowed the terroir to rediscover its identity. ❞

PEOPLE - The winery's headquarters are housed in the family's historic cellar at Monleale, a place of great conviviality where wine lovers and friends are always welcome.

VINEYARDS - Walter has built up his property through a process of recovery and acquisition. Spread around Monleale and environs, the vineyards grow all the main Tortona grape varieties. Some are over 30 years old. The most common grape is timorasso, followed by barbera, croatina, freisa and moscato. The management is painstaking and scrupulous, based on good healthy pragmatism.

WINES - Walter was a pioneer of a new conception of Timorasso. In his cellar he still keeps a few labels from the early 1990s, spectacularly fresh, complex wines that show all the grape's potential. The ambitous **Derthona Sterpi 2011** (O 4,000 bt) is powerful and well-structured with lively nuances of petrol. **Derthona Costa del Vento 2011** (O 6,000 bt) is grassy with a slightly bitter finish. **Derthona Montecitorio 2011** (O 4,000 bt), which has nothing to do with the palace of the same name in Rome, seat of the Italian Chamber of Deputies, is subtle and fragrant, made with a selection of grapes from a beautiful vineyard. The reds submitted were more than impressive.

vino slow **DERTHONA 2011** (O 40,000 bt) A base version of Timorasso, crystalline and long with definite salty notes. We prefer this lighter style, which lifts the acidity of this magnificent grape variety.

PEOPLE - Susanna Galandrino is a leading player on the Nizza Monferrato scene. When she and her husband Alberto Adamo started producing and bottling wine in 2002, she immediately leapt to the fore as a spokesperson for the whole terroir, promoting the Nizza sub-zone in particular. In the cellar Susanna and Alberto can count on the reliable backing of Giuliano Noè and Beppe Rattazzo.

VINEYARDS - The cellar is situated on the hill known as Bricco di Nizza, a very good winegrowing area. Some of its vineyards, all relatively young in age are also spread out over the hill. Worth a visit is the lovely, particularly steep vineyard at Calamandrana. Under the supervision of Piero Roseo, Susanna oversees the vineyards without recourse to chemicals.

WINES - The cellar produces mainly Barbera in a number of different versions. **Barbera d'Asti La Gena 2011** (● 10,000 bt) has good concentration with a succulent, smooth finish. This year's version **Barbera d'Asti La Lippa 2012** (● 10,000 bt) is refreshing, a pleasure to drink. **Monferrato Rosso Chiesavecchia 2010** (● 3,000 bt) is an effective assemblage of barbera, nebbiolo, cabernet and merlot. We also liked **Moscato d'Asti 2012** (O 3,300 bt) with its pleasing oxidative nuances. **Brachetto d'Acqui 2012** (● 3,300 bt) is made with grapes from a few vine rows in the Calamandrana vineyard.

vino slow **BARBERA D'ASTI SUP. NIZZA LE NICCHIE 2010** (● 7,000 bt) A textbook narrative vin de terroir, the fragrant, harmonious marriage of the typicality of the grape with the depth of the Nizza Monferrato marl.

FERTILIZERS organic-mineral, mineral, natural manure, compost, green manure
PLANT PROTECTION copper and sulphur
WEED CONTROL chemical, mechanical
YEASTS native
GRAPES 100% estate-grown
CERTIFICATION none

FERTILIZERS none
PLANT PROTECTION copper and sulphur
WEED CONTROL mechanical
YEASTS selected
GRAPES 100% estate-grown
CERTIFICATION none

SAN MARTINO ALFIERI (AT)

Marchesi Alfieri

Piazza Alfieri, 28
tel. 0141 976015
www.marchesialfieri.it
alfieri@marchesialfieri.it

SAN MARZANO OLIVETO (AT)

Carussin

Regione Mariano, 27
tel. 0141 831358
www.carussin.it
ferrobruna@inwind.it

---

21 ha - 100,000 bt | **10% discount**

PEOPLE - It's impossible not to be fascinated by a tour of the castle of San Martino Alfieri, surrounded by a park of rare beauty in which the cellars of this meritorious Asti winery are situated. The owners, sisters Antonella, Emanuela and Giovanna San Martino, have entrusted the technical management to Mario Olivero, who combines solid credentials with a great passion for the job. He is assisted by Christian Carlevero and Piero Roseo.

VINEYARDS - The company owns 150 hectares of land of which only 21 are planted with vines, a fact that says a lot about the San Martino family's approach to agriculture. The vineyards vary in age and the one given over to the Barbera Alfiera is over 70 years old. Besides barbera, the other grapes grown are pinot nero, which produces good results here, nebbiolo and grignolino. Agronomic practices are increasingly guided by considerations of environmental sustainability.

WINES - Barbera d'Asti Sup. Alfiera 2010 (● 14,700 bt) is pervasive on the nose with plenty of body and acidity to on the palate to brace the fruit. **Monferrato Rosso Sostegno 2011** (● barbera, pinot nero; 3,400 bt) has close-focused aromas with verve on the palate and hints of sweet spices on the finish. **Monferrato Rosso Costa Quaglia 2010** (● nebbiolo; 3,900 bt) regales the nose with blossomy fragrances, while the palate is well-structured with nicely sweet close-knit tannins and a finish redolent of violets. **Monferrato Rosso San Germano 2010** (● pinot nero; 3,000 bt) still reveals hints of wood but flaunts good balance and just the right amount of juice on the palate. **Piemonte Grignolino Sansoero 2012** (● 4,300 bt) is refreshing and delicate.

> **vino slow** **BARBERA D'ASTI LA TOTA 2011** (● 64,000 bt) Enviable drinkability, great juice and smoothly fresh, lively fruit — a gastronomic wine at a very reasonable price.

15 ha - 80,000 bt | **10% discount**

❝ Carussin emits positive energy. It's a "think tank" in which they devise, discuss and put into practice ideas and projects for a new form of agriculture based on observation, care for the land, carefreeness, sharing and fusion. You can't get slower than that! ❞

PEOPLE - Bruna Ferro, her husband Luigi and theirs sons Matteo and Luca are the heart and soul of a winery that is also an educational farm — with a class of 12 donkeys — and a rest stop.

VINEYARDS - Knowledge handed down from previous generations and the desire to cross new frontiers for natural wine inspired Bruna and Luigi to create a farm that is already a model for many locals. Harmony reigns among the vine rows with grassing, mowing when necessary, minimal working of the soil, and so on. All set inside a frame of healthy pragmatism.

WINES - As always, the wines of Carussin respond to rigorous criteria and necessitate a little time and patience to give of their best. The label that impressed us the most is Barbera d'Asti Lia Vì 2012 (● 16,000 bt) with its aromas of red berries and undergrowth and blunt, juicy palate — an enjoyable Everyday Wine. Also excellent is **Barbera d'Asti Asinoi 2012** (● 40,000 bt), which offers aromas of rust and ripe cherry. The red **La Tranquilla** (● barbera; 15,000 bt) is complex and rich with an encore of earthy notes. **Carica l'Asino 2012** (○ cortese, carica l'asino; 2,500 bt) is still sweetish due to the fact that the fermentation is still incomplete.

FERTILIZERS organic-mineral, compost
PLANT PROTECTION chemical, copper and sulphur
WEED CONTROL chemical, mechanical
YEASTS selected
GRAPES 100% estate-grown
CERTIFICATION none

FERTILIZERS biodynamic preparations, green manure
PLANT PROTECTION copper and sulphur
WEED CONTROL mechanical
YEASTS native
GRAPES 100% estate-grown
CERTIFICATION organic

Castello di Tassarolo 🐌

Via Alborina, 1
tel. 0143 342248
www.castelloditassarolo.it
info@castelloditassarolo.it

La Colombera 🍾

Frazione Vho
Strada Comunale per Vho, 7
tel. 0131 867795
www.lacolomberavini.it
info@lacolomberavini.it

---

17 ha - 120,000 bt   **10% discount**

❝ Wines that are light years away from technically in all its forms, wines that combine spontaneity with enjoyability. The agriculture is exemplary and performed with sensitivity and intelligence. **❞**

PEOPLE - This fairytale castle, owned by the Spinola family since the 14th century, is situated in the small village of Tassarolo. But if you wish to visit the wine cellar itself, you'll have to travel another kilometer or so. When you get there, Massimiliana and her partner Henry Finzi Constantine will offer you a simple, open welcome.

VINEYARDS - The company's 20 hectares stretch over a plateau at an altitude of 300 meters. They have been cultivated since 2006 in accordance with biodynamic criteria. One distinctive feature is the use of horses in the vineyard, a practice Henry intends to develop further to eliminate mechanical machinery altogether — or almost.

WINES - The excellent Gavi del Comune di Tassarolo Spinola 2012 (○ 40,000 bt) has crisp, crunchy fruit and a piquancy that makes for great dynamism — a perfect Everyday Wine. Also good is **Monferrato Rosso Cuvée 2012** (● barbera, cabernet sauvignon; 10,000 bt), with notes of red berries and hints of chewiness. **Gavi del Comune di Tassarolo Il Castello 2012** (○ 30,000 bt) offers fruity, vegetal aromas with an encore of aromatic herbs and a palate of refined grip thanks to its pleasant tanginess. **Piemonte Barbera Titouan 2012** (● 10,000 bt) is mature and ethereal with an even body and a slightly understated finish. **Gavi del Comune di Tassarolo Alborina 2012** (○ 6,000 bt) gives aromas of fruit and garden vegetables.

---

20 ha - 60,000 bt

PEOPLE - Who knows whether Edoardo, born in 2013, is already bubbling over with passion for wine? It's a question one is bound to ask given the fearless enthusiasm his mom, the friendly, solar Elisa, pours into the management of the family winery in the hills over Tortona. Elisa has inherited her interest for the sector from her dad Piercarlo, still at the forefront in the vineyards and the peach orchards.

VINEYARDS - The vineyards surround the cellar in a natural amphitheater, perfect for winegrowing, in the hills above the town. They occupy an area of 14 hectares in which vines alternate with other crops such as peaches, plums, chickpeas and cereals. Most of the land planted with vines is given over to timorasso, a grape in which the cellar has a lot of faith. Over the last few years Elisa and Piercarlo have moved step by step towards sustainable agriculture.

WINES - La Colombera is a convivial place open to anyone on the lookout for good, sincere wine (the unbottled stuff is excellent too). Elisa, who relies on the precious consultancy of Piero Ballario, once more submitted very effective wines, the Timorassos first and foremost. **Colli Tortonesi Timorasso Il Montino 2011** (○ 4,000 bt) is a crystalline version of notable finesse and intensity; it's a hymn to the terroir that fully deserves the Great Wine symbols. **Colli Tortonesi Timorasso Derthona 2011** (○ 12,000 bt) is elegant and mineral with intriguing notes of petrol. **Colli Tortonesi Cortese Bricco Bartolomeo 2012** (○ 10,000 bt) is pleasant and fruity. Closing with a red, **Colli Tortonesi Croatina La Romba 2011** (● 5,000 bt) is earthy with good intensity.

FERTILIZERS biodynamic preparations, green manure
PLANT PROTECTION copper and sulphur, organic
WEED CONTROL mechanical
YEASTS native
GRAPES 100% estate-grown
CERTIFICATION organic

FERTILIZERS natural manure, green manure
PLANT PROTECTION copper and sulphur
WEED CONTROL mechanical
YEASTS native
GRAPES 100% estate-grown
CERTIFICATION none

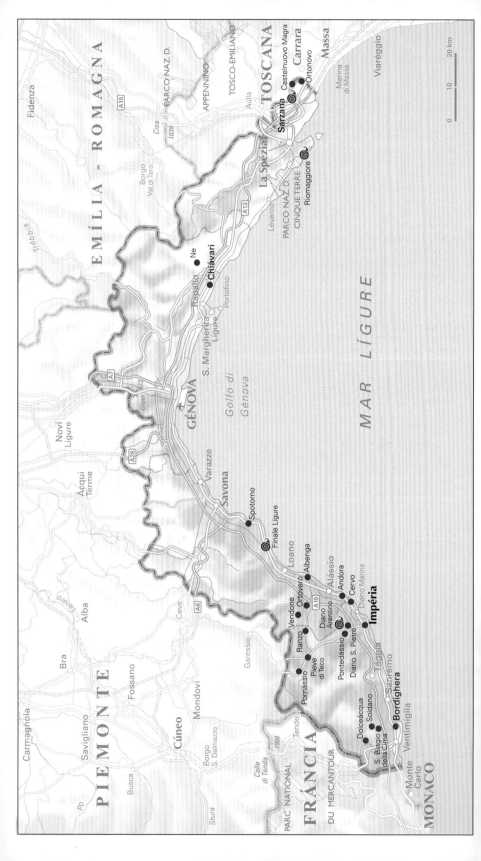

LIGURIA

Though Ligurian wine is receiving increasing consideration, its diversity and individuality still don't get the recognition they deserve. Though output is relatively low, the region still has a lot to say, especially in view of the fact that the number of quality wineries has increased sizably, not a new trend exactly but one that is growing tangibly. This is happening despite the fact that viticulture is no easy business here, practiced as it is on land with structural drawbacks, such as altitude (346 hectares of the total area are over 500 meters high), terracing and steep slopes (971 hectares out of 2,113 have gradients of over 30°), while the majority of wineries own areas of less than an hectare, 20 per cent can count on one to three hectares and only 7 per cent cover larger areas. The landscape speaks for itself: Ligurian vineyards, hemmed in by the sea to the front and the mountains to the rear, are made up of a myriad of tiny fragmented plots. Working them is a particularly arduous task (witness the verticality and relative inaccessibility of those in the Cinque Terre) and a meritorious one from the point of view of the conservation of the land, hence of the cultural and environmental heritage. Mainly white wines are produced, with vermentino and pigato grapes to the west, bosco, albarola and, again, vermentino to the east. The lumassina variety is also being revived and the bianchetta genovese re-evaluated. The main red grapes are rossese di Dolceacqua, with which firm-structured, character-packed wines are made, ormeasco and ciliegiolo, common round Genoa and on the Riviera di Levante to the east, where sangiovese, pollera and canaiolo are also grown. The 2012 harvest ended a poor growing year from the point of view of quantity due to problems in the flowering period, high temperatures and lack of rain. All this has had an adverse effect on yields, not so much in terms of the number of grapes as of their juice content. Overall, however, the quality is good with peaks of excellence here and there.

snails

58 MARIA DONATA BIANCHI
58 CASCINA DELLE TERRE ROSSE
59 SANTA CATERINA

bottles

59 VISAMORIS

DIANO ARENTINO (IM)

Maria Donata Bianchi ⊚↵

Località Valcrosa
Via Merea
tel. 0183 498233
www.aziendaagricolabianchi.it
info@aziendaagricolabianchi.com
📠—0

4 ha - 23,500 bt

66 Attentive, eco-friendly viticulture, hard work between the vine rows and in the cellar, excellent land-rooted wines —Emanuele Trevia is one of the most interesting names on the Vermentino scene and the Ligurian wine world in general. 99

PEOPLE - Behind the cellar's commendable achievements is the passionate work of people like enologists Marta, Emanuele's daughter, and the seasoned Walter Bonetti. The cellar also includes an agriturismo which Emanuele's wife Donatella Bianchi runs with great savoir-faire.

VINEYARDS - The vineyards are situated in hills with a long tradition of winemaking. Diano Castello, where the two vineyards dating back 50 years, the oldest, and the one given over to red grapes, are situated has always claimed to be the first place to cultivate the vermentino grape. In an enviable position in nearby Diano Arentino, the largest vineyard — about 15 years old with an area of three hectares — is where most of the white grapes are grown. The slopes here are gentle as opposed to steep.

WINES - Production centers round native white grapes. The cellar's two reds, made with the syrah and granaccia grapes, weren't released this year. The whites are wines of character with a strong sense of place. The lightly fruity **Antico Sfizio 2012** (O vermentino; 1,000 bt) is full of verve, its full-bodied attack refreshed by just the right amount of acidity. **Riviera Ligure di Ponente Pigato 2012** (O 8,500 bt) has fruity notes with a rich follow-through on the palate.

> **vino slow** RIVIERA LIGURE DI PONENTE VERMENTINO **2012** (O 13,000 bt) One of the best whites of all, eloquent on the nose, juicy and variegated on the palate, where it combines the freshness typical of the grape with beautifully balanced complexity and style.

FERTILIZERS green manure
PLANT PROTECTION copper and sulphur
WEED CONTROL mechanical
YEASTS selected
GRAPES 100% estate-grown
CERTIFICATION none

FINALE LIGURE (SV)

Cascina delle Terre Rosse ⊚↵

Via Manie, 3
tel. 0196 98782

5.2 ha - 23,000 bt

66 An environment-friendly winery in one of the most spectacular vineyards on the western Ligurian coast. A company that, without blowing its own trumpet, places the emphasis on sheer hard work. 99

PEOPLE - The winery was founded in 1970. For a number of years now it has been managed by Vladimiro Galluzzo, who has turned it into one of the most significant in the region, producing excellent wines right from the outset. His collaborators are his wife Paola, whose presence is as discreet as it is fundamental, enologist Giuliano Noè and agronomist Gianni Forte.

VINEYARDS - The south and southwest-facing locations of the vineyards in the Le Banche district, whose terraces grow vines planted 20-30 years ago, and Monte, with narrow terraces on 40° gradients, and the mild, marine climate of the Manie plateau in general are conducive to the cultivation of the pigato and vermentino grapes. The same varieties also grow on 40-year-old vines in a one-hectare vineyard with white clay soil in Pietra Ligure.

WINES - The wines are very good indeed. Packed with personality, they capture the essence of the western Ligurian landscape. **Riviera Ligure di Ponente Pigato 2012** (O 8,800 bt) is rich and forthright with bundles of fruit and almonds on the nose and a long, harmonious follow-through on the palate. **Apogeo 2012** (O pigato; 2,900 bt) is full-bodied, well-structured and rich in flavor with pervasive fruity, aromatic notes. Worthy of some attention, **Riviera Ligure di Ponente Vermentino 2012** (O 4,700 bt) is delicate and complex, endowed with delicious freshness and alluring flavor. **Acerbina 2012** (O lumassina; 1,900 bt) subtly renders the grape variety, hence lively freshness and an understated sensation of grassiness.

FERTILIZERS green manure
PLANT PROTECTION copper and sulphur
WEED CONTROL mechanical
YEASTS selected
GRAPES 100% estate-grown
CERTIFICATION none

VisAmoris

Strada Privata Molino Javè, 23
tel. 348 3959569
www.visamoris.it
visamoris@libero.it

Santa Caterina

Via Santa Caterina, 6
tel. 0187 629429
andrea.kihlgren@alice.it

3.5 ha - 26,000 bt   **10% discount**

PEOPLE - Rossana Zappa and Roberto Tozzi actually do other jobs, but they're always ready and willing to give up their free time to follow their winery, which came into being partly by chance. After falling in love with this corner of Liguria, they fell in love with its wine. Then they met enologist Giuliano Noè and started to invest heavily. Now, nine years on, they are producing grapes and wines exactly as they imagined.

VINEYARDS - The winery is now going organic. It owns three vineyards, one on a hillside, one on a plateau and one on a wide terrace near Rio Vasia, inland, northwest of Imperia. The calcareous-pebbly and clayey soil contribute to the structure and the flavor of the wines, while the different locations give multi-pass ripening and different acid-sugar ratios.

WINES - The thread that sews the winery's bottles together is the pigato grape in all its shapes and forms. **Riviera Ligure di Ponente Pigato Verum 2012** (O 5,000 bt), which continues to stand out for aromatic richness and structure, is fresh and juicy and unwinds dynamically into an almondy finish. Just as good is **Riviera Ligure di Ponente Pigato Domè 2012** (O 15,000 bt), which has fresh fruity aromas and lingering, delicately salty flavor. **Vis Amoris Brut Millesimato 2010** (O pigato; 3,000 bt) has great potential and **Dulcis in Fundo 2011** (O pigato; 600 bt) combines freshness and measured sweetness.

> **vino slow** RIVIERA LIGURE DI PONENTE PIGATO SOGNO **2011** (O 2,500 bt) A truly great white which moves from delicate blossomy notes to aromatic herbs and minerality, more pronounced on the full-flavored, beautifully textured palate. A wine built to last.

7.5 ha - 30,000 bt

66 Calm and slowness but also inexorable rhythm — these, we believe, are the characteristics of Andrea Kihlgren,who has been making complex wines, excellent and never humdrum, in the Sarzana hills for 20 years. The same characteristics are reflected in the wines themselves, which take more time than others to soften out and reach the degree of evolution desired. 99

PEOPLE - With is wife Alessandra, Andrea follows the whole winemaking process personally from, vineyard to cellar.

VINEYARDS - All the cellar's production is concentrated into five properties. The main one is Santa Caterina, where the soil is clayey and, besides the vineyard, planted mostly with vermentino grapes, there are also small orchards and olive groves. Soils are cover-cropped and periodically treated with vegetable composts, on view in heaps beside the single vineyards.

WINES - Barring a moderate amount of sulphur dioxide, no enology products are used in the cellar. The white wines are fermented in steel vats, while the reds are aged in wood barrels. **Colli di Luni Vermentino 2012** (O 11,000 bt) is refreshing and fruity, a pleasure to drink. **Colli di Luni Albarola 2012** (O 500 bt) has delicate balsamic notes and hints of crushed fruit with a warm, dry finish. After aging all winter on fine lees, **Colli di Luni Vermentino Poggi Alti 2012** (O 3,600 bt) offers ripe fruit and minerals. Moving on to the reds, **Golfo dei Poeti Rosso Ghiaretolo 2010** (● merlot, cabernet sauvignon; 3,200 bt) has notes of red berries, spiciness and fine tannins. Ripe fruit comes to the fore in the easy-to-drink **Liguria di Levante Rosso Fontananera 2011** (● merlot, ciliegiolo; 3,060 bt).

FERTILIZERS green manure
PLANT PROTECTION copper and sulphur, organic
WEED CONTROL mechanical
YEASTS selected
GRAPES 100% estate-grown
CERTIFICATION none

FERTILIZERS natural manure, compost, biodynamic preparations, green manure
PLANT PROTECTION copper and sulphur
WEED CONTROL mechanical
YEASTS native
GRAPES 100% estate-grown
CERTIFICATION none

LOMBARDY

It would be a mistake to offer an overview of winemaking in the region without mentioning the Milan Expo, which is now just round the corner. It is due to be held in 2015 and the expectations around it are as numerous as the ideas. It's the hope of all concerned that it will make Milan a showcase for local areas and quality agrifood supply chains.

The event will constitute an opportunity for Italy and, above all, for Lombardy. It will give the region an unprecedented chance to show off the distinctive features of its agriculture, hence to reclaim its rural identity and demonstrate how the economic model of good local farming can serve as an antidote to the crisis.

In the Franciacorta district, a place of constant ferment, ready and willing to welcome new scenarios with pragmatism and scientific purpose, more and more cellars, including the most famous, are moving towards organics. Further proof, if any were needed, of how, besides being a reliable alternative to invasion by supermarkets, quality wine is the real economic driving force of the area.

Team spirit shines through once again in the Valtellina, this year thanks to the ability of wineries and consortia to convey an image of cohesion. This is an approach by which the sustainability of a local area can be measured. In the glass, the Sforzatos reached high levels of excellence.

The pages devoted to the Oltrepò Pavese zone exemplify the philosophy of our guide — original, hence open to criticism — which reserves special care for small and medium wineries that maintain their identity and sense of belonging in an area that is still paying for the mistakes it made in the past. *Slow Wine* has a lot of belief in the potential of the area and the labors of the many winemakers who make it buzz. The spotlight is now on the Metodo Classico, the classic method, on Cruasé, first and foremost, which still shows plenty of scope for improvement.

Lugana confirms itself as a strong wine in a strong selling area. In this case too, credit is due to the teamwork shown by wineries that have worked together to give their products a precise local identity.

We also believe in the Valtenèsi project, which albeit not yet shared by everyone, seeks to raise pride in Groppello and Chiaretto.

News just in from the Bassa of Brescia, an important farming district, is that the Capriano del Colle DOC is soon to be renamed Montenetto to further emphasize its bond with the local area. Last but not least, the latest reports on Moscato di Scanzo, a pearl of Bergamo winemaking, are positive, while the new Terre Lariane district continues to hold its own, especially with its white wines.

snails

63	TOGNI REBAIOLI
64	IL PENDIO
64	DIRUPI
65	AR.PE.PE.
65	FAY
67	PODERE IL SANTO
67	AGNES

bottles

63	NINO NEGRI

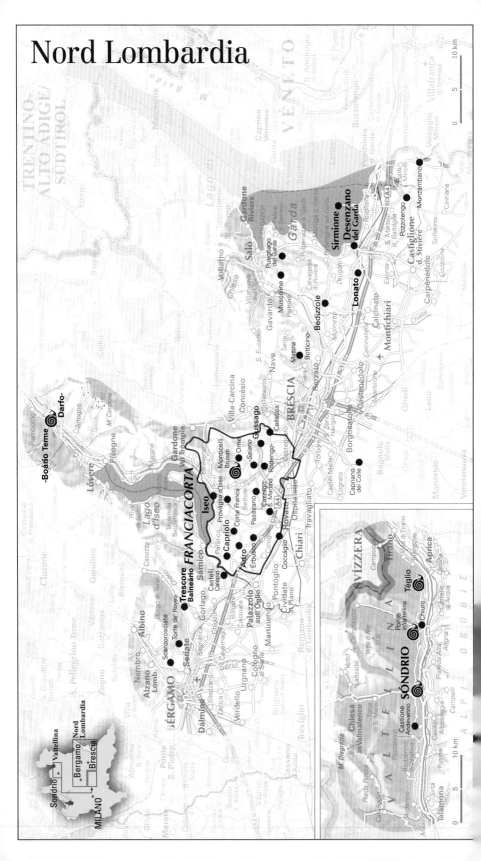

CHIURO (SO)

Nino Negri

Via Ghibellini, 3
tel. 0342 485211
www.ninonegri.it
negri@giv.it

36 ha - 800,000 bt `10% discount`

PEOPLE - There would be no Valtellina wine at all if it weren't for Nino Negri. The winery, which boasts the highest output in the valley, has been run for more than 40 years by the enologist Casimiro Maule, who deserves the credit for making it a model of quality and for giving voice to the hundreds of local winemakers. The impeccable enological style evidences the grandiosity of the mountain nebbiolo grape.

VINEYARDS - A tour of all the Nino Negri vineyards takes some time. The company's properties are vast and include veritable Valtellina crus. Take the gorgeous Fracia vineyard at Chiuro, for example, or Sassella, criss-crossed by dry stone walls. A team of experts adopt avant-garde agronomic methods and also oversee the vineyards of grape suppliers.

WINES - Casimiro's enological experience is condensed into the wines from which the qualities of the various grape varieties are coaxed out by clever use of wood. The two labels of Sforzato, the wine with which the company has made the Valtellina famous round the world, were both impeccable. The Great Wine symbol goes to the local icon par excellence, **Sforzato di Valtellina 5 Stelle 2010** (● 30,000 bt), elegant, austere, typical. Almost on a par is **Sforzato di Valtellina Carlo Negri 2010** (● 30,000 bt). **Valtellina Sup. Vigneto Fracia 2010** (● 13,000 bt) is good but still reveals traces of wood. **Valtellina Sup. Sassella Le Tense 2010** (● 70,000 bt) is juicy, fragrant and warm. **Valtellina Sup. Inferno Carlo Negri 2010** (●30,000 bt) is terrific too.

DARFO BOARIO TERME (BS)

Togni Rebaioli

Frazione Erbanno
Via Rossini, 19
tel. 0364 529706
www.togni-rebaioli.it
info@togni-rebaioli.it

3.5 ha - 12,000 bt

66 The revolutionary Valcamonica farmer, Enrico Togni, has a CV which includes; making a job out of mountain agriculture, raising the profile of local grape varieties, constantly putting himself on the line and fighting to give voice to his native valley. 99

PEOPLE - Enrico's struggle to support wine culture in the Valcamonica is, literally, an uphill task. He manages his small winery with the precious support of his family, especially his wife Cinzia and daughter Martina.

VINEYARDS - As a result of years of constant hard work in the fragile Valcamonica environment, most of Enrico's vineyard is terraced. His agronomic choices don't adhere to rigid naturalist theory. Enrico simply relies on his knowledge of farming handed down to him by his grandfather and his own sensitivity as a warden of the valley. This year has brought major innovations, one of which double-grafting the various vines with erbanno grapes.

WINES - The latest harvests have confirmed improving quality in all the wines. Credit for this must go to Enrico's friend Nico Danesi for his support in the cellar, but above all, to Enrico's own experience and ability to talk to young Italian producers. This year we had to make do with two labels, since Enrico deemed the others unready and postponed their release. He also intends to reduce his range and bank on the erbanno grape. Albeit full of alcoholic strength, the compact, fruity **Lambrù 2010** (● marzemino, barbera, merlot; 6,500 bt) is refreshing and quaffable. Intriguing and more focused every year, **1703 2010** (● 1,100 bt) is a successful attempt to lift the nebbiolo grape.

FERTILIZERS manure pellets, natural manure, green manure
PLANT PROTECTION chemical, copper and sulphur
WEED CONTROL chemical, mechanical
YEASTS selected, native
GRAPES 70% bought in
CERTIFICATION none

FERTILIZERS none
PLANT PROTECTION copper and sulphur
WEED CONTROL mechanical
YEASTS native
GRAPES 100% estate-grown
CERTIFICATION none

MONTICELLI BRUSATI (BS)

Il Pendio

Via Panoramica, 50
tel. 030 6852570
www.ilpendio.com
info@ilpendio.com

3 ha - 15,000 bt

❝❝ Terraced vineyards, olive groves, a variegated farming landscape and craftsmanship of every kind make Il Pendio unique. What impresses the most is its unconventional originality and bond with the land. ❞❞

PEOPLE - Il Pendio gravitates round Michele Loda, a real "slow" character and an adamant supporter of a winemaking model that speaks the language of purity.

VINEYARDS - Michele's deserves to be defined as mountain viticulture. The landscape is unusual, a long way from monoculture, but also from the gentle rolling hills of Franciacorta. At the highest point of the denomination (450 meters), the vineyards are planted on terraces and interspersed with woodland. The soil is also different; it is richer in white rock, a characteristic that justifies the decision to produce still wine too.

WINES - Coherence reigns in the cellar, where all operations are performed by Michele personally, by hand. As we mentioned, the cellar also produces a line of still wines in accordance with local culture and tradition. One such is the red **La Beccaccia 2008** (● 1,000 bt), a monovarietal cabernet franc, at once elegant and enriched by a veil of huskiness that makes it truly intriguing. In the cellar we also tasted a number of sparkling wines, noteworthy among which is the mineral, fragrant and drinkable Franciacorta Pas Dosé Il Contestatore 2008. **Franciacorta Extra Brut Brusato** (○ 5,000 bt), the cellar's standard-bearer, is intriguing more for its curiousness, freshness and silkiness than its approachability.

FERTILIZERS natural manure
PLANT PROTECTION copper and sulphur
WEED CONTROL mechanical
YEASTS native
GRAPES 100% estate-grown
CERTIFICATION none

PONTE IN VALTELLINA (SO)

Dirupi

Località Madonna di Campagna
tel. 0342 050667
www.dirupi.com
info@dirupi.com

4.5 ha - 20,000 bt

❝❝ Like a tidal wave, the volatile, volcanic young duo Pierpaolo Di Franco and Davide Fasolini, nicknamed "Birba" and "Faso", have overwhelmed the Valtellina wine world with their optimism, freshness and passion. What can you say about them? "Well done!" for a start. ❞❞

PEOPLE - This year the two have added a significant new chapter to their already original story. Not only have they consolidated their business, they have also come up with a much awaited novelty: their first Sforzato label.

VINEYARDS - Pierpaolo and Davide, both graduates in viticulture and enology, are both dry stone wall fans. They love exchanging ideas with fellow winemakers from the Valtellina and the rest of Italy, and they are eager to find out more and develop their ideas about new models of agriculture (they are currently dabbling in organics in the Grumello zone). Precise, scrupulous, low-profile, rooted to the land and its peculiarities, prepared to come to terms with all the problems it poses — the Dirupi philosophy in nuce.

WINES - Dirupi wines close-focused, well-crafted have a style of their own and capture the essence of their terroir. The long awaited **Sforzato di Valtellina 2011** (● 1,000 bt) shows how Birba and Faso's feeling for the Valtellina is growing more and more intimate. It's a curious, narrative, charismatic wine that looks upwards but also groundwards, raises expectations and, above all, spurs debate. **Rosso di Valtellina Olé 2012** (● 6,000 bt) is an appealing expression of local daily life, easy-going but never humdrum. **Valtellina Sup. Ris. 2010** (● 2,700 bt) is ambitious and rich, a wine to store in the cellar.

> **vino slow** IL VALTELLINA SUP. DIRUPI 2011 (● 11,000 bt) The label that set the boys' exciting progress in motion: a sharp, focused, blunt rendering of mountain nebbiolo.

FERTILIZERS none
PLANT PROTECTION chemical, copper and sulphur, organic
WEED CONTROL chemical, mechanical
YEASTS selected
GRAPES 100% estate-grown
CERTIFICATION none

SONDRIO

Ar.Pe.Pe.

Via del Buon Consiglio, 4
tel. 0342 214120
www.arpepe.com
info@arpepe.com

12 ha - 60,000 bt | **10% discount**

66 A unique, singular interpretation of mountain nebbiolo. The result of a late harvest, this original winery captures the essence of the terroir. 99

PEOPLE - With their clear, modern ideas, Isabella and Emanuele Pelizzati are consolidating the winery, which rose to fame thanks to their father Arturo. Thy are assisted by brother Guido and a staff of young people.

VINEYARDS - Emanuele is to be admired for the pride he puts into his vineyards. "At all events, visiting vineyards, ours and those of our fellow winemakers, is a moral obligation which helps one understand the true value of the terroir." From the Buon Consiglio property, over the cellar, to Rocce Rosse, in the heart of the Sassella district, Ar.Pe.Pe.boasts an intricate mosaic of vineyards, some very old, which it manages with pragmatism and common sense.

WINES - In recent years Isabella and Emanuele have developed a distinctive model with wines of strong personality. Their famous "grand reserves", which alternate with the "small" ones, are the result of commitment in the vineyards, constant care and attention and a special knack of living up to expectations. Without going over the top, as this year's range of just three labels demonstrates. Eleven harvests on, the monumental **Valtellina Sup. Sassella Rocce Rosse Ris. 2002** (● 18,000 bt) is still placing the onus on elegance and length. **Rosso di Valtellina 2011** (● 30,000 bt) is the terroir's visiting card.

> **vino slow** VALTELLINA SUP. SASSELLA ULTIMI RAGGI 2006 (● 4,900 bt) A unique, singular interpretation of mountain nebbiolo. The result of a late harvest, this original wine captures the essence of the terroir.

FERTILIZERS organic-mineral, manure pellets, natural manure
PLANT PROTECTION chemical, copper and sulphur
WEED CONTROL mechanical
YEASTS native
GRAPES 100% estate-grown
CERTIFICATION none

TEGLIO (SO)

Fay

Località San Giacomo di Teglio
Via Pila Caselli, 1
tel. 0342 786071
www.vinifay.it
info@vinifay.it

13 ha - 50,000 bt

66 Reliability, land-rootedness, competence, constructive criticism and collaboration — the secrets of Fay, a model for the many local producers concerned about quality. 99

PEOPLE - Marco Fay and his family, dad Sandro and sister Elena are the emblem of the rebirth of winemaking in the area. His straightforward, pragmatic philosophy lays the basis for the innovation and success of this historic Valtellina cellar.

VINEYARDS - Marco studies, Marco observes, Marco interprets the Valtellina landscape — why dry stone walls?, he wonders — drawing his own conclusions and, of course, coming away with a few doubts. He talks with friends and colleagues, he puts forward ideas and spreads them (for example, the importance of altitude in assessing grape quality). He's also level-headed, with his feet on the ground, the operational arm of a way of making wine still based on common sense.

WINES - Without the Carteria and Ca' Morey crus, the two wines that have strengthened the cellar's bond with the Valgella terroir, this year's range was reduced to a minimum. Having said that, the average level of the other wines was high, as **Sforzato di Valtellina Ronco del Picchio 2009** (● 8,000 bt), balsamic, well-structured and soft, demonstrates. Just as impressive was **Valtellina Sup. Costa Bassa 2010** (● 15,000 bt), succulent, typical, with beautifully textured tannins, an expression without frills of the nebbiolo grape harvested at an altitude of 300-450 meters. **La Faya 2010** (● 4,000 bt) is unusual but it works, an unorthodox take on nebbiolo, merlot and syrah. **Valtellina Sup. Sassella Il Glicine 2010** (● 3,600 bt) is fruity and richly extracted.

FERTILIZERS natural manure
PLANT PROTECTION chemical, copper and sulphur
WEED CONTROL chemical, mechanical
YEASTS native
GRAPES 100% estate-grown
CERTIFICATION none

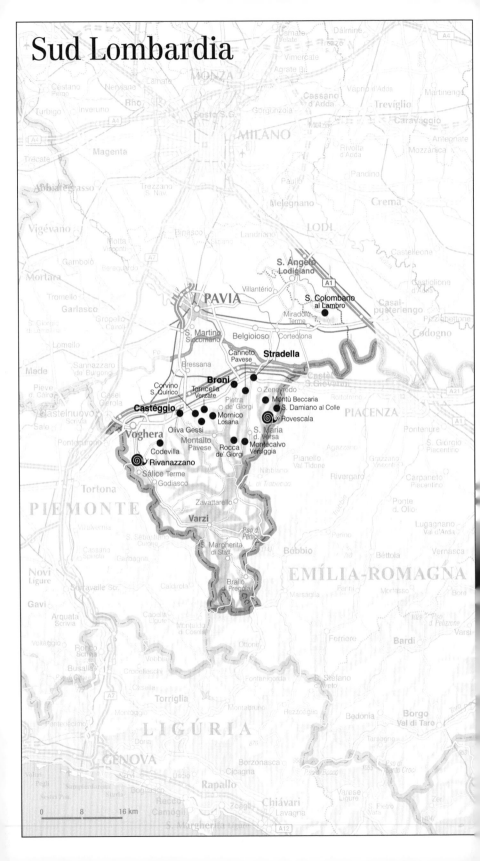

Sud Lombardia

Podere Il Santo

Via Kennedy, 36
tel. 0383 92244
www.ilsanto.biz
info@ilsanto.biz

---

5 ha - 6,000 bt

66 Closely bound up with the local land and culture, impermeable to productivist visions and monocultures, Eugenio Barbieri's winery is an "intangible" example of how peasant civilization can be adapted to the present. A rare, indeed unique model, but also a convincing one. 99

PEOPLE - Eugenio runs the company with his wife Sabina. Theirs is a closed-loop business in which viticulture rounds off a whole range of farming work and is well worth a visit.

VINEYARDS - Eugenio's vineyards are all situated in the hills round Rivanazzano on the border with Piedmont. They are interspersed with native cereal crops grown to feed cattle, pigs, hens and ducks in a harmonious context of synergic agriculture in which every element has a role to play. In the vineyards Eugenio has revived the tradition of planting some crops to revitalize the soil.

WINES - If and when you visit the winery, don't expect to see Eugenio busy among barrels and vats and fermenters and all the other cellar paraphernalia. Yet, essential though it is, the place still manages to be a wine institution. It produces two labels, both perfect examples of natural winemaking with extralong macerations and aging in old barrels and cement vats. **Rairon 2007 (●** 2,000 bt), a monovarietal made with rare grapes, is intriguing and deep: its volatile acidity may cause brows to be raised, but it actually adds character and personality. Potent, racy and alcoholic with amazing acidity, **Novecento 2005 (●** 4,000 bt) is a singular but successful interpretation of the barbera grape.

FERTILIZERS manure pellets
PLANT PROTECTION copper and sulphur
WEED CONTROL mechanical
YEASTS native
GRAPES 100% estate-grown
CERTIFICATION none

Agnes

Via Campo del Monte, 1
tel. 0385 75206
www.fratelliagnes.it
info@fratelliagnes.it

---

21 ha - 120,000 bt   **10% discount**

66 Obsessive care for the centenarian vineyards and special attention to the crus are the cornerstones of this exemplary cellar, a driving force for the whole Oltrepò district. 99

PEOPLE - Agnes and her brothers Sergio and Cristiano manage the family winery, set up in 1912, meticulously — which means, among other things, spending long hours out in the vineyards. The declared objective is to make quality wines that are as land-rooted as possible.

VINEYARDS - Three quarters of the vineyards, which have an average age of 60, are given over to croatina, the prime grape in Rovescala. Another 30 or so native varieties are also grown. The average altitude of the vineyards is 280 meters and the soil is mostly clay. The Loghetto vineyard, planted in 1906, deserves a special mention. A walk among its secular vines is an experience not to be missed.

WINES - As we wait for the project for a Metodo Classico made with pinot nero and meunier grapes, the fruit of years of aging on yeasts, to materialize, the range of different interpretations of croatina is once more up to the mark. **Possessione del Console 2011 (●** 10,000 bt) is intense, rich and fruity, while **O.P. Bonarda Millennium 2008 (●** 3,000 bt), produced only in the most favorable growing years, is warm and complex. **O.P. Bonarda Cresta del Ghiffi 2012 (●** 13,000 bt) offers good value for money and a pleasure to drink.

> **vino slow** **LOGHETTO 2012 (●** 1.500 bt) As ever one of Italy's most intriguing wines. Deep and delightful and, as the label says, "almond-edged", it captures the spirit of the centenarian vines it comes from and the man who makes it.

FERTILIZERS green manure
PLANT PROTECTION copper and sulphur
WEED CONTROL mechanical
YEASTS native
GRAPES 100% estate-grown
CERTIFICATION none

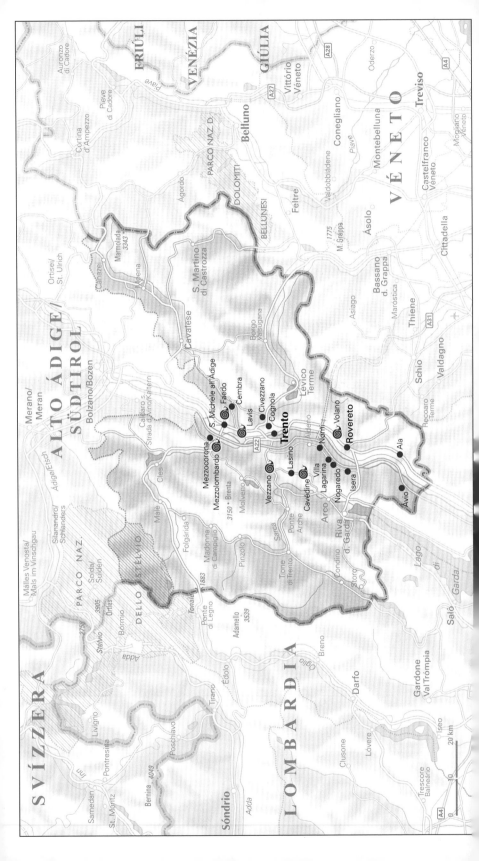

TRENTINO

The Trentino is a controversial region. Over the last 30 years, the wine scene has seen profound changes, and native varieties that, in the 1980s, represented 60 per cent of total output, now account for only 20 per cent. Suffice it to think of the dramatic decline of schiava, which in 1980 was the most cultivated variety in the Trentino and occupied 34 per cent of the total area planted with wines; now it occupies a measly 4 per cent. Worse still, lambrusco a foglia frastagliata (with jagged leaves) has dropped from 12.6 per cent to a paltry 0.5 per cent, just 53 hectares!

This is all the result of the internationalization of cultivated varieties, a process encouraged by cooperative cellars banking on more standardized wines that respond to the globalized taste of the market. Native grapes have been supplanted by chardonnay, which now occupies an area of 2,865 hectares, and pinot nero for the production of Trentodoc, which covers 245 hectares. The area covered by pinot grigio, finally, increased from 1.6 per cent of the total to 23, the equivalent of 2,351 hectares.

These stats and the wines now on the market have led many people to claim that what the Trentino lacks is identity. But it's our belief that, amid this productive confusion, there are wines (and producers) that are bucking the trend, that, notwithstanding internationalization, there are winegrowing areas producing great terroir-dedicated wines, that grapes like the much maligned nosiola deserve to be reevaluated and promoted.

Now a few general observations on our tastings. Starting with the reds, we weren't particularly taken by the Teroldego 2011s, characterized by limp fruit and not perfectly mature. Much more interesting were Lagrein, Marzemino and Schiava. The Trentodoc weren't exactly on top form, but the Nosiolas, Incrocio Manzonis and Müller Thurgaus all performed well.

The 2012 vintage was in no way memorable. An unseasonably warm March was followed by a cold wet April, during which frosts held back the flowering of the vines. Then came a summer memorable for its lack of rain and continual heatwaves (christened, incidentally, with the most improbable names, from Hannibal and Charon to Lucifer, Caligula and others besides). The rains eventually arrived in September and caused sharp swings in temperature. In general, all this translated into a lower production of grapes and difficulties for bunches to ripen perfectly. Luckily, these problems were less marked in hillside vineyards and, despite everything, the overall quality of wines was satisfactory with a number of significant peaks of excellence.

snails 🐌

70 GINO PEDROTTI
70 POJER & SANDRI
71 MASO FURLI
72 VIGNAIOLO FANTI
72 FORADORI
73 EUGENIO ROSI

bottles 🍾

73 FERRARI

CAVEDINE (TN)

Gino Pedrotti

Frazione Pietramurata
Via Cavedine, 7
tel. 0461 564123
www.ginopedrotti.it
info@ginopedrotti.it

5 ha - 22,000 bt

66 The Pedrottis embody all the principles of an old farming family. Well-rooted in the land on which they live, they respect it and get the best out of it every day. Because this is their history and this is their life. 99

PEOPLE - Gino and Rosanna Pedrotti and their children Giuseppe, Tullia and Clara run a bar-osteria serving local specialties accompanied by the wine they produce in their vineyards. Anyone visiting the Valle dei Laghi will be familiar with the historic business.

VINEYARDS - The eight small vineyards are situated round the cellar, where mostly red grapes are grown, and the terraces overlooking Lake Cavedine, where two hectares of nosiola are planted. Old pergola-trained vines alternate with other more recent Guyot-trained ones. Work in the vineyards is entrusted to Giuseppe, who follows biodynamic principles with profound respect for soil-vine-environment equilibrium.

WINES - The wines encapsulate the identity of the terroir. The exemplary **Nosiola 2011** (O 5,000 bt) is tangy and full of the juice of ripe fruit, while **Auro 2009** (● cabernet franc, merlot; 2,900 bt) is taut and intense. **Aura 2010** (O nosiola, chardonnay; 1,600 bt) is firmly structured and wonderfully drinkable, and shows good balance between softness and acidity. Schiava Nera 2011 (● 3,000 bt) is unusual: brief drying on the vine and aging in steel vats give life to a wine with pleasantly well-rounded fruit and rich in freshness. It's a great Everyday Wine.

> **vino slow** TRENTINO VINO SANTO 2000 (O 4,268 bt) An exemplary wine born of the great Trento tradition of nosiola raisining. Very delicate and spicy, dense and vibrant, it's 13 years old but it's still youthful, well-balanced and refreshing.

FERTILIZERS natural manure, biodynamic preparations, green manure
PLANT PROTECTION copper and sulphur
WEED CONTROL mechanical
YEASTS native
GRAPES 100% estate-grown
CERTIFICATION organic

FAEDO (TN)

Pojer & Sandri

Località Molini, 4
tel. 0461 650342
www.pojeresandri.it
info@pojeresandri.it

30 ha - 250,000 bt

66 Quick-fire, volcanic, ingenious — these adjectives and more besides describe the work of this Trento winery and the people who run it. Their aim is to express as well as possible the quality and identity of viticulture in the hills of Faedo and the Val di Cembra. 99

PEOPLE - The leading players in the winery are partners Mario Pojer and Fiorentino Sandri, two friends who set out on this journey together in the 1970s and still follow it today with fervor, innovative capacity and a knack for "listening to" the land.

VINEYARDS - Innovation is everywhere, especially in the field. The viticulture Mario and Fiorentino favor is attentive, deeply rooted in what the terroir has to offer. Worthy of note is the project under way at Grumes, in the upper Cembra valley, where abandoned land planted with inter-specific vines is being reclaimed. Resulting experiments with vinification are producing interesting and original results.

WINES - An exemplary range as always. The excellent **Besler Bianck 2008** (O incrocio Manzoni, kerner, riesling; 8,000 0.5 lt bt) is a Great Wine that combines elegance and cut with a spicy, citrussy palate, full of flavor and tanginess. The 2012 whites have suffered slightly from the warm growing year and their characteristic acid sinew is less assertive than usual. **Filii 2012** (O 12,000 0.5 lt bt) is a recherché, low-alcohol blend of riesling and its "offspring"— müller thurgau, kerner and incrocio Manzoni — and releases intense scents of apple and hedgerow, while **Müller Thurgau Palai 2012** (O 40,000 bt) is subtle and deftly aromatic. **Rosso Faye 2010** (● cabernet sauvignon e franc, merlot, lagrein; 6,000 bt) is beautifully austere and full-bodied. Last but not least, the sweet, opulent **Essenzia 2009** (O 16,000 bt) is made with raisined grapes.

FERTILIZERS manure pellets, natural manure
PLANT PROTECTION copper and sulphur
WEED CONTROL mechanical
YEASTS selected, native
GRAPES 100% estate-grown
CERTIFICATION none

LASINO (TN)

Pravis

Frazione Madruzzo
Località Biolche
tel. 0461 564305
www.pravis.it
info@pravis.it

30 ha - 20,000 bt **10% discount**

PEOPLE - From the cellar, surrounded by vineyards, it's possible to enjoy a view over the Valle dei Laghi, the Valley of the Lakes, and Castel Madruzzo. Thanks to the insight and obstinacy of three Lasino winemakers, Pravis describes one of the prettiest areas of the Trentino region in its wines. Erika Pedrini is the winery's young enologist. She works with equal confidence in vineyard and cellar, animated by her curiosity to try out different grape varieties and innovative cultivation techniques.

VINEYARDS - The frate, terraces planted with vines and supported by dry stone walls, the steep marly limestone slopes overlooking Lake Cavedine, the clay and silt of the the Sarche plain — different soil conditions and positions make it possible to cultivate many varieties. For some years now, the cellar has been experimenting with "piwi", an abbreviation of the German "pilzwiderstandsfähig", inter-specific vine varieties resistant to diseases such as mildew, powdery and downy.

WINES - The company's wine are characterized by freshness and flavor. From Lasino come the reds made with traditional grapes. **El Filò 2008** (● groppello noneso; 3,600 bt) is redolent of berries and soil on the nose, proud and earthy on the palate, while **Destrani 2010** (● franconia; 3,600 bt) is spicy, vegetal and fragrant. **Nosiola Le Frate 2012** (○ 6,600 bt) has a sweet, mineral nose with hints of apple and fresh grapes and a full-favored, well-rounded mouthfeel. We were intrigued by **Naran Bianco 2012** (○ solaris; 4,600 bt), produced with "piwi" solaris grapes, which has pronounced notes of pepper and tart and fresh, juicy flavor.

vino slow **L'ORA 2010** (○ 3,300 bt) A very special take on nosiola made with grapes part-withered and part-fermented in acacia barrels. It offers the nose toasty and sweet honey notes with hints of wax and butter and a very savory, beefy palate

FERTILIZERS natural manure, compost
PLANT PROTECTION copper and sulphur
WEED CONTROL mechanical
YEASTS selected
GRAPES 100% estate-grown
CERTIFICATION none

LAVIS (TN)

Maso Furli

Località Furli
Via Furli, 32
tel. 0461 240667
www.masofurli.it
masofurli@alice.it

4 ha - 16,000 bt

❝ Ingenious, experimentalist, pure — this is Marco Zanoni, a bold, perfectionist winemaker who, with great passion, describes his local area through charismatic wines of unmistakable style. ❞

PEOPLE - In 1997 Marco stopped selling his grapes to the Cantina di Mezzocorona and began making and bottling his own wine. Thinking back to the prices Trentino wine cooperatives paid for grapes in those days, it may sound like a crazy decision to make. But Marco had a dream of his own, that of making wines to confirm the potential of the terroir. Such was his conviction that he didn't hesitate to put himself on the line.

VINEYARDS - Marco thus set to work on his four hectares of land with great eco-awareness — hence without the use of chemicals — inventing the most wild and wonderful machinery to perform vineyard operations without compressing the soil overmuch. The vineyards are grassed and cover-cropped and the vines are never topped. The main aim is to let the grapes acquire a natural equilibrium of their own.

WINES - To appreciate Maso Furli's long-living, potent, stylish wines to the full, it's advisable to let them age for a few years. **Chardonnay 2011** (○ 2,600 bt) has an intense, citrussy and a juicy palate with distinct acidity. Also very good, **Rosso Furli 2009** (● cabernet, merlot; 1,200 bt) is pervasive and refreshing and will achieve maximum expressiveness with a further period of aging. **Sauvignon 2011** (○ 4,700) impresses with its mouthfilling flavor.

vino slow **MANZONI BIANCO 2011** (○ 1,500 bt) A wine of great character with aromas of freshly mown grass, basil and peach, and a palate distinguished by grip and explosive minerality. A great interpretation of a very interesting grape variety.

FERTILIZERS biodynamic preparations, green manure
PLANT PROTECTION copper and sulphur
WEED CONTROL mechanical
YEASTS selected
GRAPES 100% estate-grown
CERTIFICATION organic

LAVIS (TN)

Vignaiolo Fanti

Località Pressano
Piazza G. N. della Croce, 3
tel. 0461 240809
www.vignaiolofanti.it
info@vignaiolofanti.it

4.2 ha - 16,000 bt

66 The friendly, modest Alessandro Fanti is a winemaker who cultivates his vines with simplicity and love, producing deep, forthright wines that raise the spirits of the drinker. 99

PEOPLE - Alessandro Fanti took over the reins of the family winery from his father Giuseppe in 1991. He decided immediately to drastically cut yields in the vineyard to produce terroir-dedicated grapes. The cellar is situated at the center of the small village of Pressano.

VINEYARDS - The vineyards are split up into different plots in the area between Pressano and Sorni. For Alessandro it's vital to limit treatments in the vineyard to a minimum and he restricts himself to the use of copper and sulphur. By contrast, a great deal of manual labor (under-vine soil working, rolling-up of the shoots) is fundamental for top quality, especially on the very steep parcels.

WINES - All the hard work is rewarded by the pleasantness of the wines. **Isidor 2010** (○ incrocio Manzoni; 2,700 bt) is once more a masterpiece: assertive with explosive minerality accompanied by intense hints of grapefruit and spring flowers, it's already a Great Wine and is sure to improve in the bottle. A tannic blend of cabernet and merlot, **Portico Rosso 2010** (● 2,400 bt) is redolent of berries. **Incrocio Manzoni 2011** (○ 3,400 bt) has intense aromas of citrus fruit and pencil lead, pronounced flavor and firm structure.

> **vino slow** Nosiola **2011** (○ 4,200 bt) Ready already and extremely pleasing, we believe this wine will grow with age. It's an impeccable combination of elegance and freshness with pervasive flavor. A master class in the interpretation of the nosiola grape.

MEZZOLOMBARDO (TN)

Foradori

Via Damiano Chiesa, 1
tel. 0461 601046
www.elisabettaforadori.com
info@elisabettaforadori.com

24 ha - 160,000 bt

66 In Elisabetta's handshake you feel the rapport she, the "signora del Teroldego", has with the land. Her hands are at once strong and delicate, used to caressing the vines and pampering them. 99

PEOPLE - Elisabetta Foradori's journey towards eco-friendly viticulture began in 1984. It was then that, after her father's death, she took over the family company. Convinced of the potential of teroldego, she immediately set into motion an important massal selection project.

VINEYARDS - The historic vineyards are all scattered over the Piana Rotaliana, a plain of alluvial origin, and are given over exclusively to teroldego. The white varieties — the native nosiola and incrocio Manzoni — are cultivated on the hill of Cognola on the Fontanasanta estate. Here the vineyards grow on clayey soil and are surrounded by woods. All the vineyards stand in grass, topping is banned and interventions are limited to a minimum.

WINES - Elisabetta's aim in the cellar is to preserve the vitality of the fruit in her wine, which speaks of the land in which it was born. To make the process as natural as possible, for some years now she has been using tinajas, Spanish amphorae. This is how Teroldego Morei, Teroldego Sgarzon and Nosiola Fontanabianca are made, all three wines that we shall review in future when they reach the right level of expression. In the husky, somewhat compact and austere **Teroldego 2011** (● 90,000 bt), the fruit gives a nice encore on the finish. Forthright, clenched and dry, **Teroldego Granato 2010** (● 20,000 bt) is fruitier and spicier and tinged by sweetness from the wood.

FERTILIZERS natural manure, biodynamic preparations
PLANT PROTECTION copper and sulphur
WEED CONTROL mechanical
YEASTS selected
GRAPES 100% estate-grown
CERTIFICATION organic

FERTILIZERS compost, biodynamic preparations
PLANT PROTECTION copper and sulphur
WEED CONTROL mechanical
YEASTS native
GRAPES 100% estate-grown
CERTIFICATION biodynamic, organic

TRENTO

Ferrari

Via del Ponte di Ravina, 15
tel. 0461 972 311
www.cantineferrari.it
info@ferrarispumante.it

120 ha - 4,500,000 bt   **10% discount**

PEOPLE - When, in 1952, Bruno Lunelli bought a tiny cellar producing a meager number of bottles of Metodo Classico in Trento from Giulio Ferrari, little did he know how successful the place was going to become over the years. Today it's his cousins Marcello, Matteo and Camilla Lunelli who manage Ferrari, with the seasoned and talented enologist Ruben Larentis in charge of the cellar.

VINEYARDS - The Lunellis' vineyards spread out over the hills round Trento on different masi, or farms. A previous role is played by Pianizza, which has always supplied the chardonnay grapes for the Riserva del Fondatore. Also worthy of note is the vast vineyard that surrounds Villa Margon, where the restaurant of the same name is situated. The agronomic management is entrusted to Diego Trainotti and Luca Pedron, who apply a form of low-impact viticulture that verges on the organic.

WINES - Ferrari wines are characterized by finesse, elegance and depth. Though the cult wine, Trento Brut Giulio Ferrari Riserva del Fondatore, was missing this year, the overall quality was nonetheless very high indeed. The excellent **Trento Extra Brut Riserva Lunelli 2006** (○ 24,600 bt), for example, is assertive, sharp and delicious on the palate with consistent acidity and impeccable depth and elegance: it's a Great Wine. **Trento Extra Brut Perlé Nero 2006** (○ 19,400 bt), made exclusively with pinot nero grapes, is taut, solid and flavorful with zesty tanginess. **Trento Brut Perlé Rosé 2007** (◐ 36,500 bt) is clear-cut, very clean and deep with a firmly structured palate on which redcurrants and raspberries give a resounding encore. **Trento Brut Maximum** (○ 619,000 bt) has distinct aromas of iodine and toasted hazelnuts and is dry on the palate.

FERTILIZERS manure pellets, natural manure, biodynamic preparations, green manure
PLANT PROTECTION chemical, copper and sulphur
WEED CONTROL mechanical
YEASTS selected
GRAPES 70% bought in
CERTIFICATION none

VOLANO (TN)

Eugenio Rosi

Via Tavernelle, 3 B
tel. 0464 461375
tamaramar@virgilio.it

6.3 ha - 22,000 bt

66 Eugenio Rosi is like a fine chiseller. He turns his grapes into wine in a minimalist cellar where what counts is not technology but sensitivity and care. 99

PEOPLE - After working as an enologist for other cellars, n 1999 Eugenio began his artisan vine dressing career with a few vineyards in the most unspoiled parts of the Trentino.

VINEYARDS - The marzemino grows at Volano, in the Ziresi district, at Noriglio are the pinot bianco, old ungrafted nosiola vines and a new terraced vineyard. The red grapes grow over Rovereto. At Vallarsa, in the woods at an altitude of 750 meters, there is a small chardonnay vineyard. Everywhere one notes a viticulture based on observation, study and natural interpretation of the needs of the plants, all respected and tended one by one.

WINES - All the wines are impeccable, expressive, packed with personality, so it's hard to say which is the best. **Poiema 2010** (● 6,700 bt) is a personal interpretation of the marzemino grape: it offers intact, fleshy fruit with hints of briarwood and leather, all followed up by a deep, well-turned palate of delicious, very delicate flavor. **Cabernet Franc 9DieciUndici** (● 1,300 bt), produced with grapes from three harvests, is compact with a clinched yet powerfully fruity palate: still youthful, it is sure to grow with age. **Anisos 2010** (● pinot bianco, nosiola, chardonnay; 3,200 bt) has a nice tangy tone and lightweight tannins that enhance its character and thoroughly dry the palate.

> **vino slow** ESEGESI 2009 (● cabernet sauvignon, merlot; 8,500 bt) Almost a terroir-dedicated Bordeaux transplanted in Trentino. Earthy, sound with an austere, well-judged palate, it has a long finish redolent of quinine and mountain herbs.

FERTILIZERS natural manure, green manure
PLANT PROTECTION copper and sulphur
WEED CONTROL mechanical
YEASTS native
GRAPES 100% estate-grown
CERTIFICATION organic

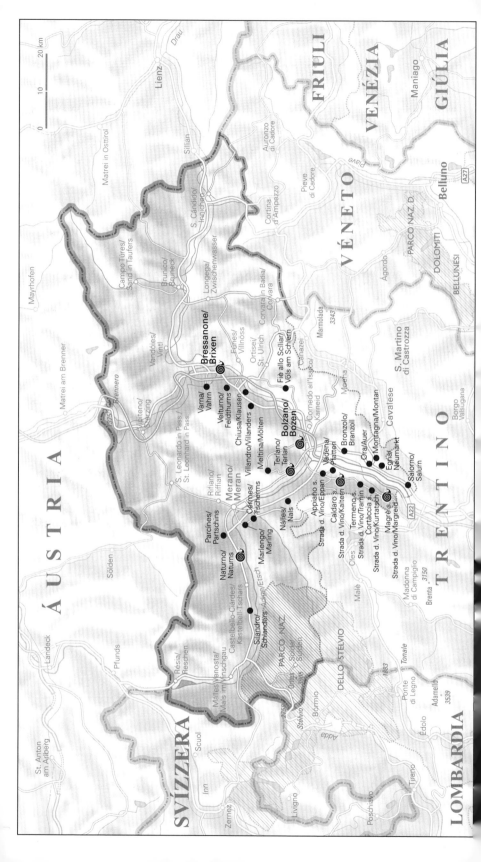

ALTO ADIGE

In Alto Adige 5,300 hectares of land are planted with vines, an area that represents barely 1 per cent of the Italian total. Yet, thanks to diversified production of consistently superlative quality, the region has nonetheless carved out a niche role for itself at the top end of the wine market. Albeit associated in the popular imagination with white wines, it turns out an impressively complete range in every typology, from light whites to full-bodied reds, from spumantes to sweet wines, with everything else in-between. This hasn't always been the case. Viticulture in Alto Adige has ancient roots but in its history has experienced ups and downs. Just 30 years ago its "mass-produced" wines were for the most part still being exported, unbottled, to Switzerland.

The amazing turnaround may have been induced by unfortunate circumstances, such as the collapse of traditional markets and the consequent need to formulate alternative strategies, but it is above all the farsightedness and professionalism of a large number of producers, supplemented by their proverbial ability to play as a team, that has made the Alto Adige one of Italy's most highly-rated wine-producing areas. It's true that its extremely variegated terrain, made up largely of mountains reaching altitudes of 1,150 meters, is very good for grape-growing. The soil varies from clayey to lightly sandy, often rocky and rich in minerals, and, notwithstanding the northern latitude, the climate is surprisingly mild with good day-to-night temperature swings.

The 2012 vintage returned to high levels, especially as far as white wines are concerned; though not as refined and eloquent as in 2010, they are fresher and heftier than the 2011 vintage. In reality, 2012 was a somewhat warm growing year in which late-September rains delayed the ripening of the grapes, or at least of the late varieties. The truth is that alcohol proof tended to be lower, acidity higher and the fruit more clearly defined. It's still early to pass a precise judgment on the reds, but Schiava and Lagrein promise to be stylish and scented.

To be honest, we've begun to have doubts about the precise role of the lagrein grape. Is it really the great native long-aging variety it's cracked up to be? On many an occasion we've been more impressed by the younger versions which, though they may be simpler and a tad *sauvage*, are much more quaffable in the glass. By contrast, we are delighted to see that Schiava, an everyday wine par excellence and the pillar of the wine economy for decades before falling out of favor, now has a group of faithful followers once more. We are still of the idea that Pinot Bianco is the white wine that best characterizes the region, or at least the Val d'Adige, while in the Valle Isarco we particularly enjoyed our tasting of Sylvaner of super finesse and grip —not to mention of certain Val Venosta Rieslings, some of which were awe-inspiring.

snails 🐌

76	NUSSERHOF - HEINRICH MAYR
77	KUENHOF - PETER PLIGER
78	MANINCOR
80	TENUTAE LAGEDER
80	UNTERORTL - CASTEL JUVAL
81	CANTINA TERLANO

bottles 🍾

76	CANTINA GIRLAN
77	WALDGRIES - CHRISTIAN PLATTNER
79	CASTELFEDER
79	PETER DIPOLI
81	CANTINA TRAMIN

Cantina Girlan

Località Cornaiano
Via San Martino, 24
tel. 0471 662403
www.girlan.it
info@girlan.it

Nusserhof
Heinrich Mayr

Via Josef Mayr-Nusser, 72
tel. 0471 978388

215 ha - 1,000,000 bt | **10% discount**

3.5 ha - 15,000 bt

PEOPLE - The Girlan cellar has a long history. It was set up in 1923 and has developed further since then. The original 15th-century building has been extended without ruining its architectural style. The latest high-tech addition is the new vinification department, inaugurated with the 2011 harvest. There are 200 members who supply grapes from about 220 hectares of vineyards. The president is Helmut Meraner, the director Oscar Lorandi, the enologist Gerhard Kofler.

VINEYARDS - Most of the vineyards are in the Cornaiano zone. In the historic schiava property in the Gschleier district, some of the pergola-trained vines are 90 years old. Pinot nero is grown in the famed Mazzon area, while aromatic varieties are to be found on the gravelly limestone of Montiggl, at an altitude of 500 meters.

WINES - Though the range of labels is extensive, the cellar's production stands out for its wines of great quality and terroir-dedicated eloquence. Simple yet simultaneously flavorful, rich and dynamic, the timeless A.A. Schiava Fass N°9 2012 (● 120,000 bt) is once more an excellent Everyday Wine. **A.A. Schiava Gschleier 2011** (● 16,000 bt) is more structured. The complex, stylish **A.A. Pinot Nero Trattman Ris. 2010** (● 18,000 bt) is redolent of strawberries, red berries and spices on the nose, while the palate has gutsy tannins and a dry finish; it's deservedly a Graet Wine. Moving on to the whites, **A.A. Pinot Bianco Plattenriegel 2012** (○ 50,000 bt) shines with no-nonsense fruit and body. No less delightful is the sweet **Gewürztraminer Pasithea Oro 2011** (○ 4,000 bt), a passito with a tropical tone, just the right degree of sweetness and pronounced flavor.

❝ He is shy and retiring, she outgoing and stylish; their wines are the sum of their two different personalities. Heinrich and Elda possess the strength to withstand all the many difficulties they are forced to address, from bureaucratic folly to overbuilding. They do so stoically, with determination and without fuss. **❞**

PEOPLE - Even the gray industrial suburbs of Bolzano have a heart of green. The Nusserhof winery is at once a minor treasure and a major message of resistance. It has belonged to the Mayr family since 1788, and Heinrich and his wife Elda keep it alive with great love and dedication.

VINEYARDS - The company has been organic since 1994, not fanatically so but with careful, well-pondered vine management. Three hectares of alluvial, porphyry-rich soil are planted with lagrein, teroldego and blatterle grapes. On the Trautmannhof farm in the Santa Maddalena area are the over 80-year-old vineyards which grow the grapes, mostly schiava, for Elda.

WINES - A.A. Lagrein Ris. 2009 (● 12,500 bt) is a complex, charismatic wine that will take some time to achieve perfect balance: it has aromas of soil, briarwood and red-currants with conspicuous tannins and a nice spicy finish. The new B........ vintage is still aging, a victim of a piece of red-tape gone wild whereby it's illegal to write its real name on the label; namely blatterle, the old variety from which it is made, unjustly erased from the wine grape register.

vino slow **ELDA 2010** (● old local grape varieties; 4,000 bt). A seductively pleasant wine, at once simple and spacious.

FERTILIZERS natural manure
PLANT PROTECTION copper and sulphur, organic
WEED CONTROL mechanical
YEASTS selected
GRAPES 100% estate-grown
CERTIFICATION none

FERTILIZERS green manure
PLANT PROTECTION copper and sulphur
WEED CONTROL mechanical
YEASTS native
GRAPES 100% estate-grown
CERTIFICATION organic

Waldgries Christian Plattner

Località Santa Giustina, 2
tel. 0471 323603
www.waldgries.it
info@waldgries.it

8.2 ha - 65,000 bt

PEOPLE - A visit to Christian Plattner's maso, or farm, inherited by his grandfather at the start of the last century, is like taking a step back in time. The buildings in the old part date back to 1242 and hardly anything has changed since then. To enter the rooms where the Riservas are aged you have to climb down time-worn stairs, but recently completed extension work now makes it easier to work and stock the bottles.

VINEYARDS - After studying enology at Laimburg in Germany and receiving a diploma in enotechnology, Christian took over the running of the maso, situated in the Santa Maddalena district, in 1994. "I began working with organic methods," he tells us, "but the schiava is just too disease-prone." Besides the vineyards round the farmhouse, Waldgries also owns parcels at Appiano, where the sauvignon grapes grow and at Ora, where the heavy, silty soil is ideal for lagrein.

WINES - A.A. Santa Maddalena Cl. 2012 (● 25,000 bt) is fresh and well-balanced with aromas of red berries and a dry finish. Christian was very satisfied with the vintage "It's Santa Maddalena as it should be," he says. We say it's a fine Everyday Wine. The intriguing **A.A. Moscato Rosa 2010** (● 2,500 bt) is stylish and savory, one of the most eloquent wines in its category. **A.A. Lagrein Mirell 2011** (● 4.500 bt) owes some of its richness and concentration to partial drying of the grapes, while **A.A. Lagrein Ris. 2011** (● 8,000 bt) is fresh with notes of talcum powder. **A.A. Sauvignon 2012** (○ 8,000 bt) is concentrated and acid, the fruit of extreme maturation.

vino slow **A.A. Santa Maddalena Cl. Antheos 2012** (● 4,000 bt) Made from old clones of different varieties of schiava, a wine that is profound, densely concentrated and packed with character. One of the noblest, most aristocratic renderings around of the schiava grape.

FERTILIZERS natural manure
PLANT PROTECTION chemical, copper and sulphur, organic
WEED CONTROL mechanical
YEASTS selected
GRAPES 10% bought in
CERTIFICATION none

Kuenhof Peter Pliger

Località Mara, 110
tel. 0472 850546
pliger.kuenhof@rolmail.net

65 ha - 35,000 bt

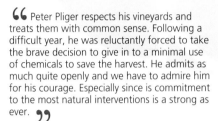

❝ Peter Pliger respects his vineyards and treats them with common sense. Following a difficult year, he was reluctantly forced to take the brave decision to give in to a minimal use of chemicals to save the harvest. He admits as much quite openly and we have to admire him for his courage. Especially since is commitment to the most natural interventions is a strong as ever. ❞

PEOPLE - In the 1980s Peter and his wife Brigitte took over the reins of the family cellar. Since then they have never ceased to put themselves to the test in their pursuit of natural vineyard management methods.

VINEYARDS - Being in contact with the vines is fundamental for Pliger. He observes them, he supports them, he intervenes when problems arise. If winegrowing in the Valle Isarco is no easy matter at the best of times, working the vineyard on the splendid but steep Lanher hill is a daunting task. Here they grow riesling at an altitude of 500-700 meters and sylvaner even higher up. All the various operations are performed by hand.

WINES - The approach in the cellar is to respect the grapes the vineyard has produced, transforming them into wines with a sense of place. The hallmark of Peter's wines is a combination of sharp tanginess and ageability. They are matured exclusively in steel tanks and large acacia wood barrels. Forthrightly mineral and succulent **A.A. Valle Isarco Riesling Kaiton 2012** (○ 11,000 bt) is as intriguing and elegant as ever. We are curious to taste it again in a year or so. **A.A. Veltliner 2012** (○ 6,000 bt) is fresh and dynamic.

vino slow **A.A. Valle Isarco Sylvaner 2012** (○ 8,000 bt) A wine of huge personality, complex on the nose with definite flinty notes and a palate that combines richness and acidity in a perfect amalgam.

FERTILIZERS natural manure
PLANT PROTECTION copper and sulphur, organic
WEED CONTROL mechanical
YEASTS native
GRAPES 100% estate-grown
CERTIFICATION none

CALDARO/KALTERN (BZ)

Manincor

San Giuseppe al Lago, 4
tel. 0471 960230
www.manincor.com
info@manincor.com

50 ha - 280,000 bt

66 Exceptional wines with a strong sense of place and lots of soul, all reasonably priced and made with conviction in accordance with the criteria of biodynamic agriculture. Let's not forget that we are speaking about one of the largest private cellars in the region. Chapeau! 99

PEOPLE - Michael Goëss-Enzenberg has been running Manincor since 1991. With great determination but also disarming humility and patience, he has revitalized a winemaking tradition that goes back to 1698. Since 2008 he has been able to count on the collaboration of the sensitive, seasoned enologist Helmut Zozin.

VINEYARDS - The finest grapes are grown at Terlano on the Lieben Aich and Turmhof estates, where the warm, sunny microclimate and sandy porphyry soils are conducive to the cultivation of pinot bianco, chardonnay and sauvignon. Red grapes prosper near Lake Caldaro alongside the modern underground cellar.

WINES - Not content to make precise wines with local grape varieties, Helmut Zozin also seeks finesse and depth of expression. While not devoid of power, his bottles are invitingly drinkable. The best example is **A.A. Terlano Pinot Bianco Eichhorn 2012** (O 12,500 bt) with its suite of fruity aromas and dynamic, long, layered palate. **A.A. Terlano Réserve della Contessa 2012** (O pinot bianco, chardonnay, sauvignon; 43,000 bt) is full-bodied but supple, lively and very leisurely. At once light and sure-footed, **A.A. Pinot Nero Mason 2011** (● 12,500 bt) impresses for its finesse. Well-rounded and complex, **A.A. Terlano Chardonnay Sophie 2012** (O 17,600 bt) is an eminently quaffable wine braced by stand-out minerality.

> **vino slow** CASSIANO 2011 (● 19,000 bt) An elegant blend of merlot and cabernet franc with small amounts of other international grapes: solid and taut with intriguing earthy spiciness.

FERTILIZERS compost, biodynamic preparations, green manure
PLANT PROTECTION copper and sulphur
WEED CONTROL mechanical
YEASTS native
GRAPES 100% estate-grown
CERTIFICATION biodynamic, organic

CERMES/TSCHERMS (BZ)

Hartmann Donà

Raffeinweg, 8
tel. 329 2610628
hartmann.dona@rolmail.net

4.2 ha - 35,000 bt

PEOPLE - Calm, laid-back with an air of wisdom and serenity — Hartmann Donà isn't just any consultant enologist. His wines are precise, never technical; they have soul depth and expressive purity, the fruit of a well-reasoned agronomic approach, sustainable without being dogmatic. He makes his presence felt precisely with his knack of staying behind the scenes. After studying at the University of Geisenheim in Germany, for many years he worked as an enologist at the Cantina Terlano. He began vinifying his own grapes in 2000.

VINEYARDS - The historic family vineyard is in Cornaiano, where robust, well-structured pinot nero grapes grow on morainal limestone soil. In San Valentino, in the hills above Merano Hartmann rents a steep vineyard planted with pinot bianco and chardonnay, varieties which he admires for the transparent way in which they express the terroir. In view of the sizable demand he has been buying grapes from trusted vine dressers for a second line of high-level monovarietal wines.

WINES - **A.A. Sauvignon 2012** (O 3,500 bt) has a deep nose of great breadth and expressive naturalness. The palate is solid and laid-back, the acidity well-integrated in a body whose impact is assertive and full, while the back palate is lighter thanks to pronounced tanginess. **A.A. Terlano Chardonnay 2012** (O 5.000 bt) is intriguingly delicate on the nose and has a long mineral finish. Broad, elegant and deep, **Donà Blanc 2009** (pinot bianco, chardonnay; 5,000 bt) is artfully aged on small wood. **Donà Rouge 2009** (● 6,500 bt), a highly personal interpretation of the schiava grape with small additions of pinot nero and lagrein, offers intriguing dark, earthy, spicy notes and surprises the palate with its fresh, solid tannic component, capable of lending dimension and length without compromising its drinkability. The still youthful **Donà Noir 2009** (● pinot nero; 2,500 bt) is robust.

FERTILIZERS manure pellets
PLANT PROTECTION copper and sulphur
WEED CONTROL mechanical
YEASTS selected, native
GRAPES 30% bought in
CERTIFICATION none

Castelfeder

Via Portici, 11
tel. 0471 820420
www.castelfeder.it
info@castelfeder.it

55 ha - 400,000 bt

PEOPLE - Castelfeder was established by Alfons Giovannet in 1970. It has been run since 1989 by his son Günther, whose own children are playing an increasingly active part in the business. Ivan, who studied enology in Italy and Germany has been supervising the technical side since 2005, and Ines has been in charge of sales since 2008. In 2011 their vineyards in the Alto Adige were supplemented by the purchase of another 6.5-hectare plot in the Moselle. It produced its first bottles with the 2013 harvest.

VINEYARDS - The cellar owns ten hectares of vineyards and rents another ten. Sixty or so grape suppliers also work 35 hectares of land. Schiava, pinot nero, sauvignon and gewürztraminer vines grow on clay-limestone soil, lagrein, chardonnay, pinot grigio and pinot bianco on sandy soil. Ivan has a great passion for the land and he selects what he deems the best plots for each individual variety. He verifies his theories with numerous micro-vinifications in the cellar.

WINES - **A.A. Pinot Bianco Tecum 2011** (○ 1.433 magnum), the product of careful grape selection, is matured in steel vats and produced with native yeasts. It's a wine of great body and style. **A.A. Chardonnay Burgum Novum Ris. 2010** (○ 8,500 bt), which we mistakenly reviewed last year, proves to be a Great Wine, rich and symmetrical with luscious, elegant flesh and excellent aging potential. **A.A. Pinot Grigio 15er 2012** (○ 15,000 bt) is very varietal and a joy to drink, like the fresh and fragrant **A.A. Schiava Breitbacher 2012** (● 5,000 bt). **A.A. Pinot Nero Burgum Novum Ris. 2010** (● 8,000 bt) is well-balanced, refreshing and stylish with great aging capacity, as our tasting of vintages from more than 20 years ago demonstrated. **A.A. Lagrein Burgum Novum Ris. 2010** (● 9,000 bt) is deep, dense and austere with notes of fruit, flowers and spice.

FERTILIZERS none
PLANT PROTECTION chemical, copper and sulphur
WEED CONTROL chemical, mechanical
YEASTS selected
GRAPES 65% bought in
CERTIFICATION none

Peter Dipoli

Via Villa, 5-I
tel. 0471 813400
www.peterdipoli.com
vino@finewines.it

4.7 ha - 40,000 bt

PEOPLE - Peter Dipoli absolutely adores the wine world. He's something of an all-rounder, working as a distributor as a consultant and as lobbyist, in the best possible meaning of the term. He's also a great character, often seen as something of a polemicist. Not that Peter deals only in words; he's also a man of action who refuses to accept compromises when it comes to defending his ideals. In 1988 he made his own dream come true by establishing a winery of his own devoted entirely to the production of great vins de terroir. We have to say he's made a good job of it.

VINEYARDS - In 1988 when he bought the steep Voglar vineyard in Penon, above Cortaccia, Peter had very clear ideas about what he wanted to make of it. He thus uprooted the schiava vines and replaced them with sauvignon. The combination of a noble grape variety, soil rich in gravelly limestone of Dolomitic origin and a microclimate in which the high altitude creates a considerable temperature range is perfect. Over the years the Voglar vineyard has been expanded and more vines have been planted at Magrè, where the clay-limestone soil and warm climate are ideal for Bordeaux varieties. In good growing years the Egna vineyard produces Merlot Fihl.

WINES - Once more this year we were totally impressed by **A.A. Sauvignon Voglar 2011** (○ 25,000 bt), made with perfectly ripe grapes and fermented on fine lees in acacia wood barrels for six months. Forget "cat's piss", forget vegetality — this is a wonderful wine dominated by generous, pure, firm fruit. Though the well-structured, deep, mineral palate is already expansive, it's sure to age well for some years to come. Even better was **A.A. Merlot-Cabernet Yugum 2010** (● 7,000 bt), skillfully aged first in barriques, then in the bottle, a wine of intriguing, earthy complexity, well-structured, healthy and juicy. This classic terroir-dedicated Bordeaux blend really is a Great Wine.

FERTILIZERS none
PLANT PROTECTION chemical, copper and sulphur
WEED CONTROL chemical, mechanical
YEASTS selected
GRAPES 100% estate-grown
CERTIFICATION none

MAGRÈ/MARGREID (BZ)

Tenutae Lageder 🐌

Vicolo dei Conti, 9
tel. 0471 809 500
www.aloislageder.eu
info@aloislageder.eu

50 ha - 280,000 bt

66 Alois Lageder has made this historic Alto Adige cellar a local institution, unerringly ahead of the rest. He is a pioneer of the holistic approach, always in pursuit of maximum sustainability, in the vineyard, in the cellar and also in the surrounding environment. 99

PEOPLE - After 45 years' service the old kellermeister Luis Von Delleman is handing the baton to the highly qualified, pragmatic youngster Georg Meißner, an expert on biodynamics and a lecturer and researcher at Geisenheim University.

VINEYARDS - The cellar's own vineyards, which provide the grapes for the Tenute Lageder line, are scattered across some of the most prestigious areas of Magrè (Löwengang, Casòn), Bolzano (Lindenburg) and Lake Caldaro (Römigberg). Slowly but surely, all the various parcels are receiving biodynamic certification. For the Alois Lageder line, a hundred or so vine dressers are following the cellar's instructions to make their own agriculture more sustainable.

WINES - The excellent **A.A. Chardonnay Gaun 2012** (○ 22,700 bt) veers between density and minerality. The classy **A.A. Cabernet Löwengang 2009** (● 12,700 bt) has pleasantly husky aromas of earthy spices and a lean, assertive palate. **A.A. Lagrein Lindenburg 2009** (● 11,850 bt) is generous on the nose with a well-structured palate and no-nonsense tannins. **A.A. Pinot Grigio Porer 2012** (○ 49,300 bt) is refined and subtle, soft and pure. The flavorsome **Beta Delta 2012** (○ pinot grigio, chardonnay; 20,800 bt) brims over with rich, succulent fruit.

vino slow **A.A. Chardonnay Löwengang 2010** (○ 34,000 bt) A wine that thrilled us with its masterful use of wood, transparent fruit and long, lingering, delicately salty finish.

FERTILIZERS compost, biodynamic preparations, green manure
PLANT PROTECTION copper and sulphur, organic
WEED CONTROL mechanical
YEASTS native
GRAPES 100% estate-grown
CERTIFICATION biodynamic, organic

NATURNO/NATURNS (BZ)

Unterortl - Castel Juval 🐌

Località Stava/Staben
Juval 1 B
tel. 0473 667580
www.unterortl.it
familie.aurich@dnet.it

4 ha - 32,000 bt

66 Martin Aurich and his wife Gisela produce their miniscule range of high-quality artisan wines with enviable application and intelligence, not to mention real passion. Hence unique, limpid wines that are the mirror of this singular terroir, the fruit of an extreme viticulture which, in their capable hands, seems like child's play. 99

PEOPLE - The cellar belongs to the famous mountaineer Reinhold Messner, but has been managed by the Aurich family since 1992.

VINEYARDS - The hill of Juval is dominated by the castle of the same name, under which vineyards twist and turn upwards round the small estate to an altitude of 850 meters, clinging to the gneiss rocks like swallows' nests. The area is one of the driest in the Alto Adige, where the föhn wind further influences the microclimate. Here day-to-night temperature swings hold back the ripening of the grapes and help to preserve their acidity.

WINES - Steel, seen as essential for preserving the expressive transparency of the grapes, prevails in the cellar. Rich and soft, **A.A. Valle Venosta Riesling Windbichl 2011** (○ 2,200 bt) makes up in depth for what it lacks in grip. The no less excellent **A.A. Valle Venosta Pinot Bianco 2012** (○ 6,500 bt) is fine and well-balanced. **A.A. Valle Venosta Müller Thurgau 2012** (○ 4,000 bt) is fresh, typical and scented with remarkable dryness and length. **A.A. Valle Venosta Pinot Nero 2011** (● 7,000 bt) is subtle but still somewhat severe. Young, fruity and spicy **Gneis 2012** (● pinot nero, zweigelt, others; 3,000 bt) is endowed with an enjoyable palate.

vino slow **A.A. Valle Venosta Riesling 2012** (○ 6,100 bt) A wine that captivates for its rock-like purity and intense, textured, salty palate. The work of a great master.

FERTILIZERS organic-mineral, natural manure, compost
PLANT PROTECTION chemical, copper and sulphur, organic
WEED CONTROL mechanical
YEASTS selected
GRAPES 100% estate-grown
CERTIFICATION none

TERLANO/TERLAN (BZ)

Cantina Terlano

Via Colli d'Argento, 7
tel. 0471 257135
www.cantina-terlano.com
office@cantina-terlano.com

150 ha - 1,200,000 bt

66 The wine cooperatives of the Alto Adige are seen as a model the world over. Now with maximum sustainability in the vineyard, exceptional quality, reliability and a wine archive that goes back half a century — Terlano is raising the bar even higher. 99

PEOPLE - Founded in 1893, the cellar has always specialized in white wines. The great cellarman Sebastian Stocker worked at Terlano from 1955 to 1993 and his legacy is now in the capable hands of kellermeister Rudi Kofler.

VINEYARDS - The terroir of Terlano has regaled us with truly great white wines over the years. Where does its secret lie? In the red rocks of porphyritic origin? Or the dry, warm microclimate? In altitudes of well nigh 1,000 meters? In the hour upon hour of daily sunshine? Whatever, the fact is that its wines have a character and an aging capacity unique among Alto Adige wines. The 143 winegrowers religiously comply with a rigid protocol of agricultural practices under the guidance of Norbert Spitaler.

WINES - Solidity, rocky minerality and enduring quality are the common denominators of Terlano's wines. **A.A. Chardonnay Rarità 2000** (O 3,500 bt) is once more a top player, a Great Wine of incredible integrity, profound, elegant and long. **A.A. Pinot Bianco 2012** (O 70,000 bt) is delicate and floral, while A.A. Terlano Cl. 2012 (O 230,000 bt) is more linear and subtle, drinkable and satisfying, a perfect Everyday Wine. **A.A. Terlano Nova Domus 2010** (O 25,000 bt) is a harmonious symphony of tropical and spicy aromas, which come in with an encore on a creamy, leisurely palate.

> vino slow **A.A. TERLANO PINOT BIANCO VORBERG RIS. 2010** (O 80,000 bt) A great classic that has earned the most glowing epithets down the years. Elegant, close-knit, creamy, pervasive, refined, rich and many others besides.

FERTILIZERS mineral, compost, biodynamic preparations
PLANT PROTECTION chemical, copper and sulphur, organic
WEED CONTROL mechanical
YEASTS selected
GRAPES 100% estate-grown
CERTIFICATION none

TERMENO/TRAMIN (BZ)

Cantina Tramin

Strada del Vino, 144
tel. 0471 096633
www.cantinatramin.it
info@cantinatramin.it

245 ha - 150,0000 bt

PEOPLE - Manager and enologist Willi Stürz has brought this historic wine cooperative, which now boasts 270 members, into the spotlight over the last ten to 15 years. He has done so with constant hard work and foresight. The new high-tech structure is where all the winemaking operations are carried out and is also used to welcome the many wine tourists who come to the area.

VINEYARDS - All the vineyards have been catalogued and classified according to the grapes they grow. They are located on the slopes, sometimes dizzyingly steep, round Termeno and on the other side of the valley. The soil composition is as variable as in the rest of the Alto Adige region. Porphyry is prominent but some terrains are also calcareous-dolomitic, morainal and clayey. In order to allow them to perform to the best of their ability, a variety of viticultural practices are used, all very eco-friendly. The number of organically managed hectares is growing.

WINES - The A.A. Sauvignon 2012 (O 120,000 bt) is very good indeed, an Everyday Wine of crisply defined aromas, intense and fresh-tasting. Freshness and flavor also feature in **A.A. Pinot Bianco Moriz 2012** (O 55,000 bt) and the richer, maturer **A.A. Bianco Stoan 2012** (O chardonnay, sauvignon, pinot bianco, gewürztraminer; 40,000 bt). A wonderful range of wines is produced with gewürztraminer, the Termeno native grape par excellence. **A.A. Gewürztraminer 2012** (O 300,000 bt) is elegantly aromatic and supple on the palate. Denser and spicier, **A.A. Gewürztraminer Nussbaumer 2012** (O 70,000 bt), is balanced and complex, subtle and delicate. **A.A. Gewürztraminer V.T. Terminum 2011** (O 4,500 bt) is sweet, unctuous and oily, revived by a lively streak of acid and tinged by intense notes of apricot and candied pineapple — a Great Wine.

FERTILIZERS organic-mineral, natural manure, compost, biodynamic preparations, green manure
PLANT PROTECTION chemical, copper and sulphur, organic
WEED CONTROL chemical, mechanical
YEASTS selected, native
GRAPES 100% estate-grown
CERTIFICATION none

VENETO

Despite the fact that bizarre climate conditions in 2012 caused a drop in production that ranges from an average of 5 per cent to troughs of 15 per cent, with a total output of about eight million hectoliters the Veneto is still Italy's number one winemaking region. When we speak about Veneto wine, it's necessary to mention the huge efforts of winemakers over the last few years to achieve excellent quality. Though the process has been faster and more conspicuous in some of the more important denominations, such as Valpolicella and Soave, it has gradually extended to lesser kown ones such as Colli Euganei and Lessini Durello in particular.

In western Veneto, Bardolino is being rediscovered with the exaltation of the corvina variety, which regales wines with enjoyable drinkability. Worth recording too is the growing appeal of the fresh Chiaretto, spumante version included. The Custozas, assemblages of white varieties, are less expressive than in previous years and are struggling to find a well-defined style of their own. In the Valpolicella, Amarone production continues to grow, increasingly and successfully banking on the recognizability of the various subzones. The same can't be said of Ripasso, commercially successful maybe, but, in our opinion, lacking in precise identity. Albeit hard to come by these days, the base table Valpolicellas we tasted were very good. In the Soave and Gambellara zones, garganega suffered the adverse effects of this year less than it did those of the last and it boasts a few excellent Everyday Wines, plus one or two pleasant surprises among the "evolved whites" from the 2011 vintage. Durello, from the ancient Lessinia native variety, is starting to capture the attention of markets, especially in the excellent Metodo Classico version. In the Colli Berici, they are gambling on tai rosso against international varieties, while the Colli Euganei proved once more to be a good growing area for Bordeaux grapes. In eastern Veneto, sales continued to grow in the vast Prosecco production area with peaks of excellence in the Prosecco Superiore zones of Conegliano-Valdobbiadene and Asolo, and we have deliberately chosen to review exclusively wine companies in these two historic areas. In the province of Treviso, finally, it's worth mentioning two rather neglected zones: Piave, with its rustic raboso grape, and Montello Colli Asolani, with convincing Bordeaux blends.

snails 🐌

85	Le Fraghe
87	Corte Sant'Alda
88	Monte dall'Ora
88	Villa Bellini
91	La Biancara
92	Prà
93	Fongaro
93	Leonildo Pieropan
95	Ca' Orologio
96	Vigneto Due Santi
100	Casa Coste Piane
101	Silvano Follador
101	Sorelle Bronca

bottles 🍾

86	Allegrini
86	Cav. G.B. Bertani
87	Giuseppe Quintarelli
92	Gini

coins €

89	Cavalchina
89	Monte Del Frà
91	Domenico Cavazza
96	Il Mottolo
100	Bortolomiol

Valpolicella
e Veneto occidentale

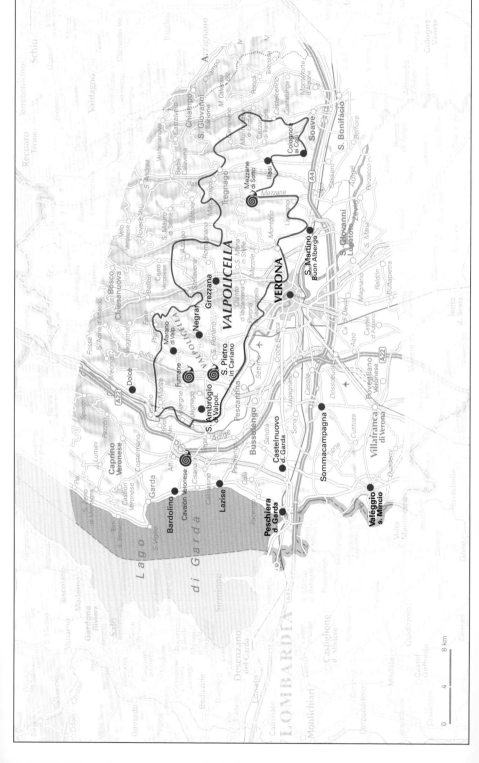

Giovanna Tantini

Località I Mischi
Via Unità d'Italia 10
tel. 045 7575070
www.giovannatantini.it
info@giovannatantini.it

12 ha - 25,000 bt **10% discount**

PEOPLE - In 2000 Giovanna Tantini was at a crossroads: make the most of her law degree or, following her instinct and passion, take over the reins of the family farm? She chose to take the second route and, under the guidance of agronomist Federico Curtaz and enologist Attilio Pagli, immediately planted new vineyards. Since then the winery's quality has improved consistently.

VINEYARDS - The winery's 12 hectares are divided between the communes of Castelnuovo del Garda and Sona. About half of them are very close to the cellar. Adamant that great wines are born in the vineyard, Giovanna immediately adopted an innovative and meticulous approach to winegrowing, which enabled her to produce high quality corvina grapes even down on the plain, where the land is theoretically less favorable for growing than that of the hills. The 2000 plantings are trained using the Guyot system, which has also been progressively introduced to the older high-trained vineyards.

WINES - A Bardolino that challenges the passing of time — that's how Giovanna likes to regard and define her wine, which she will release a year later than normal for the denomination. Our recent tasting of the old vintages convinced us that she's right. Bardolino 2011 (● 10,000 bt) is no exception to the rule and deserves the Everyday Wine symbol: the sensory profile is broad and complex with notes of fine spices and tobacco that are strong without overwhelming the living, fresh, crisp fruit, while the palate is nicely poised between lightness, depth and flavor. Also good is the simpler, more linear **Bardolino Chiaretto 2012** (● 7,000 bt), beautifully fragrant with supple dynamism on the palate.

FERTILIZERS none
PLANT PROTECTION chemical, copper and sulphur
WEED CONTROL chemical, mechanical
YEASTS selected
GRAPES 100% estate-grown
CERTIFICATION none

Le Fraghe   🌀

Località Colombare, 3
tel. 045 7236832
www.fraghe.it
info@fraghe.it
🚃—0

30 ha - 120,000 bt **10% discount**

❝ "My father wasn't a winemaker," says Matilde Poggi, "but I've been in contact with wine ever since I was a kid because he and my uncle had a cellar. My father used to look after the vineyards that I took over in 1984, when I formed my winery. In almost 30 years of harvests I've learned a lot about this terroir inland from Lake Garda. ❞

PEOPLE - From this year the dynamic, tireless Matilde is also president of the Italian Federation of Independent Winemakers.

VINEYARDS - The company has been certified organic since last year. Its land covers an area of 30 hectares and is divided into a number of plots. The oldest vineyards are around the ancient family home, which Matilde, who has six brothers, has converted into a wine cellar. The others are situated within a radius of a couple of kilometers at the foot of Monte Moscal, at Rivoli, at Affi, where the Brol cru has deep morainal soil, and at Montalto.

WINES - These wines are characterized by pleasantness and drinkability and are excellent at the table with food. "For me, wine is an everyday drink," says Matilde, "and should always go with food." There's no solipsism about this; conviviality is welcome, especially if it is backed up by value for money. Bardolino 2012 (● 60,000 bt) has luscious fruit, inviting spices, and a juicy palate that makes it enjoyable in the glass; in short, an excellent Everyday Wine. The deliciously refreshing **Bardolino Chiaretto Rodon 2012** (◉ 20,000 bt) and the harmonious **Garganega Camporengo 2012** (○ 25,000 bt) are both stopped with screw caps. "I wanted to preserve the freshness of my wines without any further evolution," explains Matide. The new entry, **Bardolino Cl. Brol Grande 2011** (● 4,000 bt), is barrel-aged for a year. **Cabernet Quaiare 2011** (● 10,000 bt) still has slightly clenched tannins that hold back the fruity base; it will still take a little time to develop.

FERTILIZERS manure pellets, green manure
PLANT PROTECTION copper and sulphur, organic
WEED CONTROL mechanical
YEASTS selected
GRAPES 100% estate-grown
CERTIFICATION organic

FUMANE (VR)

Allegrini

Via Giare, 5
tel. 045 6832011
www.allegrini.it
info@allegrini.it

GREZZANA (VR)

Cav. G.B. Bertani

Via Asiago, 1
tel. 045 8658444
www.bertani.net
bertani@bertani.net

100 ha - 700,000 bt

PEOPLE - The Allegrini family has been in the Valpolicella since the 16th century and the cellar was established in 1854. The deus ex machina was Giovanni Allegrini, who began bottling in the mid 20th century. A man of great professional stature, he showed acute foresightedness in 1979 when he bought the two vineyards that have since become symbols for the international wine world. Giovanni's son Franco took over the reins in 1983. He now oversees the vineyards and the cellar, while his sister Marilisa is in charge of sales.

VINEYARDS - The unique vineyards are managed with consolidated know-how constantly enhanced by new research (the latest arrival, as far as sustainable agriculture is concerned, is zonation). The cellar owns 100 hectares in the Valpolicella classica zone between Fumane — where the Palazzo della Torre vineyard surrounds a Renaissance villa — Sant'Ambrogio, with its celebrated Grola and Poja vineyards, Mazzurega and San Pietro in Cariano, home to the Monte dei Galli and Villa Giona estates.

WINES - It's impossible to compress the Allegrini winemaking and entrepreneurial history into a few lines. Their contribution to the Valpolicella renaissance in the 1980s was decisive and their wines are always recognizable and identitary. Refined, juicy, harmonious and well-poised between structure and fresness, **Amarone della Valpolicella Cl. 2009** (● 120,000 bt) is once more a Great Wine. **Recioto della Valpolicella Cl. Giovanni Allegrini 2010** (● 20,000 bt) is also excellent. **Palazzo della Torre 2010** (● corvina, rondinella, sangiovese; 300,000 bt) combines lightness and substance on an approachable palate. **La Grola 2010** (● corvina, corvinone, oseleta, syrah; 200,000 bt) is spicy and stylish. **La Poja 2009** (● corvina; 14,000 bt) is forthright and warm, all-embracing and mouthfilling.

220 ha - 1,600,000 bt

PEOPLE - A large-scale company for the size of its vineyards and the number of bottles it produces, it still conserves the character it had when it was established by the Bertani brothers more than 150 years ago. The recent takeover by the Tenimenti Angelini group has in no way impinged on the management. The wines have never lost the typical Veneto soul the family has always been proud of, a soul that can be especially appreciated if one has the fortune to taste the old vintages.

VINEYARDS - The company owns land at Valpantena, where Villa Arvedi is located, at Soave, on Lake Garda, and in the Valpolicella, where its headquarters, Villa Novare, is situated. Only a third of it is given over to winegrowing, the rest consisting of woods and meadows and a few olive groves. Viticulture moves in two directions: environmental sustainability and the pursuit of good balance in the vines to ensure healthy, ripe grapes.

WINES - The new management hasn't changed the interpretation of the terroir and the wines thus continue to be characterized by finesse and dynamism. The nicely balanced **Valpolicella Cl. Villa Novare 2012** (● 75,000 bt) is a joy to drink. **Valpolicella Valpantena Secco Bertani 2011** (● 400,000 bt) is delicate and stylish with a juicy, tangy, lingering palate. The excellent **Valpolicella Cl. Sup. Vigneto Ognisanti 2011** (● 30,000 bt) has a refreshing balsamic streak on the nose and a fleshy, laid-back plate with a gratifying finish — a Great Wine at a bargain price. **Soave Sereole 2012** (○ 100,000 bt) is refreshing and subtle.

| vino slow | **AMARONE DELLA VALPOLICELLA CL. 2006** (● 40,000 bt) A historic label of impeccable, measured style — as always. The aromas are fine and fruity, the palate beautifully precise with perfectly balanced acid verve and fleshy structure. |

FERTILIZERS natural manure
PLANT PROTECTION chemical, copper and sulphur, organic
WEED CONTROL mechanical
YEASTS native
GRAPES 100% estate-grown
CERTIFICATION none

FERTILIZERS organic-mineral, manure pellets, natural manure
PLANT PROTECTION copper and sulphur
WEED CONTROL mechanical
YEASTS selected
GRAPES 100% estate-grown
CERTIFICATION none

MEZZANE DI SOTTO (VR)

Corte Sant'Alda

Località Fioi
Via Capovilla, 28
tel. 045 8880006
www.cortesantalda.it
info@cortesantalda.it

19 ha - 80,000 bt	10% discount

66 "The wine is an expression of my way of life," says Marinella Camerani. Never has a statement been so clearly backed up by the facts. Marinella produces sincere wines born of a deep love of the land. 99

PEOPLE - Since the first label was released from her father's vineyards in 1986, Marinella has never stopped trying to do better. She had the company certified organic in 2003, biodynamic in 2010. A careful experimentalist, after aging wines on wood and steel now she intends to try her hand with amphorae. Her husband Cesar helps her in the vineyard and her daughter lends a hand with the rest of the business.

VINEYARDS - The vineyards cover 12 hectares on calcareous land surrounded by woods in the Fioi hills. There are another two hectares on Monte Tombole and another hectare and a half, productive from this year, at Castagnè, where Steiner's concepts of agricultural individuality will be applied.

WINES - At the moment Marinella is consciously making changes and more are on the way. The wines, albeit elegant, close-focused and approachable, could still achieve more, character-wise. For some time now every wine comes from a specific vineyard, chosen for a series of specific factors, defined by careful zoning. **Valpolicella Sup. Ripasso Campi Magri 2010** (● 20,000 bt) has velvety tannins. **Amarone della Valpolicella Corte Sant'Alda 2009** (● 14,000 bt) is developing but still needs a little more time to grow. **Recioto della Valpolicella Corte Sant'Alda 2011** (● 2.000 bt) and **Soave Vigne di Mezzane 2012** (○ 12,000 bt) both toe the company line.

> **vino slow** VALPOLICELLA CÀ FIUI 2012 (● 25,000 bt) A fresh, fruity vintage Valpolicella, easy and enjoyable to drink. A convincing interpretation of the typology.

FERTILIZERS compost, biodynamic preparations
PLANT PROTECTION copper and sulphur
WEED CONTROL mechanical
YEASTS native
GRAPES 100% estate-grown
CERTIFICATION biodynamic, organic

NEGRAR (VR)

Giuseppe Quintarelli

Via Cerè, 1
tel. 0457 513241
giuseppe.quintarelli@tin.it

12 ha - 60,000 bt

PEOPLE - Fiorenza Quintarelli, her husband Giampaolo and their sons Francesco and Lorenzo have accepted the inheritance left by the great Bepi, the "cherry whisperer", with all the commitment they can muster. The story of the winery is a long one, which emerged from the fascinating, dramatic "short twentieth century" into the new millennium with the proactive force of youth, as its wines demonstrate.

VINEYARDS - Most of the vineyards are in the valley of Negrar, one of the five communes of the classic Valpolicella zone. The rest of the property is split up among Sant'Ambrogio, Marano and Montorio, in the Val Squaranto northeast of Verona. All the classic grapes — corvina, corvinone, rondinella, molinara and others besides — are cultivated using the pergola and Guyot training systems.

WINES - The house style continues to be a formidable kaleidoscope of finesse and elegance — pure velvet. Hence inimitable wines that compete with the world's finest. The cream of the crop is **Recioto della Valpolicella Cl. 2001** (● 3,500 bt), which validates our argument on its own. Explosive fruit, infinite nuances — a veritable nectar of the gods and a magnificent Great Wine! **Alzero 2004** (● cabernet sauvignon and cabernet franc, merlot; 3,000 bt), made with raisined grapes, was submitted again for tasting: it had fresh, sharp tones of blossom and delicious fruit jam. Magnificent! **Valpolicella Cl. Sup. 2004** (● 15,000 bt) releases scents of undergrowth accompanied by ethereal notes. **Primo Fiore 2009** (● cabernet, corvina, corvinone; 10,000 bt) is very good indeed, as is **Bianco Secco 2012** (○ garganega, trebbiano, sauvignon, chardonnay, saorin; 9,000 bt).

FERTILIZERS natural manure
PLANT PROTECTION chemical, copper and sulphur
WEED CONTROL mechanical
YEASTS native
GRAPES 100% estate-grown
CERTIFICATION none

Monte dall'Ora

Via Monte dall'Ora, 5
tel. 045 7704462
www.montedallora.com
info@montedallora.com

6.5 ha - 30,000 bt

66 Thanks to the daily care and attention (and action) Carlo Venturini and Alessandra Zantedeschi devote to their wine, Monte dall'Ora has become one of the most virtuous Valpolicella cellars. 99

PEOPLE - Carlo and Alessandra's life project got under way in 2000, when the couple decided to move from Verona to the Castelrotto hills. Here they bought and tidied up the vineyards, then restructured the wine cellar-cum-farmhouse. The decision to adopt organic methods was immediate.

VINEYARDS - The terraced vineyards round the house are like lush, well-kept gardens: besides vines, they also grow cherry trees, olive trees, wild herbs and flowers, breed farmyard animals and keep a horse (which roams freely among the vine rows, thus acting as a "natural weedkiller". The aim is to cultivate the plants in harmony, leaving them to find their own balance, a sine qua non of healthy, high-quality grapes.

WINES - The wines maintain a precise character and physiognomy while, at the same time, clearly "feeling" their vintages. An exemplary case is **Valpolicella Cl. Saseti 2012** (● 12,000 bt), tarter and subtler than usual but still fruity and flavorful. **Valpolicella Cl. Sup. Camporenzo 2010** (● 9,000 bt) is dry and austere, while **Valpolicella Cl. Sup. Ripasso Saustò 2009** (● 6,500 bt) tends to open slowly in the glass before offering spiciness and a spruce, tangy palate. As excellent as ever, **Recioto della Valpolicella Cl. Sant'Ulderico 2009** (● 2,000 bt) has an intense, complex nose with a succession of ripe berries, spices, quinine and aromatic herbs. **Amarone della Valpolicella Cl. Stropa 2006** (● 1,800 bt) is a masterpiece of refinement and depth, incomparably fleshy and mineral with complex, ever-changing aromas. It's truly a Great Wine.

FERTILIZERS	compost, biodynamic preparations
PLANT PROTECTION	copper and sulphur, organic
WEED CONTROL	mechanical
YEASTS	native
GRAPES	100% estate-grown
CERTIFICATION	organic

Villa Bellini

Località Castelrotto di Negarine
Via dei Fraccaroli, 6
tel. 0457 725630
www.villabellini.com
villabellini@villabellini.com

4 ha - 5,000 bt

66 When they open the doors of Villa Bellini, Cecilia Trucchi and her husband Marco welcome you into a secret world. The 18th-century building, the gardens and the vineyard with its old perimeter walls, still intact, conjure up a way of living respectful of humanity and of nature. 99

PEOPLE - This couple of architects are patiently restructuring the villa, their dream since they bought the property in 1987.

VINEYARDS - Every season regales us with new emotions in a vineyard that has always been managed with organic methods. With years of experience under her belt, Cecilia has clear ideas about what to expect and what to receive from her four hectares of land, which she boldly chose to largely replant in 2007. The estate faces southeast and the vines are planted on the dry stone wall terraces, known locally as marogne, typical of the Valpolicella.

WINES - **Valpolicella Cl. Sotto Fresche Frasche 2012** (● 2,000 bt) has a name (literally "under fresh fronds") that encapsulates the identity of this wine, a pleasant table companion that goes well even with fish. The nose has fresh, never overpowering cherry fragrances and a smooth, perfectly balanced palate.

> **vino slow** **VALPOLICELLA CL. SUP. TASO 2010** (● 3,000 bt) A wine that opens with customary refined style in the glass. On the nose, aromas of spices, ripe fruit and cocoa interweave to create a complex, deep bouquet. On the plate, the tannins are well-balanced, making for soft, rounded, long, harmonious drinkability. The only flaw is the limited number of bottles produced this year. But, after all, it's only fair that nature should occasionally make its own demands!

FERTILIZERS	compost, biodynamic preparations
PLANT PROTECTION	copper and sulphur
WEED CONTROL	mechanical
YEASTS	native
GRAPES	100% estate-grown
CERTIFICATION	organic

SOMMACAMPAGNA (VR)

Cavalchina

Frazione Custoza
Località Cavalchina
tel. 045 516002
www.cavalchina.com
cavalchina@cavalchina.com

50 ha - 320,000 bt

PEOPLE - The Nerozzi family property on the hill of San Pietro at Sommacampagna is an oasis of greenery and silence, just a short distance from Lake Garda and all its traffic. After replanting the many vineyards, Sergio and his son Carlo, both architects, began producing wine in the 1980s with labels that soon became a focus for the local area. Since 2000 Carlo has been carrying on the business with the expert consultancy of enologist Federico Giotto.

VINEYARDS - The cellar is surrounded by lush vineyards with long, neat and tidy vine rows, precision also being the leitmotiv of all Cavalchina wines. The vines grow on the typical soil of the rolling morainal Garda hills, popular not only among lovers of scented, easy-drinking wines but also among cyclists. An obelisk at the entrance to the cellar dates from 1866 and commemorates the history of the Risorgimento and the wounding in battle of Prince Amedeo di Savoia.

WINES - The wines are more traditional than the hi-tech cellar might lead to believe. An authentic sense of place is conveyed by the juicy, gutsy **Custoza 2012** (O 180,000 bt), the fresh, supple **Bardolino Chiaretto 2012** (☉ 50,000 bt) and Bardolino 2012 (● 60,000 bt), beautifully fruity and charismatic, as ever one of the best examples of the typology, hence deserving of recognition as an Everyday Wine. **Custoza Sup. Amedeo 2011** (O 20,000 bt) is complex, refined and mineral. **Ripasso della Valpolicella Torre d'Orti 2011** (● 20,000 bt) and **Amarone della Valpolicella Torre d'Orti 2009** (● 10,000 bt) are both distinguished and ambitious, elegant and full-bodied. Excellent value for money, they are sure to benefit from a few more years in the cellar.

FERTILIZERS organic-mineral
PLANT PROTECTION chemical, copper and sulphur
WEED CONTROL mechanical
YEASTS selected
GRAPES 100% estate-grown
CERTIFICATION none

SOMMACAMPAGNA (VR)

Monte Del Frà

Strada Custoza, 35
tel. 045 510490
www.montedelfra.it
info@montedelfra.it

174 ha - 1,000,000 bt

PEOPLE - We aren't joking when we say that the best thing that can happen to the visitor to Monte Del Frà is to be treated like a dog. The fact is that the first thing we noticed on our arrival at the owners' villa was a group of 13 foundlings being fed and pampered in the garden. Maybe it was out of respect for the spirit of hospitality of the monks who have lived on this hill for centuries. Marica Bonomo, tasked by the family with the communication and promotion side of the business, is proud of the new tasting room and kitchen. It will stage gastronomic, literary and artistic evenings devoted to wine. The cellar is always open, Sundays included.

VINEYARDS - Most of the vineyards are on the morainic hills south of Lake Garda: the Lena di Mezzo vineyard occupies 18 hectares in the Valpolicella Classica zone produces extremely elegant wines. The company is very modern from the agronomic point of view with vineyards divided by microzones and designed for mechanical harvesting. Its Bardolino and Custoza are models of correctness and pleasantness and are exported to as many as 42 countries.

WINES - The ever reliable **Custoza Sup. Ca' del Magro 2011** (O 60,000 bt) is made with grapes grown on poor soil, which guarantee good aging prospects and complexity. Custoza 2012 (O 550,000 bt), a full-flavored, juicy Everyday Wine, and **Bardolino 2012** (● 200,000 bt) are both pleasant, fragrant and direct. **Valpolicella Cl. Sup. Tenuta Lena di Mezzo 2011** (● 50,000 bt) ushers in the most stylish, prestigious wines. It is followed by the soft and well-rounded **Amarone della Valpolicella Cl. Tenuta Lena di Mezzo 2009** (● 30,000 bt) and the grandiose **Amarone della Valpolicella Cl. Scarnocchio 2008** (● 8,500 bt), which is still full of youthful brawn and fighting spirit, but is sure to mellow to perfection as it grows up.

FERTILIZERS organic-mineral
PLANT PROTECTION chemical, copper and sulphur
WEED CONTROL mechanical
YEASTS selected
GRAPES 100% estate-grown
CERTIFICATION none

Terre della garganega

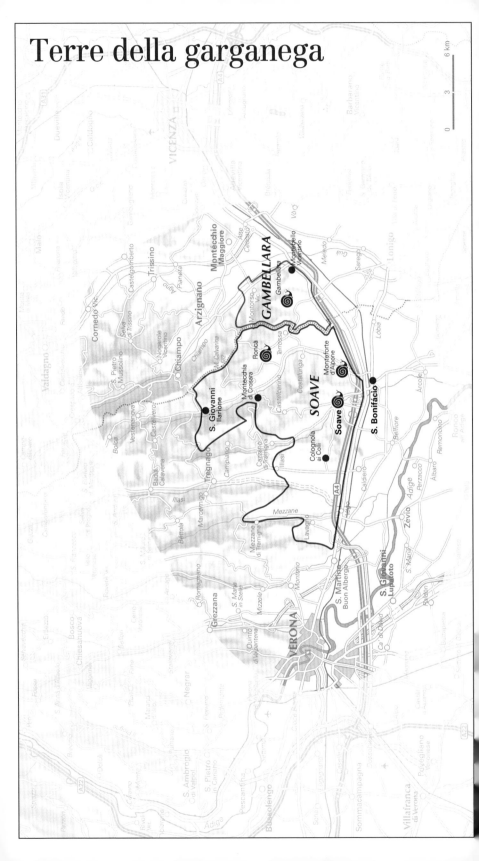

GAMBELLARA (VI)

La Biancara

Frazione Sorio
Contrada Biancara, 14
tel. 0444 444244
www.biancaravini.it
biancaravini@virgilio.it

12 ha - 60,000 bt

66 Rivers of adjectives have been used to describe Angiolino Maule, one of the leaders of the natural wine movement. He's a farmer who devotes an enormous amount of care — not to mention self-criticism — to his work. That my not sound a lot but, in any event, it stands for everything. 99

PEOPLE - Angiolino Maule explains the difference between the kind of fertility sought in farming over the last half a century — quantity-driven with the use of fertilizers and plant protection products that have poisoned the soil — and fertility based on quality, which yields fewer but tastier, more fragrant and complete fruits and presupposes healthy, living biodiverse soil. This signifies responsibility towards the land and towards consumers of the present and future generations.

VINEYARDS - The whole family, meaning Angiolin's wife and three children, work in the winery with commitment and curiosity towards the goal of zero-impact agriculture. In the vineyards they use copper and sulphur very sparingly and generally prefer to grass them.

WINES - The wines are all well-focused and genuine (meaning only native yeasts in the cellar and a limited use of sulphur). They might almost be defined as "wines with a conscience" and they always reflect the company's eagerness to experiment and change. **Bianco Masieri 2012** (O 20,000 bt) is simple and sincere, while **Bianco Sassaia 2012** (O 20,000 bt), fermented in oak barrels without temperature control and filtration, is more complex, broad, supple and very mineral.

> **vino slow** RECIOTO DI GAMBELLARA 2009 (O 2,000 bt) An auteur interpretation of the typology: before being bottled, it ferments for 15 days on the skins and ages for three years. Complex and fluid, it has intact, all-embracing fruit, supported by tangy, acid sinew that lengthens the palate enjoyably.

FERTILIZERS compost, green manure
PLANT PROTECTION copper and sulphur, organic
WEED CONTROL mechanical
YEASTS native
GRAPES 100% estate-grown
CERTIFICATION organic

MONTEBELLO VICENTINO (VI)

Domenico Cavazza €

Frazione Selva
Via Selva, 22
tel. 0444 649166
www.cavazzawine.com
info@cavazzawine.com

150 ha - 890,000 bt

PEOPLE - This historic Vicenza winery was founded in 1928, when Giovanni Cavazza bought his first vineyards at Selva di Montebello. Now Stefano and Andrea of the fourth generation of the family run the place with the agronomist Francesco, the enologist Giancarlo and the cellar manager Giovanni. Large though the company may have become, the family-style management continues.

VINEYARDS - With its 160 hectares, the Cavazzas' winery is one of the largest in the province. The vineyards are divided between two distinct zones. At Gambellara and Selva di Montebello, they grow white grape varieties on volcanic soil. On the hill of Alonte, in the Colli Berici, the Cavazza have bought the stupendous Tenuta Cicogna estate, where red varieties grow on sandstone with traces of limestone. Interventions in the vineyards are kept to a minimum.

WINES - The Cavazzas' wines express the potential of the two terroirs and the varietal characteristics of the grapes to perfection. **Gambellara Cl. La Bocara 2012** (O 95,000 bt), for example, is fresh and dynamic with assertive minerality. The delicate **Colli Berici Tai Rosso 2012** (● 35,000 bt) is redolent of raspberry and deliciously refreshing. **Colli Berici Cabernet Costiera 2010** (● 14,500 bt) has stylish vegetality and brash tannins and is worth following in the future. **Fornetto Rosso 2010** (● 14,000 bt) is a singular blend of cabernet, merlot and the native tai rosso.

> **vino slow** GAMBELLARA CL. CREARI 2011 (O 15,000 bt) A personal and effective interpretation of late-harvest garganega grapes. The nose is deeply mineral with luscious ripe fruit, while the palate has plenty of grip, refreshed by vibrant acid backbone. A white wine of massive character and guaranteed aging prospects.

FERTILIZERS organic-mineral, mineral, manure pellets, natural manure
PLANT PROTECTION chemical, copper and sulphur
WEED CONTROL mechanical, chemical
YEASTS selected
GRAPES 100% estate-grown
CERTIFICATION none

MONTEFORTE D'ALPONE (VR)

Gini

Via Matteotti, 42
tel. 0457 611908
www.ginivini.com
info@ginivini.com

MONTEFORTE D'ALPONE (VR)

Prà

Via della Fontana, 31
tel. 045 7612125
www.vinipra.it
info@vinipra.it

---

55 ha - 200,000 bt

24 ha - 300,000 bt | **10% discount**

PEOPLE - The Gini family have been growing wines at Monteforte since the 17th century. Their old farming wisdom was handed down from generation to generation until 1980, when the late Olinto, a respected figure locally, released their first label. Olinto's son Sandro is an enologist and has been working at the winery since the early 1980s. He oversees the vineyards while his brother Claudio and son Matteo take care of the cellar.

VINEYARDS - The organically certified winery's property covers an area of 55 hectares, half of which in the favorable Soave Classico growing areas and half at a Campiano (Cazzano di Tramigna). The first group of vineyards is pergola-trained on volcanic soil and the vines, some ungrafted, have an age that varies from 60 to 120. The second, planted with pinot nero grapes in 1988 (other varieties were added in 2000), are Guyot-trained and grow on clayey-calcareous soil.

WINES - Winemaking tradition, good growing soil and old vineyards — plus innovation, research and technology. In the wines, in Soave Classico in particular, all this translates into longevity and uniqueness. The nicely complex **Soave Cl. La Froscà 2012** (O 20,000 bt) has texture and promising character. **Soave Cl. 2012** (O 120,000 bt) is tangy and supple, while **Gran Cuvée Brut 2008** (O garganega, pinot nero, chardonnay; 10,000 bt) is reliable. Rounding off the range (though at least another two splendid Recioto di Soaves might have been mentioned) is the promising **Campo alle More 2009** (● pinot nero; 5,000 bt).

66 "Love the vineyard and cultivate it with wisdom and humility." Graziano manages his vineyards with innovative techniques that have a very low impact on the environment. He uses machinery that has led him to stop using chemicals and recover a biodiversity that risked being lost. **99**

PEOPLE - Graziano Prà has always been a firm believer in the quality of the produce of the Soave zone. After the death of his father, he graduated in enology and decided to return to the family farm. With care and enthusiasm he began producing wines with a style of their own, designed to promote, respect and preserve the local area. This is why he is acknowledged as one of the most important Soave producers.

VINEYARDS - The vineyards are scattered over the finest hills in the Soave zone: Foscarino, Montegrande and Froscà. The red grapes are cultivated on the organically-managed Morandina estate, in the Valpolicella.

WINES - Prà's wines have always been distinguished by elegance. **Soave Cl. Otto 2012** (O 150,000 bt) is simple and linear with indisputable freshness. Scents of ripe apples and pears and vanilla pervade **Soave Colle Sant'Antonio 2009** (O 7,000 bt). Of the red wines we tasted, we particularly enjoyed **Valpolicella Sup. La Morandina 2011** (● 5,000 bt).

vino slow SOAVE CL. STAFORTE 2011 (O 6,600 bt). Structure, savor and aromatic complexity for a wine of sumptuous refinement.

vino slow SOAVE CL. CONTRADA SALVARENZA VECCHIE VIGNE 2011 (O 15,000 bt) This historic Soave label is the happy result of the decision to get the best out of the oldest vineyards. Deeply mineral with intense flavor, it has a long, well-balanced and delicately textured palate.

vino slow SOAVE CL. MONTEGRANDE 2012 (O 15,000 bt) Well-rounded and refreshing with an awesomely long mineral palate. We don't need to waste many words on this wine: it's simply a dream come true.

FERTILIZERS natural manure, green manure
PLANT PROTECTION copper and sulphur, organic
WEED CONTROL mechanical
YEASTS native
GRAPES 100% estate-grown
CERTIFICATION organic

FERTILIZERS organic-mineral, natural manure
PLANT PROTECTION chemical, copper and sulphur
WEED CONTROL mechanical
YEASTS selected
GRAPES 100% estate-grown
CERTIFICATION none

Fongaro

RONCÀ (VR)

Via Motto Piane, 12
tel. 045 7460240
www.fongarospumanti.it
info@fongarospumanti.it

12 ha - 80,000 bt

❝ With exemplary coherence the Fongaros promote the durella grape and manage their winery using organic methods with respect for the Lessinia area. ❞

PEOPLE - The winery came into being in 1975, the fruit of Guerrino Fongaro's notion that the durella grape, highly acidic and previously used to produce rough, barely drinkable wines, might work for Metodo Classico bottle fermentation. He was right and his grandsons Matteo and Alessandro are carrying on his good work with great enterprise and passion.

VINEYARDS - The arbor-trained vineyards are situated on the hills round the cellar at altitudes of 300 to 500 meters. The basalt soil of volcanic origin is typical of the eastern part of the Lessinia zone. Since 1985 the company has adopted organic methods, which preserve the environment and maintain the natural balance of the durella grape, rustic but very delicate and necessitating great care and attention.

WINES - At the outset the company banked heavily on the Metodo Classico, but since then its range has extended to include a number of different labels, all made with durella, that bring out the range of expression of this native "mountain" grape. We were impressed by the excellence of **Lessini Durello M. Cl. Brut Etichetta Nera 2007** (○ 10,000 bt), which ferments on yeasts for 40 months: all-embracing and creamy on the palate, it has a bouquet of citrus and dried fruits which veer enjoyably towards spice and balsam. Also very good is **M. Cl. Brut Etichetta Bianca** (○ 20,000 bt), a cuvée of durella and incrocio Manzoni, in which mineral freshness and satisfying fruitiness predominate. Of the wines reviewed last year and still available on the market, we recommend M. Cl. Pas Dosé Etichetta Verde 2009, with its exquisitely dry complexity.

FERTILIZERS natural manure, green manure
PLANT PROTECTION copper and sulphur
WEED CONTROL mechanical
YEASTS selected
GRAPES 100% estate-grown
CERTIFICATION organic

Leonildo Pieropan

SOAVE (VR)

Via Camuzzoni, 3
tel. 045 6190171
www.pieropan.it
info@pieropan.it

40 ha - 380,000 bt

❝ Leonildo Pieropan embodies the history of Soave in the last 40 years. The tenacity and belief with which he has presented the wine to the world, overcoming the diffidence caused by its dubious reputation in the past, are the fundamental ingredients of its present success. ❞

PEOPLE - Today Leonildo can count as ever upon the help of his wife Teresita and of their highly motivated sons Dario and Andrea, who are entrusted with the vineyards recently inaugurated in the Valpolicella to produce red wines.

VINEYARDS - The Calvarino vineyard is so steep, working it brings to mind the suffering associated with a hill its name evokes — Calvary. Here the soil is basaltic-tufaceous, hence of volcanic origin. The La Rocca vineyard, which is more calcareous and clayey, stretches to the foot of Soave castle. The diversity of soils and microclimates explains the clear difference between the two crus. The viticulture is virtuous, designed to produce healthy, ripe grapes and preserve the fertility of the soil and the vitality of the vines.

WINES - The wines are of the highest standard as always. It's never easy to establish the one we like the most but this year, by a neck, the palm of Great Wine goes to **Soave Cl. La Rocca 2011** (○ 35,000 bt) for its fullness, never top-heavy or static but, rather, dynamic, caressing and magnificently typical. **Soave Cl. Calvarino 2011** (○ 45,000 bt) offers the nose mineral and floral notes, while on the palate it combines verve, elegance, assertiveness and a length worthy of the very best versions. More approachable and ready to uncork is Soave Cl. 2012 (○ 300.000 bt), an Everyday Wine with thereness, impressive acidity and flesh to match.

FERTILIZERS none
PLANT PROTECTION copper and sulphur
WEED CONTROL mechanical
YEASTS selected
GRAPES 100% estate-grown
CERTIFICATION none

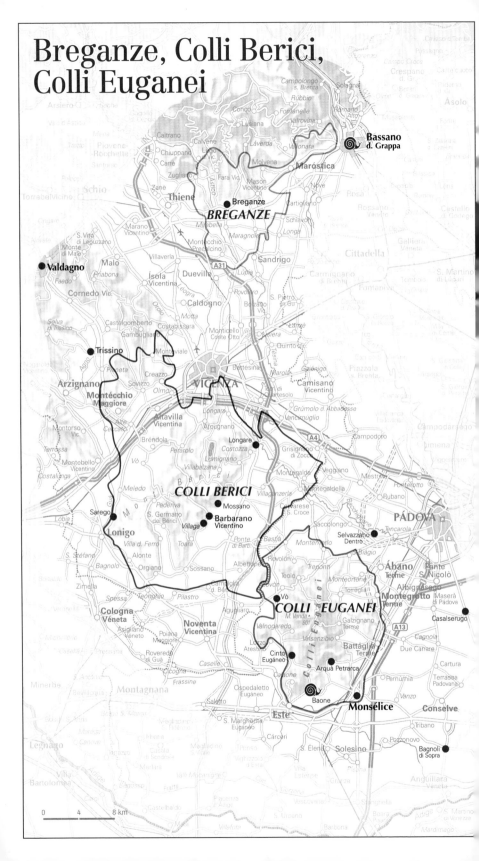

Breganze, Colli Berici, Colli Euganei

ARQUÀ PETRARCA (PD)

Vignalta

Via Scalette, 23
tel. 0429 777305
www.vignalta.it
info@vignalta.it

BAONE (PD)

Ca' Orologio

Via Ca' Orologio, 7 A
tel. 0429 50099
www.caorologio.it
info@caorologio.com

---

50 ha - 200,000 bt

---

12 ha - 28,000 bt

PEOPLE - Vignalta, the focus for the Colli Euganei zone, came into being "way back" in 1986, just when the new wave that was to inundate Italian viticulture and enology was starting to swell. It grew up with ideas and courage and a broad, open vision of the challenge ahead. Lucio Gomiero, the heart and soul of the company, rode the new wave and made a significant contribution to the rebirth and affirmation of his own local area.

VINEYARDS - We were taken on our tour of the Vignalta world by cellarman Michele Montecchio. We set out from Arquà Petrarca, where the wine cellar and some of the vineyards are situated, and went on to explore the best hillside locations. The volcanic soil contains lime and trachyte, decisive for diverse wines of consistently high quality.

WINES - The expressiveness typical of the Euganean terroir is the thread that sews the wines together. The symbol of the zone, the smooth, stylish Colli Euganei Rosso Gemola 2009 (● merlot, cabernet franc; 26,000 bt) is a Great Wine. Still very young but already enjoyable, it's sure to last. Following in its footsteps, **Marrano 2008** (● 26.000 bt) is a classic blend of merlot and cabernet sauvignon with a bouquet of aromatic herbs and a full, lingering body. **Colli Euganei Rosso Ris. 2009** (● merlot, cabernet sauvignon; 100,000 bt) is the team's holding midfielder, well worth its price. **Colli Euganei Chardonnay 2011** (○ 3,000 bt) is characterized by a certain oakiness. **Colli Euganei Fior d'Arancio Passito Alpinae 2009** (○ 4,000 0.375 l bt) and the debut wine **Brut Nature** (○ raboso, chardonnay; 3,000 bt) are both valid.

66 This is one of the most significant wineries in the Colli Euganei. It owes its prestige to the pragmatic, never uncritical perfectionism and determination of owner Maria Gioia Rosellini, whose sole aim is to treat the vineyards and the surroundings environment well. **99**

PEOPLE - Ca' Orologio was born in 1995 when the then youthful Maria Gioia decided to turn her life around. Achieved the move from "urban mother" to rural winemaker. Achieved by buying the farming estate with adjoining 156th-century villa and soon converting the latter into an elegant agriturismo with space for a small but functional wine cellar.

VINEYARDS - The estate came with a two-hectare vineyard of very old vines. New plantings were soon added on two hillsides not very far away, but very different the one form the other. The soil at Calaone is of volcanic origin, while at Ca' Orologio the vineyard stands on broad terraces without supporting walls where the soil is rich in calcareous flakes. Since 1999 the cellar has been applying the principles of organic farming.

WINES - All-embracing, well-rounded and warm, **Colli Euganei Rosso Calaòne 2011** (● merlot, cabernet, barbera; 12,000 bt) has gorgeous fruity flesh, well supported by effective acidity and flavor with a pleasant balsamic note on the finish. **Relògio 2011** (● carmenère, cabernet franc; 4,000 bt) is leafy and earthy on the nose with notes of undergrowth and ripe red berries, while the palate is well-rounded, mellow almost, with plenty of flavor on the finish to balance its hefty structure. The lighter, suppler **Lunisole 2010** (● 2,000 bt) is made from barbera grapes from a vineyard planted almost 40 years ago on volcanic soil; its bouquet is open and expressive with ripe fruit to the fore, its palate is well-turned and marked by a streak of acidity that lengthens the mouthfeel.

FERTILIZERS manure pellets, green manure
PLANT PROTECTION chemical, copper and sulphur
WEED CONTROL mechanical, chemical
YEASTS selected
GRAPES 100% estate-grown
CERTIFICATION none

FERTILIZERS biodynamic preparations, green manure
PLANT PROTECTION organic
WEED CONTROL mechanical
YEASTS native
GRAPES 100% estate-grown
CERTIFICATION organic

BAONE (PD)

Il Mottolo €

Via Comezzara, 13
tel. 347 9456155
www.ilmottolo.it
ilmottolo@fastwebnet.it

BASSANO DEL GRAPPA (VI)

Vigneto Due Santi

Viale Asiago, 174
tel. 0424 502074
www.vignetoduesanti.it
info@vignetoduesanti.it

6.5 ha - 16,500 bt · **10% discount**

PEOPLE - The Colli Euganei are one of the Veneto's up-and-coming winegrowing areas. The credit for this must go to a series of companies that have completely overhauled the approach to productive quantity and quality. One such is Il Mottolo, a name which derives from a dialect term for a rock formation of calcareous origin. The winery was established in 2003 by Roberto Dalla Libera and Sergio Fortin, bowled over by the beauty of an area where nature reigns supreme.

VINEYARDS - The vineyards are growing and prospering under the supervision of agronomist Filippo Giannone. Human intervention is meticulous, respectful and non-invasive. The Baone and Arquà Petrarca terroir, where the vineyards are situated, has limestone and clayey soil and is packed with potential. The vines rim the slopes of Monte Cecilia and face south and southeast. They are trained with a mixture of the spurred cordon, Guyot and "casarsa" systems.

WINES - The idea of wine developed at Il Mottolo puts the priority on the freshness and drinkabiity produced by the favorable local soil and weather conditions. It's a concept that enologist Flavio Prà always bears in mind. A practical example of it is **Colli Euganei Rosso Serro 2010** (● 3,500 bt), with a bouquet tinged with violets and forest fruits and a body of fine-grained tannins. Close on its heels comes **Vignanima 2010** (● carmenère, merlot; 2,500 bt), which has redcurrant, bramble and chocolate on the nose and a rich, fleshy, lingering palate. Full-flavored, satisfying and supple, Colli Euganei Merlot Comezzara 2011 (● 4,500 bt) is a perfect Everyday Wine. **Colli Euganei Cabernet Vigna Marè 2011** (● 3,500 bt) is crisp and delicious. **Colli Euganei Moscato Fior d'Arancio Passito Vigna del Pozzo 2011** (○ 1,000 bt) and **Le Contarine 2012** (○ moscato, garganega; 2,500 bt) are both very good indeed.

18 ha - 100,000 bt · **10% discount**

❝ For years now Adriano and Stefano Zonta have been running this winery with unflagging passion and deep belief in the area's winegrowing tradition, respect for the land and the criteria of sustainability. ❞

PEOPLE - Adriano and Stefano share out equally the work in the vineyard and the simple, functional cellar, where they welcome visitors with their excellent wines. Their winery is a focus for the Bassano zone and a welcome discovery for the many outsiders who visit.

VINEYARDS - The vineyards are split up into different parcels on the ridge that descends from the Marsan district to the entrance to the Valsugana. They grow on calcareous morainal soil with fossil deposits. They are surrounded by woods and olive groves and management with a minimum of intervention and, though organic certification has yet to be received, maximum respect for the balance of the vines. In the lovely Due Santi vineyard beside the cellar, there are vines that reach almost 65 years of age.

WINES - Freshness, drinkability and accessible pricing characterize the whole range. Breganze Merlot 2010 (● 20,000 bt) is an exemplary Everyday Wine: caressing, textured and juicy, its lightness makes it ideal at the table. On the same level is **Breganze Cabernet 2010** (● 25,000 bt), more compact and dry. The company's flagship wine, **Breganze Cabernet Vigneto Due Santi 2010** (● 16,000 bt) is complex, full-bodied and assertive but still young. A wine not to be missed is the white **Malvasia Campo dei Fiori 2012** (○ 3,500 bt), made with grapes from the old vineyards: elegant, spicy and mineral, it is sure to evolve. **Breganze Bianco Rivana 2012** (○ friulano; 6,000 bt) is approachable and floral.

FERTILIZERS none
PLANT PROTECTION chemical, copper and sulphur
WEED CONTROL mechanical
YEASTS selected
GRAPES 100% estate-grown
CERTIFICATION none

FERTILIZERS natural manure
PLANT PROTECTION chemical, copper and sulphur
WEED CONTROL mechanical
YEASTS selected
GRAPES 100% estate-grown
CERTIFICATION none

CINTO EUGANEO (PD)

Marco Sambin

Frazione Valnogaredo
Via Fattorelle 20 A
tel. 349 3625965
www.vinimarcus.com
info@vinimarcus.com

3 ha - 7,200 bt

PEOPLE - The short history of the Sambin winery began with the new millennium. Marco, the owner, was teaching psychology at Padua University, but his passion led him to the nearby Colli Euganei: hence nature, a sense of freedom, memories of Petrarch. It was inevitable that he should marry wine, made here since antiquity, and set out on an adventure that has been exciting right from the very first steps.

VINEYARDS - Recovery of previously abandoned land, the farsighted application of biodynamic criteria, a measured use of sulphur, minimalist cellar techniques — these are the guidelines for the winery's agronomic and enological work. The cellar is situated in the Valgonaredo district of the commune of Cinto Euganeo, in the western part of the denomination, facing the Colli Berici. The vineyards are planted on clayey limestone and cover an area of three hectares out of a total of four.

WINES - Each one of Marco's wines bears the name in Latin of a member of his family, the noble De Norcen da Feltres. Until last year there was only one label; now others have been released, all from tiny amounts of grapes. **Isabel 2012** (☉ merlot; 300 bt) is a rosé with delicate hints of fresh herbs and sour cherries. **Micael 2011** (● merlot; 500 bt) is intense and engrossing with notes of bramble and chocolate. **Johannes 2011** (● syrah; 500 bt) is delicately spicy with notes of violet and woodland vegetation on the nose and a full-flavored balsamic palate. The superlative **Marcus 2010** (● cabernet sauvignon and cabernet franc, merlot, syrah; 6,000 bt) is an austere, compact Great Wine that explodes with fruit and flowers on the nose and follows through with a silky, pervasive palate. **Francisca 2009** (● cabernet sauvignon; 600 bt) is an excellent passito. Congratulations to the agronomist-enologist Guido Busatto.

SELVAZZANO DENTRO (PD)

La Montecchia
Conte Emo Capodilista

Via Montecchia, 16
tel. 049 637294
www.lamontecchia.it
lamontecchia@lamontecchia.it
🍷 🚜

30 ha - 130,000 bt   **10% discount**

PEOPLE - It's always a pleasure to meet Giordano Emo Capodilista, a descendant of an important Veneto noble family. An enlightened, ironic man of the world, Giordano began developing his family's old Montecchia estate in 1992. His passion for viticulture has driven him to embark upon an intelligent regeneration operation to recover old grape varieties.

VINEYARDS - The vineyards are located in two different places: Baone and Montecchia itself, where the wine cellar is. Baone was bought in 2001. Here the old terraces sit on limestone soil and grow varieties revived by the owner and new plantings of cabernet sauvignon and carmenère. On the red soil of Montecchia grows the little known moscato fior d'arancio grape. The vines are cultivated with maximum respect for the vineyard, without chemical weed control and systemic treatments.

WINES - Balance and richness of flavor are the common traits of wines that capture the essence of the Euganean Hills, overtly and consistently. Concentrated and elegant, **Colli Euganei Rosso Villa Capodilista 2010** (● 6,500 bt) will mellow its austere tannins in the course of time. **Colli Euganei Cabernet Sauvignon Ireneo 2010** (● 6,000 bt) marries power and freshness on a tangy, spicy palate. The young, fragrant Godimondo 2012 (● cabernet franc; 24,000 bt) stands out for forthrightness and drinkability: it's an excellent Everyday Wine. Potent and fresh with complex aromas of citrus fruit with a hint of bitterness on the finish, **Colli Euganei Fior d'Arancio Passito Donna Daria 2011** (○ 4,000 bt) has great character. **Colli Euganei Fior d'Arancio Spumante 2012** (○ 30,000 bt) has measured sweetness and a fragrant palate.

FERTILIZERS natural manure, green manure
PLANT PROTECTION copper and sulphur, organic
WEED CONTROL mechanical
YEASTS native
GRAPES 100% estate-grown
CERTIFICATION none

FERTILIZERS none
PLANT PROTECTION chemical, copper and sulphur
WEED CONTROL mechanical
YEASTS selected, native
GRAPES 100% estate-grown
CERTIFICATION none

Colline del Prosecco, Piave e Veneto orientale

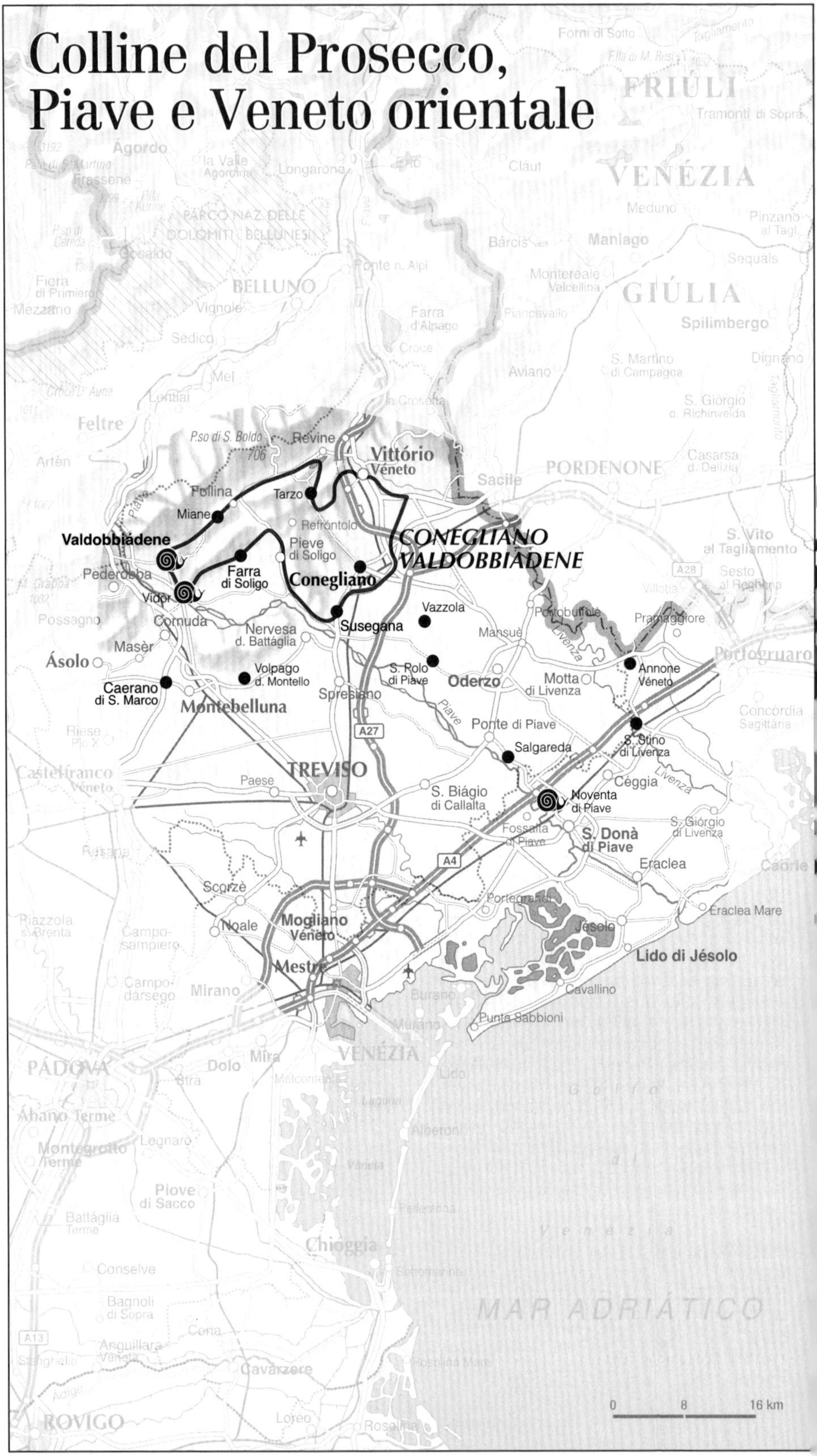

CONEGLIANO (TV)

Zardetto

Via Martiri delle Foibe 18,
tel. 0438 394969
www.zardettoprosecco.com
info@zardettoprosecco.com

SUSEGANA (TV)

Valdellövo

Frazione Collalto
Via Cucco, 29
tel. 0438 981232
www.valdellovo.it
info@valdellovo.it

22 ha - 1,000,000 bt

10 ha - 70,000 bt

PEOPLE - Fabio Zardetto is the dynamic heir of a family that has been producing wine for over 100 years. His grandfather Ernesto was a winegrower and the warden at the Enological School in Conegliano, but it was his father Pino, an enologist, who set up the business proper in the late 1960s. Today Fabio, and his brother Filippo are passionate producers of Prosecco Superiore, which represents almost half the new cellar's production.

VINEYARDS - The company rents 20 hectares of vineyards, all on excellent winegrowing land in different localities — San Pietro di Feletto, Carpesica and Santo Stefano — whose grapes are vinified separately. Recently it bought two hectares in a pretty natural amphitheater at Cozzuolo. Here the old parcels, which produce a number of great varieties, are in the middle of the organic certification process.

WINES - The wines all have strong personalities and embody the areas of origin of the grapes. The excellent Valdobbiadene **Prosecco Sup. Brut Rive di Ogliano Tre Venti 2012** (○ 10,000 bt), made with the grapes from Carpesica, has firm, tangy, spicy structure. Just as intense is **Valdobbiadene Prosecco Sup. Dry Fondego 2012** (○ 50,000 bt), which the San Pietro soil enriches with notes of ripe fruit and softness. **Valdobbiadene Sup di Cartizze 2012** (○ 10,000 bt) has stylish blossomy, citrussy nuances, fused in a creamy, all-embracing mouthfeel. Simpler but with beautifully balanced flavor, **Valdobbiadene Prosecco Sup. Brut Refosso 2012** (○ 200,000 bt) is almost crisp on the palate, while **Valdobbiadene Prosecco Sup. Extra Dry Molin** (○ 150,000 bt) has very pleasant fresh floral nuances.

PEOPLE - Benedetto Ricci has inherited his passion for wine from his family. His grandfather was one of the promoters of the "Strada del Vino Bianco" and his father, who studied enology in Conegliano, managed a cellar for years. He opened the winery in partnership with his brother Luca in 2000, and since 2008 has been running it with his wife Clotilde Camerotto with more than flattering results. His consultant in the cellar is Federico Giotto.

VINEYARDS - When you walk into the small plot surrounded by dense woodland on the hill of Collalto, you feel as if you are being catapulted out of time. Here there are two hectares of old glera, bianchetta and verdiso grapes, some planted as many as 50 and 60 years ago, which provide the scions for the more recent eight-hectare Crode vineyard. The high-trained plantings are coaxed along with great care. Humus and green manure are used and treatments are limited.

WINES - Benedetto and Clotilde have achieved excellent results so far, as confirmed by the range they submitted for tasting. Conegliano Valdobbiadene Prosecco Sup. Extra Dry Anno Zero 2012 (○ 15,000 bt) is one of the finest examples of its typology and a perfect Everyday Wine. Well-balanced and very delicate on the palate, it has a fine flavorsome follow-through with notes of wisteria and apple. On a par with it is the deep, mineral **Conegliano Valdobbiadene Prosecco Sup. Brut Zero Nove 2012** (○ 7,000 bt). The excellent **Prosecco sui lieviti Glera col Fondo Non Filtrato 2011** (○ 8,000 bt) is juicy, deft and thirst-quenching. Worth tasting too is **Conegliano Valdobbiadene Prosecco Frizzante Bade 2011** (○ 3,000 bt), the result of natural secondary fermentation with the addition of dried glera must: substantial and flavorful, it has a pleasantly bitter finish.

FERTILIZERS organic-mineral, natural manure, compost
PLANT PROTECTION copper and sulphur
WEED CONTROL mechanical
YEASTS selected
GRAPES 100% estate-grown
CERTIFICATION converting to organics

FERTILIZERS compost, green manure
PLANT PROTECTION chemical, copper and sulphur
WEED CONTROL chemical, mechanical
YEASTS selected
GRAPES 100% estate-grown
CERTIFICATION none

VALDOBBIADENE (TV)

Bortolomiol €

Via G. Garibaldi, 142
tel. 0423 974911
www.bortolomiol.com
info@bortolomiol.com

VALDOBBIADENE (TV)

Casa Coste Piane

Frazione Santo Stefano
Via Coste Piane, 2
tel. 0423 900219
casacostepiane@libero.it

4.5 ha - 2,000,000 bt

PEOPLE - The inheritance of Giuliano Bortolomiol, the man who banked on the potential of the Valdobbiadene terroir and spumante production in the postwar years, has been accepted by his widow and their daughters Elvira, Giuliana, Luisa and Maria Elena. With great passion they monitor every single aspect of production. But that's not all; they also invest in projects of social and humanitarian value and in cultural activities relating to art and wine.

VINEYARDS - The 70 historic grape suppliers are supervised by the agronomist Giovanni Pascarella and have to comply with a strict vine dressing protocol aimed at sustainability and the production of grapes of excellent quality. Another enologist, Gianfranco Zanon, is in charge of production management. The cellar's own four hectares are certified organic and its Filandetta vineyard, in the heart of the Valdobbiadene zone, is well worth a visit.

WINES - Impeccable style and exemplary elegance are the traits that characterize the range. The excellent **Valdobbiadene Prosecco Sup. Brut Ius Naturae 2012** (O 16,000 bt) is an organic wine combining ripe fruit with delicate minerality. Also very good indeed is **Valdobbiadene Prosecco Sup. Brut Motus Vitae Rive di San Pietro di Barbozza 2011** (O 7,000 bt) is a long Charmat with very fine perlage and wonderful follow-through. With its munchy, spicy texture, Valdobbiadene Prosecco Sup. Brut Prior 2012 (O 140,000 bt) is a paradigm for the typology, a flavorful, fragrant Everyday Wine. **Valdobbiadene Prosecco Sup. Extra Dry Banda Rossa 2012** (O 100,000 bt) is creamy and refreshing. **Valdobbiadene Prosecco Sup. Extra Dry Senior** (O 300,000 bt) is blossomy and austere, while **Valdobbiadene Prosecco Sup. di Cartizze Dry 2012** (O 35,000 bt) is austere.

6 ha - 60,000 bt

❝ Behind Loris Follador is the collective story of the many farmer-grape growers who he has forged and backed down the years. He has done so with heart and stubbornness, convincing them not to abandon the tradition of spontaneous second fermentation in the bottle. Today he thoroughly deserves to be recognized as the leading ambassador of this ancient method. ❞

PEOPLE - In 2013 Loris Follador celebrated 20 years of working with the Casa Coste Piane brand. Today he is helped in his job by his wife Sandra and their sons Adelchi and Raffaele.

VINEYARDS - Casa Coste Piane is situated at Fol, a tiny hamlet near Santo Stefano in the Valdobbiadene, to all intents and purposes a Prosecco premier cru and a place of fairytale natural beauty. The sea of green that sweeps over the rugged but noble hills in the months leading up to the grape harvest regenerates the soul. Loris tends his vineyards with passion, respecting nature to preserve its peculiarities.

WINES - The good 2012 grape harvest made it possible to produce wines with a lot of identity. The vineyards are cultivated at altitudes of 300 to 400 meters on clayey soils with a base of marl, sand and traes of sandstone. We were impressed by **Brichet Frizzante Naturalmente 2012** (O 4,000 bt), which is fragrant, creamy and taut. **Valdobbiadene Prosecco Sup. Extra Dry San Venanzio 2012** (O 3,000 bt) is full of flavor.

> **vino slow** **VALDOBBIADENE PROSECCO SUP. FRIZZANTE NATURALMENTE** (O 38,000 bt) The "sur lie" or "on the leas" technique — "col fondo" in local parlance — continues to be the cornerstone of this typology and this wine's distinctive feature is digestibility. Also striking is the freshness that permeates it. Fine and delicate, it releases intense nuances of acacia, while on the palate it is clear-cut and typical with notes of hazelnut, walnut and almond.

FERTILIZERS natural manure
PLANT PROTECTION copper and sulphur
WEED CONTROL mechanical
YEASTS selected
GRAPES 70% bought in
CERTIFICATION organic for the cellar's own vineyards

FERTILIZERS organic-mineral, natural manure
PLANT PROTECTION copper and sulphur
WEED CONTROL mechanical
YEASTS native
GRAPES 100% estate-grown
CERTIFICATION none

Silvano Follador 🐌

Frazione Santo Stefano
Via Callonga, 11
tel. 0423 900295
www.silvanofollador.it
info@silvanofollador.it

3.5 ha - 25,000 bt

❝ Silvano Follador is an independent winemaker who spurns convention. He has embraced the philosophy of biodynamics enthusiastically but not uncritically, with creativity, courage and sensitivity — virtues that are, alas, on the verge of extinction, not only in the wine world. ❞

PEOPLE - It wasn't an easy choice for Silvano. After overseeing the vineyards he inherited from his grandfather for a few years and also making wine with bought-in grapes, in 2004 he decided to restrict production solely to his own grapes and to adopt biodynamic practices. All this has made him one of the most articulate interpreters of the terroir. He is helped in his work by his father and sister Alberta.

VINEYARDS - The oldest vineyards near the cellar are worth the journey on their own. Covered with spontaneous plants, they are very old and sit at the foot of the Cartizze hills. The most recent plantings are at San Giovanni di Valdobbiadene. All the vineyards are followed with constant attention to the preservation of biodiversity and the intactness of the soil, which is reinforced with green manure cropping and natural substances.

WINES - Silvano manages to transmit his deep respect for the land into his wines: wines that are essential, in which the terroir can be perceived immediately. Well-structured and creamy, **Valdobbiadene Prosecco Sup. Brut Nature 2012** (○ 19,000 bt) has refined scents of white peach. On a second tasting, Valdobbiadene Prosecco Sup. Brut Dosaggio Zero 2010, which we reviewed last year, proves once more to be a Metodo Classico of great finesse.

> **vino slow** **VALDOBBIADENE SUP. DI CARTIZZE BRUT NATURE 2012** (○ 6,600 bt) A wine that never fails to amaze for its exemplary finesse and profound mineral structure. This vintage appears slightly softer than others but has the same very delicate texture.

FERTILIZERS natural manure, biodynamic preparations
PLANT PROTECTION copper and sulphur, organic
WEED CONTROL mechanical
YEASTS selected
GRAPES 100% estate-grown
CERTIFICATION none

Sorelle Bronca 🐌

Frazione Colbertaldo
Via Martiri, 20
tel. 0423 987201 987009
www.sorellebronca.com
info@sorellebronca.com

20 ha - 250,000 bt | **10% discount**

❝ A wine company that beat the rest by a mile in realizing that organic agriculture wasn't just an extra to stick on labels for show, but a sine qua non for quality wines that fully encapsulate their terroir of origin. ❞

PEOPLE - Sisters Antonella and Ersiliana Bronca have inherited a family winemaking tradition that was inaugurated almost a century ago by their grandfather Martino. The production manager is Piero Balcon, Antonella's husband, now flanked by Ersiliana's young daughter Elisa, an enologist, in the cellar.

VINEYARDS - The main body of vineyards is situated at Rua di Feletto, where mainly red grapes are grown. The glera grapes come from numerous parcels on the steep slopes round Colbertaldo, particularly the historic Particella 68, a very old, very steep, well-positioned, well-ventilated vineyard. Piero, a tireless winemaker, has established organic cultivation everywhere, respecting the rhythms and the needs of the vineyards, not to mention the biodiversity of the surrounding countryside.

WINES - The Proseccos are made with the technique of secondary fermentation with the addition of must, which gives them greater fragrance. As wines like the assertive, taut and citrussy **Valdobbiadene Prosecco Sup. Brut 2012** (○ 109,000 bt) and the softer, caressing **Valdobbiadene Prosecco Sup. Extra Dry 2012** (○ 107,000 bt) prove. **Valdobbiadene Prosecco Sup. Brut Particella 68 2012** (○ 11,200 bt) explodes with fresh ripe fruit on the nose, following up with perfectly balanced, tangy deep palate with luscious juiciness. **Colli di Conegliano Rosso Ser Bele 2010** (● cabernet sauvignon and cabernet franc, merlot, marzemino; 3,800 bt) displays its usual elegance ad texture.

FERTILIZERS natural manure, green manure
PLANT PROTECTION copper and sulphur
WEED CONTROL mechanical
YEASTS selected, native
GRAPES 100% estate-grown
CERTIFICATION converting to organics

FRIULI VENEZIA GIULIA

Last year we related the difficulties many Friulan producers spoke to us about when we visited them at their cellars. The problem was climate change which, in 2011 and 2012, had brought summers with very high temperatures and no rain.

We also explained how all this had been evident in our tastings of wines from the 2011 harvest, generally unaromatic and alcoholic without the complexity of taste that prolongs length in the mouth.

Our tastings of the 2012 wines suggest that producers have found rapid solutions to the problem of climatic "upheaval", submitting wines that were aromatically well-defined with just the right amount of alcohol. All in all, they treated us to a fine display of professionalism and skill in managing the agronomic side of their work.

It was decided that from now on the Colli Orientali del Friuli —for convenience, traditionally abbreviated as COF — will be called Friuli Colli Orientali. In this way the name is brought into line with most of the region's other denominations, which always put "Friuli" in front of the specific local areas. For a certain period of time producers will be able to opt for one or the other, after which Friuli Colli Orientali will become compulsory. To avoid confusion, in this guide we have decided to use the term Friuli Colli Orientali, abbreviated as FCO, for all the labels in question.

snails 🐌

105	MEROI
105	MIANI
108	I CLIVI
109	LE DUE TERRE
110	RONCO DEL GNEMIZ
111	VIGNAI DA DULINE
113	BORGO SAN DANIELE
113	EDI KEBER
115	KANTE
115	SKERK
116	ZIDARICH
116	GRAVNER
117	LA CASTELLADA
117	DAMIJAN PODVERSIC
118	RADIKON
119	SKERLJ

bottles 🍾

108	LE VIGNE DI ZAMÒ
109	AQUILA DEL TORRE
111	VOLPE PASINI
114	RONCO DEL GELSO
114	VENICA & VENICA
118	VIE DI ROMANS
119	ZUANI

coins €

106	PAOLO RODARO
106	SIRCH
107	CANUS
107	GIGANTE
110	VISTORTA

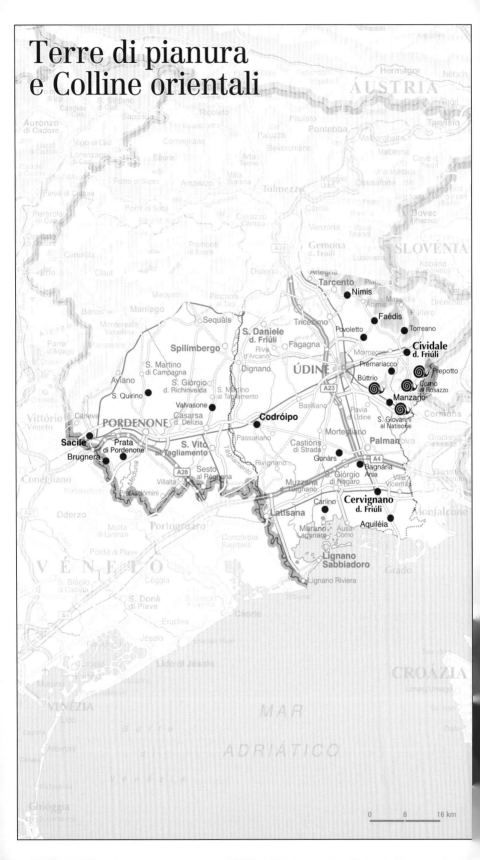

Terre di pianura
e Colline orientali

Meroi

Via Stretta, 6 B
tel. 0432 674025
www.meroidavino.com
info@meroidavino.com

Miani

Via Peruzzi, 10
tel. 0432 674327

---

15 ha - 30,000 bt

" Father and son team Paolo and Damiano Meroi are the team behind this small cellar, which they run efficiently and with passion. No wonder it's known and respected in every corner of the world in which the culture of fine wine is strong. "

PEOPLE - The high standard of quality and drinkability of all the labels is a guarantee for those on the lookout for deep, richly complex wines. Heirs to a family tradition of wine-growing, the Merois are assisted in the vineyards and in the cellar by the experienced and helpful Mirko Degan.

VINEYARDS - Where necessary systemic treatments are carried out to avoid passing too often between the vine rows in the wet, which would compress the soil and risk asphyxiating the roots. Low yields and painstaking care for the single vines make for great grapes, from numerous, diversified clones, in the cellar.

WINES - The measured use of the finest French oak adds just the right personality and life to the wines. The sublimely recognizable **FCO Refosco P.R. Vigna Dominin 2010** (● 1,800 bt) is compact, commendably self-assured and full of grip with a bouquet of red berries. The heftier, more tannic **FCO Merlot Vigna Dominin 2010** (● 1,500 bt), packed with balsamic notes, will take longer to develop, but with appropriate bottle-aging it will pull out all the eloquence of a vintage as tough as it is intriguing. We thoroughly enjoyed our tasting of **FCO Verduzzo Friulano 2011** (○ 600 bt), a great rendering of a delicate grape: thanks to unpronounced sweetness, it has subtle progression, elegance and fluency.

---

13 ha - 11,500 bt

" The name Miani means more than premium labels highly prized in every corner of the planet. It also stands for a man and a lifetime totally dedicated to his vineyards in an all-embracing rapport of love and profound respect. "

PEOPLE - Enzo Pontoni embarked on his adventure in the early 1990s, when he started working his mother Edda Miani's vineyards, few that they were. In a short space of time, without seeking the limelight, he was to become one of the world's best known and loved Friulan producers.

VINEYARDS - Enzo oversees a vast number of small vineyards, especially at Buttrio, where the Vigna delle Zitelle property is now taking shape, much to the delight not only of Enzo himself but also of his friend and colleague Paolo Meroi. He also owns a four-hectare vineyard at Rosazzo and another, on a very steep slope, at Corno di Rosazzo. Enzo spends an inordinate amount of time out in the country, adopting methods that are practically organic with great care and attention.

WINES - Vinifications are performed vineyard by vineyard exclusively in small wood casks. 2012 was a warm growing year, which meant that some major labels had to be shelved. **FCO Friulano 2012** (○ 2,600 bt) has a palate that is at once linear, almost sharp, and weighty, complex and tremendously rich in flavor. Yet even more complex is **FCO Friulano Filip 2012** (○ 1,000 bt), outstandingly elegant and minerally. **FCO Sauvignon 2012** (○ 900 bt), made with the grapes earmarked for Banel and Saurint, neither of which was produced, has intact fruit and creamy flesh without any vegetal notes. The uber-stylish **FCO Chardonnay 2012** (○ 600 bt) is arguably the best of the bunch by virtue of its long, overwhelming progression on the palate.

FERTILIZERS manure pellets, natural manure
PLANT PROTECTION chemical, copper and sulphur
WEED CONTROL mechanical
YEASTS selected
GRAPES 100% estate-grown
CERTIFICATION none

FERTILIZERS natural manure
PLANT PROTECTION copper and sulphur
WEED CONTROL mechanical
YEASTS selected, native
GRAPES 100% estate-grown
CERTIFICATION none

Paolo Rodaro

Località Spessa
Via Cormons, 60
tel. 0432 716066
www.rodaropaolo.it
info@rodaropaolo.it

Sirch

Via Fornalis, 277
tel. 0432 709835
www.sirchwine.com
info@sirchwine.com

50 ha - 200,000 bt · **10% discount**

25 ha - 150,000 bt

PEOPLE - The first vineyards were bought in 1967 by Edo and Gigi, the father and uncle of Paolo Rodaro. All descend from a family that has been farming in the area since the mid 19th century or thereabouts. After buying 26 hectares of land from Conte Romano in 2002, Paolo is now the sole owner of a total of 121 hectares, 50 of which are vineyards that he manages personally. His is, de facto, one of the vastest wine estates in Friuli.

VINEYARDS - The company applies conventional viticulture sensibly and conscientiously with a short production chain, renewable energy and eco-sustainability. More specifically, it and another 12 in the Colli Orientali del Friuli zone are taking part in the Perleuve-coordinated VTS project, designed to replace anti-botrytis sprays and chemical insecticides and reduce treatments to a bare minimum.

WINES - We recommend **FCO Pignolo Romain 2007** (O 6,000 bt) which, albeit made with grapes over-ripened on the vine, is nonetheless well-balanced with contained juicy extracts. It's a wine full of energy, from the bouquet of black berries to the pleasantly dry palate, on which alcoholic and tannic astringency comes to the fore. Of the whites, we enjoyed the terroir-dedicated FCO Friulano 2012 (O 40,000 bt), deeming it worthy of the Everyday Wine symbol. The nose has typical, buttery aromas, while the palate stands out for its coherent, fluid drinkability. The finish is vegetal and recalls the grape's relationship with sauvignon. The well-conceived stylish and delicate **FCO Malvasia 2012** (O 4,000 bt) is wonderfully creamy and elegant. Worth buying too is **FCO Picolit 2010** (O 1,000 bt), well-integrated by welcome freshness.

PEOPLE - In the 1980s, the Sirchs used to produce wine to sell unbottled (a taglietti, in the local dialect) in their bar in Cividale. It was in 2002 that brothers Luca and Pierpaolo began bottling. On that occasion they released 8,000 bottles but since then they have made huge bounds forward. They recently charged the Campanian group, Feudi di San Gregorio, of which Pierpaolo is CEO, with the distribution of their wines.

VINEYARDS - The vineyards are split into small plots between Prepotto, Cladrecis e Gramogliano, zones with different soil and weather conditions. Piepaolo, also co-founder of an important agronomic consultancy company called Preparatori d'Uva, respects these conditions with optimal vineyard management. The farmers from whom the company buys a small percentage of its grapes work in accordance with the same philosophy.

WINES - Luca's work in the cellar can be summed up as the pursuit of freshness, cleanness and varietal consistency. The standard of all the wines tasted was good, and the whites stood out in particular. Two of them achieved outstanding levels: **FCO Malvasia 2012** (O 5,300 bt) is pleasingly spicy, well-balanced and long, **FCO Pinot Grigio 2012** (O 26,000 bt) is blossomy and fruity with nice complexity and freshness in the glass. Better still is FCO Friulano 2012 (O 27,000 bt), which has citrussy notes fused with pennyroyal and rosemary; warm on the palate with assertive acidity and flavor, it's a Great Wine. **FCO Ribolla Gialla 2012** (O 19,000 bt) and **FCO Sauvignon 2012** (O 20,000 bt) are both beautifully textured, the second standing out for its aromatic finesse and pleasant tanginess.

FERTILIZERS organic-mineral, mineral, manure pellets, natural manure, green manure
PLANT PROTECTION chemical, copper and sulphur
WEED CONTROL chemical, mechanical
YEASTS selected
GRAPES 100% estate-grown
CERTIFICATION none

FERTILIZERS organic-mineral, natural manure, green manure
PLANT PROTECTION chemical, copper and sulphur
WEED CONTROL mechanical
YEASTS selected
GRAPES 10% bought in
CERTIFICATION none

CORNO DI ROSAZZO (UD)

Canus

Via Gramogliano, 21
tel. 0432 759427
www.canus.it
info@canus.it

CORNO DI ROSAZZO (UD)

Gigante

Via Rocca Bernarda, 3
tel. 0432 755835
www.adrianogigante.it
info@adrianogigante.it

9 ha - 45,000 bt   **10% discount**

PEOPLE - The company's visiting card is more like a picture postcard. It sits on a hilltop surrounded by a landscape of vineyards, winding roads, expanses of woodland to the north inhabited by wildlife, and Monte Matajur, still capped with snow on the day of our visit. The owner Dario Rossetto oversees the cellar while his "teammate", the personable Simone Desabbata manages the vineyards.

VINEYARDS - This is the first year of conversion to organics. Under-vine weed control has been abandoned and now the low spurred cordon-trained vines will require more attention if they are to withstand pressure from the environment. The new challenge necessitates a change in habits and likely, as Simone points out, machinery to mole-plow and turn over the soil as the tractor will be passing more frequently than before.

WINES - At the forefront in our tastings was the new, very reasonably priced Ronco del Gris line, the average quality of which is more than satisfactory. In particular, we recommend the excellent *Pinot Grigio Ronco del Gris 2012* (O 3,000 bt). This delightful Everyday Wine has has intense aromas with delicate spiciness and green grassy nuances. The bright and breezy palate has amazingly broad, rich and fruity after-aromas. The enjoyable **Bianco Flôr di Cuâr Ronco del Gris 2012** (O friulano; 1,200) is characterized by a minerally bouquet with notes of candied fruit. Of the same high standard but slightly simpler is **Chardonnay Ronco del Gris 2012** (O 1,300 bt). The star of the traditional line, **Ribolla Gialla di Rosazzo 2012** (O 3,500 bt), is discreetly vertical despite its hefty alcohol component.

25 ha - 110,000 bt

PEOPLE - Adriano Gigante is a winemaker's winemaker, passionate about his work, to which he brings all the old traditional know-how handed down to him by past generations, especially his grandfather Ferruccio, founder of the company in 1957. Inspired by contacts with other producers and farmers, Adriano has developed a contemporary winery in which quality viticulture with low environmental impact embraces a concept of tourist hospitality based on sustainability.

VINEYARDS - Twenty-five hectares of land are planted on the ponca terraces of the hill of Rocca Bernarda. Adriano has stopped using chemical weedkillers and concerns himself increasingly with the health of the soil, the main factor for the quality of the vine. This is wonderful winegrowing land, especially the vineyard inherited from Ferruccio, which is almost a hundred years old.

WINES - The winery's cult label, FCO Friulano Vigneto Storico 2012 (O 10,000 bt) stole the limelight once more. Its spacious, soft attack is immediately infused with a very delicate, palate-refreshing streak of tanginess. It's a very well-balanced Great Wine, muscular but also stylish and deep. It pips to the post its "big brother" **FCO Friulano 2012** (O 15,000 bt), which has a slightly different style: equally full-favored, it has a leaner, less deep structure with a dry, taut finish and pleasing aromas of ripe fruit and bitter almonds. **FCO Sauvignon 2012** (O 15,000 bt) has extremely varietal aromas with distinct hints of tomato leaf and sage and keeps the same tone on the palate.

FERTILIZERS organic-mineral, manure pellets, natural manure
PLANT PROTECTION copper and sulphur
WEED CONTROL mechanical
YEASTS selected
GRAPES 10% bought in
CERTIFICATION converting to organics

FERTILIZERS organic-mineral, natural manure
PLANT PROTECTION chemical, copper and sulphur
WEED CONTROL mechanical
YEASTS selected
GRAPES 100% estate-grown
CERTIFICATION none

CORNO DI ROSAZZO (UD)

I Clivi

Località Gramogliano, 20
tel. 328 7269979
www.clivi.it
iclivi@gmail.com

MANZANO (UD)

Le Vigne di Zamò

Località Rosazzo
Via Abate Corrado, 4
tel. 0432 759693
www.levignedizamo.com
info@levignedizamo.com

10 ha - 40,000 bt	10% discount

67 ha - 250,000 bt	10% discount

66 "In the cellar you work with what you've got. Any complexity comes from the grapes themselves". These few words suffice to explain the virtuous idea of wine and winemaking that the Zanussos have in mind. 99

PEOPLE - Ferdinando Zanusso developed his knowledge of wine doing a job that often took him to France, where he sampled labels from every terroir. Hence his own personal idea of wine which, suitably adapted to his own area, he has passed on to his son and long-time collaborator Mario. The resulting wines are moderate on alcohol, savory and mineral.

VINEYARDS - Barring the ribolla vineyard, all the others have high average ages and grow old clones. The extreme naturalness of the growing methods adopted and the lovely landscape are worth the winding hillside drive it takes to get to them. The old double-arched cane plantings of tocai friulano are, in a word, monumental. In the Collio district the Brazzan vineyard is also hard to reach on account of its steepness.

WINES - In the cellar spontaneous fermentations, low temperatures and non-induced malolactic fermentations are de rigueur. The resulting wines are extremely dry, lean, well-balanced and devoid of gratuitous concentration. **Collio Bianco Clivi Brazan 2001** (O friulano, malvasia istriana; 6,500 bt) offers a broad suite of aromas and prolonged bottle-aging makes it a wine of great complexity and lively acid sinew. The rich texture of **Collio Malvasia Vigna 80 anni 2011** (O 3,000 bt) on the palate detracts nothing from its stunning brightness and style.

vino slow **FCO FRIULANO CLIVI GALEA 2011** (O 3,500 bt) Yet another impressive version of the label. A subtle, stylish wine, linear and complete, with an intriguingly dry palate and great richness of flavor.

PEOPLE - The Zamò family entered the Friuli wine world in 1978. It was then that the late Tullio bought the first hectares of vineyard at Ipplis, before going on, despite ups and downs, to extend his property and become a leading player on the scene. Today the company is in the capable hands of his sons Pierluigi and Silvano, joint-owners with Oscar Farinetti's Eataly group. Adriano Qualizza is the vineyard manager, Alberto Toso the cellar manager.

VINEYARDS - The property is split up into three main estates: the historic Vigna del Leon, over 30 years old, between Ipplis and Rocca Bernarda, where the old sauvignon, malvasia and pinot bianco vineyards grow on a hilltop characterized by a considerable temperature range; the youngest vineyards which surround the cellar, a stone's throw from the Abbey of Rosazzo; the five-hectare red grape vineyard at Buttrio. Great care is taken in the vineyard to avoid the useless and damaging recourse to chemicals.

WINES - The superb **FCO Merlot Vigne Cinquant'anni 2009** (● 5,000 bt) is a red of great texture and character with eloquent fruit and soft, caressing tannins. Citrussy and taut, **FCO Friulano Vigne Cinquant'anni 2011** (O 7,500 bt) is lighter-bodied than usual. **FCO Friulano 2012** (O 13,300 bt) is extremely fresh and piquant with a full, balsamic palate, enhanced by a typically almondy finish. The delicately varietal **FCO Sauvignon 2012** (O 12,000 bt) is supple and rich on the palate with a nice encore of citrus fruit.

vino slow **COF ROSAZZO BIANCO RONCO DELLE ACACIE 2010** (O chardonnay, friulano; 9,800 bt) An oxidative maturing wine of great stylishness and sumptuous silkiness, blossomy and delicate, subtle and deep. A historic label for a Friulan wine that smacks of Burgundy.

FERTILIZERS none
PLANT PROTECTION copper and sulphur
WEED CONTROL mechanical
YEASTS native
GRAPES 100% estate-grown
CERTIFICATION organic

FERTILIZERS manure pellets, humus
PLANT PROTECTION copper and sulphur, organic
WEED CONTROL mechanical
YEASTS selected
GRAPES 100% estate-grown
CERTIFICATION none

POVOLETTO (UD)

Aquila del Torre

Frazione Savorgnano del Torre
Via Attimis, 25
tel. 0432 666428
www.aquiladeltorre.it
info@aquiladeltorre.it

18 ha - 50,000 bt — **10% discount**

PEOPLE - Brother and sister Michele and Francesca work in a corner of paradise, their "office" consisting of due south-facing ridges terraced with vineyards and offering a view over the whole of Friuli. Here are the company headquarters and the cellar built by their father Claudio Ciani. Francesca, the sales manager, also runs the b&b. Michele works in the vineyard and the cellar in collaboration with the experienced consultant agronomist Andrea Pittana.

VINEYARDS - The vineyards are unique in the Friuli region: a single plot of 20 hectares with vine rows up to a kilometer in length. The terraces were built following rational analysis of the technical machinery available on the market. Moving from the bottom upwards we find sauvignon, then refosco at the center, where the heat is concentrated, and, at the top, picolit and riesling. In this final section of the vineyard, temperatures may swing by 20°C in the course of a single day.

WINES - The cellar is spacious and the red grapes follow a different path to white ones, which constitute the majority. Since the 2012 harvest, all have fermented spontaneously with native yeasts. **FCO Friulano AT 2012** (O 8,000 bt) is enjoyable and delicate; its sappiness is accompanied by freshness and pressure and the palate closes on an intriguing creamy note. The grape variety is immediately recognizable in **FCO Picolit 2011** (O 1,500 bt), which has honey on the nose, its sweetness braced by welcome freshness. Impressive too is the dry, grassy **Oasi 2011** (O picolit; 1,300 bt), drinkable from the first sip with a stylish toastiness that will help it to grow. **FCO Sauvignon Blanc AT 2012** (O 8,000 bt) is packed with personality and rich in texture.

FERTILIZERS natural manure, compost
PLANT PROTECTION copper and sulphur
WEED CONTROL mechanical
YEASTS native
GRAPES 100% estate-grown
CERTIFICATION converting to organics

PREPOTTO (UD)

Le Due Terre

Via Roma, 68 B
tel. 0432 713189
fortesilvana@libero.it

5 ha - 18,000 bt

66 Want to know the secret of this wonderful winery? The answer is that, while to staying extremely busy and dynamic, it has never changed dimension and modus operandi. 99

PEOPLE - Silvana Forte and Flavio Basilicata's adventure began in the 1990s when they got together and shared their passion for wine. Since then they have accumulated experience and developed their ideas, though their initial style and rigor have remained intact. Today their daughter is playing an increasingly active role in the business.

VINEYARDS - The vine rows run along the small terraces that wind up to the hilltop on which the house-cum-cellar stands. On one side the soil is red, on the other marly. It is this sharp difference in the space of just a few meters that inspired the cellar's name, which means "Two Soils". Viticultural techniques are basic and no fertilizers, herbicides or insecticides are used, everything being left to observation, timely manual intervention and respect for nature.

WINES - Interventions are kept to a minimum in the cellar too: meaning spontaneous fermentations, sulphur additions only at bottling, no clarification, only light filtration. Austere but by no means short on softness, **FCO Merlot 2011** (● 3,000 bt) has a bouquet of ripe fruit and a beautifully creamy palate. **FCO Rosso Sacrisassi 2011** (● 7,000 bt) blends the roughest, most austere traits of refosco with the spicy elegance of schioppettino and offers a stylish, measured, infinitely toothsome palate.

vino slow FCO BIANCO SACRISASSI 2011 (O friulano, ribolla gialla; 5,000 bt) A blend of friulano and ribolla gialla grapes with a very strong sense of place. Refined and subtle on the nose, it explodes in the mouth with massive minerality, without losing any of its elegant, aristocratic style.

FERTILIZERS none
PLANT PROTECTION copper and sulphur
WEED CONTROL mechanical
YEASTS native
GRAPES 100% estate-grown
CERTIFICATION none

Vistorta €

Via Vistorta, 82
tel. 0434 71135
www.vistorta.it
vistorta@vistorta.it

Ronco del Gnemiz

Via Ronchi, 5
tel. 0432 756238
www.roncodelgnemiz.com
serena@roncodelgnemiz.com

---

80 ha - 200,000 bt | **10% discount**

PEOPLE - The winery of Count Brandolino Brandolini d'Adda has been in his family for more than two centuries. Today it is run by Alec Ongaro, the production manager, in collaboration with the French enologist Samuel Tinon. The wines are French in style too, reminiscent of those of Bordeaux, where the count used to own Chateau Greysac, an important step in his training and experience.

VINEYARDS - The winery is shared between two companies: Vistorta, which owns 34 hectares of Guyot- and spurred cordon-trained vines of merlot from different French clones; Conte Brandolini, on whose 44 hectare the other grape varieties are grown. The management of the vines, which grow on clayey, pebbly soil, and of other crops, is organically certified.

WINES - The white grapes come from Conte Brandolini, on the border with Veneto. Classic vinification and bottling by growing year make for fresh, vigorous wines. One such is **Friuli Grave Friulano 2012** (O 13,000 bt), golden in color with notes of powdered chamomile, dried flowers and interesting acidity and flavor which add depth and linearity. Also full-bodied ad full-flavored is **Friuli Grave Chardonnay 2012** (O 17,500 bt), which has citrussy fragrance and a dynamic palate. The excellent Friuli Grave Sauvignon 2012 (O 20,000 bt) is pervaded by classic hints of tomato leaf with subtle nuances of oranges and lemons — a beautifully supple and satisfying Everyday Wine. Class and elegance denote **Friuli Grave Merlot Vistorta 2010** (● 13,000 bt), produced with grapes from Vistorta, just outside Sacile. A full-bodied distinctly Bordeaux-style wine.

14 ha - 25,000 bt

❝ Serena and Christian are true stewards of their land. They tread and respect it every day, happy to receive whatever nature yields and capable of translating every positive nuance into wine. **❞**

PEOPLE - Partners in life, Serena Palazzolo and Christian Patat are the untiring driving force behind this historic cellar, which looks onto the Abbey of Rosazza. Set up by the Palazzolo family in the 1960s, the business was taken over by Serena in the mid 1990s.

VINEYARDS - When we made our visit, the vineyards were all standing in grass and completely waterlogged. We were forced to zigzag among the vine rows, where the cellar's favorite grape, sauvignon, prevails, to a jazz-like rhythm. Mechanical weed control operations were hard to carry out in a wet start to the season. But eventually everything was to return spick and span, with one bunch per shoot on the red vines and two per shoot on the white.

WINES - After tasting the classics from 2011 for the last edition of this guide, this year we sampled the Sol and Peri selections. The highly concentrated **FCO Sauvignon Peri 2011** (O 5,000 bt) has a spacious, complex nose and a layered fruity flavor with delicate aromatic undertones. In the fullness of time the wine's delicacy and spiciness, devoid of vegetal notes, will make it even more exciting to drink. The stylish **FCO Chardonnay Sol 2011** (O 5,000 bt) and warm **FCO Sauvignon Sol 2011** (O 5,000 bt), both young and promising, are more clenched wines.

> **vino slow** **FCO BIANCO SAN ZUAN SOL 2011** (O friulano; 5,000 bt) Pleasantly citrussy on the nose, where elegant nuances fuse with attractive notes of oak, taut and nicely refreshing on the palate, a wine that is the result of well-gauged vinification.

FERTILIZERS manure pellets, natural manure, compost
PLANT PROTECTION copper and sulphur
WEED CONTROL mechanical
YEASTS selected
GRAPES 100% estate-grown
CERTIFICATION organic

FERTILIZERS natural manure, compost, biodynamic preparations
PLANT PROTECTION copper and sulphur
WEED CONTROL mechanical
YEASTS selected
GRAPES 100% estate-grown
CERTIFICATION biodynamic, organic

Vignai da Duline 🐌

SAN GIOVANNI AL NATISONE (UD)

Località Villanova
Via IV Novembre, 136
tel. 0432 758115
www.vignaidaduline.com
info@vignaidaduline.com

8 ha - 22,000 bt

66 For Lorenzo and Federica winemaking is first and foremost a "political project" and, secondly, a form of art, seen as the active and dialectic contemplation of nature based on solid agronomic bases. 99

PEOPLE - It was a decision made with the heart that led Lorenzo Mocchiutti and his partner Federica Magrini to dedicate their life project to the land in 1997.

VINEYARDS - Besides the two hectares dating from the 1920s that he inherited from his grandfather Lorenzo also oversees the Ronco Pitotti vineyard — a six-hectare organic bijou bounded by woodland in the hills near Manzano — entrusted to him by his friend Francesco Valori in 2001. The watchword is total respect for the land, the aim being to preserve its microbiological fertility and transmit its essence to the wine.

WINES - We predict a great future for **Morus Nigra 2011** (● refosco; 2,000 bt), characterized by pronounced fruitiness, velvety tannins and excellent cleanness. We suggest waiting a few years to enjoy this great interpretation of refosco at its best. **FCO Chardonnay Ronco Pitotti 2011** (○ 2,200 bt) is balanced and complex.

vino slow MORUS ALBA **2011** (○ 2,950 bt) As Federica says, this wine is "a balancing act not only between different grapes but also between different terrains". It's made with 60 per cent malvasia istriana grapes from Duline and 40 per cent grapes from an old sauvignon clone in Ronco Pitotti. Aged separately in barriques, the two grapes combine to offer stylish aromas and a splendidly mineral palate.

FERTILIZERS none
PLANT PROTECTION copper and sulphur
WEED CONTROL mechanical
YEASTS native
GRAPES 100% estate-grown
CERTIFICATION organic

Volpe Pasini

TORREANO (UD)

Frazione Togliano
Via Cividale, 16
tel. 0432 715151
www.volpepasini.net
info@volpepasini.it

52 ha - 400,000 bt   **10% discount**

PEOPLE - Volpe Pasini is a historic name in Friuli winemaking. The family sold the company, complete with cellar and vineyards, in the mid 1990s to Emilio Rotolo, a Calabrian doctor who, with characteristic passion, energy and insight, revamped its production and image. Today Dr Rotolo is assisted by his son Francesco. Over the last two harvests the company has developed a new productive approach thanks to enologist Lorenzo Landi, who has improved the quality and character of the wines.

VINEYARDS - The vineyards are scattered around the area. Especially worthy of note are Zuc, a splendid terraced, south-facing amphitheater, and the imposing Prepotto, where the red grapes ripen. The viticulture practiced is attentive and meticulous with much mechanization to permit prompt and effective interventions in the vineyard

WINES - Two brands stand out above the others: Zuc di Volpe is reserved to the most prized labels, Villa to the more economical line. Towering above the rest is **FCO Sauvignon Zuc di Volpe 2012** (○ 11,000 bt), recherché and recognizable in style, with huge richness and complexity on the nose and a linear, juicy, tangy palate. It's already a Great Wine and will grow even greater with time. As always, **FCO Pinot Bianco Zuc di Volpe 2012** (○ 10,000 bt) is a wine of consummate elegance, subtle on the nose with a silky, deep palate. The excellent **COF Pinot Grigio Zuc di Volpe 2012** (○ 13,000 bt) is endowed with rich, full-flavored, zesty fruitiness and good grip. All the labels in the more economical range are well-crafted. We recommend **FCO Sauvignon 2012** (○ 22,000 bt), juicy, varietal and quaffable, and **FCO Merlot Togliano 2010** (● 36,000 bt), which has fresh fruit and a soft finish.

FERTILIZERS natural manure
PLANT PROTECTION chemical, copper and sulphur, organic
WEED CONTROL chemical, mechanical
YEASTS selected
GRAPES 100% estate-grown
CERTIFICATION none

Collio, Isonzo e Carso

Borgo San Daniele

Via San Daniele, 16
tel. 0481 60552
www.borgosandaniele.it
info@borgosandaniele.it
⌐0

Edi Keber

Località Zegla, 17
tel. 0481 61184
edi.keber@virgilio.it
⌐0

---

18 ha - 56,000 bt | **10% discount**

❝ Brother and sister Alessandra and Mauro Mauri inherited their land from their grandfather in 1990. They were young then and full of enthusiasm. With their heads filled with projects for the future, they behave as if they still are today. **❞**

PEOPLE - Mauro monitors production from the vineyard to the cellar, while Alessandra supervises administration and communication. Together they have created a winery with a precise local identity.

VINEYARDS - The vineyards are situated mainly in the Cormons portion of the Isonzo DOC zone. Over the years the Mauris have restructured, extended and replanted them in accordance with the principles of high-quality agriculture and with full respect for the health of the soil (plus a few biodynamic practices): meaning dense plantings, low yields, and treatments with sulphur, copper and nothing else. Organic certification is now on its way.

WINES - Mauro wants to improve the terroir and make human intervention in the wine less evident so that each single year has its own identity. The whites from 2011 are more concentrated and ostentatious than the more expressive 2010, but possess a lot of naturalness. On its debut the new **Friuli Isonzo Malvasia 2011** (○ 7,000 bt) stands out for its aromas of wisteria and a stylish palate with salty tones. **Friuli Isonzo Pinot Grigio 2011** (○ 13,000 bt) is a classic for style and flavor. **Arbis Ros 2007** (● 10,000 bt) is no longer a cuvèe but is made with 100 per cent pignolo: gritty, deep and austere, it needs more time in the bottle to give of its best.

> **vino slow** **FRIULI ISONZO FRIULANO 2011** (○ 13,000 bt) Somewhat slow to open out, the wine proceeds to give itself totally, with complex aromas and a splendidly rounded palate, to the drinker who is patient enough to wait for it.

12 ha - 50,000 bt | **10% discount**

❝ Edi Keber deserves a round of applause for the team spirit he has brought to the area, but also for the awareness he has instilled about work in the vineyard: he has shown that every action taken reverberates in the surrounding environment. **❞**

PEOPLE - A border winemaker who knows no boundaries, Edi has achieved goals and taken decisions innovative for the Collio district. Today his forward-looking vision has been inherited and carried on by his talented son Kristian.

VINEYARDS - Looking from the valley floor towards the cellar, the gaze takes in the malvasia vineyards below, then the tocai and finally the ribolla. In these hillside vineyards, the Kebers work with a canola oil-fueled tractor and atomizers that salvage and recycle treatments. "The vineyard shouldn't be a garden," warns Kristian during our visit, but you can see a special touch: the balance between grapes and leaves demonstrates the harmony of the vines.

WINES - The name of Edi Keber is well-known, associated in the wine world and beyond with the tocai friulano grape. Seventy per cent of his cellar's vineyards derive from clones, some from the Rolat wine district and others from the vines that used to be Stanislao Keber's. Today Edi and Kristian are busy getting the best out of the terroir through its native grape varieties. For some years now they have produced only one wine, a perfect emblem of the area. A postcard from Zegla with a sunny 2012 postmark.

> **vino slow** **COLLIO BIANCO 2012** (○ 50,000 bt) Made with friulano, ribolla gialla and malvasia istriana grapes, all fermented in traditional cement tanks. Terroir, vinification and must selection are interconnected. The nose releases a elegant bouquet of fragrances, the palate is complex, stylish, well-rounded and full of flavor.

FERTILIZERS natural manure, humus
PLANT PROTECTION copper and sulphur
WEED CONTROL mechanical
YEASTS native
GRAPES 100% estate-grown
CERTIFICATION converting to organics

FERTILIZERS natural manure, none
PLANT PROTECTION copper and sulphur
WEED CONTROL mechanical
YEASTS selected
GRAPES 100% estate-grown
CERTIFICATION converting to organics

Ronco del Gelso

CORMONS (GO)

Via Isonzo,117
tel. 0481 61310
www.roncodelgelso.com
info@roncodelgelso.com

25 ha - 150,000 bt

PEOPLE - Giorgio Badin is a living testimony to the fact that commitment, talent and consistency ultimately produce results. Over the last 20 years or so, this vigneron has turned the two hectares of his family's small winery into 25, making the place one of the best-known and admired in the Isonzo area. Recently, he has also installed a photovoltaic plant and a heating system fueled by vine shoots in the cellar.

VINEYARDS - A great connoisseur of the local area, Giorgio made his dream come true by planting vines on every piece of free land he could find round the town of Cormons. His 25 hectares are thus a mosaic in which he knows every shade and tiles by heart. The single plots are well kept and easily recognizable by the uniformity of the training systems and the alternation of grassed and harrowed vine rows.

WINES - Quality at a more than reasonable price — this is Giorgio's reward for his obsessive pursuit of the perfect wine. Intriguing, albeit not particularly complex aromas of peach and apricot characterize **Friuli Isonzo Pinot Bianco 2012** (O 5,000 bt), together with a palate with nice grip and acid thrust. **Friuli Isonzo Rive Alte Sauvignon Sottomonte 2012** (O 26,000 bt) seduces the nose with aromas of panettone and raisins, while the well-balanced, honey-flavored palate makes it a good dessert wine. Also valid is **Friuli Isonzo Friulano Toc Bas 2012** (O 33,000 bt), which has an intriguing attack on the nose. Though the palate is slightly less lively than in previous versions, the price it has paid for a long hot summer, it's an enjoyable tipple just the same.

FERTILIZERS organic-mineral, mineral, manure pellets, biodynamic preparations, humus
PLANT PROTECTION chemical, copper and sulphur, organic
WEED CONTROL chemical, mechanical
YEASTS selected
GRAPES 100% estate-grown
CERTIFICATION none

Venica & Venica

DOLEGNA DEL COLLIO (GO)

Località Cerò, 8
tel. 0481 61264
www.venica.it
venica@venica.it

37 ha - 262,000 bt

PEOPLE - The Venica family began making wine in 1930 when they bought a farm and the vineyards round it at Dolegna. Since then production has grown in size and quality and now their winery is known the world over. Today brothers Gianni and Giorgio oversee the vineyards and the cellar respectively, while Gianni's dynamic wife Ornella devotes herself to corporate image work.

VINEYARDS - The vineyards extend over an area of a few square kilometers round the cellar: five large parcels on steep hillsides (whose denomination appears on the label) and three on the valley floor. The most closed-in, warm hollows have been earmarked for red grapes, the white ones growing in colder spots where day-to-night temperature swings are more pronounced. High-tech machinery optimizes Gianni's painstaking, meticulous approach to viticulture.

WINES - A range of top level wines with peaks of excellence here and there. Like **Collio Pinot Bianco 2012** (O 15,000 bt), whose style is as subtle and elegant as ever, all silky substance and assertive flavor. The same tone, though with greater grip and depth, is to be found in **Collio Friulano Ronco delle Cime 2012** (O 20,000 bt), delicate and caressing with hints of almond and fresh flowers. **Collio Sauvignon Ronco delle Mele 2011** (O 40,000 bt) keeps it customary style, with intense vegetal and citrussy notes lifting its contained, dynamic body. With its subtle, lingering fragrance, **Collio Malvasia 2012** (O 6,500 bt), is very pleasant indeed. Last but not least, the excellent **Refosco Bottaz 2010** (● 4,000 bt) is built on fresh, fulsome fruit refreshed by biting acidity, which enlivens and prolongs flavor.

FERTILIZERS mineral, natural manure
PLANT PROTECTION chemical, copper and sulphur
WEED CONTROL chemical, mechanical
YEASTS selected
GRAPES 100% estate-grown
CERTIFICATION none

Kante

Frazione San Pelagio
Località Prepotto, 1 A
tel. 040 200255
kante@kante.it

13 ha - 45,000 bt

66 Edi Kante is an artist without a school, without a patron. He responds only to his two inspiring muses; viticulture and enology. A rare connoisseur of the terroir and its potential, he has been in vineyards ever since he learned to walk. 99

PEOPLE - A visit to the cellar is an experience that won't leave you cold. Like a tasting of old vintages, yet to be released, that reveal the extraordinary qualities of an area, at once beautiful and impossible.

VINEYARDS - Every square meter of the vineyards has been clawed back from the wild, rugged Carso territory. But now the vines complement and enhance the landscape. The winery's 13 hectares, of which six are over the border in Slovenia, are managed with rare mastery and remarkable sensitivity when it comes to selecting the right varieties and interpreting them. Everything is in place, everything expresses the microclimatic characteristics of every clod of earth.

WINES - The cellar boasts a considerable historical memory. A perfect marriage between functionality and design, it is built 18 meters underground and houses minor treasures, there for the lucky visitor to discover. Both the base line and the reserves offer constant value for money. The pleasantly quaffable **M. Cl. Brut KK** (O chardonnay, malvasia) offers attractive notes of kefir and puff pastry, which combine beautifully with a very delicate perlage. We also had the pleasure to taste some very exciting new wines soon to be released. We recommend in particular the fantastic Sauvignon Riserva 2006!

> **vino slow** VITOVSKA VITIGNO ANTICO 2010 (O) One of the finest interpretations of Carso's great native grape: delicate and full of thrust with hints of citrus fruit and mint, it boasts a palate of great style and depth.

FERTILIZERS natural manure
PLANT PROTECTION copper and sulphur
WEED CONTROL mechanical
YEASTS selected
GRAPES 100% estate-grown
CERTIFICATION none

Skerk

Frazione San Pelagio
Località Prepotto, 20
tel. 040 200156
www.skerk.com
info@skerk.com

7 ha - 20,000 bt   **10% discount**

66 The sun is shining and Sandi Skerk is busy in the cellar. The atmosphere oozes spontaneity ad energy. Beyond the rock walls of the cellar one sees the sea, which has the appearance of cold marble pearled with condensation. It's here, among these "contrasts" that Sandi has shaped himself and shapes his wines. 99

PEOPLE - After graduating in engineering, he decided to go on cultivating the family vineyards, previously overseen by his father Boris. The small scale of the enterprise allows the family, who also run an osmiza, or farm shop, to follow every stage of production with due care and attention.

VINEYARDS - Sandi is a winegrower by choice. He has regenerated his family's vineyards, converting the 40-year-old pergolas to lower training systems and training the new ones with canopy-bush ones. Low temperatures in the flowering season have reduced the number of grapes, but emergency irrigation may not be necessary. Sandi has already halved the use of copper hydroxide and is now testing new anti-mildew products.

WINES - All the wines were aged for a year in oak barrels and casks, always in contact with noble sediments. After slow decanting through the winter, they were then bottled without clarification or filtration. **Terrano 2011** (● 3.000 bt) is scored by a vein of refreshing acidity.

> **vino slow** OGRADE 2011 (O vitovska, malvasia, sauvignon, pinot grigio; 6,000 bt) The nose is very well-rounded, packed with warmth and spiciness, infused with blossomy and marine undertones. The palate is lean-edged and forthright, balanced and braced by lively acidity. A wine that's already a pleasure to drink and will, we believe, complete its evolution in the years to come.

FERTILIZERS manure pellets, natural manure, green manure, humus
PLANT PROTECTION copper and sulphur, organic
WEED CONTROL mechanical
YEASTS native
GRAPES 100% estate-grown
CERTIFICATION organic

Zidarich

Frazione San Pelagio
Località Prepotto, 23
tel. 040 201223
www.zidarich.it
info@zidarich.it

8 ha - 28,000 bt

66 Artisan winemaker Benjanim Zidarich is firm believer in the specificity of the Carso and his small family cellars. Which is why he fights, day in, day out, to assert his values. 99

PEOPLE - Benjamin's adventure got underway when he began cultivating a half-hectare patch of vineyard. After which, with the tenacity and farsightedness typical of the area and its people, he built up this model winery. The view over the Gulf of Trieste from the terrace of the family osmiza is breathtaking.

VINEYARDS - The problems posed by winegrowing in the Carso are evident in the vineyard. Excessive red tape — six offices for a new vineyard against four for a new house! — is the most glaring of a whole mass of restrictions that prevent viticulture from growing. In Friuli Venezia Giulia it isn't as easy as it ought to be to replant old vineyards. And the problems are even greater on the steep slopes of the Carso ridge.

WINES - No fashions, just good, healthy products — these are Benjamin's principles, based on respect for the grape and minimum intrusion in the cycles of nature. The well-structured grape mix of **Prulke 2011** (O sauvignon, vitovska, malvasia; 4,500 bt) gives wonderfully clean flavors, rich in extract, aromatic herbs, and fresh and dried fruit, seducing the nose with faint nuances of violet and rhubarb. The vibrant **Vitovska 2011** (O 12,000 bt) is full of tannic weight and its lively nose develops after-aromas that range from ripe fruit to bitter orange, all enfolded by notes of incense.

vino slow **MALVASIA 2011** (O 5,000 bt) The juiciest of wines with a nose packed with fruit, sweet and fresh. The extremely deep palate reveals Carso limestone, lively tannins and a refreshing balsamic vein.

FERTILIZERS natural manure
PLANT PROTECTION copper and sulphur
WEED CONTROL mechanical
YEASTS native
GRAPES 100% estate-grown
CERTIFICATION none

Gravner

Frazione Oslavia
Località Lenzuolo Bianco, 9
tel. 0481 30882
www.gravner.it
info@gravner.it

16 ha - 38,000 bt

66 Ten years ago Luigi Veronelli said Josko Gravner was the best winemaker in the world. Josko must have taken him very seriously indeed, seeing how every day - since then, but obviously even before - he has done everything possible to make those words true. 99

PEOPLE - Josko Gravner's career has radically transformed the way people think about wine in Friuli and throughout the world. He began to make wine with his family's grapes at the age of 16. Photographs from the early 1980s show him standing beside his first stainless steel vats, in pictures from the 1990s he is bending over the barriques in which he used to age his Chardonnays and Sauvignon, lauded by international critics. Now he makes wine only in amphorae according to traditions whose roots are literally biblical.

VINEYARDS - Josko has phased out the grapes he regards as "extraneous". Today in his vineyards in Oslavia and Hum, in neighboring Slovenia, he cultivates just two historic native varieties: his beloved ribolla gialla and the red pignolo. For over 25 years he has never used chemical in his vineyards, which he works manually with a care that stems from his great sensitivity towards the overall health of the eocsystem.

WINES - In Josko's view, neither Breg 2006 nor Ribolla Gialla 2006 is ready yet, Pignolo still less so. This is why he is holding back the first tastings of the new vintages until the end of 2013. In the meantime, Breg Anfora 2005 and Ribolla Anfora 2005, still on sale, are maturing well in the bottle.

FERTILIZERS none
PLANT PROTECTION copper and sulphur
WEED CONTROL mechanical
YEASTS native
GRAPES 100% estate-grown
CERTIFICATION none

La Castellada

Località Oslavia, 1
tel. 0481 33670
nicolobensa@virgilio.it

Damijan Podversic

Via Brigata Pavia, 61
tel. 0481 78217
www.damijanpodversic.com
damijan.go@virgilio.it

---

10 ha - 25,000 bt

❝ La Castellada is the symbol of the simple, eventful story of a farming family in Oslavia. Anyone who says that "farmers never change" should go to the Bensas and ask them to tell it. ❞

PEOPLE - Like many other farms in the Collio district, La Castellada started out by producing unbottled wine for the family osteria. The first bottling began in 1985, but the real leap forward in quality dates to the 1990s, a period of great collective ferment in Oslavia. Nicolò Bensa, who set up the winery with his brother Giorgio, is now assisted by his son Stefano.

VINEYARDS - The vineyards are situated on either side of the ridge of the hill overlooking Oslavia. To the right, on the cooler, better located slope, the vineyards look across to Monte Sabatino and Slovenia. To the left small valleys descend to the plain and the sea. The vineyards have always been managed sustainably and the philosophy is to allow the grapes to ripen completely while maintaining levels of acidity that ensure assertive and long-living wines.

WINES - Minor adjustments in the cellar have made the aromas of recent vintages more delicate without detracting anything from Castellada's typically rounded style. **Collio Bianco 2008** (○ pinot grigio, chardonnay, sauvignon; 5,000 bt) is intense and leisurely, possibly more linear than the spectacular 2006, a well-crafted wine if ever there was one. The novelty this year is a long-macerated wine made with grapes from old vineyards: **Collio Bianco Riserva Vrh 2006** (○ chardonnay, sauvignon; 2,000 bt) shuns convention but rewards the attention it demands with complexity and huge personality.

> **vino slow** COLLIO SAUVIGNON 2008 (○ 2,000 bt) All the elegance of maceration. Hence a well-rounded, complex palate of white peach, candied fruit, mint and fennel.

FERTILIZERS manure pellets, green manure, humus
PLANT PROTECTION copper and sulphur
WEED CONTROL mechanical
YEASTS native
GRAPES 100% estate-grown
CERTIFICATION none

---

10 ha - 30,000 bt

❝ Let Damijan Podversic explain his three secrets for quality grapes: "Great seeds, great varieties, great soil". A mature grapeseed is the foundation for good tannins, grape skins for aroma. All the rest is hard work — always keeping an eye on the moon. ❞

PEOPLE - Damijan began working his father's vineyard when he was a slip of a lad, then moved on to vineyards of his own. Today he still has the same enthusiasm and tenacity as he had then.

VINEYARDS - The vines and the soil are impeccably looked after. The cellar's vineyard on Monte Calvario is surrounded by woodland and adopts the bush-training system on the canopies, which Damijan calls palmette. "We play second fiddle to nature," is his philosophy. Every 40 crates of select perfectly ripened white grapes, he sets off for the cellar in Scriò, where he ferments them on the skins.

WINES - For Damijan, "unless wine's great, you don't drink it". After three months' maceration in truncated cone-shaped vats the grapes are pressed, after which they are aged first on steel then in barrels and, finally, bottled. **Nekaj 2009** (○ friulano; 4,000 bt) is pleasant and juicy. **Malvasia 2009** (○ 4,000 bt) is young and muscular. **Kaplja 2009** (○ chardonnay, friulano, malvasia; 8,000 bt) is complex, dry, with good nose-palate consistency. It's worth taking note of the 2005, 2010 and 2012 vintages in which most wines were made from grapes with noble rot.

> **vino slow** RIBOLLA GIALLA 2009 (○ 8,000 bt) Yet another impeccable Ribolla: refreshing and flavorful with a tannic finish. Whether you uncork it immediately or leave it in the cellar, it's a wine not to be missed.

FERTILIZERS green manure, none
PLANT PROTECTION copper and sulphur
WEED CONTROL mechanical
YEASTS native
GRAPES 100% estate-grown
CERTIFICATION organic

GORIZIA (GO)

Radikon

Località Tre Buchi, 4
tel. 0481 32804
www.radikon.it
info@radikon.it

MARIANO DEL FRIULI (GO)

Vie di Romans

Località Vie di Romans, 1
tel. 0481 69600
www.viediromans.it
viediromans@viediromans.it

---

11 ha - 30,000 bt

66 The father-and-son team of Stanko and Saša Radikon combine experience and healthy ambition, tradition and innovation. Opposites attract and maybe that explains their well-deserved success. **99**

PEOPLE - Thanks to the bold decisions of Stanko, a pro-natural and pro-maceration winemaker, since the early 1990s the cellar has become an institution in the region and beyond. Now he and Saša have moved on, identifying further room for improvement.

VINEYARDS - The vineyards are tended impeccably, especially considering the position in which they are located, with steep slopes especially in the three hectares that surround the winery headquarters. The agronomic approach is so naturalist as to often appear fatalistic. But on land where others would see nothing but problems, Stanko and Saša sense the potential for more stupendous harvests.

WINES - In the cellar long spontaneous fermentations in large wooden casks are in; sulphur additions, clarification and filtration are out. Maceration times and methods vary: longer for "classic" wines, shorter for the two labels which acknowledging his son's eagerness to follow new roads, Stanko calls "Saša's wines". The excellent, rich, drinkable **Slatnik 2011** (O chardonnay, friulano; 8,000 bt) has strong well-integrated scents of blossom, aromatic herbs and spices, and a juicy, well-sustained palate. **Pinot Grigio 2010** (O 8,000 bt) is denser and harder on the palate, eloquent and complex on the nose. The 2007 wines — Ribolla Gialla, Oslavje and Jakot — will take time to express themselves, so we'll speak about them another time.

---

50 ha - 250,000 bt

PEOPLE - Owner Gianfranco Gallo represents the third generation of a farming family that has been working this land for at least two centuries. To the farm he has inherited he has brought passion and in-depth knowledge of viticulture and enology. He began bottling his wine in 1978, then set about performing research and experiments in the cellar. Ten years later he decided he wanted to make wine for each parcel of land to capture their single characteristics. That was in 1989: since then Gianfranco has become a true "cru pioneer".

VINEYARDS - Fifty hectares of land are planted with vines, all tended with impeccable care along the lines of the great French models. Plantings are dense with 6,500 vines per hectare trained with the bilateral spurred cordon system, 50-70 centimeters from the ground. Gianfranco is keen to respect the local terroir and puts himself at the service of the climate and the soil by maintaining the organic activity of the terrain.

WINES - "It's wrong to teach a technique as an end unto itself: all it is is a vehicle for conveying the terroir." With these few, well-chosen words, Gianfranco sums up the wines and the style of Vie di Romans, a model for the region in particular and Italian white wines in general. Rich and honeyed, seductive and stylish, **Friuli Isonzo Rive Alte Chardonnay Ciampagnis Vieris 2011** (O 38,300 bt) was most enjoyable. Well-calibrated with beautifully judged acidity and flavor, it's a Great Wine. Excellent too was the almost copper-colored **Friuli Isonzo Rive Alte Pinot Grigio Dessimis 2011** (O 27,300 bt) with its hints of rose and butter and tangy, full-flavored, enfolding palate. **Dut'Un 2010** (O 4,200 bt) is an assemblage of chardonnay and sauvignon with warm, intense aromas of hay and blossom and luminous, harmonious flavor. **Friuli Isonzo Malvasia Dis Cumieris 2011** (O 8,300 bt) is refined and flavorful.

FERTILIZERS natural manure, compost, green manure
PLANT PROTECTION copper and sulphur
WEED CONTROL mechanical
YEASTS native
GRAPES 100% estate-grown
CERTIFICATION none

FERTILIZERS organic-mineral, manure pellets, humus
PLANT PROTECTION chemical, copper and sulphur
WEED CONTROL chemical
YEASTS selected
GRAPES 100% estate-grown
CERTIFICATION none

Zuani

Località Giasbana, 12
tel. 0481 391432
www.zuanivini.it
info@zuanivini.it

Skerlj

Frazione Sales, 44
tel. 040 229253
www.agriturismoskerlj.com
info@agriturismoskerlj.com

---

12 ha - 70,000 bt

PEOPLE - Zuani is the baby of Patrizia Felluga, Marco Felluga's first child, and it was born to crown her dreams in 2001. Some of the existing vineyards were maintained and new ones were planted with the scientific support of Attilio Scienza and Donato Lanati, who analyzed the soil to assess its potential and suitability for specific grape varieties. Patrizia's son and daughter, Caterina and Antonio Zanon, also play an active part in every department.

VINEYARDS - The vineyards are planted between the Collio district in Italy and the Brda in Slovenia. The hills straddling the national border are of Eocene origin and the weather and soil conditions are similar on both sides. The soil, which contains marl and sandstone of marine origin, is good for the vineyards, hence for the wines they produce, all minerally, textured and long-lasting. The Zuani crus are to be found in the best locations on the slopes round Giasbana.

WINES - Two wines are produced, both white and both recognizable by their stylish labels. One is steel-fermented, the other aged in barriques for eight to nine months. Both are made with the native friulano and the international pinot grigio, chardonnay and sauvignon grapes. The excellent **Collio Bianco Zuani Ris. 2010** (O 10,000 bt), made with late-harvested grapes, has a nose dominated by aromatic herbs and a silky, zesty palate. It is sure to reap the benefits of more time in the cellar.

> **vino slow** **COLLIO BIANCO VIGNE 2012** (O 60,000 bt) Yet another master class for a wine that's rapidly becoming one of the symbols of the Collio. Intensity, complexity and finesse are the qualities that define the bouquet, which has hints of peaches and apricots, oranges and lemons. The appetizing, harmonious palate has a generous attack and a rich finish, freighted with acidity and flavor.

1.6 ha - 3,500 bt

66 Matej Skerlj is a young winemaker whose character reflects that of the area he lives in. He lets his wines do the talking without wasting words. Any other talk would only break the marvelous silence of the Carso. 99

PEOPLE - Matej and his sister Kristina also run their family's osmiza, a typical Carso farm shop-cum-inn where they serve wine, cured meats and classic local dishes.

VINEYARDS - Guyot-trained vines, fruit canes tied by hand with willow twigs, highly mineralized red soil —walking through the vineyards is like a stroll through a country garden. We find all this and more both in Matej's own vineyards and on the properties the local old-timers entrust to him.

WINES - Simple and functional, no gratuitous modern gadgetry — the cellar reflects the producer. And it's the ideal place for him to make the wines the way he likes to. Human intervention is reduced to a minimum given the superlative quality of the primary ingredients. One interesting practice, now a tradition, is that of washing the Slavonian wood barrels with warm water and quince. Without wishing to detract from the oh-so-**Carso Terrano 2010** (● 800 bt), very typical with a great sense of place, the cellar's pièce de resistance are its macerated whites. Splendid too is **Malvasia 2010** (O 800 bt), fleshy and rich with nicely balanced fruit from nose to palate, where distinct hints of apricot make it a pleasure to drink.

> **vino slow** **VITOSKA 2010** (O 800 bt) A masterful interpretation of the grape with pleasant notes of citrus fruits and ginger on the nose and a well-rounded, juicy, typical palate of deep complexity and flavor.

FERTILIZERS manure pellets, natural manure
PLANT PROTECTION chemical, copper and sulphur
WEED CONTROL mechanical
YEASTS selected
GRAPES 100% estate-grown
CERTIFICATION none

FERTILIZERS natural manure
PLANT PROTECTION copper and sulphur
WEED CONTROL mechanical
YEASTS native
GRAPES 100% estate-grown
CERTIFICATION none

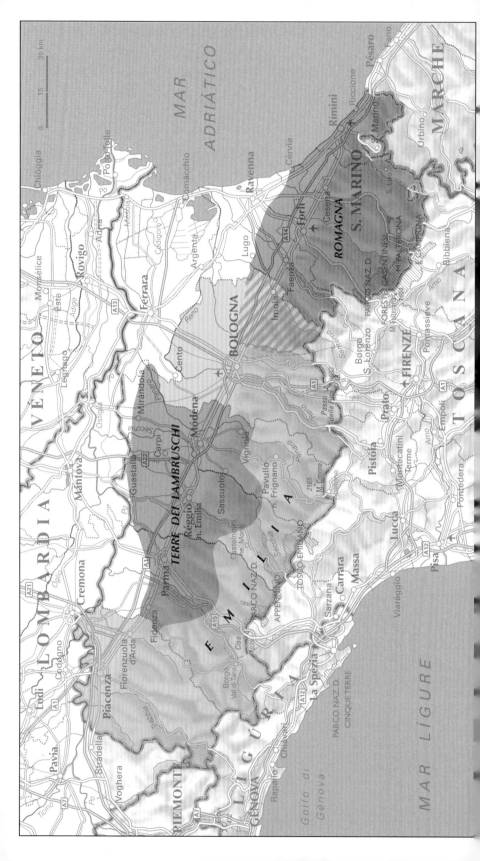

EMILIA ROMAGNA

The region has a large number of production zones with very different grape varieties and weather and soil conditions. In the northernmost area, the hills over Piacenza, home to the famed Gutturnio, we saw a sharp rise in the number of quality labels made with native grapes, among which precious passitos. Here, as in the Emilian provinces of Parma, Reggio Emilia and Modena, which we have denominated Terra dei Lambruschi, there is a strong, firmly-rooted tradition of fizzy wines, born to accompany the rich, tasty local cooking. Apropos, we are delighted to note the growing interest of producers and consumers for the old method of second fermentation in the bottle, largely roused by Vittorio Graziano, a fervid supporter of the tradition.

Moving southwards, the Colli Bolognesi zone runs along the east side of the Apennines. Here the most significant wines are made with pignoletto, a native grape of huge potential, as yet not fully expressed.

Romagna, finally, is the land of sangiovese and albana. It is split up into different subzones with different levels of output. Here we can see an increasingly pronounced tendency towards sustainable, clean viticulture. This is one of the reasons why we awarded a new Snail symbol to Villa Venti, a winery extremely representative of the *Slow Wine* philosophy.

Considering the different typologies, the vintages we tasted went from 2003 (a few Piacenza passitos) to 2012, the most represented. The growing year famously recorded seven anticyclones, hence warm, dry weather. The result was high sugar concentration, precocious ripening and a big drop in the quantity of grapes produced (partly due to spring-time frost), countervailed by an improvement in quality. Less wine, then, but better.

The two Riserve 2010 di Sangiovese di Romagna were slightly below par compared with the 2008 and 2009 vintages. They were the products of a cool, damp year of wines that, albeit interesting for their pronounced acidity, in some cases were sometimes lean and lightweight.

snails @⟲

125 CAMILLO DONATI
127 VIGNE DEI BOSCHI
127 FATTORIA ZERBINA
128 PAOLO FRANCESCONI
129 VILLA VENTI

bottles ▮

125 CLETO CHIARLI
128 GALLEGATI
129 TORRE SAN MARTINO

coins €

123 BARACCONE
123 LUSENTI

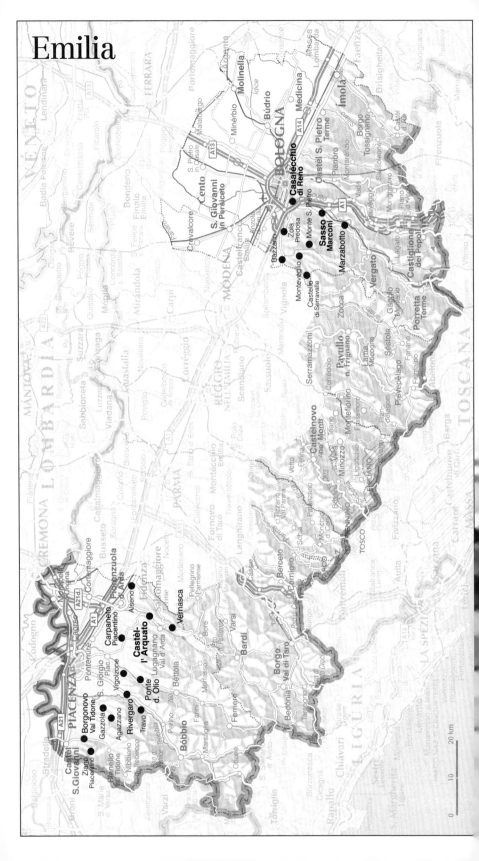

Baraccone

Località Cà Morti, 1
tel. 0523 877147
www.baraccone.it
info@baraccone.it

Lusenti €

Località Casa Piccioni di Vicobarone, 57
tel. 0523 868479
www.lusentivini.it
info@lusentivini.it

---

10 ha - 40,000 bt   **10% discount**

17 ha - 120,000 bt

PEOPLE - If you happen to be in the Ponte dell'Olio area (the name means "Oil Bridge" and in the old days the bridge in question, over the River Nure, was used by oil merchants from Genoa) don't miss the chance to visit Baraccone. You'll be welcomed by Andreana Burgazzi, the life and soul of the winery, which sits on one of the highest slopes of the Valnure, since 1995. She is helped in the vineyard by Serghei Railean under the supervision of agronomist Roberto Abate.

VINEYARDS - The vineyards are situated at an altitude of 400 meters. All enjoy excellent southeast-facing positions and were planted in 1999. A vineyard planted in 2007 started to produce a couple of years ago and for the moment its grapes are used to make Gutturnio Frizzante. This year Andreana conducted some experiments with organics but, though she embraces the approach ideologically, she is not yet prepared to abandon systemic products completely.

WINES - The wines of Andreana and enologist Stefano Testa are sewn together by a common thread: robust but never heavy, they are beautifully fruity on the nose and well-rounded on the palate. The top of the class is once more Gutturnio Sup. Colombaia 2011 (● 11,500 bt), a shining example of everything the typology is capable of: full-bodied without being hard, mouth-filling, long and rounded, it's an excellent Everyday Wine. Following in its footsteps, **Gutturnio Frizzante Ri' More 2012** (● 11,500 bt) is fruity and well-balanced with an acidity that prolongs the palate. **Gutturnio Ronco Alto Ris. 2008** (● 3,000 bt) has well-structured tannins, a spicy bouquet with hints of liquorice and a stylish finish. **Filiblù 2007** (● 1.500 bt) is an effective Cabernet Sauvignon made with dried grapes. **Zagaia Frizzante 2012** (○ 10,000 bt) is fresh and fruity.

PEOPLE - Lodovica Lusenti and Giuseppe Ferri are helped in the cellar by the valiant Anderson do Nascimento. With the passing of time they are managing to effectively convey the care and attention with which their company is directing its work towards a respectful approach to the environment. This respect has translated into the decision to switch to organics.

VINEYARDS - The company's production focuses on the malvasia, croatina and barbera grapes. The vineyards are scattered round the Ziano district. The two main plots are a five-hectare vineyard in Pozzolo Piccolo with the oldest croatina and barbera vines, which go back over 50 years, and a six-hectare vineyard round the cellar in Casa Piccioni, which grows mainly pinot nero, ortrugo and malvasia grapes.

WINES - Lusenti produces a range of enjoyable, well-crafted typical wines. C.P. Malvasia Frizzante Emiliana 2012 (○ 3,000 bt), produced with the technique of second fermentation in the bottle is once more an excellent Everyday Wine: it offers notes of citrus fruit on the nose, racy structure and a fragrant dry finish. **Gutturnio Frizzante 2012** (● 35,000 bt) has munchy fruit and a beefy palate. **C.P. Gutturnio Sup. Cresta al Sole 2009** (● 5,500 bt) is richer and fuller. The hugely impressive **Cabernet Sauvignon Villante 2009** (● 1,500 bt) has notes of bell pepper typical of the variety and a very structured palate with an interesting long finish. **Martin 2011** (● barbera, croatina, merlot; 3,500 bt) is pleasantly fruity. **C.P. Malvasia Passito Il Piriolo 2010** (○ 2,000 bt) has notes of dates on the nose and an opulent, full-flavored palate.

FERTILIZERS natural manure
PLANT PROTECTION chemical, copper and sulphur
WEED CONTROL mechanical
YEASTS selected
GRAPES 100% estate-grown
CERTIFICATION none

FERTILIZERS natural manure
PLANT PROTECTION copper and sulphur
WEED CONTROL mechanical
YEASTS selected
GRAPES 20% bought in
CERTIFICATION converting to organics

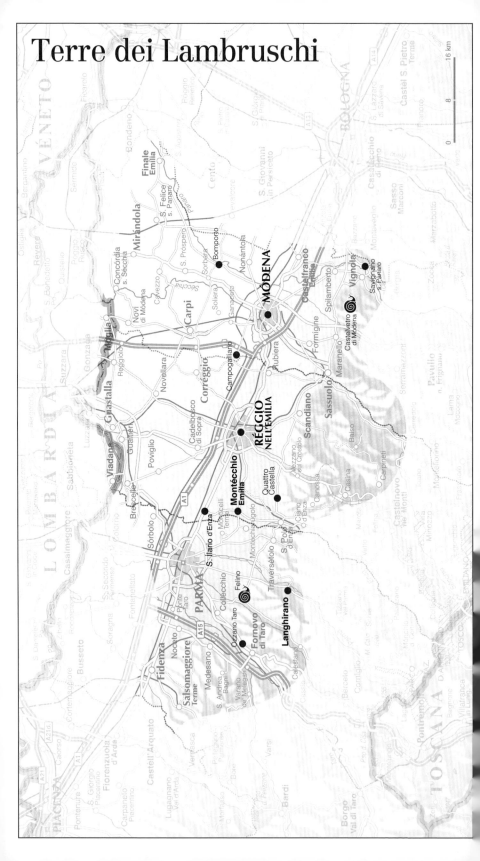

Terre dei Lambruschi

Cleto Chiarli

Via Belvedere, 8
tel. 059 3163311
www.chiarli.it
italia@chiarli.it

100 ha - 900,000 bt   **10% discount**

PEOPLE - No one could dispute that the Chiarli family, who began producing Lambrusco in their original cellar in Modena in 1860, have "written the history" of the wine. Some years ago the present owners, brothers Anselmo and Mauro, began overhauling the company and completed their project with the building of a new cellar at Castelvetro for the vinification of grapes from their own estates.

VINEYARDS - The vineyards in the hills round Castelvetro grow on clayey soil that gives the grasparossa grape richness and fleshiness, whereas the lean, loose sandy-silty soil of the plainland round Sozzigalli and Soliera by the River Secchia, the heart of the Sorbara production area, instill the acidity and finesse characteristic of the variety.

WINES - Enologist Franco De Biasi's mastery and in-depth knowledge of the area give us a superlative range with impeccable aromatic focus. Two are top performers: Lambrusco di Sorbara del Fondatore 2012 (● 12,000 bt), which, according to tradition, undergoes second fermentation in the bottle, is spacious, deep, and full-flavored, while Lambrusco Grasparossa di Castelvetro Vigneto Cialdini 2012 (● 50,000 bt) restores the typical huskiness of the grape variety with a full, dry palate. Both are excellent Everyday Wines. The well-crafted **Lambrusco di Sorbara Vecchia Modena Premium M.H. 2012** (● 60,000 bt) has lots of wild strawberry on the nose and an assertive, forthright palate. **Lambrusco Grasparossa di Castelvetro Villa Cialdini 2012** (● 80,000 bt) is equally good.

Camillo Donati

Frazione Bambiano
Via Costa, 3 A
tel. 0521 637204
www.camillodonati.it
camillo@camillodonati.it

12 ha - 70,000 bt

66 Camillo Donati still says "I live wine, I don't make it". He adds that, "I'm the first to drink my wine and I hope other perceptive people with a conscience will drink it too. Which is why I'm very careful about what ends up in my bottles." Hence his decision to work as naturally as possible. 99

PEOPLE - The family cellar was opened by Camillo Donati's grandfather Orlando in 1930. Camillo has been running it for almost 20 years with the help of his wife Francesca and niece Monia. For the last two years they have been making wine in a small new, functional cellar, all naturally second-fermented in crown-capped bottles.

VINEYARDS - The vineyards are divided between the Bottazza and Sant'Andrea estates in the hills near the cellar. For more than ten years, Camillo has adopted certified organic methods and a biodynamic approach to agriculture in an attempt to capture the most natural sense of place possible.

WINES - The "whims" of nature have produced expressive, early-drinking wines this year. One such is the fragrant, flavorful **Il Mio Sauvignon 2012** (○ 5,000 bt) and the dry **Il Mio Trebbiano 2012** (○ 4,800 bt). The same characteristics are shared by the luscious, expressive **Il Mio Malvasia** (○ 22,000 bt), full of flesh and complex on the nose, Il Mio Barbera 2010 (● 7,000 bt) is a fine Everyday Wine, refreshing and evolved to a tee. Camillo's wines improve with time in the bottle as we found out retasting Il Mio Lambrusco 2010, now at a fascinating stage in its evolution, in which callow aromas have given way to stylish spicy notes and the palate has stayed as vibrant and assertive as before.

FERTILIZERS natural manure
PLANT PROTECTION chemical, copper and sulphur
WEED CONTROL chemical, mechanical
YEASTS selected
GRAPES 100% estate-grown
CERTIFICATION none

FERTILIZERS none
PLANT PROTECTION copper and sulphur
WEED CONTROL mechanical
YEASTS native
GRAPES 100% estate-grown
CERTIFICATION organic

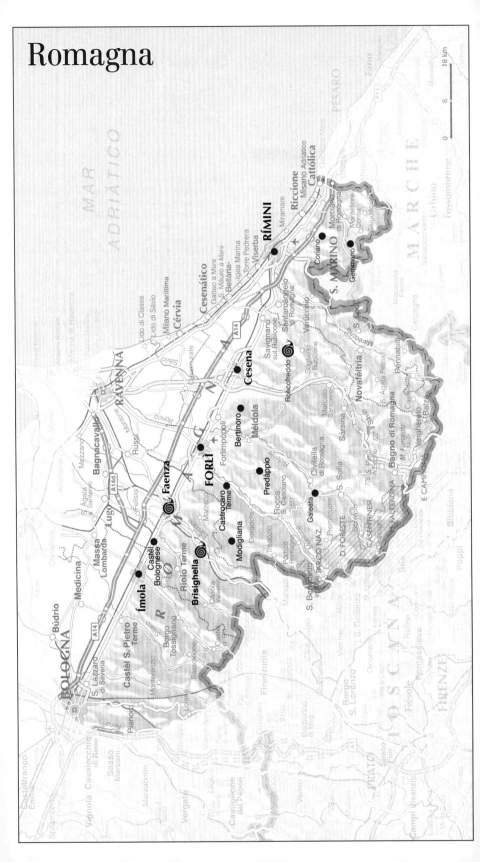

BRISIGHELLA (RA)

Vigne dei Boschi

Via Tura, 7/A
tel. 0546 51648
www.vignedeiboschi.it
vignedeiboschi@alice.it

FAENZA (RA)

Fattoria Zerbina

Frazione Marzeno
Via Vicchio, 11
tel. 0546 40022
www.zerbina.com
info@zerbina.com

65 ha - 15,000 bt   **10% discount**

29 ha - 200,000 bt

66 Paolo Babini and Katia Alpi are enthusiastic winemakers who know their job well. They oversee work in the vineyards and the cellar personally. What drives them is their conviction that only natural vine dressing can bring out the specific characteristics of the area. 99

66 Rigor and passion are the keys to the world of Maria Cristina Geminiani. Professional in every detail, from production to public relations, she feels a visceral love for Romagna and its land. 99

PEOPLE - The Vigne dei Boschi project, which began in 1989, aims to produce wines that reflect the distinctive features of the Valpiana area in the hills south of Brisighella.

VINEYARDS - The locations of the vineyards on dry, well-ventilated hilltops surrounded by woods and olive groves were chosen with the utmost care. Altitudes reach as high as 450 meters and the marly, sandy soil endows the grapes with plenty of extracts and an interesting range of aromas. True to the old Romagna tradition, the sangiovese vines are bush-trained.

WINES - These two producers make wines that stand out for their aromatic complexity and elegance. Without overdoing things, they interpret the terroir and see nature as a treasure of inestimable value that needs to be preserved. The release of Poggio Tura 2009, not yet mature but already very expressive, has been postponed. We thus tasted **Monteré 2011** (O 2,500 bt), made with albana grapes and stylishly tannic. The nose betrays oxidative traces from maceration and aging in barriques, the palate is zesty with bundles of fresh, fragrant fruit. **16 Anime 2011** (O 3,000 bt) is a Riesling of great acidity, depth and length with a definite aroma of petrol. **Longré 2008** (● 2,000 bt), made with syrah grapes, has intense spicy, earthy notes and a generous, fleshy palate with a refined minerally finish.

PEOPLE - Maria Cristina has the inquisitive, pragmatic character typical of people from the Brianza district of Lombardy, where she was born. This is one of the factors behind the improved quality of wine in this area, the homeland of her grandfather Vincenzo, where she came to live and take over the cellar in the 1980s.

VINEYARDS - In Maria Cristina's unconscious, tradition and innovation have always been intertwined. In agriculture that means using the single-pole bush training system, once the most common in the Romagna hills. Today the system, sometimes in its candelabra version, is the only one adopted for red grape varieties. Part of the credit for the development of the project must go to seasoned agronomist Remigio Bordini.

WINES - Innovation is the second concept that governs day-to-day thinking. Witness the decision to vinify dried albana grapes with noble rot. **Albana di Romagna Passito Scaccomatto 2009** (O 2,650 bt) is supple with notes of botrytis and an elegant uncloying finish. **Albana di Romagna Passito Arrocco 2009** (O 4,400 bt) maintains the subtle style of Scaccomatto but veers towards sweeter notes of chestnut honey. The welcome new entry **Romagna Albana Bianco di Ceparano 2012** (O 8,500 bt) plays on the contrast between a sweet fruity attack and an acid-rich finish, while the fruity, refreshing, zesty **Romagna Sangiovese Sup. Ceregio 2012** (● 120,000 bt) proves once more that it is a wine to be relied on.

FERTILIZERS biodynamic preparations, green manure
PLANT PROTECTION copper and sulphur, organic
WEED CONTROL mechanical
YEASTS native
GRAPES 100% estate-grown
CERTIFICATION biodynamic, organic

FERTILIZERS organic-mineral, manure pellets, green manure
PLANT PROTECTION chemical, copper and sulphur
WEED CONTROL chemical, mechanical
YEASTS selected
GRAPES 100% estate-grown
CERTIFICATION none

Paolo Francesconi 🐌

Località Sarna
Via Tuliero, 154
tel. 0546 43213
www.francesconipaolo.it
info@francesconipaolo.it

Gallegati 🍾

Via Lugo, 182
tel. 0546 621149
www.aziendaagricolagallegati.it
info@aziendaagricolagallegati.it
⌐0

8.5 ha - 20,000 bt   **10% discount**

6 ha - 15,000 bt

❝ Paolo Francesconi provides living proof that organic farming is possible even in difficult conditions, even when the advantages of altitude are missing. Sure, it takes a lot of hard work to make good, healthy wine here, but Paolo does the job supremely well. ❞

PEOPLE - This small winery came into being in 1992 in the hills west of Faenza when, after working for years at other cellars, Paolo decided to take over the family estate and dress the wines a "different" way.

VINEYARDS - Everything seems perfect when you visit the winery, a little oasis of a place bounded by hedges, where every element plays a vital role in achieving the desired balance: a microsystem in which the vineyard, the land and the fauna live in perfect harmony. In the old Lamone riverbed, the vines, Guyot-trained for the albana grape and cordon-trained for sangiovese, rest on soil rich in red clay with strata of gravel beneath.

WINES - Native yeasts, natural fermentations, no temperature control and limited use of sulphur allow the wines to express themselves intimately, reflecting the terroir and the grapes. Aged exclusively in steel vats, **Romagna Sangiovese Sup. Limbecca 2011** (● 11,000 bt), is redolent of fresh, crunchy fruit. The wonderfully drinkable **Luna Nuova 2011** (○ trebbiano, 1,500 bt) has a fleshy, mineral palate. The passito **D'Incanto 2012** (● centesimino; 1,900 bt) is as full of flavor as ever, while **Vite in Fiore 2011** (○ albana; 1,200 bt) has a bouquet of white flowers and a lean body.

vino slow	**ARCAICA 2012** (○ albana; 1,000 bt) A splendid wine made with albana grapes macerated on the skins for 90 days. A fine bouquet of dried flowers and yellow fruit is followed by a juicy, dry palate braced by lively acidity and measured tannins.

PEOPLE - The affable and cordial Gallegati brothers have been running this fine family winery since 1998. Their land is split into two estates: in the Faenza countryside they grow kiwi fruit and persimmons, in the Monte Coralli district in the hills round Brisighella, they grow sangiovese and albana grapes. Adamant supporters of quality winemaking, have espoused the criteria of sustainable agriculture, limiting their interventions in the field.

VINEYARDS - The vineyards are in the hills at an altitude of about 200 meters, rimmed by woodland and gulleys in a steep and rugged landscape of extraordinary beauty. They grow on mixed clay-limestone soil and are mostly spurred cordon-trained. Spontaneous grassing helps attenuate the heat in summer. Particularly evocative is the low-yield albana vineyard.

WINES - Gallegati's wines are powerful and well-structured, though not without elegance, and capture the essence of the land round Faenza. The excellent **Sangiovese di Romagna Sup. Corallo Nero Ris. 2010** (● 8.500 bt) has a bouquet of plums and roses and a deep, fleshy, juicy palate with distinctive acidity and an interesting minerally finish. **Colli di Faenza Rosso Corallo Blu Ris. 2010** (● 3,000 bt) is concentrated and leisurely with refined notes of herbs and stylish tannins. The best of the bunch is **Albana di Romagna Passito Regina di Cuori 2010** (○ 1,500 bt), which has a complex nose of figs and candied apricots and a sumptuously full-bodied palate with bundles of acidity. An exemplary traditional Albana and a flavorful Great Wine.

FERTILIZERS biodynamic preparations, green manure
PLANT PROTECTION copper and sulphur
WEED CONTROL mechanical
YEASTS native
GRAPES 100% estate-grown
CERTIFICATION organic

FERTILIZERS mineral
PLANT PROTECTION chemical, copper and sulphur
WEED CONTROL chemical, mechanical
YEASTS selected
GRAPES 100% estate-grown
CERTIFICATION none

MODIGLIANA (FC)

Torre San Martino

Località Casone
Via San Martino in Monte
tel. 06 69200627
torresanmartino@gmail.com

10 ha - 18,000 bt

PEOPLE - Formerly Tenimenti San Martino in Monte, this admirable winery, established in 2001, has changed its name. The management, under the Costa family, who are also the owners, with Remigio and Francesco Bordini in charge of matters agronomic and enological, has remained unchanged. The aim continues to be the conservation of a quasi-"archaeological" style of farming with respect for the area's history, environment and landscape.

VINEYARDS - All the vineyards are grouped in a single plot at an altitude of 350 meters. At their heart is an old bush-trained sangiovese property, planted in 1922 on steep marly land. The place and its pool of original clones have been patiently salvaged and have provided the material for the younger vineyards. The high planting density of both red and white varieties, soil composition and good hillside locations are all conducive to the production of good quality grapes.

WINES - Torre San Martino's wines are generous, exemplary and elegant, not to mention built to last. The excellent **Romagna Sangiovese Vigna 1922 Ris. 2010** (● 3,000 bt) is a wine you can trust: it has heavyset structure buttressed by tannins and freshness, still somewhat exuberant on account of its youthfulness but also a guarantee of longevity. Romagna Sangiovese Gemme 2012 (● 3,000 bt) doesn't pale in comparison, anything but. Suppler but already well-balanced with plenty of stuffing, it's deservedly an Everyday Wine. The two whites are pure cut-glass: in **Colli di Faenza Vigne della Signora 2012** (○ albana, chardonnay, sauvignon; 3,000 bt), the varietal presence of the native grape is conspicuous, while **Colli di Faenza Chardonnay 2012** (○ 3,000 bt) privileges freshness and fruit.

FERTILIZERS manure pellets
PLANT PROTECTION copper and sulphur
WEED CONTROL chemical, mechanical
YEASTS selected
GRAPES 100% estate-grown
CERTIFICATION none

RONCOFREDDO (FC)

Villa Venti

Frazione Villa Venti
Via Doccia, 1442
tel. 0541 949532
www.villaventi.it
info@villaventi.it

7 ha - 27,500 bt | **10% discount**

66 Rethinking vine growing to nurture the characteristics of the terroir necessitates reverting to organics, but that's not enough in itself. Mauro Giardini and Davide Castellucci are adamant that it also takes a grand creative design to get the best out of nature and turn it into good wine. 99

PEOPLE - In 2003 Mauro and Davide decided to make the dream they had cherished for so long come true and set up the cellar. Not that it was easy: the steep hillsides that overlook the small town of Longiano had previously only been covered with fallow woodland, so Mauro and Davide had to work hard (with the invaluable help of agronomist Remigio Bordini) to get Villa Venti into shape.

VINEYARDS - The vineyards are situated round the cellar cum farmhouse, also an agriturismo, at an altitude of about 200 meters on soil composed mainly of red and sandy clay. The first sangiovese plantings (trained with the trident system, a modified version of the bush) was recently joined by another of famoso, an interesting white variety native to Romagna. The agricultural methods used are strictly organic.

WINES - The unique climate, — warm and Mediterranean but also well ventilated — produces rich, healthy grapes which, once optimally ripe, make direct, assertive wines of great but never forced complexity. One such is the austere, composed Romagna Sangiovese Longiano Primo Segno 2011 (● 20,000 bt), which improves and perfects its character with long aging in the bottle, though it already deserves to be recommended as a reliable Everyday Wine. **Felis Leo 2009** (● sangiovese, merlot, cabernet; 3,000 bt) is fleshier, solid, mellowed by aging on wood. **Romagna Sangiovese Sup. Maggese 2010** (● 2,000 bt), finally, is more austere and lean-edged.

FERTILIZERS none
PLANT PROTECTION copper and sulphur
WEED CONTROL mechanical
YEASTS selected
GRAPES 100% estate-grown
CERTIFICATION organic

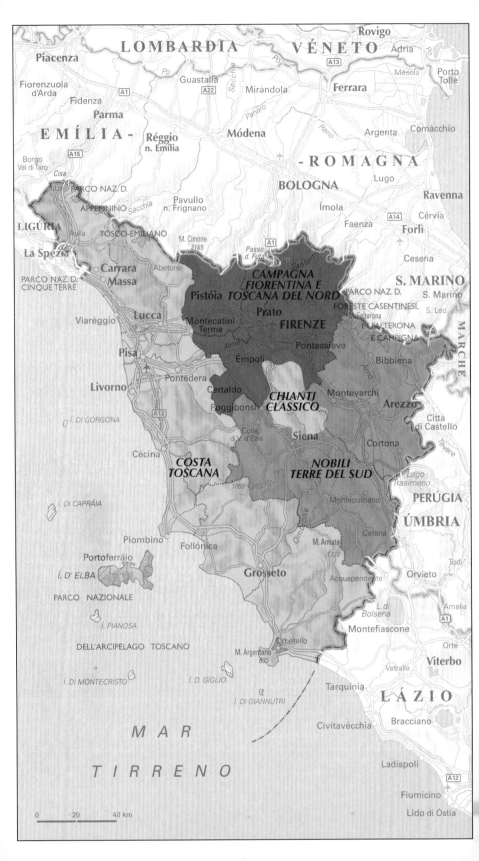

TUSCANY

The first thing that catches the eye when analyzing winegrowing in the region is the consistent quality of the principal denominations; this despite a series of problematic grape harvests, as was the case of 2008 in Montalcino and 2010 at Bolgheri. Yet our work, unique for a wine guide, has allowed us this year to appreciate another, maybe less immediately evident aspect, the fruit of four years of traveling round winegrowing areas. We have, in fact, uncovered a hidden world of production with features that combine to draw a more nuanced physiognomy for Tuscan wine. We are referring to young cellars that have invested mainly personal skills and love of the land with a dual intent: to avoid wasting the natural and cultural legacy they have inherited and to balk the socioeconomic trends of recent years. To cite a few examples, wine companies such as Ottomani, Calafata, Istine and Ornina are new models of viticulture in which the youth of their owners and work centered on the rediscovery of existing vineyards come together as one. Today the main denominations evidence a significant contradiction between the excellent quality they express and the crisis of domestic markets. In other words, they tend to be successful outside the national boundaries. It is to be hoped that this "grassroots" viticulture can ultimately become a new socioeconomic model capable, albeit on a small scale, of reconstructing a cohesive fabric of people, exchanges and culture and ensuring a future and a base for growth. We are confident that it can and are proud to say as much.

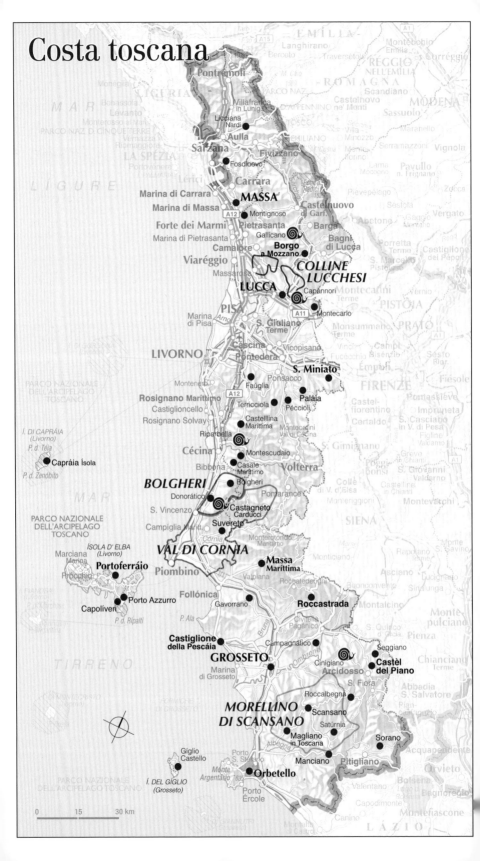

Tenuta San Guido

Località Capanne, 27
tel. 0565 762003
www.sassicaia.com
info@sassicaia.com

87 ha - 740,000 bt

PEOPLE - The legend of Sassicaia, the iconic label of the 1990s wine boom, has been amply celebrated in literature. But its shining star has moved the spotlight away from the sensible work Mario Incisa della Rocchetta has done in promoting agriculture as a system for protecting and promoting the environment. The production of wine, of "that" wine in particular, is a consequence of his approach, which continues to be valid today for Tenuta San Guido.

VINEYARDS - Despite the size of the property, as many as 87 hectares of which are planted with wines, the agronomic approach here has always sought minimal impact on the environment through interventions tailor-made for each vineyard. The most important of all are, of course, those of Sassicaia at Castiglioncello. Completely replanted, they descend through different soil and climate conditions to the Via Aurelia below.

WINES - A focus for the denomination, never matched, never mind improved upon in terms of elegance, **Bolgheri Sassicaia 2010** (● cabernet sauvignon and cabernet franc; 200,000 bt) is aged for 18 months in old and new barriques. The bouquet of blackcurrants is tinged with tertiary notes of tobacco and soil, the palate is dynamic and graceful with finely weaved tannins. A Great Wine if ever there was one. **Guidalberto 2011** (● cabernet sauvignon, merlot, petit verdot; 240,000 bt) has concentrated body and character with hints of ripe red berries buttressed by liquorice and vanilla. The palate is complex, mouthfilling and dense, more opulent than linear. **Le Difese 2011** (● cabernet sauvignon, sangiovese: 300,000 bt) has a vegetal, spicy nose and an approachable, eloquent palate.

FERTILIZERS organic-mineral, natural manure, green manure
PLANT PROTECTION chemical, copper and sulphur
WEED CONTROL mechanical
YEASTS native
GRAPES 10% bought in, wine bought in
CERTIFICATION none

Poggio Trevvalle

Località Arcille
Podere Ex E.M., 348
tel. 0564 998142
www.poggiotrevvalle.it
valle@poggiotrevvalle.it

13.5 ha - 60,000 bt   **10% discount**

PEOPLE - After they'd completed their studies, Umberto and Bernardo Valle were forced to take over their family farm in the Tavoliere area of Puglia, which used to produce vegetables for the canning industry. In 1998 they gave life to their dream of producing quality wine. To do so they chose an area in Tuscany that was still relatively unknown, the Maremma. There they bought the Capecchi estate from one of the first assignees of reclamation work.

VINEYARDS - The property spreads out over the two local DOC zones, Montecucco and Morellino di Scansano. The vineyards are contour-planted on a north-south vertical, in an ideal position for the grapes to ripen with the bunches that remain turgid and are well protected by the leaf canopy. The oldest plantings date from 1993, the most recent, given over entirely to sangiovese, from 2006.

WINES - The Valle brothers' wines are characterized by great palate-nose cleanness and good drinkability. **Morellino di Scansano Passera 2012** (● 40,000 bt) is a clear expression of the local tradition and offers aromas of fresh fruit with a tannic palate and tangy finish. **Rafele 2009** (● cabernet sauvignon, merlot; 3,000 bt) is more complex with clean vegetal and fruity aromas and a flavorful, dynamic leafy palate. Morellino di Scansano Poggio Trevvalle 2011 (● 5,000 bt) has notes of fruit and spice with a lean, well-balanced, juicy palate — a very pleasing Everyday Wine. **Montecucco Poggiotrevvalle 2011** (● sangiovese, merlot, cabernet; 5,000 bt) has hints of fruit and lively acidity. **Rosato Poggiotrevvalle 2012** (☉ sangiovese; 3,000 bt) is approachable and pleasing.

FERTILIZERS manure pellets, green manure
PLANT PROTECTION copper and sulphur
WEED CONTROL mechanical
YEASTS native
GRAPES 100% estate-grown
CERTIFICATION organic

CAPANNORI (LU)

Tenuta di Valgiano

Frazione Valgiano
Via di Valgiano, 7
tel. 0583 4022710
www.valgiano.it
info@valgiano.it

22 ha - 80,000 bt   **10% discount**

❝ This winery, set up in 1993 by Moreno Pettini, Laura Collobiano and the enologist Saverio Petrilli, is now a synonym of a form of viticulture that pursues equilibrium between vine, human being and terroir. Not only in the productive context, but also as part of a complex organic cycle. ❞

PEOPLE - Worth a mention is the winery's solidarity with many local farmers. Together they have formed a sort of collective movement in Lucca to promote environmental sustainability, of which the winery is a leading advocate.

VINEYARDS - The vineyards surround the estate, with Pizzorne on one side and the Lucca plain on the other. The vines are stimulated through green manure cropping and biodynamic treatments to replicate the characteristics of the soil, which has a composition of "alberese" limestone soil and "macigno toscano" sandstone which, respectively, contribute to the structure and finesse of the wine.

WINES - Over the last few years Valgiano's wines have developed a strong personality which, like it or not, reflect undeniable unconventionalism and freedom of expression. **Colline Lucchesi Palistorti 2011** (● syrah, sangiovese, merlot; 60,000 bt) is a wine with spicy aromas and fleshy fruit, which gives an encore on the palate. **Palistorti Bianco 2012** (○ vermentino, trebbiano, malvasia; 7,500 bt) is more delicate with delectable scents of blossomy.

> **vino slow** COLLINE LUCCHESI TENUTA DI VALGIANO 2010
> (● syrah, sangiovese, merlot; 10,000 bt) One of the best vintages ever, a wine that expresses its complexity with notes of balsam and red berries, which tend to evolve into earthier, almost truffly tones. On the palate it has verve and elegance with plenty of close-knit tannins to define its huge body.

FERTILIZERS biodynamic preparations, green manure
PLANT PROTECTION copper and sulphur, organic
WEED CONTROL mechanical
YEASTS native
GRAPES 100% estate-grown
CERTIFICATION biodynamic

CASTAGNETO CARDUCCI (LI)

I Luoghi

Località Campo al Capriolo, 201
tel. 0565 777379
www.iluoghi.it
info@iluoghi.it

3.5 ha - 12,000 bt

❝ I Luoghi is an example of virtuous viticulture and excellent quality. The company's contribution has proved vital in adding vivacity and freshness to the prestigious Bolgheri denomination. ❞

PEOPLE - It's rare in Bolgheri to be welcomed by someone who actually makes wine and is also the owner of the company you are visiting. I Luoghi offers a new take on the typical Bolgheri winery. We were taken round by the two people behind it, Stefano Granata and his wife Paola De Fusco. The couple share everything: from hard work in the vineyard to vinification to choice of grape blends for the wines.

VINEYARDS - The company owns 3.5 hectares of vineyards divided into two plots. The composition of the soil in each is roughly the same, namely loose with copious sand. Having said that, the two vineyards have distinct personalities, which are well reflected in the grapes. Agronomic practices are reduced to a minimum with limited use of copper and sulphur and the utmost attention to pruning and care for the vegetation.

WINES - On the coast the 2010 growing year was very different from the preceding two. In a cool year in which high acidity added extra elegance to the wines, late-August rain meant that the grapes took longer to ripen. This was one of the reasons, together with shorter aging on wood, why the fascinating **Bolgheri Sup. Podere Ritorti 2010** (● cabernet sauvignon and franc, merlot, syrah; 9,000 bt) is already gorgeous.

> **vino slow** BOLGHERI SUP. CAMPO AL FICO 2010 (● cabernet sauvignon and franc; 3,000 bt) Matured on small wood, thanks to the freshness of fruit redolent of quinine and Mediterranean scrub, a wine that maintains a finesse and a linearity virtually unique in the category.

FERTILIZERS green manure
PLANT PROTECTION copper and sulphur, organic
WEED CONTROL mechanical
YEASTS native
GRAPES 100% estate-grown
CERTIFICATION converting to organics

CINIGIANO (GR)

Salustri

Località La Cava
Frazione Poggi del Sasso
tel. 0564 990529
www.salustri.it
info@salustri.it

15 ha - 100,000 bt | **10% discount**

❝ A guardian of old farming wisdom, Leonardo Salustri has developed his viticulture in a modern enological context, one in which knowledge like his is often, mistakenly, seen as dated. ❞

PEOPLE - Leonardo Salustri's is one of the most vibrant, reliable wineries in the Montecucco zone. His viticulture is a sort of bridge between two eras. Thanks to his top class wines, this Poggi del Sasso winemaker has realized all the potential of his native area.

VINEYARDS - Harmony between past and future is evident in the agronomic management of the company. Salustri is a lover of old vineyards and it is precisely in the oldest plantings that he grows his best grapes. For years now, he and his son Marco have been working on a research and experimentation project on the best sangiovese clones with the University of Pisa. One of the best adapted of these has been christened Salustri.

WINES - In the cellar Marco has inherited all his father's sensitivity and talent. **Montecucco Santa Marta 2010** (● 25,000 bt) has blossomy freshness with a juicy palate braced by tannins. One of the best examples of Vermentino, **Narà 2012** (○ 15,000 bt) ages in steel vats. It has alluring aromas of fruit with almost iodine balsamic fullness. Vibrant on the palate it has an acid sinew that enhances its rigid body. **Montecucco Marleo 2011** (● 20,000 bt) is fantastically drinkable.

vino slow **MONTECUCCO GROTTE ROSSE 2010** (● 5,000 bt) A pedigree Sangiovese made with a selection of grapes from the oldest vineyards. Its nose of dried flowers is followed up by an alluring palate, warm but rich in acid contrast and hints of spice.

FERTILIZERS green manure
PLANT PROTECTION copper and sulphur
WEED CONTROL mechanical
YEASTS native
GRAPES 100% estate-grown
CERTIFICATION organic

GALLICANO (LU)

Podere Concori

Frazione Fiattone
Località Concori, 1
tel. 0583 766374
www.podereconcori.com
info@podereconcori.com

3.5 ha - 12,000 bt

❝ Podere Concori has worked hard to protect and promote an area unknown to many but rich in farming history. The wines it produces are full of crystalline expressive elegance and capture the essence of this remote and precious place. ❞

PEOPLE - Gabriele Da Prato is Garfagnana through and through. A former restaurateur, this proud, volcanic winemaker works with passionate determination day by day to realize the huge potential of his native Garfagnana district in the province of Lucca.

VINEYARDS - What strikes one most about Gabriele's vineyard is the light. Diffuse and bright, it is reflected on the leaves and among the vine rows. The soil is fertile and rich in humus, partly thanks to biodynamic practices, loose lower down and mineral and pebbly higher up. The magnificent Piezza vineyard in front of the farmhouse, a small steep terraced plot, produces the syrah grapes for the company's first cru.

WINES - The wines are characterized by cleanness and precision, as well as very fragrant fruit. Gabriele scores rightaway with the first release of **Vigna Piezza 2011** (● syrah; 1,600 bt). An assertive wine on nose and on palate, it's spicy and nicely fleshy, broad and juicy with magnificent tannins and a soft, silky finish. The succulent, well-balanced **Pinot Nero 2011** (● 1,600 bt) has notes of aromatic herbs. **Podere Concori Bianco 2012** (○ pinot bianco, chenin blanc; 3,000 bt) bowled us over with its notes of spring flowers and sage.

vino slow **MELOGRANO 2011** (● syrah, ciliegiolo, carrarese, maraccina, merlot; 8,000 bt) The company's flagship wine, a combination of aromatic complexity, made up of spice and fruit, and a delectably laid-back, joyously gratifying palate.

FERTILIZERS natural manure, biodynamic preparations, green manure, humus
PLANT PROTECTION copper and sulphur
WEED CONTROL mechanical
YEASTS native
GRAPES 100% estate-grown
CERTIFICATION biodynamic

ORBETELLO (GR)

La Parrina €

Frazione Albinia
Località La Parrina
tel. 0564 862626
www.parrina.it
info@parrina.it

RIPARBELLA (PI)

Caiarossa

Località Serra all'Olio, 59
tel. 0586 699016
www.caiarossa.com
info@caiarossa.com

---

67 ha - 150,000 bt

PEOPLE - La Parrina is a large farm of 500 hectares in the southern Maremma in Tuscany, just a few kilometers from the coast. Here viticulture is just one of many activities, which also include livestock breeding, horticulture and oil and cheese production. Run by the Spinola family, the farm presence ensures the conservation of agricultural knowledge, the landscape and the environment.

VINEYARDS - The vineyard is part of a broader system and fits in perfectly with the picturesque Tuscan landscape. The various plots have been planted on the best growing hills and every parcel has its own distinctive position and soil conditions. The density of about 5,000 vines per hectare and excellent climatic conditions — the vicinity of the sea and good air circulation — mean that the use of chemicals can be cut to a bare minimum.

WINES - Parrina's wines are reliable and their quality is consistent. We particularly liked the ones made with native grapes, such as **Costa dell'Argentario Ansonica 2012** (○ 30,000 bt), which matures briefly in barriques, offering pleasantly light flavor and blossomy impact on the nose. Parrina Vermentino 2012 (○ 7,000 bt) ages on steel and remains for a few months on the fine lees. We recommend it as an Everyday Wine. The excellent **Parrina Sangiovese 2012** (● 40,000 bt) has a nose of withered flowers and fruit jam and a warm, alcoholic palate with stand-out tannins. The concentrated **Parrina Radaia 2010** (● 3,000 bt), a monovarietal Merlot aged in new barriques, is deep, warm and pervasive.

---

32 ha - 80,000 bt

❝ With its alternative, sustainable approach to agriculture and original, full-flavored wines, Caiarossa represents the avant-garde on the Tuscan coast. ❞

PEOPLE - The Dutch entrepreneur Eric Alba Jelgersma embarked on this project in 2002. It is directed by enologist Dominique Genot and has always been conducted in accordance with organic and biodynamic principles, combining the advantages of the two schools of thought. In sum, this means lowering the impact of agricultural practices and taking care of the land.

VINEYARDS - The vineyards open up onto the natural amphitheater that surrounds the cellar. They grow on heterogeneous soil, the composition of which ranges from clayey and gravelly, ideal for varieties such as syrah, to stony, excellent for cabernet sauvignon. The sangiovese vines grow on sharply saline red earth. The spurred cordon training system is the most commonly used and yields total about 40 quintals per hectare.

WINES - The wines stand out for their eloquence and are all beautifully poised between intensity and finesse. **Pergolaia 2011** (● sangiovese, cabernet sauvignon e franc, merlot; 45,000 bt) has plenty of body but it's also extremely enjoyable by virtue of its refreshing juiciness and approachable tannins. **Caiarossa Bianco 2011** (○ chardonnay, viognier; 2,000 bt) offers toasted and ripe fruit aromas on the nose and a broad, full-flavored palate. **Oro di Caiarossa 2010** (○ petit manseng; 800 bt) is a passito with a nose of almonds and candied fruits and a fresh, tangy palate.

> **vino slow** **CAIAROSSA 2010** (● cabernet franc and sauvignon, merlot, sangiovese, petit verdot, syrah; 46,000 bt) A nose rich in fleshy fruit and delicate spiciness and a well-balanced, lean, minerally palate whose finish is harmonized by silky tannins.

FERTILIZERS organic-mineral, green manure
PLANT PROTECTION chemical, copper and sulphur
WEED CONTROL chemical, mechanical
YEASTS selected
GRAPES 100% estate-grown
CERTIFICATION none

FERTILIZERS natural manure, biodynamic preparations
PLANT PROTECTION copper and sulphur, organic
WEED CONTROL mechanical
YEASTS native
GRAPES 100% estate-grown
CERTIFICATION biodynamic, organic

Sassotondo

Frazione Sovana
Località Pian dei Conati, 52
tel. 0564 614218
www.sassotondo.it
info@sassotondo.it

11 ha - 50,000 bt **10% discount**

PEOPLE - Sassotondo is a magnificent spot. The visitor who arrives on this open plateau along the winding roads round Pitigliano is taken aback by its view over the Maremma. Edoardo Ventimiglia and Carla Benini came here in 1990. Their idea of viticulture is indissolubly linked to a life philosophy that exalts harmony between humans and the nature that surrounds them. This sensitivity soon led to organic certification.

VINEYARDS - On our walk round the vineyards with Carla, we noted how the company's approach of "listening to the land" has achieved balanced grape growth. Under our feet the soil was characterized by tufa, the footprint of every wine. The company's ciliegiolo is a massal selection from the "legendary" San Lorenzo vineyard with 30-year-old vines facing Pitigliano, bought in 1991.

WINES - Edoardo and Carla aim for elegance and drinkability in their wine, but they also like to experiment to figure out to interpret their grapes best. The top-rate **Maremma Ciliegiolo 2011** (● 15,000 bt) is almost piquant on the nose, easy to digest and fresh in the mouth. The excellent **Bianco di Pitigliano Isolina 2012** (○ 3,000 bt): has a nose of withered flowers and a flavorsome, juicy plate. **Numero 10 2009** (○ trebbiano; 600 bt) has a bouquet of summer flowers and a well-developed, rich-flavored palate. **Tufo Bianco 2012** (○ 6,000 bt) is also impressive.

vino slow SAN LORENZO 2010 (● ciliegiolo; 3,000 bt) A wine made with grapes from a vineyard that Carla and Edoardo literally saved from oblivion. Blossomy and spicy with a graceful, richly textured palate — we judged this to be one of the purest versions to date.

FERTILIZERS biodynamic preparations, green manure
PLANT PROTECTION copper and sulphur
WEED CONTROL mechanical
YEASTS native
GRAPES 100% estate-grown
CERTIFICATION organic

Casanova della Spinetta

Località Casanova
Via Provinciale Terricciolese
tel. 0587 690508
www.la-spinetta.com
toscana@la-spinetta.com

65 ha - 225,000 bt

PEOPLE - The first descriptions of a grape variety known as "sangioveto" date back to 1590, when a certain Gianvettorino Soderini defined it as "juicy and very full of wine". It was in 2001 that the Rivetti family, previously famous for their success in Piedmont, ventured down to the Pisan hills in Tuscany to try their hand with local grapes, among which the above-mentioned sangioveto-sangiovese. In their 65-hectare natural amphitheater, the Rivetti practice Tuscan viticulture while sticking to their own principles.

VINEYARDS - The vineyards round the wine cellar are a sight for sore eyes. The tight-packed vines are spurred cordon-trained with only a few fruit canes. The plants are pushed beyond their limits, though they never exceed 6,500 per hectare on mainly sandy soil. In the cellar wines are barrel- and bottle-aged to soak up the essence of the terroir.

WINES - Sangiovese Sassontino 2004 (● 6,000 bt) evidences this terroir's great suitability for the Tuscan grape variety par excellence; its delicate blossomy and earthy fragrances and complex, harmonious palate make it a Great Wine. **Vermentino 2012** (○ 32,000 bt) is a white worthy of the "red carpet", bright, refined, summer and pleasing. The stylishly balsamic **Nero di Casanova 2009** (● sangiovese; 140,000 bt) veers towards fresh notes of Mediterranean maquis. **Gentile di Casanova 2008** (● prugnolo gentile; 15,000 bt) denotes a palate-nose balance to match its name. The enjoyable, well-rounded, racy **Colorino di Casanova 2008** (● 15,000 bt) hits the nose with vanilla and orange blossom. The top-of-the range **Chianti Ris. 2008** (● 23,000 bt) is complex with spice on the nose and a long palate with young tannins that are bound to grow.

FERTILIZERS natural manure, compost, green manure
PLANT PROTECTION copper and sulphur
WEED CONTROL mechanical
YEASTS native
GRAPES 100% estate-grown
CERTIFICATION none

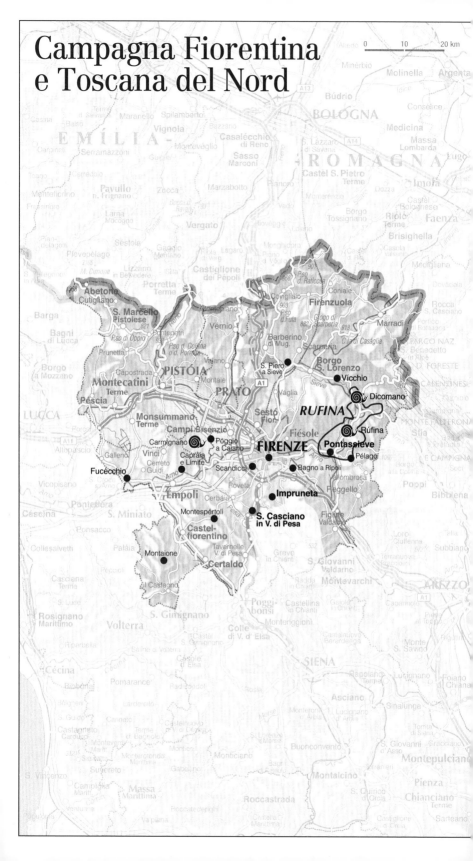

Campagna Fiorentina e Toscana del Nord

CARMIGNANO (PO)

Fattoria di Bacchereto
Terre a Mano

Via Fontemorana, 179
tel. 055 8717191
terreamano@gmail.com

8 ha - 23,000 bt

66 After making the radical decision in favor of sustainable viticulture, Rossella Bencini Tesi interprets the prestigious Carmignano denomination in wines of great personality and eloquent naturalness. 99

PEOPLE - A highly motivated company that aims for maximum naturalness in all its products, from wine to olive oil to its exquisite dried figs. Marco Vannucci is the enologist and Silvio Nuti works in the cellar and the vineyards, while Alberto "Bibi" Guidotti is a jack-of-all-trades, a self-taught polyglot with thousands of stories to tell.

VINEYARDS - The limited amount of land planted with vines is divided into eight plots in a large olive grove with about 9,000 trees. Five of the vineyards surround the manor house and enjoy considerable temperature ranges. Precisely in view of the microclimatic differences between the vineyards, each is worked and harvested separately with ad hoc vinification.

WINES - The cellar is fitted out with basic equipment such as a grape press and French wood casks for aging the wine. The wines are fermented with native yeasts and are neither filtered nor clarified. Fortified by constant stirring of the lees, they are endowed with great body and texture. **Sassocarlo 2011** (○ trebbiano, malvasia; 3,000 bt) is an excellent, delicate white with a complex bouquet and long palate. **Carmignano Terre a Mano 2010** (● sangiovese, cabernet sauvignon, canaiolo; 10,000 bt) has a delicate nose and a well-structured palate and is ready to uncork. **Vin Santo di Carmignano 2003** (○ trebbiano, malvasia; 1,300 bt) is powerful and creamy with pronounced dried fruit, lingering on the palate with penetrating but never cloying sweetness.

DICOMANO (FI)

Fattoria Il Lago

Frazione Campagna, 18
Località Citerna
tel. 055 838047
www.fattoriaillago.com
info@fattoriaillago.com

21 ha - 50,000 bt

PEOPLE - Fattoria Il Lago is situated on the extreme edge of the lovely Rufina area. The Spagnoli bought the farm in the 1960s to produce wine and provide tourist accommodation. Today brothers Filippo and Francesco run the place which, enologically speaking, is enjoying success for its reliability and consistent quality.

VINEYARDS - The vineyard has carved out a niche for itself within the broader farm, in which woods and lakes ensure vital temperature control. The vineyards form a mosaic whose different tiles are planted on the best hillsides available. In the part nearest the woods, the pinot nero vineyard has the lowest average temperature. The sangiovese grapes are planted on soil rich in limestone and clay.

WINES - Fabrizio Moltard offers precious collaboration in the cellar, where the wines are fermented in stainless steel vats and barrel-aged. The engrossing **Syrah 2009** (● 2,500 bt) combines fragrant varietal scents with deep texture and balance. Made with grapes first dried, then pressed, **Pian dei Guardi 2008** (● sangiovese; 6,000 bt) has a nose of fruit jam and a palate of close-knit tannins. The commendable steel-aged Chianti Rufina 2011 (● 30,000 bt) has floral fragrances and a juicy, harmonious palate; it's a worthy Everyday Wine. Barrel-aged for 14 months, the deeper, more complex **Chianti Rufina Ris. 2007** (● 4,000 bt) has a dynamic palate refrained by slightly unfocused tannins. **Vin Santo del Chianti Rufina 2001** (● 2,500 bt) is ethereal, delicate and very long indeed.

FERTILIZERS green manure
PLANT PROTECTION copper and sulphur, organic
WEED CONTROL mechanical
YEASTS native
GRAPES 100% estate-grown
CERTIFICATION organic

FERTILIZERS organic-mineral
PLANT PROTECTION chemical, copper and sulphur
WEED CONTROL chemical, mechanical
YEASTS selected
GRAPES 100% estate-grown
CERTIFICATION none

DICOMANO (FI)

Frascole

Località Frascole, 27 A
tel. 055 8386340
www.frascole.it
frascole@frascole.it
⌐—0

---

16 ha - 50,000 bt | **10% discount**

66 Enrico Lippi, who works in the vineyards and cellar, and his wife Elisa Santoni are the heart and soul of Frascole. They have raised the profile of this, a jewel of a place set in the gorgeous Rufina landscape, through their love of the land and wines of exceptional quality. 99

PEOPLE - Now that it has added new labels to its range, Frascole has become one of the most interesting cellars on the Tuscan wine scene.

VINEYARDS - The vineyards are situated in two areas with different microclimates and are an average 15 years old, though one small portion goes back 50 years. A number of different plots are on steep gradients and are split up into small parcels to make them manageable. The characteristics of the different blocks come out in harmonious, well-balanced, beautifully delicate wines in the cellar.

WINES - We are at pains to point out how good quality characterizes all the wines submitted, an exception more than a rule that rewards Enrico for all his hard work. Two new labels made their debut this year. The first, **In Albis 2011** (O trebbiano; 1,800 bt), the result of an assemblage of five typologies of trebbiano, has stylish texture and is leisurely on both nose and palate. The second is the deep, highly scented **Limine 2008** (● merlot; 2,000 bt), full of finesse and acidic length. The top class **Vin Santo del Chianti 2004** (O trebbiano, malvasia; 1,000 bt) is impressive for texture and aroma. Chianti Rufina 2011 (● 30,000 bt) offers substance and balance at a reasonable price — it's one of this year's best Everyday Wines. **Bitornino 2011** (● sangiovese, canaiolo, trebbiano; 15,000 bt) is terroir-dedicated, simple and light in both texture and price.

FERTILIZERS manure pellets, green manure
PLANT PROTECTION copper and sulphur
WEED CONTROL mechanical
YEASTS native
GRAPES 100% estate-grown
CERTIFICATION organic

LUCCA

Fabbrica di San Martino €

Frazione San Martino in Vignale
Via Pieve Santo Stefano, 2511
tel. 0583 394284
www.fabbricadisanmartino.it
info@fabbricadisanmartino.it
⌐—0

2.2 ha - 12,000 bt

PEOPLE - Giuseppe Ferrua and his wife Giovanna Tronci made a real life choice when, in 2002, they decided to sell their successful restaurant business to devote themselves entirely to farming on this patch of land overlooking Lucca. Here they have restored their 20 hectares of woodland, olive groves and vineyards to the natural state. The scene is dominated by a magnificent 18th-century villa on the top of the hill.

VINEYARDS - There are only 2.2 hectares of vines, some of which over 600 years old, with mixed native grape varieties, as was the custom in those years. Giuseppe guards them jealously, patiently replacing gaps with replants from scions. The vineyard is surrounded by woodland in which free-range Garfagnina cattle graze, "bringing slowness and increasing the biodiversity".

WINES - The wines of Fabbrica di San Martino are slow too: slow to develop, slow to mature, slow to express all their naturalness. **Colline Lucchesi Arcipressi Rosso 2012** (● sangiovese, malvasia, ciliegiolo; 3,000 bt), made with grapes from the old vineyard, matures in steel vats only and offers fresh scents, nice fruit and plenty of flavor on the finish. **Colline Lucchesi Fabbrica di San Martino Rosso 2010** (● sangiovese, canaiolo, colorino; 4,000 bt), steel-vat fermented before being aged for 12 months in wood barrels, is floral, a little mature and taut on the palate.

| vino slow | FABBRICA DI SAN MARTINO BIANCO 2011 (O vermentino, trebbiano, malvasia; 3,000 bt) Poised between style and craftsmanship, a true masterpiece. It is vinified in mid-sized casks after brief maceration on the skins and stays six months on the lees. The nose brims over with tropical fruit and the palate develops harmoniously and pervasively. |

FERTILIZERS green manure
PLANT PROTECTION copper and sulphur
WEED CONTROL mechanical
YEASTS native
GRAPES 100% estate-grown
CERTIFICATION biodynamic, organic

RUFINA (FI)

Fattoria Selvapiana

Località Selvapiana, 43
tel. 055 8369848
www.selvapiana.it
selvapiana@tin.it

60 ha - 240,000 bt

❝ Kindness and professionalism are the qualities with which the increasingly eco-sensitive Federico Giuntini runs a company that has become a focus, not only for the specific denomination but also for the sangiovese grape in general. ❞

PEOPLE - Federico is in charge of the cellar where he fondly preserves bottles of a hundred years and more. Enologist Franco Bernabei protects the specific properties of the grape in the cool, humid climate of the Rufina zone.

VINEYARDS - The terroir extends over two ridges on which the vineyards are set out in different locations. Here the soil is very pebbly with some clay. On raised-up ground in the middle of the estate soars a well-preserved medieval sighting tower. The average age of the vines is high, and some of them are 45 years old. Their yield is now relatively poor but the grapes still manage to be of the highest quality.

WINES - The wines of Selvapiana are scented and juicy with enormous elegance thanks to the cool Apennine climate. Despite the unfavorable growing year, **Chianti Rufina Bucerchiale Ris.** 2010 (● 26,000 bt), made with grapes from an old vineyard, was excellent once more. **Pomino Villa Petrognano 2011** (● sangiovese, cabernet, merlot; 6,000 bt) from the smallest, highest Tuscan DOC zone, is refreshing, fruity and well-balanced. Chianti Rufina 2011 (● 140,000 bt) is again an unbeatable wine in terms of value for money — a splendid Everyday Wine. **Syrah 2011** (● 1,800 bt) offers nicely crisp tannins and aromas of sweet spices. **Vin Santo del Chianti Rufina 2005** (○ trebbiano, malvasia; 2,000 bt) has all the traditional stylish aromas of dried fruit with refreshing acidity and an uncommonly leisurely finish.

FERTILIZERS organic-mineral, natural manure, green manure
PLANT PROTECTION copper and sulphur
WEED CONTROL mechanical
YEASTS native
GRAPES 100% estate-grown
CERTIFICATION converting to organics

SAN CASCIANO IN VAL DI PESA (FI)

Villa del Cigliano

Via Cigliano, 17
tel. 055 820033
www.villadelcigliano.it
n.montecchi@villadelcigliano.it

25 ha - 35,000 bt | 10% discount |

PEOPLE - Niccolò Montecchi began working in his family's wine company a few years ago and since then the improvement in quality has been evident. Today this young winemaker is faced with an even tougher task: namely imprinting the character of the terroir on his wines. The road he has undertaken, one of sustainability and the promotion of native grapes, is sure to lead him to excellent results.

VINEYARDS - Villa del Cigliano owns 60 hectares of land, of which about 25 are planted with vines. The vineyards have wide plant spacing and run round the cellar, crossing a hill whose soil is composed of "galestro" marl and clay. The age of the vines varies from 15 to 20 years. One of the first things Niccolò did when he joined the company was to improve the agronomic management. He is convinced, in fact, that the quality of wine is a direct consequence of the quality of viticulture.

WINES - The policy is to retain the pleasing, relaxed flavor of Chianti Classico, while adding deeper texture through more thorough work in the field. Hence maximum attention to aging, which is performed without small wood. **Chianti Cl. 2011** (● 25,000 bt) inherits vanilla notes from the aging process that are gradually replaced by balsamic florality and a broad, concentrated body. **Demodé 2012** (◉ sangiovese; 2,500 bt) is very pleasing in the glass.

| vino slow | **CHIANTI CL. RIS.** 2009 (● 3,000 bt) A splendid oak barrel-aged wine. Its aromas of almost dried flowers accompany well-extracted tangy, juicy texture. |

FERTILIZERS natural manure, green manure
PLANT PROTECTION chemical, copper and sulphur
WEED CONTROL mechanical
YEASTS native
GRAPES 100% estate-grown
CERTIFICATION none

Chianti Classico

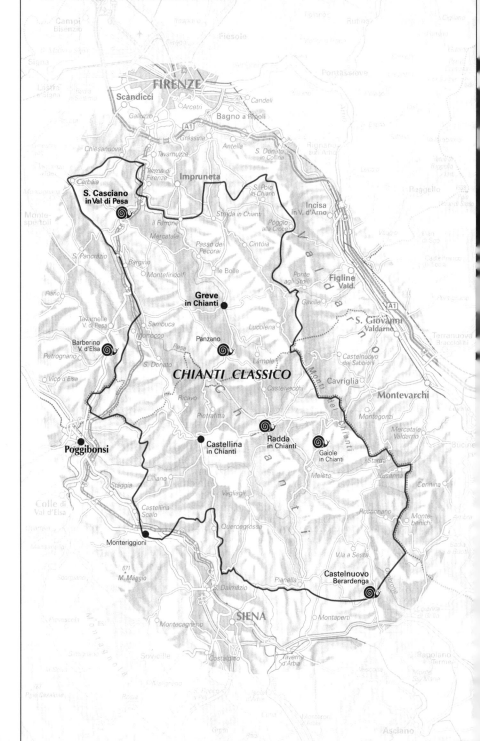

BARBERINO VAL D'ELSA (FI)
Castello della Paneretta €
Strada della Paneretta, 35
tel. 055 8059003
www.paneretta.it
paneretta@paneretta.it

BARBERINO VAL D'ELSA (FI)
Castello di Monsanto 🍾
Via Monsanto, 8
tel. 055 8059000
www.castellodimonsanto.it
monsanto@castellodimonsanto.it

22 ha - 100,000 bt | **10% discount**

70 ha - 400,000 bt | **10% discount**

PEOPLE - First impressions suggest a shy, ingoing person, but once you start talking all his eagerness to recount his passion and love of his job flood to the fore. Enrico Albisetti oversees his family's property in one of the most beautiful corners of the Chianti Classico denomination: 300 hectares of unspoiled nature among woods, olive groves and vineyards. His collaborators are consultant Nicola Berti, Marco Guiggiani and Gianluca Tapinassi.

VINEYARDS - Enrico took us round two of his company's most prestigious crus, Torre a Destra, planted in 2001, and Torre a Sinistra, replanted in 2010 with grafts of sangiovese from a massal selection. Their names, Right of the Tower and Left of the Tower, derive from the fact that they are situated on either side of a road that leads to a centuries-old sighting tower. The soil contains a large amount of maroon-colored ferrous "galestro".

WINES - We like the wines for the way in which they are simultaneously deft and delicate, straight-talking and sincere. They're like certain young girls who have little to say but have eyes that cut to your soul. Take **Terrine 2007** (● sangiovese, canaiolo; 6,500 bt) with its stylish aromas and a delicate suite of tannins that adds depth and fragrance. The company is justly proud of **Canaiolo 2009** (● 2,600 bt), a successful attempt to ennoble a native grape too often relegated to a bit part. **Chianti Classico Ris. 2009** (● 18,000 bt) follows the furrow of tradition with intact nuanced aromas, combining power and structure with flavor and welcome freshness. **Chianti Cl. 2010** was produced in limited quantities and is already sold out. The **Chianti Cl. 2011** (● 49,000 bt) is now on sale.

PEOPLE - It was in 1962 that Aldo Bianchi re-established ties with his never forgotten place of origin by buying this splendid Chianti estate. First his son Fabrizio, then in the last few years his granddaughter Laura have made the place a focus for lovers of the traditional wines of this part of Tuscany. We were accompanied on our visit by the company's enologist Andrea Giovannini.

VINEYARDS - The vineyards are as well kept as gardens and are fertilized mainly with leguminous manure. The soil has the composition typical of the Chianti zone with a high percentage of "galestro" marl mixed with clay and, in some places, chalky substances. The most famous vineyard, Poggio, is one of the denomination's most authentic crus. Viewing it from the top of the hill gave us a sense of the beauty of the landscape and the importance of human labor in preserving it over the course of time.

WINES - The wines are meticulously crafted and austere, untouched by passing fashion and exceptionally long-lasting. This was demonstrated in the vertical tasting of Chianti Cl. Ris. Il Poggio, organized to celebrate the company's 50th anniversary. **Chianti Cl. Ris. Il Poggio 2009** (● 18,000 bt) lives up to its fame with a complex, nuanced aromatic timbre and a burly, incisive palate packed with taste and charisma that ends in a grand finale. **Chianti Cl. 2011** (● 30,000 bt) is simpler, still young but already highly drinkable. The fragrant, captivating **Chianti Monrosso 2011** (● 100,000 bt) comes at a very reasonable price. **Chardonnay 2011** (○ 15,000 bt) is mineral on the nose, taut and harmonious.

| **vino slow** CHIANTI CL. RIS. 2010 (● 130,000 bt) A splendid wine with an intriguing bouquet of pencil lead and flowers, blood-rich and savory. In the mouth it expands into a wonderfully long, harmonious finish. |

FERTILIZERS natural manure
PLANT PROTECTION chemical, copper and sulphur
WEED CONTROL mechanical
YEASTS selected
GRAPES 100% estate-grown
CERTIFICATION none

FERTILIZERS organic-mineral, green manure
PLANT PROTECTION chemical, copper and sulphur
WEED CONTROL mechanical
YEASTS selected
GRAPES 100% estate-grown
CERTIFICATION none

BARBERINO VAL D'ELSA (FI)

Isole e Olena

Località Isole, 1
tel. 055 8072763
isolena@tin.it

CASTELLINA IN CHIANTI (SI)

Villa Pomona €

Località Pomona, 39
Strada Chiantigiana S.R. 222
tel. 0577 740930
www.fattoriapomona.it
villapomona@virgilio.it

---

45 ha - 200,000 bt

4.5 ha - 13,000 bt | **10% discount**

66 Paolo De Marchi has restored the old village of Isole e Olena, promoting it through wines of extraordinary quality that have once more drawn general attention to the growing potential of this area in the heart of the Chianti Classico zone. 99

PEOPLE - At one time Isole and Olena were two separate farms. It was in 1956 that De Marchi bought what remained of the two settlements and lumped everything together. Documents citing Olena in particular date back to the 12th century.

VINEYARDS - The initial idea, fruit of Paolo's international experience, was to plant both native and international grapes, seeking to pinpoint the best soil and weather conditions for each. The vineyard is immersed in an unspoiled landscape and extends over 45 hectares at an altitude of almost 400 meters on soil rich in marl. The cellar has always sought to recover vines found in loco and test their aptitude for quality.

WINES - If it's true that the terroir is stronger than the grape and that the wines made with allochthonous grapes are all of the highest standard, the quintessence of enology as applied to Isole e Olena is the cellar's interpretation of sangiovese. **Cepparello 2010** (● sangiovese; 38,000 bt) has deep earthy, blood-rich aromas and a gently tannic palate that evokes pleasure and a sense of place. It's once more a Great Wine and has enormous potential to evolve. **Chianti Cl. 2011** (● 137,000 bt), one of the best wines of the harvest, has a blossomy nose and a palate in which freshness and warmth interweave to create a supple, fragrant texture. The technically exemplary **Cabernet Sauvignon 2007** (● 4,000 bt) offers a bouquet of blackcurrant with balsamic hints and a juicy palate that is full of impetus.

PEOPLE - When Monica Raspi is talking about her winery she abbreviates its name to the that of the place where the vineyards are located: Pomona. For her, Pomona stands for more than just a business; it's also part of her life, a place where viticulture has become the destination of a journey without a return ticket. Tasting her wines, we reckon her choice was the right one.

VINEYARDS - You leave the house, you cross the road and, all of a sudden, you find yourself at the center of the company's five-hectare vineyard. Monica has been managing the vineyard firsthand for ten years now. It was her meeting with the agronomist Ruggero Mazzilli that made her dream of organics come true. The crest on which the vineyard sits has soil composed of "galestro" marl and clay and is excellent grape-growing land: it has thus been possible to introduce organic methods without traumatic dispersions of energy.

WINES - We are no longer taken aback by this winery's performances. Every year they reflect the variability of grape harvests with superlative wine quality. Yet there's always a plenty to be concerned about. The protracted fermentation of the grapes from the 2011 harvest, for example, had Monica worried until the summer after. **Chianti Cl. 2011** (● 10,000 bt) has scents of ripe fruit, brambles in particular, and the palate is dynamic and accomplished with full flavor and strong tannins containing the concentrated texture.

---

vino slow **CHIANTI CL. RIS. 2010** (● 3,300 bt) The wine ages in large oak barrels. Made with grape from a 30-year-old vineyard, it has blossomy depth with blood-rich reverberations. It has more extracts than in the past, but loses none of its expression and terroir-dedicated sweep.

FERTILIZERS organic-mineral, natural manure, compost
PLANT PROTECTION copper and sulphur
WEED CONTROL mechanical
YEASTS selected
GRAPES 100% estate-grown
CERTIFICATION none

FERTILIZERS natural manure, green manure
PLANT PROTECTION copper and sulphur
WEED CONTROL mechanical
YEASTS native
GRAPES 100% estate-grown
CERTIFICATION organic

CASTELNUOVO BERARDENGA (SI)

Fattoria di Fèlsina

Via del Chianti, 101
tel. 0577 355117
www.felsina.it
info@felsina.it

CASTELNUOVO BERARDENGA (SI)

Querciavalle €

Località Pontignanello, 6
tel. 0577 356842
www.agricolalosi.it
info@agricolalosi.it

75 ha - 500,000 bt | 10% discount

22 ha - 150000 bt

❝ Fèlsina is one of Tuscany's agricultural treasures. It owes its existence to the insight of Domenico Poggiali. In the mid 1960s he bought the estate to stop it being split up into bits, which would have been disastrous, and turned it into a model for the local area. ❞

PEOPLE - Caterina Mazzocolin and Giovanni Poggiali are the pioneering leaders of a company that owns two agricultural gems: the Fattoria di Fèlsina farm itself and the Castle of Farnetella in Sinalunga.

VINEYARDS - The company owns 11 plots, each with its own distinctive characteristics, each capable of adding complexity to its flagship grape, sangiovese. Subject to massal selection since 1983 and progressively replanted by Giovanni in 1993, the sangiovese, or sangioveses, of Fèlsina capture a deep sense of the Castelnuovo Berardenga terroir.

WINES - The range shines for consistent quality. We liked **Fontalloro 2010** (● sangiovese; 43,000 bt) a lot. Aged for three years in barriques, it releases blood-rich, ferrous aromas over a broad, vertical palate with sumptuous tannins — a classic Great Wine. **Chianti Cl. Rancia Ris. 2010** (● 47,000 bt), made with grapes from the same vineyard, is as excellent as ever. Aged for a year in new and second-use barriques, it has blossomy, balsamic aromas with a whiff of tobacco. The no-nonsense first impact on the palate contributes delightful overall complexity. **Chianti Cl. 2011** (● 240,000 bt) has a bouquet of ripe fruit and a broad palate with pronounced alcohol. The well-crafted **Maestro Raro 2010** (● cabernet sauvignon; 6,000 bt) is aged for a year in barriques and has beautifully deep vegetality and succulent juiciness.

PEOPLE - The Losi family's history as owners of Querciavalle began when great-grandfather Tranquillo, a sharecropper with the Bacci family, bought a piece of land. From 1954 to the 1970s they only produced wine at Querciavalle, selling it to other local producers, then they started to bottle it. Today the family winery is run by Pietro Losi and his brother Paolo, helped by Pietro's children, Valeria and Riccardo.

VINEYARDS - The vineyards, some of which 80 years old, are situated against the splendid backdrop of the charterhouse of Pontigano and look across to the towers of Siena, which stand out on the horizon. The soil varies and includes traces of clay, tufa, and "galestro" and "alberese" marl. The sangiovese clones needed for replanting were obtained from the oldest vineyards. A survey with the University of Florence has revealed the presence of old clones, the fruit of crossings with French grapes.

WINES - **Chianti Cl. Millenium Ris. 2008** (● 10,000 bt) is complex with notes first of leather and tobacco, then of cherry and chocolate. On the palate it is juicy and intense with lots of freshness, ready for a long life in the bottle. **Chianti Cl. Ris. 2010** (● 20,000 bt) is made with a selection of grapes from the old vineyards and aged in large barrels: it has sweet spices, ripe fruit and a pleasing finish. **Chianti Cl. 2011** (● 50,000 bt) is balanced and enjoyable. **Vigna della Capanna 2011** (● 15,000 bt) is a monovarietal easy-drinking Sangiovese whose soft palate sets off the edginess of the grape. Rosso del Cavalier Tranquillo 2011 (● sangiovese, canaiolo, malvasia and trebbiano; 20,000 bt), inspired by the classic Chianti recipe, is an excellent Everyday Wine. **Vin Santo del Chianti 2000** (O 5,000 bt) is succulent and never cloying.

FERTILIZERS biodynamic preparations, green manure
PLANT PROTECTION copper and sulphur
WEED CONTROL mechanical
YEASTS selected
GRAPES 100% estate-grown
CERTIFICATION converting to organics

FERTILIZERS natural manure, green manure
PLANT PROTECTION copper and sulphur
WEED CONTROL mechanical
YEASTS selected
GRAPES 100% estate-grown
CERTIFICATION none

Badia a Coltibuono

Località Badia a Coltibuono
tel. 0577 746110
www.coltibuono.com
info@coltibuono.com

70 ha - 250,000 bt

66 Thanks to its deep empathy with the land, which it defends with sensitive organic farming and viticulture and promotes with wines of outstanding quality, the company is at the very top of Italian winemaking. 99

PEOPLE - Badia a Coltibuono has belonged to the Stucchi Prinetti family for generations. Today, besides being the guardians of a century and more of history, sister and brother Emanuela and Roberto are also the main brains behind of the company's rise to quality.

VINEYARDS - At Coltibuono what organic management means most of all is maintaining the vitality of the soil to ensure the longevity of the vines and the general well-being of the ecosystem. The estate is seen as a complex organism in which the 70 hectares of vines, situated at Monti in Chianti at an altitude of 300-500 meters, interrelate with the surrounding environment.

WINES - The most important point to note is the quality of the wines, capable of combining a sense of belonging with splendid naturalness of expression. **Chianti Cl. 2011** (● 200,000 bt) is aged in large wood barrels. Paradigmatic for the typology, it releases blossomy notes followed by a taut, juicy palate. **Sangioveto 2009** (● sangiovese; 6,500 bt) has flower-petal delicacy and balsamic breadth on a vertical, fine, perfectly measured palate. **Vin Santo del Chianti Cl. 2006** (○ 10,000 bt) ages for four years in oak half-barriques. It smacks of undergrowth, dried mushrooms and hazelnuts and has a sweet acid palate.

vino slow CHIANTI CL. RIS. 2009 (● 40,000 bt) A wine aged for two years in oak casks and barrels of different sizes. It evokes the essence of the terroir with a delicate nose of citrus fruit and blossom, which leads into a deft, juicy body. Not to be missed.

FERTILIZERS natural manure, compost, green manure
PLANT PROTECTION copper and sulphur, organic
WEED CONTROL mechanical
YEASTS native
GRAPES 100% estate-grown
CERTIFICATION organic

Riecine

Località Riecine
tel. 0577 749098
www.riecine.it
info@riecine.com

11 ha - 50,000 bt

66 There have been lots of new developments at Riecine, plus the confirmation of a fact we knew already: that we can continue to bank on the talent of Sean O'Callaghan for wines that are a faithful expression of Chianti Classico. 99

PEOPLE - The new management has embarked on a necessary process of renovation. The most evident revolution is the building of a new cellar to replace the old ones, which had grown too cramped for the company's needs.

VINEYARDS - Agronomic dynamism is the quality that most characterizes the work of Sean, whose cosmopolitan experience has led him to shun all vineyard management dogma and opt for an empiric approach based on experience, insight and eco-sustainability. The company own 12 hectares planted with vines near the cellar and in the Vertine and Casina districts. The landscape is dominated by woodland, altitudes are high and the soil is stony.

WINES - As of next year, Riecine will discontinue production of the Riserva to create a monovarietal Sangiovese, the expression not of a denomination but of a place. This may not be the direction we would like the terroir to move in, but we respect the company's decision. **Chianti Cl. 2010** (● 38,000 bt) releases balsamic fruit with plenty of energy and sweetness. The mouthfeel is broad and succulent with dynamic taste ensured by a touch of splendid acidity that contributes raciness and length.

vino slow CHIANTI CL. RIS. 2009 (● 7,000 bt) A shining example of the company's style. Suspended midway between classicism, based on austere tannins and light body, and modernism, the result of notes of ripe fruit on the nose and a juice-rich palate, this is a classy, personality-packed wine that really works.

FERTILIZERS compost, biodynamic preparations, green manure
PLANT PROTECTION copper and sulphur
WEED CONTROL mechanical
YEASTS native
GRAPES 100% estate-grown
CERTIFICATION organic

Rocca di Castagnoli 🍷

Località Castagnoli
tel. 0577 731004
www.roccadicastagnoli.com
info@roccadicastagnoli.com

220 ha - 780,000 bt   **10% discount**

PEOPLE - Rocca di Castagnoli was established in 1981 by Calogero Calì, a lawyer with winemaking passion and vision. Besides the historic nucleus, which corresponds to the splendid hamlet of Castagnoli, near Gaiole in Chianti, he owns other autonomous wineries in the Chianti Classico and Maremma districts in Tuscany and in Sicily. This "constellation" of vineyards is managed with great professionalism by Rolando Bertacchini.

VINEYARDS - The vineyards reach altitudes of 850 meters in an exceptional variety of different positions. Castello di San Sano, in the commune of Gaiole, is characterized by stony soil. Tenuta di Capraia, at Castellina in Chianti, has tufaceous sandy soil with traces of clay. The estate in the Maremma district is situated at the heart of the Morellino denomination. The grapes from all the vineyards are interpreted with great attention to sustainability.

WINES - The quality of the wines is remarkable and puts the group among the best large-scale winemakers in Italy. The splendid **Chianti Cl. Castello di San Sano Guarnellotto Ris.** 2010 (● 25,000 bt) has satisfying aromatic freshness and depth: for us, it's this year's Great Wine. **Stielle 2009** (● sangiovese), a potent wine that will become more flavorsome as time goes by, is made with grapes from one of the company's crus. **Chianti Cl. Poggio a' Frati Ris.** 2010 (● 30,000 bt) expresses splendidly clean floral scents and is relaxed and pervasive on the palate. **Chianti Cl. Rocca di Castagnola 2011** (● 300,000 bt) is fragrant, pleasing and supple. A special favorite of ours is **Castello di San Sano Borro al Fumo 2009** (● sangiovese, malvasia lunga del Chianti; 2,000 0.5 l bt), which has a gentle blossomy nose and a deft palate. **Castello di San Sano Chianti Cl. 2011** (● 200,000 bt) is very approachable.

FERTILIZERS organic-mineral, manure pellets
PLANT PROTECTION chemical, copper and sulphur
WEED CONTROL mechanical
YEASTS native
GRAPES 100% estate-grown
CERTIFICATION none

San Giusto a Rentennano 🍷

Località San Giusto a Rentennano
tel. 0577 747121
www.fattoriasangiusto.it
info@fattoriasangiusto.it

31 ha - 70,000 bt

PEOPLE - One page in the history of the Chianti wine renaissance has been written by San Giusto a Rentennano. The winery is still considered symbol of Chianti Classico for the expressive exactness and stylistic consistency of its wines, all endowed with huge aging potential. It is managed by Luca Martini di Cigala, who oversees matters agronomic, helped by his brother, who runs the cellar.

VINEYARDS - You realize Luca is a very skilled winemaker when he starts talking about his vineyards. These are located on three different hillsides: the first looks over the River Arbia and has "alberese" and "galestro" soil which, respectively, give wines body and finesse ; the second grows on tufa, sand and rock; the third, opposite Monti in Chianti, has clay-rich soil. Organic methods have been used since 2001.

WINES - Across the various typologies, San Giusto's sangiovese grapes are always genuine, full of naturalness and freshness, structure and alcohol, characteristics that morph into superb finesse with age. The barrique-aged **Percarlo 2009** (● sangiovese; 12,900 bt) is a wine of unique charm that alternates spicy and earthy notes; fresh and intense, it caresses the palate with faint hints of minerals before being lifted by a delicately tannic finish. It's a Great Wine. The excellent **La Ricolma 2010** (● merlot; 4.000 bt) has an exciting nose and a juicy, well-sustained palate with a full, lingering finish. **Chianti Cl. Le Baroncole Ris.** 2010 (● 10,500 bt) stands out for the eloquence of its fruit, flavor and length. **Chianti Cl.** 2011 (● 35,200 bt) is a reliable wine with satisfying, sinewy, typical flavor.

FERTILIZERS natural manure, compost, green manure
PLANT PROTECTION copper and sulphur, organic
WEED CONTROL mechanical
YEASTS native
GRAPES 100% estate-grown
CERTIFICATION organic

Podere Castellinuzza

Località Lamole
Via Petriolo, 21
tel. 055 8549052
castellinuzza@yahoo.it

Querciabella

Via di Barbiano, 17
tel. 055 85927777
www.querciabella.com
info@querciabella.com

4,5 ha - 7,000 bt

106 ha - 300,000 bt   **10% discount**

PEOPLE - Arriving at Castellinuzza, we've always been struck by the beauty of the place. It's situated in the Lamole district, an oasis in the heart of the Chianti Classico zone. The owner of this small winery, Paolo Coccia, is animated by great passion, which he has passed on to his daughter Serena, who helps him with the administrative side of the business, and his wife Luisa Cavigli, who oversees the cellar and retail sales.

VINEYARDS - Paolo proudly takes us for a walk through vineyards, his kingdom: from the almost 100-year-old vine rows still bush-trained, to the ones planted 47 years ago and trained with the local Chianti arch system, to the most recent ones of 16 years protected by the surrounding woodland. The soil is quite loose with "galestro" marl resting on mattaione, a friable stone that allows the vine roots to delve deep. The vines are all constantly monitored without recourse to chemicals.

WINES - Soil composition, high altitude, northwest- and southwest-facing positions, and an excellent microclimate add unique properties to the wines. Fermentation and aging in cement vats maintain and lift the varietal components of the fruit and the terroir. This year the Riserva 2010 and Rosso 2011 weren't produced, but Chianti Cl. 2011 (● 7,000 bt) was, impressing us with its aromatic complexity and richness notwithstanding the particularly warm growing year. Its aromas are mineral and balsamic, spicy and fruity while the palate has dynamic character full of freshness and polished tannins. It's a perfect Everyday Wine. During our visit we also had the pleasure to taste some older vintages, which confirmed all these wines' potential.

PEOPLE - Respect for the environment and entrepreneurial vision are the qualities that have allowed Querciabella to assert itself as a model in the Chianti Classico zone. The Castiglioni family believes in sustainable viticulture and espoused biodynamics ten years ago. After fine-tuning their agronomic methods, they aim to exalt the different aptitudes of their vineyards, which include some of the finest crus in the denomination.

VINEYARDS - The heart of the cellar's land is the hill of Ruffoli in the commune of Greve in Chianti. The vineyards climb to the highest hilltops in the Chianti Classico denomination. Altitude and conduciveness for wine-growing also characterize the other Chianti vineyards at Gaiole and Radda. Another 30 hectares are situated in the Maremma to round off a complex set of properties to which Querciabella applies biodynamics with the utmost conviction.

WINES - The cellar's terroir gives rise to stylistically exemplary wines. **Camartina 2010** (● cabernet sauvignon, sangiovese; 15,000 bt) ages for about two years in wood barrels of which 40 per cent are new; connoted by depth of flavor and crystalline fruity aromas, it's a Great Wine. Poised between finesse and concentration, **Batàr 2011** (○ chardonnay, pinot bianco; 10,000 bt) is once again one of the best whites in Tuscany. **Chianti Cl. 2011** (● 90,000 bt), made with sangiovese grapes grown in the hills of Radda and Ruffoli, has aromas of citrus fruit and a deft palate with flavorsome tannins. On its debut, **Turpino 2010** (● cabernet franc, syrah, merlot; 20,000 bt), a blend of Chianti and Maremma grapes, is refreshing and pleasing. **Palafreno 2010** (● merlot; 3,500 bt) is nicely complex.

FERTILIZERS organic-mineral
PLANT PROTECTION copper and sulphur
WEED CONTROL mechanical
YEASTS selected
GRAPES 100% estate-grown
CERTIFICATION none

FERTILIZERS compost, biodynamic preparations, green manure
PLANT PROTECTION copper and sulphur
WEED CONTROL mechanical
YEASTS native
GRAPES 100% estate-grown
CERTIFICATION biodynamic

Castello dei Rampolla 🐌

Via Case Sparse, 22
tel. 055 852001
castellodeirampolla.cast@tin.it

Fontodi 🐌

Via San Leolino, 89
tel. 055 852005
www.fontodi.com
fontodi@fontodi.com

---

32 ha - 80,000 bt

66 By virtue of sensitive agronomic choices designed to preserve the life of the soil and the superlative quality of its wines, Castello dei Rampolla should be regarded as a model for Italian winemaking to follow. 99

PEOPLE - The sister-and-brother team of Maurizia and Luca Di Napoli Rampolla have inherited the company, which has been in the family for more than three centuries. In 1965 their father Alceo began to convert what was then a farm into a winery. Maurizia and Luca now run the company with biodynamic methods.

VINEYARDS - The vineyards enjoy an enviable south-facing position round the family villa at an altitude of 300 meters. The mostly marly soil is only worked lightly in summer and the grass is mowed by hand. The majority of the vineyards date from the 1990s, though there is still a portion of cabernet planted in 1978. The celebrated Vigna d'Alceo vineyard is bush-trained, while the other vineyards are cordon-trained.

WINES - A charismatic winery that refuses to give in to market standardization and produces wines that are strongly terroir-dedicated. **Sangiovese 2011 (●** 1,000 bt) is precise on the nose and palate. **Chianti Cl. 2011 (●** 36,000 bt) has delicate aromas, juicy flavor and a pleasantly refreshing finish. The sumptuous **Sanmarco 2009 (●** cabernet sauvignon, sangiovese, merlot; 20,000 bt) has a nose of blackcurrant with streaks of balsam and a palate of deftly interlaced complexity and concentration — a Great Wine. **Trebianco 2011 (○** sauvignon blanc, traminer, chardonnay; 1,000 bt) produces intense aromas and tangy flavors without the use of sulphur. The delicate, stylish **D'Alceo 2009 (○** cabernet sauvignon, petit verdot; 13,000 bt) is full and concentrated in the mouth with a grand finale of welcome fruity encores.

FERTILIZERS biodynamic preparations
PLANT PROTECTION copper and sulphur, organic
WEED CONTROL mechanical
YEASTS native
GRAPES 100% estate-grown
CERTIFICATION none

---

80 ha - 300,000 bt

66 Fontodi is a prestigious Chianti Classico that has learned to approach its vast tracts of vineyard with respect for the soil and the use of old farming skills. 99

PEOPLE - The company was taken over by the Manetti family in the late 1960s. Since then he has made a significant contribution to the revival of the local area thanks to the success of its wines on the world market.

VINEYARDS - The vineyards are lumped together in a single plot in the heart of the Conca d'oro, or golden valley, near Panzano in Chianti. The agronomic system perfected by Giovanni Manetti over the years is based on the closed-cycle concept. In other words, everything used in the production process comes from inside the company itself, which seeks to do without external inputs. In the owner's view, it takes a living vineyard, meaning a vineyard rich in microbiological activity, to grow grapes of high quality.

WINES - Despite this textbook viticulture, the expressiveness of the wines was down a little this year, maybe because we tasted them a tad too early (especially since they are made to evolve). **Chianti Cl. Vigna del Sorbo Ris. 2010 (●** 20,000 bt) ages for two years in barriques, half of which new. It has aromas of soil and leather and a deep, tannic palate. **Chianti Cl. 2010 (●** 170,000 bt) releases citrus fruits and blossom on the nose and an agreeably dainty palate. **Flaccianello della Pieve 2010 (●** 55,000 bt) ages for two years in new barriques. For the moment it seems a little tight on the nose with undertones of ripe fruit, vanilla and spice, while the tannins are still hard. It's a wine that still needs time to develop. **Syrah Case Via 2010 (●** 12,000 bt) has sweet, spicy aromas, excellent concentration and dynamic juiciness.

FERTILIZERS natural manure, compost, green manure
PLANT PROTECTION copper and sulphur
WEED CONTROL mechanical
YEASTS native
GRAPES 100% estate-grown
CERTIFICATION organic

Le Cinciole

Via Case Sparse, 83
tel. 055 852636
www.lecinciole.it
info@lecinciole.it

Cinciano

Località Cinciano, 2
tel. 0577 936588
www.cinciano.it
info@cinciano.it

---

12 ha - 40,000 bt

33 ha - 200,000 bt `10% discount`

66 Viticulture that respects the life of the soil, winemaking talent, consistent quality — these are the distinctive features of one of Chianti Classico's most significant wineries. 99

PEOPLE - She's an architect and comes from Monza, he's a surveyor and comes from Rome. Their work took them to Milan in the late 1980s but neither was satisfied. They were looking for something "to click, something to do firsthand". Valeria Viganò and Luca Orsini, the heart and soul of Le Cinciole, made their dream come true in the 1990s. Everything clicked when they discovered Panzano.

VINEYARDS - As Luca sees it, it's vital to maintain the equilibrium of the vine. The soil is worked in-depth, the grass is mowed between the vine rows, compost is prepared in-house. "It's also fundamental," according to Luca, "to do everything possible to protect the plants from the caprices of the weather. In recent years we had the problem of over-ripe grapes, this year we have unevenly distributed ripeness".

WINES - The sangiovese selection has produced **Petresco 2009** (● 5,000 bt), from this year no longer a Chianti Classico Riserva, which has mature notes on the nose and well-judged wood. **Calamaione 2008** (● cabernet, merlot, syrah; 3,000 bt) is a blend of different grapes but manages to capture a sense of place. It releases a broad suite of aromas with a mid-palate of great acid energy and an impressively long finish. Last but not least, **Rosato 2012** (⊙ 2,000 bt) is a Sangiovese of some charm with a full-flavored, racy palate.

PEOPLE - The first document to mention Cinciano goes back to 1126, when the estate was given as a gift to Gotifredo, the bishop of Florence. The place stayed in the hands of the church until 1983, the year in which the Garrè bought it. Brothers Ferdinando and Ottavia administer the property with the help of Claudio Antonelli on the management side and sales manager Angelo Dalbello. Valerio Marconi oversees the vineyard and cellar with the assistance of consultant Stefano Porcinai.

VINEYARDS - The vineyards, which surround the villa, grow almost exclusively sangiovese grapes. Over the last ten years or so they have been gradually replanted. The new parcels are spurred cordon-trained, while the single-arched cane system is still used on the old 40-year-old vines. The soil is composed of sandstone and alberese, and the vineyards face southeast on gently rolling hills rimmed by woodland.

WINES - Though the company is currently overhauling its management sytems, it continues to take great care over its vineyard and cellar work the aim of which is to squeeze the best out of the grapes. **Chianti Cl. 2011** (● 25,000 bt) is flavorful and delicate, while **Pietraforte 2011** (● sangiovese, merlot, cabernet; 3,000 bt) has pleasing mineral aromas and a long, well-rounded palate. **Rosso 2011** (● sangiovese; 13,000 bt) offers good value for money and is ideal for daily drinking. **Gotifredo Rosato 2012** (⊙ sangiovese; 6,500 bt) releases delicate fruity scents and impressive freshness. The blossomy **Bianco 2012** (○ viognier, sauvignon blanc, grechetto; 6,600 bt) is poised between saltiness and sweetness on the finish.

---

vino slow CHIANTI CL. 2010 (● 25,000 bt) An elegant, harmonious wine with welcome grip. It has a stunningly aerial character, essential but capable of leaving on the palate a delicious streak of tangy acidity.

vino slow CHIANTI CL. RIS. 2010 (● 15,000 bt) All the finesse of Chianti Classico is concentrated into ths wine. The nose is elegant and earthy, the flavor enfolding, beautifully set off by the tannins, which add panache and personality.

FERTILIZERS natural manure, green manure
PLANT PROTECTION copper and sulphur
WEED CONTROL mechanical
YEASTS native
GRAPES 100% estate-grown
CERTIFICATION organic

FERTILIZERS organic-mineral
PLANT PROTECTION chemical, copper and sulphur
WEED CONTROL mechanical
YEASTS selected, native
GRAPES 100% estate-grown
CERTIFICATION none

Caparsa

RADDA IN CHIANTI (SI)

S.C. Caparsa, 47
tel. 0577 738174
www.caparsa.it
caparsa@caparsa.it

12 ha - 20,000 bt | **10% discount**

66 Caparsa's clean viticulture produces exciting wines with a genuine sense of place. The winery is a milestone in the real history of Chianti Classico. 99

PEOPLE - Paolo Cianferoni is an amazing character. When you meet him you immediately think, "What a winemaker!" It's a real pleasure to hear him rambling on about farming history and agriculture in general. He's especially interesting when he gets on to his own story and the "secrets" he picked up from the old sharecroppers who used to work on the estate.

VINEYARDS - "After replanting the vineyards, I have a visceral feeling that at last Caparsa has the imprinting I was after," says Paolo. On our visit to the Doccio a Matteo vineyard at an altitude of 480 meters we discovered that grape pips 2,300 years old were recently unearthed on the hilltop. Not bad as a confirmation of the suitability of the alberese, marl and clay soil for winemaking! The pips are now on display at the museum in Castellina in Chianti, by the way.

WINES - The cellar is well worth a visit. "I have 12 hectares of vines," says Paolo, "and produce more Chianti Classico than I actually bottle. What's left, if I don't like it, I sell unbottled." This is why he didn't produced Chianti Classico Doccio a Matteo in the 2009 vintage. **Chianti Cl. Caparsino Ris. 2009** (● 10,000 bt) lives up to its reputation with a nose compressed by spiciness finished off by hints of fruit and blossom, an acid, well-disciplined palate and a commendably assertive finish. **Rosso di Caparsa** (● sangiovese, trebbiano, malvasia; 4,000 bt) is racy with juicy fruit and an inviting, enjoyable finish. **Bianco di Caparsino 2011** (○ trebbiano, malvasia; 800 bt) is on the husky side.

FERTILIZERS manure pellets, natural manure
PLANT PROTECTION copper and sulphur
WEED CONTROL mechanical
YEASTS native
GRAPES 100% estate-grown
CERTIFICATION organic

Monteraponi

RADDA IN CHIANTI (SI)

Località Monteraponi
tel. 055 352601
www.monteraponi.it
mail@monteraponi.it

10 ha - 42,000 bt | **10% discount**

66 Michele Braganti has given a new lease of life to the property his family bought in the early 1970s. Drawing on a penchant for winegrowing he never knew he had, he has asserted himself in a brief space of time with extremely delicate, terroir-dedicated wines. 99

PEOPLE - Monteraponi is one of those villages of wild, breathtaking beauty where time seems to have stood still. The Braganti family has captured the essence of the place and conveys it flavor with a sustainable approach to winemaking in which preservation of the oldest vineyards is one of the top priorities.

VINEYARDS - The vineyards, all well located in a cool, picturesque valley, are rimmed by woodland and grow on marly limestone soil. They are naturally managed with green manure cropping and covering as opposed to topping. The grapes from the Baron Ugo vineyard, at an altitude of 560 meters vines up to 40 years old, give depth, minerality and texture, whereas those from the Campitello vineyard, at an altitude of 420 meters, have greater fruity fragrance.

WINES - The company's small cellar is practical and essential, like its vinification. The wines are craft-made, so close-focused, so terroir-dedicated, so enjoyable it's hard to pick out the best. The verdict on **Chianti Cl. Baron Ugo Ris. 2009** (● 3,000 bt) was unanimous, however. It's a pedigree wine of pure class, one of the denomination's finest. For us, it's a Great Wine. We also enjoyed the naturalness and character of **Chianti Cl. Campitello Ris. 2010** (● 4,000 bt) and the blossomy fragrance of **Chianti Cl. 2011** (● 30,000). Interesting too was the new **Trebbiano 2012** (○ 700 bt), the fruit of a special vinification and maceration technique. **Vino Rosso di Monteraponi** (● 6,000 bt) is an enjoyable blend of grapes varieties.

FERTILIZERS green manure
PLANT PROTECTION copper and sulphur
WEED CONTROL mechanical
YEASTS native
GRAPES 100% estate-grown
CERTIFICATION organic

RADDA IN CHIANTI (SI)

Montevertine

Località Montevertine
tel. 0577 738009
www.montevertine.it
info@montevertine.it

RADDA IN CHIANTI (SI)

Poggerino

Località Poggerino
tel. 0577 738958
www.poggerino.com
info@poggerino.com

---

18 ha - 80,000 bt

12 ha - 60,000 bt

" The company has sealed the bond between sangiovese and its preferred terrain, the Chianti Classico zone, and has now become one of its most admired interpreters. **"**

PEOPLE - Martino Manetti is firmly at the company helm now that the people who put it on the map have gone. After his father Sergio and Giulio Gambelli, last year Bruno Bini died. He was the factotum, the heart and soul of this legendary winery, a connoisseur of its land and cellar, to which he devoted his life. We join Martino in remembering his humility and simplicity.

VINEYARDS - Kissed by heaven! That's how we would describe the land where the company's vineyards grow, where the sangiovese grape expresses itself purely and profoundly, almost like nowhere else. The vineyards are split into different plots and stand at an altitude of 380-550 meters on loose limestone soil with traces of marl and alberese. They are managed with an entirely natural, eco-friendly approach under the expert agronomic consultancy of Ruggero Mazzilli.

WINES - Year after year, our tastings reveal the absolute value and excellence of the company's wines, which convey the peculiarities of land and vintage faithfully, immaculately and naturally. The profile of **Le Pergole Torte 2010** (● sangiovese; 24,000 bt) is fresh and crystalline, earthy and broad, the palate is stylish and sinuous, taut and linear with assertive, full-flavored, tremendously deep acidity — a Great Wine. **Pian del Ciampolo 2011** (● sangiovese, colorino, canaiolo; 25,000 bt) has better-developed fruit, a characteristic typical of the vintage.

vino slow **MONTEVERTINE 2010** (● sangiovese, colorino, canaiolo; 23,000 bt) An ever-changing nose of red berries, blossom and soil and a precise, full-flavored, complex, long palate — a wine that's Chianti to the marrow.

PEOPLE - Piero Lanza, a skilled winemaker who knows what he's about, has been running the family cellar since 1988. Displaying precocious agronomic sensibility, he understood rightaway that the quality of wine depends on the care one puts into the vineyard. Which is why he took up organic viticulture about ten years ago. Today his voice is one of the most authoritative of the entire denomination.

VINEYARDS - As we observed the vines on our visit in May, Piero explained that the uniformity of the canopy and the bright green that characterizes all the vine rows were the fruit of careful working of the soil, which he sees as the "raw material" of his wines. He sows tall fescue in the most fertile areas and clover in the others to ensure both healthy competition and the right amount of organic substances. The company cru is the Bugialla vineyard.

WINES - Tasting from the barrel wine from the portions of vineyard kept separate — which has incredible nuances of flavor — reminds one of all the energy put into the hard work in the field. **Chianti Cl. 2010** (● 40,000 bt) is a complex wine that opens on ripe fruit tones before veering towards blossomy notes. The full-flavored palate is distinguished by texture and lightness. **Labirinto 2011** (● sangiovese; 7,000 bt) comes from the lower parts of the vineyard: barrel-aged for a year, it is a dynamic interpretation of the Radda terroir. **Primamateria 2009** (● sangiovese, merlot, cabernet sauvignon; 4,000 bt) is valid too.

vino slow **CHIANTI CL. BUGIALLA RIS. 2009** (● 7,000 bt) Aged for two years in 20-hectoliter barrels and mid-sized casks, a wine with its place of origin written all over it. Blood-rich and spicy, then citrussy on the nose, it is at once deep and dynamic on the palate with tannins of rare finesse.

FERTILIZERS natural manure, compost
PLANT PROTECTION copper and sulphur, organic
WEED CONTROL mechanical
YEASTS native
GRAPES 100% estate-grown
CERTIFICATION none

FERTILIZERS green manure
PLANT PROTECTION copper and sulphur
WEED CONTROL mechanical
YEASTS native
GRAPES 100% estate-grown
CERTIFICATION organic

RADDA IN CHIANTI (SI)

Val delle Corti

Località La Croce
Case Sparse Val delle Corti, 144
tel. 0577 738215
www.valdellecorti.it
info@valdellecorti.it

7 ha - 28,000 bt **10% discount**

❝ The company was founded by Roberto's father in 1974 and Roberto took it over in 1999. His idea has always been to develop the expression and character that the local area instills into its grapes — with respect for the environment of course. ❞

PEOPLE - Val delle Corti is no longer just a pleasant surprise. These days its wines are a dead cert thanks to Roberto Bianchi, who has given them consistent quality.

VINEYARDS - The oldest vineyard is the one closest to the house. It covers an area of four hectares and grows on soil in which the surface marl makes for wearisome walking. Roberto also rents another three hectares near Radda. The vineyards face east and have an average altitude of 450 meters, a condition essential for grapes of good acidity. The low Guyot training system is replacing the spurred cordon one in the new plantings, whereas the oldest vine rows are trained with the double "cappuccio" system.

WINES - The company has been successful thanks to the finesse of its wines, all extraction, aromatic delicacy and identity. **Chianti Cl. Ris. 2009** (● 7,000 bt), which ages on wood for about two years, has aromas of slightly withered flowers with whiffs of blood and a vigorous, dense, well-balanced palate. **Lo Straniero 2011** (● sangiovese, merlot; 5,000 bt) has an approachable, fruity, harmonious tone. The immensely enjoyable **Campino 2011** (● sangiovese; 6,000 bt) is aged only on steel.

> **vino slow** **CHIANTI CL. 2010** (● 9,000 bt) True to the school of Sean O'Callaghan, the company's enologist, the wine is aged in wood casks and barrels of different sizes. It offers hints of tobacco, soil and rust against a background of crushed flower petals. The palate is rich but aerial in a contrast that improves its drinkability. A refined paradigm of the denomination.

FERTILIZERS natural manure, compost, biodynamic preparations
PLANT PROTECTION copper and sulphur, organic
WEED CONTROL mechanical
YEASTS native
GRAPES 25% bought in
CERTIFICATION converting to organics

SAN CASCIANO IN VAL DI PESA (FI)

Corzano e Paterno

Frazione San Pancrazio
Via San Vito di Sopra, 9
tel. 055 8248179
www.corzanoepaterno.it
info@corzanoepaterno.it

17.5 ha - 65,000 bt **10% discount**

❝ The Corzano e Paterno farm adopts a closed-cycle approach that encompasses everything from vine and olive cultivation to the production of forage for the sheep. Each and every operation is carried out with respect for the environment. ❞

PEOPLE - The farm is made up of two units, Corzano and Paterno, bought by company owner Wendelin Gelpke with the idea, subsequently handed down to his heirs, of turning it into a single indivisible entity.

VINEYARDS - The vineyards, which cover an area of 18 hectares, are overseeen by Aljoscha Goldschmidt and surround the company headquarters. The soil is clayey with traces of stone and the vines are Guyot- and bush-trained. All operations are carried out with full respect for the environment. Petit manseng vines were planted to add freshness to Corzanello Bianco.

WINES - The excellent **Corzano 2010** (● sangiovese, cabernet sauvignon, merlot; 6,000 bt) offers complex fruity and balsamic aromas with minerally notes and a pleasantly stylish palate of great texture and balance. The well-crafted **Chianti Terre di Corzano 2011** (● 32,000 bt) is fruity and fresh with an interesting palate. Also good is **Corzanello Rosato 2012** (⊙ sangiovese; 5,000 bt) whose fruity, leafy aromas are braced by structure and freshness. **Corzanello Bianco 2012** (○ chardonnay, sémillon, petit manseng; 22,000 bt) has tonic notes and a minerally palate.

> **vino slow** **PASSITO DI CORZANO 2001** (○ trebbiano, malvasia; 2,000 bt) Though legal cavils prevented it from having the christening it deserves, this is to all intents and purposes a Vin Santo. It's a vine with entrancing, deep aromas, full of flavor thanks to an extraordinary balance between sugar concentration and acid verve. One of the year's most exciting tastings.

FERTILIZERS natural manure
PLANT PROTECTION copper and sulphur
WEED CONTROL mechanical
YEASTS selected
GRAPES 100% estate-grown
CERTIFICATION converting to organics

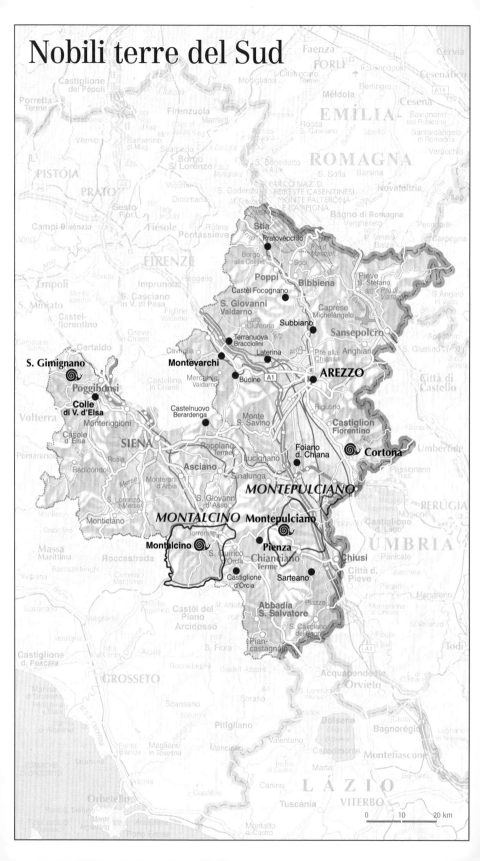

Nobili terre del Sud

BUCINE (AR)

Podere Il Carnasciale

Località Mercatale Valdarno
tel. 0559 911142
bettinarogosky@caberlot.eu

CORTONA (AR)

Stefano Amerighi

Poggiobello di Farneta
tel. 0575 648340
www.stefanoamerighi.it
info@stefanoamerighi.it

---

5 ha - 9,000 bt

PEOPLE - Podere Il Carnasciale began to make wine in 1986 when Wolf Rogosky began to grasp the potential of caberlot, a then unknown grape, a natural hybrid of cabernet franc and merlot discovered by an agronomist called Bordini in the 1970s. Today the company is managed by Bettina and Moritz Rogosky with enologist Peter Shilling and Marco Maffei. Together they use the same passion and determination as the founder to create wine that are unique anywhere in the world.

VINEYARDS - The only grape grown is caberlot, planted on four plots in different years and positions. The oldest vineyard is bush-trained, while the more recent ones adopt the cordon system. All have a high density of planting. Work in the vineyards is all-natural and treatments are reduced to a bare minimum. The yield per hectare is very low. The harvest is carried out by hand in different stages and every bunch is picked only when the grapes are perfectly ripe. The company now intends to go biodynamic.

WINES - Top quality is the aim: vineyards and wines are followed step by step and cosseted with a care approaching devotion by the whole team. In the small canteen every parcel of grapes is vinified separately to understand their peculiarities and matured on mid-toasted wood to realize all their potential. Attention to detail is everything. Careful selection and assemblage produce two unique, unforgettable wines. **Caberlot 2010** (● 3,000 magnum) is intriguing, complex, spicy, balsamic, full-bodied and elegant on the palate, but never excessive. It is a wine certain to last, produced only in magnums to favor its maturation. A Great Wine with great personality. Il **Carnasciale 2011** (● caberlot; 6,000 bt) is younger in personality, fruity and spicy with tannins well to the fore and excellent acidity.

8 ha - 13,000 bt   `10% discount`

66 On his winemaking journey, Stefano Amerighi has chosen sustainability as his traveling companion. Thanks to the consistent quality of the wines he produces with pure enological talent, the road he has embarked upon is sure to take him a long, long way. 99

PEOPLE - Passion for wine and love of the land have continued to stimulate Stefano Amerighi in his work, despite recent growing years that have been unfavorable for his beloved syrah. It's Stefano himself who performs biodynamic analyses on soil and vines, with consultant enologist Federico Staderini helping out in the cellar.

VINEYARDS - In the early noughties syrah, some sangiovese, colorino and even montepulciano grapes were planted in the Poggiobello di Farneta vineyard for grafting with the French variety now typical round Cortona. Planting density is high with about 7,000 plants per hectare. Put in a row, that's about 40 kilometers of vines! Neighboring crops are also grown biodynamically.

WINES - Stefano generally heaps all his attention on one wine alone: his Cortona Syrah, the end-result in the cellar of a great deal of specific work on grapes in the vineyards, where soil and weather conditions vary. The grapes from each of the eight parcels are vinified separately and, after maturing in cement vats for at least two months, are skillfully assembled to bring out their aroma and flavor.

> **vino slow** **CORTONA SYRAH 2010** (● 13,000 bt) A wine of deep leafy fragrances with spices and fruit well to the fore. The palate is very well-balanced with unaggressive tannins and long, warm, welcome length.

FERTILIZERS manure pellets, compost
PLANT PROTECTION copper and sulphur
WEED CONTROL mechanical
YEASTS native
GRAPES 100% estate-grown
CERTIFICATION none

FERTILIZERS biodynamic preparations, green manure
PLANT PROTECTION copper and sulphur, organic
WEED CONTROL mechanical
YEASTS native
GRAPES 100% estate-grown
CERTIFICATION biodynamic, organic

Baricci

Località Colombaio di Montosoli, 13
tel. 0577 848109
baricci1955@libero.it

5 ha - 30,000 bt

❝ Baricci's wines are the node that ideally connects past to present, a mirror of the small farming tradition that continues to bear aloft the name of Montalcino. ❞

PEOPLE - The 2008 vintage was Colombaio di Montosoli's 38th to date. Nello Baricci bought the property in 1955 in a period in which a job in a factory was the rosiest alternative to country labor. In the late 1960s, he began bottling his own wine, first Rosso di Montalcino, then, in 1971, Brunello. Today it's his grandsons Federico and Francesco who carry forward the family tradition.

VINEYARDS - The winery sits among the hills of Montosoli, one of the denomination's best growing areas, a place where viticulture is documented from the Middle Ages. Nello immediately grasped the potential of the soil here, lean but simultaneously rich in minerals, fossils and "galestro" marl, ideal for vines. He thus planted six small plots, with excellent south- and southeast-facing locations, which still constitute the nuclei of his production.

WINES - "Sangiovese is a mirror that reflects every vintage perfectly." So spoke Francesco talking about the troubled 2011 harvest and introducing **Rosso di Montalcino 2011** (● 18,000 bt), an intact, complex wine in which juicy fruit comes to the fore on a long, satifying palate.

> **vino slow** **BRUNELLO DI MONTALCINO 2008** (● 12,000 bt) A complex wine with inebriating hints of tobacco and spice and the classic Montalcino sangiovese overtones of soil and undergrowth. The palate is rich and powerful with a toughness that adds unique freshness. A shining example of the character of the sangiovese grape in Montalcino.

FERTILIZERS natural manure
PLANT PROTECTION copper and sulphur
WEED CONTROL mechanical
YEASTS native
GRAPES 100% estate-grown
CERTIFICATION none

Jacopo Biondi Santi Tenuta Greppo

Località Villa Greppo, 183
tel. 0577 848087
www.biondisanti.it
biondisanti@biondisanti.it

25 ha - 80,000 bt

PEOPLE - Sadly, Franco Biondi Santi died in April at the ripe old age of 91. The "lord of Brunello", as he was known to many, was a charismatic figure respected throughout the Italian wine world. We grieve his loss and remember him as a stalwart of values such as respect for tradition and attachment to one's place of origin. His son Jacopo is carrying on where he left off, thus ensuring that the company's strict philosophy will remain unchanged.

VINEYARDS - The vineyards are spread out over various areas and used for the wines according to age (from four to ten years for the Rosso, from 10 to 25 for the Brunello, and over 25 for the Riserva. Besides the historic Tenuta Greppo estate in Montalcino, Jacopo Biondi Santi has also owned the Tenuta del Castello di Montepò in the Maremma area — 52 hectares of cutivated mainly with the BBS11 sangiovese clone —since 1991.

WINES - "Greppo was and still is tradition, Castello di Montepò stands for innovation." That's how Jacopo sums up his idea of his company's continuity. A stand-out among the Montalcino classics is **Brunello di Montalcino Ris. 2007** (● 14,000 bt), austere, full of zip and character, very deep. Albeit still in fieri, it's already monumental, a Great Wine. **Brunello di Montalcino 2008** (● 56,600 bt) has gentle, fresh aromas but also youthful grip and spunk. **Rosso di Montalcino 2009** (● 21,100 bt) is earthy and savory, a wine of nice contrasts. The wines from Montepò are more developed with richer fruit. Worthy of note are the exuberant **Sassoalloro 2009** (● sangiovese; 150,000 bt), the austerely mature **Morellino di Scansano 2009** (● 24,000 bt) and the mouthfilling **Braccale 2010** (● sangiovese, merlot; 50,000 bt).

FERTILIZERS organic-mineral
PLANT PROTECTION chemical, copper and sulphur
WEED CONTROL mechanical
YEASTS native
GRAPES 100% estate-grown
CERTIFICATION none

Fattoi

Località Santa Restituta
Podere Capanna, 101
tel. 0577 848613
www.fattoi.it
info@fattoi.it

---

9 ha - 50,000 bt · **10% discount**

66 A typical Tuscan estate of olive groves and vineyards, with secular trees, veritable monuments to biodiversity, and wines with an outstanding sense of place. 99

PEOPLE - Ofelio Fattoi is the head of this family of Tuscan winemakers. He is still active in the vineyard and his contribution in the cellar, the fruit of years and years of experience, is still vital. His sons Leonardo and Lamberto are now in charge of the work in the fields and his granddaughter Lucia sees to hospitality and sales.

VINEYARDS - In the cellar the consultant enologist is Pietro Rivella. The vineyards face southwest and enjoy plenty of sunshine and light, as well as air from the sea breezes that blow in from the coast which is only 30 kilometers away as the crow flies. It is from the oldest plot, which was planted in the 1970s, that the best grapes are chosen to produce the Riserva.

WINES - Work on the new, partly underground aging cellar has been completed at last. It houses the 30-hectoliter oak casks in which the Brunello is aged. **Brunello di Montalcino 2008 (●** 25,000 bt) has nuanced, austere aromas. The first impact on the palate is edgy but then grows and unwinds, helped along its way by very fine tannins and sparkling acidity. We also liked **Rosso di Montalcino 2011 (●** 20,000 bt), whose bouquet releases distinct scents of blossom and cherry and contrasts deftly with the palate. Fine drinking at an affordable price.

> **vino slow** **BRUNELLO DI MONTALCINO RIS. 2007 (●** 4,000 bt) A compact, deep, elegant suite of aromas with notes of soil and iron and a vigorous, caressing palate with rich, tangy tannins and a long, lingering finish. A wine of disarmingly eloquent naturalness, steeped in the place of its birth.

FERTILIZERS organic-mineral
PLANT PROTECTION chemical, copper and sulphur
WEED CONTROL mechanical
YEASTS selected
GRAPES 100% estate-grown
CERTIFICATION none

Il Paradiso di Manfredi

Via Canalicchio, 305
tel. 0577 848478
www.ilparadisodimanfredi.com
info@ilparadisodimanfredi.com

---

2 ha - 9,500 bt

66 Il Paradiso di Manfredi is tangible proof of the poetry of the earth. It's a company almost out of time whose leading players seem to live for the task of distilling its essence into the most wonderful wines. 99

PEOPLE - Sometimes passion becomes profession. This has been the case for Florio Guerrini and his wife Rosella Martini, who used to be teachers. With the help of their daughters Silvia and Gioia, and inheriting the legacy of Rossella's father Manfredi Martini, they have built up one of the best wineries in the area.

VINEYARDS - In the vineyard, split into seven terraced plots, all with fossil-rich soil and each with climatic conditions of its own, Florio is repeating the work Manfredi did for so many years. He doesn't top the vines, he intertwines the rows (because the leaves are the lungs of the vine), he doesn't practice green covering, and he doesn't use any form of fertilizer.

WINES - "In my wines, time acts like a magic formula," says Florio, "and gives them the distinctive features of the Paradiso terroir." This is the real reason why the release of the 2006 vintage has been delayed. In the glass, **Rosso di Montalcino 2011 (●** 2,500 bt) has intense flavor with quality tannins and a refreshing, minerally finish. **Brunello di Montalcino 2008 (●** 7,000 bt) is at its eloquent best: it has aromas of damp soil and tobacco leaves and a full-bodied, supple palate in which mature streaks appear.

> **vino slow** **BRUNELLO DI MONTALCINO RIS. 2007 (●** 1,200 bt). Lustrous on the eye, original on the nose with hints of meadow herbs, iron, rust and blood, the type of aromas only Paradiso is capable of, which is why its wines are unrepeatable. The palate is also masterful with sweet tannins and graceful, unstoppable energy. It will be released in 2015.

FERTILIZERS none
PLANT PROTECTION copper and sulphur
WEED CONTROL mechanical
YEASTS native
GRAPES 100% estate-grown
CERTIFICATION none

Le Chiuse

Località Pullera, 228
tel. 055 597052
www.lechiuse.com
info@lechiuse.com

8 ha - 30,000 bt	**10% discount**

66 We were bowled over by the quality of the wines at Le Chiuse and by the exquisite manners of the owners. The cellar is a shining star in the Montalcino wine firmament. 99

PEOPLE - The company, a historic property of the "inventors of Brunello", the Biondi Santi family, is now run by their direct descendent Simonetta Valiani. Since 1986 she has produced her own wine, restoring old outbuildings and building a new underground cellar in a pretty natural environment. She is helped by her husband Niccolò Magnelli and their son Lorenzo.

VINEYARDS - Most of the vineyards surround the cellar, though there is also a one-hectare plot up towards the top of the town of Montalcino. Cultivation is impeccably manual and organic and respects both land and fruit. The soil is rich in minerals and the production of grapes per hectare is kept low to ensure quality.

WINES - Lengthy maceration and aging in old barrels characterize work in the cellar. **Brunello di Montalcino 2008 (●** 11,000 bt) has a broad, persistent, taut palate with fine tannins and promises to evolve well. The wave of innovation brought to the company by Lorenzo Magnelli materializes in **Stellare M. Cl. 2011** (Ⓖ sangiovese; 1,200) a lovely rosé spumante with a pervasive bouquet, lingering rich flavor and a soft, delicate perlage. The typical **Rosso di Montalcino 2011** (● 12,000 bt) is pleasing, fragrant and fresh.

> **vino slow** BRUNELLO DI MONTALCINO RIS. 2007 (● 6,600 bt) A thoroughbred Brunello at a bargain price. The nose has intense earthy aromas with notes of red berries, the palate is soft with composed tannins, plenty of acid energy and an impressively tangy finish. In other words, a commendable Slow Wine.

FERTILIZERS	manure pellets, green manure
PLANT PROTECTION	copper and sulphur
WEED CONTROL	mechanical
YEASTS	native
GRAPES	100% estate-grown
CERTIFICATION	organic

Pian delle Querci

Località Pian delle Querci
tel. 0577 834174 - 333 9940016
www.piandellequerci.it
info@piandellequerci.it

8.5 ha - 53,000 bt

PEOPLE - Pian delle Querci stands at the end of the dirt road that runs across the Montosoli district, in the northeast section of the denomination. At the cellar we were received by Angelina Ndreca, a former math teacher and a woman of character, the daughter-in-law of Vittorio Pinti, who bought the company in the 1960s. "It's a small company, not very famous, and run with passion by the whole company," she told us. "Which is just how we like it."

VINEYARDS - In the vineyard, a single plot in front of the cellar, work two of Angelina's brothers, Martino e Davide, under the supervision of Vittorio Pinti, who uses his experience to seek the right combination between reduction of yields and climate change to ensure ripe grapes, hence top quality wines in the cellar.

WINES - "We have a traditional approach to winemaking," says Angelina. According to her production philosophy, it's important to offer consumers "very good wine at the right price". The pedigree **Brunello di Montalcino 2008 (●** 31,000 bt) clearly conveys the typical local traits of freshness and pleasant flavor, relative assertiveness and a pleasing, though not exceptionally long finish. Reliable and enjoyable as it is, **Rosso di Montalcino 2011 (●** 14,500 bt) has already sold out! Angelina told us that the 2012 can already be ordered.

> **vino slow** BRUNELLO DI MONTALCINO RIS. 2007 (● 6,600 bt) A thoroughbred Brunello at a bargain price. The nose has intense earthy aromas with notes of red berries, the palate is soft with composed tannins, plenty of acid energy and an impressively tangy finish. In other words, a commendable Slow Wine.

FERTILIZERS	organic-mineral, natural manure
PLANT PROTECTION	copper and sulphur
WEED CONTROL	mechanical
YEASTS	native
GRAPES	100% estate-grown
CERTIFICATION	none

MONTALCINO (SI)

Podere Salicutti

Località Podere Salicutti, 174
tel. 0577 847003
www.poderesalicutti.it
leanza@poderesalicutti.it

4 ha - 18,000 bt | **10% discount**

PEOPLE - We are met by late spring rain on our arrival at Podere Salicutti. If anything, the pervading air of melancholy only adds to the incredible charm of this stupendous corner of greenery on the southeast side of the commune of Montalcino. A spellbound Francesco Leanza, a Roman by birth, bought the place in 1990 and began by restructuring the estate and the buildings. A few years later, with humility and enthusiasm, he began making wine.

VINEYARDS - Francesco has always had a sensitive approach to his vines and began implementing organic methods right from the word go. The vineyards are split into three plots where most of the land has an Austro-Alpine matrix and is composed of sedimentary rocks of marine origin. The grapes grown on the Piaggione and Teatro Brunello plots go mainly into the Brunello, those from Sorgente, where the soil is more calcareous and clayey, into Rosso and Dopoteatro.

WINES - Francesco is a cultured, polite person and his personality and character are reflected in his sober wines. Pervasive and measured, they are more stylish than muscular. In the cellar the approach is essential and interventions are limited: the grapes are fermented with native yeasts in temperature-controlled steel vats and the wines aged in wood casks and barrels. We liked the blossomy, spicy **Brunello di Montalcino Piaggione 2008** (● 8,000 bt) with its nicely contained note of warmth, and the earthy, caressing **Rosso di Montalcino Sorgente 2010** (● 6,000 bt), with its very distinct fruit. The intriguing Dopoteatro 2010 (● cabernet sauvignon, canaiolo; 1,300 bt) is grassy, lean and laid-back.

FERTILIZERS natural manure
PLANT PROTECTION copper and sulphur
WEED CONTROL mechanical
YEASTS native
GRAPES 100% estate-grown
CERTIFICATION organic

MONTEPULCIANO (SI)

Boscarelli

Frazione Cervognano
Via di Montenero, 28
tel. 0578 767277
www.poderiboscarelli.com
info@poderiboscarelli.com

14 ha - 100,000 bt | **10% discount**

66 Today, 50 years from its foundation, Boscarelli is one of the Montepulciano wineries that have helped create the perfect model for an elegant Vino Nobile of consistent quality. 99

PEOPLE - It was in 1962 that Egidio Corradi decided that the hills of Cervognano were the ideal place to practice his own personal idea of viticulture. Today his nephews Egidio, Niccolò and Luca De Ferrari are ably following in his footsteps, ensuring a rosy future for this splendid winery.

VINEYARDS - The vineyards are all situated near the cellar. At Cervognano the soil is alluvial and pebbly, the generally even terrain interrupted here and there by red-colored jags and sandier parts. The vines grow at an average density per hectare of about 7,000 and are trained with the Guyot system which, according to their owners, notably lengthens their life-cycle — an important agronomic target.

WINES - The use of oxygen in the vinification process is one of the most delicate in a wine cellar, but here they handle it well. With so much experience under its belt, Boscarell stands out for eloquent wines, a happy marriage of the depth of the fruit and a classical style of great finesse. Take **Nobile di Montepulciano 2010** (● 15,000 bt), for example, ferrous and floral, packed with acid and savory thrust. The splendid **Nobile di Montepulciano Nocio dei Boscarelli 2009** (● 4,500 bt) offers the nose dried flowers and mint. Austere and subtle, it is a Great Wine par excellence. **Nobile di Montepulciano Ris. 2008** (● 10,000 bt) has dank aromas of dried flowers and soil followed up by warm, caressing texture. **Rosso di Montepulciano Prugnolo 2011** (● 15,000 bt) is fragrant and balsamic.

FERTILIZERS natural manure, green manure
PLANT PROTECTION chemical, copper and sulphur
WEED CONTROL chemical, mechanical
YEASTS native
GRAPES 100% estate-grown
CERTIFICATION none

Podere Il Macchione

Via Provinciale, 18
tel. 347 4157687
www.podereilmacchione.it
podereilmacchione@live.it

Poderi Sanguineto I e II ⊚⌄

Frazione Acquaviva
Via Sanguineto, 2/4
tel. 0578 767782
www.sanguineto.com
sanguineto@tin.it
⌐—0

---

6 ha - 15,000 bt

3.7 ha - 30,000 bt   **10% discount**

PEOPLE - This exciting Montepulciano new winery came into being in 2005, when both-ers Simone and Leonardo Abram descended from Tentino and decided to invest their future in a six-hectare plot in the Caggiole district, excellent for winemaking. Their eco-awareness soon convinced them of the wisdom of adopting a sustainable form of high-standard viticulture that came up trumps immediately.

VINEYARDS - The Macchione nestles among the hills on the road that leads to Montepulciano. The vineyards surround the cellar in a position that not only ensures constant air circulation, but also allows the vines to rest on a number of different geological formations. At the top the clay loam is peppered with pebbles, at the bottom the soil is looser and rich in fossils.

WINES - The vineyards have different ages, varying from 15 to 50 years. The grapes from each parcel are fermented separately in cement vats, which makes it possible to monitor carefully their subsequent evolution in mid-sized casks or 15 hectoliter-vats. This range of technical equipment makes it easier to choose the best batches to allocate to the Nobile. The consultancy of enologist Mery Ferrara is always precious. **Nobile di Montepulciano Ris. 2008** (● 3,000 bt) has very deep aromas with close-focused fruit enhanced by leafier, earthy, minty notes. The palate is spacious and textured with well-integrated tannins. **Nobile di Montepulciano 2009** (● 12,000 bt) has blossom and citrus fruits on the nose with a light, juicy palate. A sumptuous interpretation of the denomination of a Great Wine.

66 Sanguineto, run by Dora Forsoni and Patrizia Brogi, both brilliant winemakers, is the place for wine lovers looking for bottles of innate natural eloquence, sense of place and authentic flavor. 99

PEOPLE - It's always a pleasure to spend an hour or two with Dora and Patrizia, who started bottling their wine in 1997. "We cater for people who love drinking wine," says the latter, "which is why the only ingredients we use are our grapes".

VINEYARDS - "Dora follows every single plant in the vineyard," it's still Patrizia talking, "and we try to make our vine rows live as long as possible. So we take a shoot from the graft to give it a future." This year they planted a hectare of land with varieties selected from the oldest vineyard.

WINES - The first step in the two women's sensitive approach to winemaking is the identification of the best grapes possible. They aren't afraid of long fermentations; Patrizia likes walking into the cellar in spring and hearing "the singing of the barrels". The end-result is wines that might take purists aback, but not people who like plenty of character in their glass. **Rosso di Montepulciano 2011** (● 17.000 bt) has deep aromas of blood-rich meat and a succulent, dynamic palate. **Nobile di Montepulciano 2010** (● 18,000 bt), aged in large wood barrels, also offers meaty notes but alternates them with tobacco and leather; the palate is laid-back with extraordinary natural eloquence.

vino slow NOBILE DI MONTEPULCIANO RIS. 2009 (● 5,000 bt) This Nobile has impressive red-blooded, blossomy aromas and a naturally expressive palate. It's a rich, fresh wine, deep and charismatic.

FERTILIZERS organic-mineral, green manure	FERTILIZERS none
PLANT PROTECTION copper and sulphur	PLANT PROTECTION chemical, copper and sulphur
WEED CONTROL mechanical	WEED CONTROL mechanical
YEASTS native	YEASTS native
GRAPES 100% estate-grown	GRAPES 100% estate-grown
CERTIFICATION none	CERTIFICATION none

SAN GIMIGNANO (SI)

Il Colombaio di Santa Chiara €

Località il Colombaio, 10 C
tel. 0577 942004
www.colombaiosantachiara.it
info@colombaiosantachiara.it
🐌—0

11 ha - 80,000 bt

PEOPLE - Il Colombaio di Santa Chiara is one of the emerging cellars on the San Gimignano wine scene. The agricultural wisdom of Mario Logi, the founder, interweaves with the energy and passion of his three sons Alessio, Stefano and Giampiero to create a perfect marriage between dynamism and constructive hard work. Speaking about the company's plans for the future, Alessio said that, "We want to build a new cellar suited to our quality requirements".

VINEYARDS - The winery's two properties are spread out between Santa Chiara and San Donato and are split up into four parcels. At Santa Chiara work is under way on the planting of a new vineyard. The soil is tufaceous, though in some parts it becomes quite clayey, and the approach adopted here is organic. "I have to say thanks to my father," says Alessio, "because it's his experience that has taught us our in-depth knowledge, hence the ability to intervene promptly in the vineyard in all circumstances."

WINES - For some years now the winery has carefully selected grapes according to the different characteristics of the vineyards, isolating the single peculiarities of those to be turned into wine. The results haven't been slow in coming. **Vernaccia di San Gimignano Selvabianca 2012** (O 40,000 bt) smacks of vanilla but its complex flavor is cushioned by over-sweetness. **Vernaccia di San Gimignano L'Albereta Ris. 2011** (O 5,000 bt) offers scents of spring flowers on palate that is complex, relaxed and leisurely. The interesting **San Gimignano Rosso Il Colombaio 2009** (● 5,000 bt) has nicely clean aromas.

> **vino slow** **VERNACCIA DI SAN GIMIGNANO CAMPO DELLA PIEVE 2011** (O 40,000 bt) A masterly interpretation of the typology with blossomy scents and flavor marked by acid verve and great texture.

FERTILIZERS natural manure, green manure
PLANT PROTECTION copper and sulphur
WEED CONTROL mechanical
YEASTS selected
GRAPES 100% estate-grown
CERTIFICATION organic

SAN GIMIGNANO (SI)

Montenidoli

Località Montenidoli
tel. 0577 941565
www.montenidoli.com
montenidoli@valdelsa.net
🐌—0

24 ha - 90,000 bt

❝ "The goodness of wine depends on the quality of the soil," says Elisabetta Fagiuoli. "This is why we have to respect the environment in which the vines, like us, grow." Her words are blunt and encompass an absolute truth. Like the splendid wines Montenidoli has been regaling us with for years and years. ❞

PEOPLE - Besides exuding charisma, this outstanding producer also possesses uncommon technical nous, which she puts into precise, simple words as though winemaking were the most natural profession in the world.

VINEYARDS - Elisabetta shows us the exact point at which the geology of the Quatenary era runs into that of the Triassic, a leap of "only" 200 million years. Here grows the bush-trained sangiovese vineyard planted by her late and never-forgotten partner Sergio Muratori, Near the cellar the Quaternary soil is more variegated with fossil-rich matrices alternating with clay.

WINES - The company's wine production seeks to promote the Montenidoli terroir with personality and elegance. **Vernaccia di San Gimignano Carato 2009** (O 6,500 bt) has aromas of spring flowers and a spacious, dynamic palate. **Vernaccia di San Gimignano Tradizionale 2011** (O 20,000 bt), which macerates on the skins at length, has aromas of iodine and a full-flavored palate. The splendid **Vinbrusco 2011** (O trebbiano, malvasia; 4,000 bt) has a delightfully simple palate. **Templare 2009** (O vernaccia, trebbiano, malvasia; 6,500 bt) is a class act. Of the reds we recommend **Chianti Colli Senesi 2009** (● 4,000 bt).

> **vino slow** **VERNACCIA DI SAN GIMIGNANO FIORE 2011** (O 20,000 bt) Aged in steel vats, a wine with delicate notes of blossom and damp stone and outstandingly pure flavor. It stylishly coaxes out all the tangy minerality of the Vernaccia zone.

FERTILIZERS green manure
PLANT PROTECTION copper and sulphur
WEED CONTROL mechanical
YEASTS native
GRAPES 100% estate-grown
CERTIFICATION organic

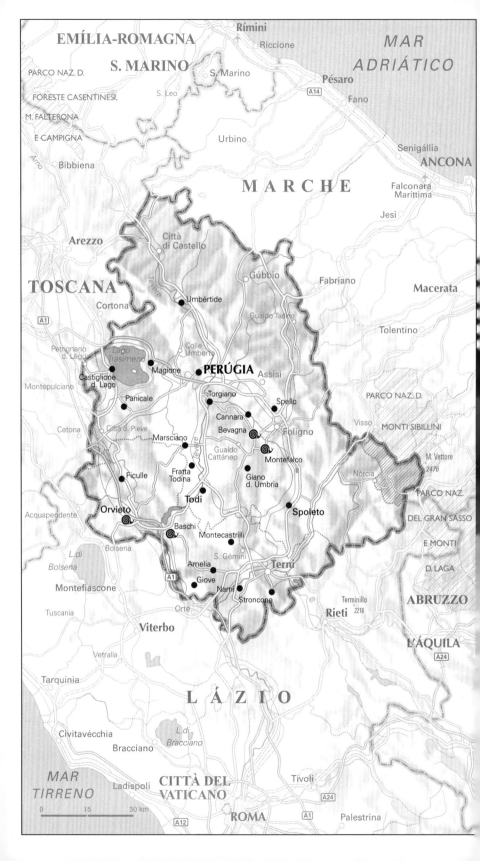

UMBRIA

Less and less wine is being produced in Umbria. This is the trend that catches one's eye reading National Institute for Statistics data on the last grape harvest. The fact is that the region is the one that has suffered the largest production decrease nationwide, an estimated drop of 20-25 per cent with respect to the 2011 vintage. The forecast merely confirms the trend recorded over the last few years. What causes most food for thought is the regional production index for 2012: 637,000 hectoliters produced compared to a million just six years ago! This constant degrowth should not be seen only as a trend associated with grape harvests, but urges reflection on the degree to which the regional winegrowing system has suffered adverse economic conditions. Despite the stats, however, the quality of the wine sector and the intellectual vivacity of its leading players still make Umbria a region of significant interest.

The Orvieto and Montefalco zones are the driving force behind regional viticulture. Orvieto appears eager to win back its place as a focus for white wine production in Central Italy, and we awarded the Snail symbol to a historic winery, Barberani-Vallesanta. Together with Palazzone, this historic family represents a pinnacle of quality for the denomination and its switch to organic viticulture provides further confirmation of their professional approach.

There isn't a great deal of news to report from Montefalco. Sagrantino is a wine with a character all of its own which, more than others, demands sensitive interpretation and technical skill. Given the commendable approach of the wineries listed in the following pages, we have sought to promote a productive style centered on aerial texture, in which the phenolic richness of the grape never overwhelms flavor. Different stylistic interpretations of trebbiano spoletino, already numerous, proliferated. Relatively unknown, this grape could be another feather in the region's productive cap. In general, Umbrian viticulture has acknowledged the need to interpret its terroirs with greater personality. These would now appear equipped to express their enological potential not only by virtue of an extreme technical approach but also, at long last, of a rediscovered sense of belonging.

snails

coins €

BASCHI (TR)

Barberani - Vallesanta 🌀↙

Località Cerreto
tel. 0763 341820
www.barberani.it
barberani@barberani.it

55 ha - 350,000 bt · **10% discount**

❝ The Barbarani cellar, which produces wines that capture the essence of the Orvieto terroir, has been an Umbrian institution for more than half a century. It has now gone organic to crown its history of excellence and sustainability. ❞

PEOPLE - The cellar makes the most of a unique microclimate, that of the nearby lake of Corbara. Today it is run by the third generation of the family in the persons of Niccolò and Bernardo, respectively enologist and sales manager.

VINEYARDS - The Barberani brothers have always appreciated natural agriculture and will receive organic certification with the 2013 harvest. All vineyard operations are performed manually, from pruning with planting of the shoots to cover cropping, from fertilizing to harvesting. The new water treatment plant is supplemented by consolidated sustainable practices in the cellar.

WINES - **Orvieto Cl. Sup. Castagnolo 2012** (○ grechetto, procanico, chardonnay, riesling; 50,000 bt) is an easy-drinking wine, fruity and fresh. The sulphur-free **Orvieto Cl. Sup. ViNoSo2 2012** (○ grechetto, procanico; 6,000 bt) stands out for its scents of tangy fruit and a certain tannic sensation. **Lago di Corbara Rosso Polvento Villa Monticelli 2008** (● sangiovese, cabernet sauvignon, merlot; 10,000 bt) is complex and penetrating. The novelty of the year is **Aleatico Passito 2007** (● 2,000 bt), which combines sweetness and pleasing tannins.

vino slow **ORVIETO CL. SUP. CALCAIA MUFFA NOBILE 2010** (○ procanico, grechetto, sauvignon; 10,000 bt) For years the Barberani have engaged in the difficult task of vinifying noble rot. The results of their efforts are evident in this wine with its temping fragrances of dried apricots, vanilla and mint, which linger over a dense palate braced by an acid sinew that enhances the overall complexity.

FERTILIZERS green manure
PLANT PROTECTION copper and sulphur
WEED CONTROL mechanical
YEASTS native
GRAPES 100% estate-grown
CERTIFICATION converting to organics

BEVAGNA (PG)

Adanti 🌀↙

Località Arquata
Via Belvedere, 2
tel. 0742 360435
www.cantineadanti.com
info@cantineadanti.com

30 ha - 160,000 bt · **10% discount**

❝ In the mid-1970s the Adanti began to adopt the virtuous practices that have made their winery a model for the wine world of Montefalco and beyond. ❞

PEOPLE - Daniele Palini, the technical soul of the cellar, is living proof that all his father Alvaro's determined hard work down the years is now being carried on with the same outstanding results.

VINEYARDS - The property is split into three plots. Arquata, an old place-name, nestles on a sunny hilltop of compact soil that enhances the color, structure and strength of the grapes. Higher up, Colcimino has skeleton-grain soil rich in sand from which the deep-rooted vines draw elegance and transfer it to the grapes. The grapes grown in Campo Letame, a vineyard south of Montefalco, characterize the terroir less but are nonetheless of consistently good quality.

WINES - Adanti produces impeccable, measured wines, a veritable paradigm for the Montefalco denomination. **Arquata 2008** (● cabernet sauvignon, merlot, barbera; 9,000 bt) is complex, juicy and linear. **Montefalco Rosso 2009** (● 60,000 bt) is pleasingly drinkable with good supporting acidity. **Montefalco Bianco 2012** (○ 20,000 bt) offers a well-balanced palate and rhythmic grip. The excellent **Grechetto dei Colli Martani 2012** (○ 10,000 bt) opens with citrus fruit and ends on a typically almondy tone.

vino slow **MONTEFALCO SAGRANTINO 2008** (● 24,000 bt) A wine that matures for 30 months in large barrels and shows off rich, stylish phenolics. It releases scents of blood oranges and graphite which prelude a fragrant progressive palate with silky tannins.

FERTILIZERS green manure
PLANT PROTECTION copper and sulphur
WEED CONTROL chemical, mechanical
YEASTS selected
GRAPES 100% estate-grown
CERTIFICATION none

Fattoria Colleallodole

Vocabolo Colle Allodole, 228
tel. 0742 361897
www.fattoriacolleallodole.it
info@fattoriacolleallodole.com

---

12 ha - 80,000 bt · `10% discount`

66 Francesco's strong character, his insight, his attachment to the land and the values handed down to him by his father have helped him put Colleallodole up there among the finest, most genuine Umbrian wineries. 99

PEOPLE - It's 1975. A journalist meets a producer and tastes his wine. He then turns to the man's teenage son and says, "Carry on your dad's work and you'll have a future ahead of you!" The journalist was Luigi Veronelli and the boy was Francesco Antano, son of Milziade. There's no doubt about it, Veronelli had vision.

VINEYARDS - Among the gently rolling hills between Bevagna and Montefalco, in the heart of the Sagrantino zone, everywhere you look you see vineyards. The excellent position and the gravelly clay soil provide the foundation for the creation of well-structured, complex wines. Francesco, a winemaker's winemaker, tends the vineyards constantly in symbiosis with nature, drawing on all his dedication, passion and experience.

WINES - Barrel-aging and native yeasts yes, filtration and temperature control no. These are the basic tenets of Francesco's winemaking philosophy. **Bianco di Milziade 2012** (○ trebbiano, chardonnay, pinot, friulano; 5,000 bt) is complex and aromatic, braced by pronounced acidity. **Montefalco Rosso 2010** (● 30,000 bt) is dry and potent, softened on the finish by the sangiovese grape's characteristic delicacy. Warm and fleshy, **Montefalco Rosso Ris. 2009** (● 3,000 bt) has an aroma of undergrowth buttressed by softened tannins. **Montefalco Sagrantino 2009** (● 8,000 bt) embodies perfect equilibrium between depth of taste and coherence of aroma. "It's not you who are good, it's the earth beneath your feet," is what Milziade used to say to Francesco.

FERTILIZERS green manure
PLANT PROTECTION copper and sulphur
WEED CONTROL mechanical
YEASTS native
GRAPES 100% estate-grown
CERTIFICATION none

Omero Moretti

Via San Sabino, 19
tel. 0742 90426
www.morettiomero.it
info@morettiomero.it

---

11 ha - 45,000 bt · `10% discount`

PEOPLE - Omero Moretti came to a decision: viticulture was to be his primary occupation. Previously he'd always been a livestock breeder as well, but in 1997 he decided to narrow his vocation for farming down to cellar management alone. Thanks to the help of his family, he has now become a standard bearer for the quality of Umbrian wines in Italy and abroad. His enologist is the experienced Luca Capaldini.

VINEYARDS - Omero is one of Umbria's first organic farmers, having received certification way back in 1991. The vineyards are spread out over the hill of Giano, from which it is possible to enjoy a magnificent view of nearby Montefalco and the plain of Foligno. The composition of the soil is mixed and the grapes grown are the native sagrantino and grechetto, along with sangiovese, merlot and malvasia. Omero oversees the grape harvest, which is carried out completely by hand, and the vinification process personally.

WINES - Moretti's competence and genuineness are reflected in his wonderfully natural, enologically correct wines. The labels even cite lines from The Odyssey (Omero is Italian for Homer). **Nessuno 2012** (○ grechetto, malvasia; 8,000 bt) combines the freshness of grechetto and the blossomy aromas of the malvasia grape with style and harmony. It's a good Everyday Wine. **Montefalco Rosso 2011** (● 15,000 bt), which offers notes of ripe red berries, is pleasantly refreshing. **Montefalco Sagrantino 2009** (● 9,000 bt) promises to approach the levels of excellence of 2008: hence complex fragrances, robust but stylish tannins and remarkable balance. The winery's new cru **Montefalco Sagrantino Vignalunga 2006** (● 600 bt) is crisp, well-rounded and long.

FERTILIZERS natural manure, compost
PLANT PROTECTION copper and sulphur
WEED CONTROL mechanical
YEASTS selected
GRAPES 100% estate-grown
CERTIFICATION organic

Antonelli San Marco 🐌

Località San Marco
tel. 0742 379158
www.antonellisanmarco.it
info@antonellisanmarco.it
🍷—o

45 ha - 300,000 bt	**10% discount**

❝ This winery's impressive history translates into lucid agricultural awareness which, in turn, expresses itself in classic vins de terroir of understated modernity. ❞

PEOPLE - The ancient origins of Filippo Antonelli's estate are visible in the austere architecture of the mansion house, which enshrines centuries of history. Out of respect for the place and its heritage, the modern wine cellar has been built below ground level, thus leaving the original appearance unaltered.

VINEYARDS - The company has been certified organic 2012. It owns 35 hectares of land at an average altitude of about 350 meters. The vines are trained using the spurred cordon and Guyot systems, new plantings exclusively with the latter. The crushed grapes enter the cellar which, as mentioned, is directly below the old house, and the debris is dumped traditionally without the use of pumps.

WINES - Quality shone in all the wines released. At the cutting-edge was **Trebbiano Spoletino 2011** (O 14,000 bt), made with maceration on the lees and barrel-fermentation of 50 per cent of the weight. **Montefalco Sagrantino Chiusa di Pannone 2007** (● 5,300 bt) is a veritable Sagrantino cru. An austere, complex wine with citrussy aromas and hefty tannins, it promises to give of its best after long aging. **Montefalco Rosso Ris. 2008** (● 13,000 bt) is supple on the palate with notes of mint and liquorice root.

> **vino slow** SAGRANTINO DI MONTEFALCO 2008 (● 33,000 bt) A wine of great sedateness thanks to elegant aromas of violet and liquorice and, above all, a taste profile in which the finesse is perfectly integrated with the length of the palate.

FERTILIZERS compost
PLANT PROTECTION copper and sulphur
WEED CONTROL mechanical
YEASTS native
GRAPES 5% bought in
CERTIFICATION organic

Paolo Bea 🐌

Località Cerrete, 8
tel. 0742 378128
www.paolobea.com
info@paolobea.com

11 ha - 55,000 bt

❝ It's the quality of the soil that generates the vine and determines the true value of the wine. This is a lesson that has been handed down for generations in the Bea family. Thanks to their winery, it is now a patrimony that belongs to us and to many wine lovers. ❞

PEOPLE - "You have to observe, listen to and try to comprehend nature, never to dominate it," says Giampiero Bea, as we stroll through his vineyards. Looked after with this philosophy, the parcels are a sight to behold, even though the grape bunches are still growing.

VINEYARDS - The vineyards sit at an altitude of about 400 meters on the best growing land in the hills of Montefalco for soil composition and position. Downhill, interspersed with maple trees, are century-old trebbiano spoletino vines. In the new cellar a cross-section model shows the stratification of the soil with clay, gravel, silt and inland pebbles.

WINES - The cellar's wines follow the seasons, giving of their best in the growing years that are theoretically the best, but also capable of reacting even in the poorer ones. A sip of **Arboreus 2010** (O trebbiano spoletino; 7,600 bt) is like eating a mouthful of the local food. The stylish opulence of the aromas is just the prelude to the juice that pervades the palate, supported by racy acidity and masterful cleanness. Not to be missed. Full-bodied and well-defined in the glass, **Montefalco Rosso Pipparello Ris. 2007** (● 8,300 bt) has a sauvage note about it. **Rosso de Vèo 2007** (● 7,200 bt), "Bea's red in dialect" is an absolute pleasure to drink.

> **vino slow** MONTEFALCO SAGRANTINO PAGLIARO 2007 (● 14,000 bt) A wine with an austere nose and palate well wrapped up in tannins. We were struck by its finesse and pure class. A paradigm for the denomination.ˈ

FERTILIZERS compost, green manure
PLANT PROTECTION copper and sulphur, organic
WEED CONTROL mechanical
YEASTS native
GRAPES 5% bought in
CERTIFICATION organic

Tabarrini

Frazione Turrita
tel. 0742 379351
www.tabarrini.com
info@tabarrini.com

16 ha - 60,000 bt | **10% discount**

66 Thanks to Giampaolo, the winery combines respect for farm work with modern entrepreneurial spirit. It's an example for the whole area. 99

PEOPLE - Giampaolo Tabarrini leads a tight-knit team of family members: his partner, who often helps him in his work, his mother Franca, who oversees hospitality, his father Nello, always generous with his advice, and his uncle Angelo. The names and the faces of a dynamic company where quality is guaranteed.

VINEYARDS - The vineyards are situated round the cellar and are spurred cordon-trained. Excellent positions and clayey-silty soil, often scatterd with inland pebbles, have made it possible to choose the best vineyards for the sagrantino crus. The old trebbiano spoletino vines, planted 60 years ago, yield the grapes for terroir-dedicated wine rooted in eras long gone by.

WINES - In the modernity of the wines one still notes a bond with the tradition of capturing the essence of their terroir of origin. **Adarmando 2011** (O trebbiano spoletino; 8,000 bt) has subtle minerality to project the fragrance of the aromas and a solid, deep palate. With its Mediterranean notes and cut-glass juiciness, **Montefalco Rosso Colle Grimaldesco 2010** (● 18,000 bt) is an exciting quaff. **Montefalco Sagrantino Campo alla Cerqua 2009** (● 1.900 bt) has amazingly complex aromas and austerity. **Montefalco Sagrantino Colle alle Macchie 2007** (● 1,900 bt) is ready to drink.

vino slow MONTEFALCO SAGRANTINO COLLE GRIMALD-ESCO 2009 (● 15,000 bt) Ostensibly the simplest of the crus submitted by Giampaolo, its aerial, well-extracted taste profile and clear-cut aromas make it our ideal Sagrantino.

FERTILIZERS manure pellets, green manure
PLANT PROTECTION copper and sulphur
WEED CONTROL mechanical
YEASTS native
GRAPES 100% estate-grown
CERTIFICATION none

Palazzone

Località Rocca Ripesena, 68
tel. 0763 344921
www.palazzone.com
info@palazzone.com

24 ha - 140,000 bt | **10% discount**

66 It's thanks to the work of this winery that we still get the chance to speak of a great Orvieto white. It's the expression of a wonderful winegrowing area that deserves promoting. 99

PEOPLE - "The company has chosen for us. It has invested us with responsibility, with its great beauty ..." So speak Giovanni and Lodovico Dubini. In the late 1970s their father planted the first vines and started producing wine in 1978. His sons took over the reins in 1984.

VINEYARDS - The vineyards are broken up into many small plots round the old building and face northeast, an ideal condition for maintaining the freshness of the grapes. The soil at Rocca Ripesena is composed of clay of sedimentary origin, a characteristic which gives the wines longevity and minerality. Over the years, Giovanni, who oversees production, has tested new techniques and reinterpreted old ones.

WINES - 2012 was a rather dry year but this didn't prevent Palazzone from creating wines of lower alcohol proof and higher quality than the previous one. **Grechetto Grek 2012** (O 7,000 bt) is deliciously lemony with a characteristic note of almonds on the finish. Orvieto Cl. Sup. Terre Vineate 2012 (O 50,000 bt) has a long palate and promises to last — an excellent Everyday Wine. Delicate with hints of honey and lime blossom, posed between flesh, flavor and freshness, **Viognier 2012** (O 4,000 bt), enjoyed one of its best vintages to date.

vino slow ORVIETO CL. SUP CAMPO DEL GUARDIANO 2011 (O 9,600 bt) A symbol of the denomination for finesse and longevity. It has deep aromas of candied fruit and spices and a mature palate with plenty of thrust and a flavorful, juicy finish.

FERTILIZERS organic-mineral, natural manure, green manure
PLANT PROTECTION copper and sulphur
WEED CONTROL mechanical
YEASTS selected
GRAPES 100% estate-grown
CERTIFICATION none

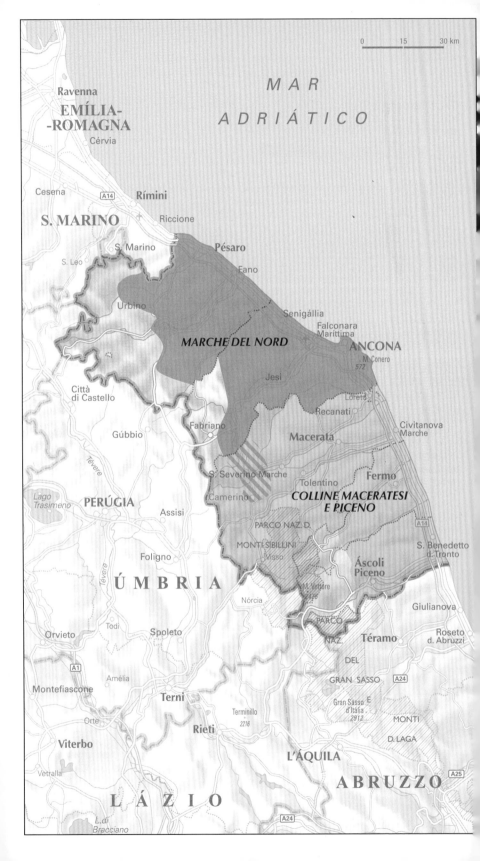

MARCHE

The Marche region is in a state of ferment. The increase in the number of producers, already recorded in the previous edition of the guide, continued. New wineries saw the light in both the Pesaro and the Piceno districts, often out of necessity, either because it's no longer profitable to sell grapes to the larger companies or, more commonly, because wine cooperatives are closing down. In this context, the most important trend is the involvement of young people, confirmation of the vitality of the farming sector and the tendency for the new generations to invest in the land for their future. It is no coincidence that many of our symbols have gone to youngsters we banked on from the outset and whose growth we have tracked: Leo Felici, Davide and Giacomo Mattioli of Poderi Mattioli, Riccardo Baldi of La Staffa, Emanuele and Daniele Colletta of Clara Marcelli.

Another sign of ferment was the creation of TerroirMarche, a consortium of Marche winegrowers which intends to promote and raise the profile of organic viticulture in the region, as well as the dissemination of crops and practices for sustainable, ethical farming. At present it has five members: Aurora of Offida, Fiorano of Cossignano, La Distesa and La Marca di San Michele of Cupramontana, Pievalta of Maiolati Spontini. Analysis of the qualitative aspects of production shows that the Verdicchio zone (Castelli di Jesi and Matelica) is again the one in best shape, with diffuse high quality in every price range. Even in the warm 2012 growing year, wines responded with aromatic brightness and balance. The Conero continues to suffer a certain lack of identity with often over-mature, over-extracted wines, sometimes without focus and expansion. In the Lacrima di Morro d'Alba zone, instead, the warm 2011 and 2012 growing years seem to have been a boon for the base wines, which display more fragrance and suppleness than the "Superiore" category. In the Pesaro zone, Bianchello seemed more on form than usual and, wines from the 2012 vintage were more substantial and fleshier. Pecorino, however, suffered the heat badly, with wines with sweet aromas, overripe fruit and an alcohol content that has hindered their development. The red wine picture is rosier and in Rosso Piceno Superiore and montepulciano-based wines we noted greater finesse, better-focused fruit and equilibrium. Let's hope the trend continues so that the principal red wine zone in the region can reacquire the consistency it deserves. Leaving aside the 2011 and 2012 vintages, which we have already mentioned, 2010 was a very cool year and added aromatic finesse and keenness.

Marche del Nord

0   10   20 km

MAR ADRIÁTICO

EMILIA-
ROMAGNA

PÉSARO

Fano

Senigállia

LACRIMA DI
MORRO D'ALBA

Falconara Maritt.

ANCONA

ROSSO
CONERO

Pérgola

Urbino
Fossombrone

Urbánia

Cartoceto

Piagge

Mondávio

Barchi

Corinaldo

Ostra Vétere

Ostra

Morro d'Alba

Monte S. Vito

S. Marcello

Bárbara

Belvedere
Ostrense

Camerano

Sirolo

Numana

Montecarotto

Póggio
S. Marcello

Offagna

Arcévia

VERDICCHIO DEI
CASTELLI DI JESI

Castèlplánio

Jesi

Maiolati Spontini

Ósimo

Castelfidardo

Porto Recanati

Loreto

Recanati

Cágli

Serra de' Conti

Sérra
Quírico

S. Pàblo di Jesi

Cupramontana

Stáffolo

Filottrano

Montefano

Apiro

Cíngoli

Fabriano

Cerreto d'Esi

VERDICCHIO
DI MATÉLICA

Matélica

Castelraimondo

Pióraco

Camerino

UMBRIA

ABRUZZO

Moroder

Via Montacuto 121
tel. 071 898232
www.moroder-vini.it
info@moroder-vini.it

28 ha - 130,000 bt `10% discount`

PEOPLE - Moroder and montepulciano form a historic wine duo in the Conero zone. Alessandro's place isn't just a winery, it's also a farm that grows cereals, fruit, vegetables and truffles. Alessandro, a great believer in the montepulciano grape, hs increased the area dedicated to it and opted for organics to improve its quality. Today he is helped by his son Marco, a competent young man with lots of ideas who is giving a new lease of life to the family brand.

VINEYARDS - The strong points of the Montacuto vineyards are the sea breezes that caress the Conero and the clay-limestone soil that ensures structure and close-knit tannins. It is in this environment that the 40-year-old vines grow alongside others planted in the 1990s. The other vineyards grow on the more compact soil of Candia, Varano and Aspio. Grassing, cover cropping, mole-plowing and organic fertilization are the methods used to work the land. The whole farm is organic.

WINES - Different vinification techniques, different containers and different aging times are all geared to a single objective: to give the montepulciano grape character and fruity aromas. The wines are eloquent, well-balanced and delightful. Rosso Conero Moroder 2010 (● 50,000 bt) is now a well-established Everyday Wine. It highlights sweet fruit, expansion and uniformity of taste. **Rosa di Montacuto 2012** (☉ montepulciano, alicante, sangiovese; 7,000 bt) has less cloying aromas at last and is more tonic than it used to be. **Elleno 2012** (○ malvasia; 6,000 bt) is a brilliant white, clear-cut with lively aromas.

> **vino slow** CONERO DORICO RIS. 2009 (● 14,000 bt) A wine that expresses all the elegance of the montepulciano grape. It stands out for its aromatic composure and fragrance, its vigorous, by no means heavy palate and its well-balanced tannins, which add extra complexity.

FERTILIZERS natural manure, green manure
PLANT PROTECTION copper and sulphur
WEED CONTROL mechanical
YEASTS selected
GRAPES 100% estate-grown
CERTIFICATION organic

Andrea Felici

Contrada Sant'Isidoro
tel. 0733 611431
www.andreafelici.it
leo@andreafelici.it

9 ha - 35,000 bt `10% discount`

" Sustainability in the vineyard and exactness in the cellar — the prerequisites for wines of improved quality with a true sense of place. **"**

PEOPLE - A lover of night life or a painstaking Apiro winemaker? There are two apparently conflicting sides to Leo Felici's exuberant personality, but his winery works on solid bases without distractions. His dad Andrea, a wise countryman and a canny worker laid the bases, Leo, a meticulous and able winemaker and communicator, added the winning touch. In his wines it's possible to breathe the air of the terroir. So let's allow him to enjoy himself!

VINEYARDS - So what do Leo and Andrea have to say: "We take obsessive care of the soil because that's where the grapes are born. There are no set rules in the vineyards because conditions are never the same in agriculture. You look at the vineyard and see what it needs, then you do what you have to do. We don't use chemicals because the vine needs stimulating and chemicals destroy its natural defenses".

WINES - Select grape varieties, close-focus and balance come out naturally in Felici wines. The terroir does its bit, then the hands of Leo and Aroldo Belelli do the rest. Verdicchio dei Castelli di Jesi Cl. Sup. Andrea Felici 2012 (○ 30,000 bt) is an excellent Everyday Wine. A triumph of aroma, it has a refined follow-through on the palate and a pleasing acid-saline symmetry.

> **vino slow** CASTELLI DI JESI RIS. CL. IL CANTICO DELLA FIGURA 2012 (○ 5,000 bt) A wine that captures the essence of the Apiro impeccably. It bubbles over minerals, wild fennel and aniseed that, unobtrusively, supplement the fruit. The palate is as exact as it is eloquent and dynamic, the savory finish plows a furrow towards the future.

FERTILIZERS natural manure, green manure
PLANT PROTECTION copper and sulphur
WEED CONTROL mechanical
YEASTS selected, native
GRAPES 100% estate-grown
CERTIFICATION organic

Santa Barbara

Borgo Mazzini, 35
tel. 071 9674249
www.vinisantabarbara.it
info@vinisantabarbara.it

70 ha - 650,000 bt | **10% discount**

PEOPLE - Santa Barbara is a dynamic company whose terroir-dedicated wines brilliantly strike the right balance between authenticity and modernity, at once a pleasure to drink and capable of pleasing the market. Stefano Antonucci, the company's founder and charismatic leader, is backed by a team of young collaborators. Together, year by year, they present a broad range of wines, all of the highest quality.

VINEYARDS - Stefano's story as a winemaker began in Barbara, the village where the cellar is situated and where he bought his first vineyard, Pignocco. Today almost all the grapes produced in Barbara go to Stefano, whose properties have spread into historic verdicchio-growing territory — Serra de' Conti, Arcevia, Montecarotto — where soil composition and locations vary.

WINES - A broad range of wines of consistent quality — Stefano never fails to hit the bull's eye. Once more a Great Wine this year, **Castelli di Jesi Ris. Cl. Stefano Antonucci 2011** (O 35,000 bt) stands out for elegance, softness never over-spicy aromas and a tonic, full-bodied palate rounded off by a full-flavored, long finish. On top form yet again, **Verdicchio dei Castelli di Jesi Cl. Le Vaglie 2012** (O 170,000 bt), delicate with a racy, full-flavored palate, is one of the best wines for years. **Pathos 2010** (● merlot, cabernet, syrah; 8,000 bt) has dense fruity aromas, soft but subtle. **Sensuade 2012** (⊙ lacrima, moscato rosso, aleatico; 5,000 bt) is alluring and flavorful, while **Sangiovese Colle Ravara 2011** (● 10,000 bt) is enjoyably drinkable. **Verdicchio dei Castelli di Jesi Passito Lina 2010** (O 2,500 bt) is at the top of its typology.

FERTILIZERS organic-mineral
PLANT PROTECTION chemical, copper and sulphur
WEED CONTROL mechanical
YEASTS selected, native
GRAPES wine bought in
CERTIFICATION none

Collestefano

Frazione Rustano
Località Colle Stefano, 3
tel. 0737 640439
www.collestefano.com
info@collestefano.com

17 ha - 89,000 bt

66 Fabio's shyness and modesty are consistent with Collestefano's ambition to quietly make simple wine that captures the essence of the Matelica terroir. 99

PEOPLE - Fabio Marchionni explains his philosophy as follows: "If a customer or a wine lover or a journalist were to call today, they would talk with me or my wife Silvia. This is Collestefano's strong point. Maybe with a secretary or a switchboard operator the communication would be more effective, but that would spell the end for our artisanship. And we want to continue being artisans".

VINEYARDS - The heart of Collestefano consists of 17 hectares of vines that the family manages with passion using sustainable methods. Plantings, old and new, of massal and clonal selections grow on gravelly limestone soil in a north-east location. Turfing, cover cropping and fertilization with manure attract microorganisms that, in turn, facilitate the life in the soil.

WINES - Collestefano isn't the cru of a well-located vineyard but a blend of grapes from the various plots, which Fabio assembles without allowing himself to be influenced by fashions or the market. In his opinion, humans have to intervene as little as possible because the wine has to have the flavor of the soil and the vintage, nothing else. His Verdicchio is among the finest from 2012, while **Rosa di Elena 2012** (⊙ sangiovese, cabernet; 4,000 bt) is delicate with a tonic, racy silhouette.

vino slow **VERDICCHIO DI MATELICA COLLESTEFANO 2012** (O 85,000 bt) A wine with Nordic aromas and Camerino-style body. Follow-up and elegance are the distinctive features of the palate which veers between acidity and salinity to ensure enjoyable drinking and a luminous future.

FERTILIZERS manure pellets, natural manure, green manure
PLANT PROTECTION copper and sulphur
WEED CONTROL mechanical
YEASTS selected
GRAPES 15% bought in
CERTIFICATION organic

MAIOLATI SPONTINI (AN)

Pievalta

Via Monteschiavo, 18
tel. 0731 705199
www.baronepizzini.it
pievalta@baronepizzini.it

26.5 ha - 125,000 bt   **10% discount**

❝ Pievalta deserves to be congratulated for ferrying verdicchio to the shores of biodynamics, thereby demonstrating that, even without using chemicals in the vineyard and cellar, it's possible to make stylish complex, varietal wines. ❞

PEOPLE - When the young Milanese enologist Alessandro Fenino was sent by Barone Pizzini to manage Pievalta — the estate it had bought in the Castelli di Jesi with the intention of converting it to biodynamics — he had no shortage of passion, humility and will to learn. In the few years since then, Alessandro has enhanced his own professional experience by learning to interpret the stubborn character of verdicchio. Today Pievalta's wines are a focus for the whole area.

VINEYARDS - Biodynamics is used at Pievalta to balance the soil and the vines and improve phytosanitary reactivity. Alessandro is no extremist and is prepared to take risks in poor growing years, his priority mission being to keep the ecosystem alive. Hence cow horn manure, selective grassing and cover cropping to reactivate the microbic life of the tufa soil of Follonica and the clay limestone of Maiolati.

WINES - The wines are reliable, recognizable and rich in personality. Verdicchio dei Castelli di Jesi Cl. Sup. Pievalta 2012 (○ 85,000 bt) is exemplary for tautness and sharpness with aromas redolent of peach, straw and aniseed — an excellent Everyday Wine. **M. Cl. Extra Brut Perlugo** (○ 20,000 bt) gets the verdicchio grape right with delicacy, close-focus and soft sparkle.

vino slow CASTELLI DI JESI RIS. CL. SAN PAOLO **2010** (○ 14,000 bt) A fusion of structure, reactivity and dynamism. The nose is what the verdicchio grape should be — peach and apricot, aniseed, minerally hints – the palate fleshy and well-rounded in a balanced, uncommonly savory context.

FERTILIZERS manure pellets, natural manure, compost, biodynamic preparations, green manure
PLANT PROTECTION copper and sulphur, organic
WEED CONTROL mechanical
YEASTS selected, native
GRAPES 100% estate-grown
CERTIFICATION biodynamic, organic

MATELICA (MC)

Fattoria La Monacesca

Contrada Monacesca
tel. 0733 672641
www.monacesca.it
info@monacesca.it

28 ha - 200,000 bt

❝ Matelica, Monacesca, Mirum: a perfect symbiosis and a credit to the terroir. Productive efficiency is the emblem of a now well-consolidated style. ❞

PEOPLE - 2013 saw the death of Casimiro Cifola, the enlightened businessman who, in 1966, bought the Farfense monastery in Matelica, now the cellar's headquarters. Aldo, his son, took over the reins some years ago and has managed the cellar with confidence, technical competence and determination ever since. La Monacesca is not only a cellar but also part and parcel of the local area.

VINEYARDS - The vineyards cover an area of 28 square meters on all sides of a hillock near the old village. On the clay and limestone soil grow verdicchio, sangiovese and some merlot and chardonnay. In one section of the vineyards, Aldo has planted 14 verdicchio clones to reproduce the massal genetic pool.

WINES - Every year we wonder whether Aldo's wines will be better than those of the year before. A high standard of quality and consistency are always a guarantee of exciting results. Albeit young and in need of further aging, **Verdicchio di Matelica Monacesca 2012** (○ 150,000 bt), rich in fruit, complex and rich with a generous, racy finish, is nonetheless very good indeed. **Camerte 2010** (● sangiovese, merlot; 30,000 bt) is a crisp, complex, high-altitude red with a juicy, supple palate whose only flaw is its extreme youthfulness.

vino slow VERDICCHIO DI MATELICA MIRUM RIS. **2011** (○ 14,000 bt) Less rich and soft than the 2010, but drier and more forthright and full of vigor. Despite the warm year, a tonic wine that expresses complexity and a long savory finish. An old-style Mirum for traditionalists.

FERTILIZERS organic-mineral, manure pellets
PLANT PROTECTION chemical
WEED CONTROL chemical, mechanical
YEASTS selected
GRAPES 100% estate-grown
CERTIFICATION none

Marotti Campi €

Via Sant'Amico, 14
tel. 0731 618027
www.marotticampi.it
wine@marotticampi.net

Umani Ronchi

Via Adriatica, 12
tel. 071 7108019
www.umanironchi.it
wine@umanironchi.it

56 ha - 206,000 bt · 10% discount

230 ha - 2,800,000 bt · 10% discount

PEOPLE - A mid 19th-century villa, a farm with 120 hectares of land, cereal crops and, as early as 1850, vineyards with 8,000 vines per hectare. This is the historical background of Marotti Campi, a thriving winery in the lush Lacrima zone. The initial choice to plant vineyards and sell grapes was soon replaced by the desire to bottle wine. At the helm today is Lorenzo, a dynamic young man who always has a suitcase in his hand, since most of the year he's abroad talking about Lacrima and Verdicchio.

VINEYARDS - A number of plots, separate but adjacent and close to the cellar, cover a total area of 56 hectares. In the Sant'Amico district, a 15-hectare property is divided in two: in one, 18-year-old lacrima vines produce the grapes for Orgiolo, in the other, directly opposite, a 25-year-old Guyot- and Sylvoz-trained vineyard grows verdicchio. On the slope below the villa, 9 hectares of verdicchio vines produce the grapes for Salmariano.

WINES - A wide range of typically reliable wines, designed for easy drinking without losing sight of the varietal characteristics. **Castelli di Jesi Ris. Cl. Salmariano 2010** (O 26,000 bt) is a Great Wine. It has finesse on the nose enhanced by slight hints of pepper, followed by a docile, educated palate with sweet notes that, far from being out of place, help to create balance. **Lacrima di Morro d'Alba Sup. Orgiolo 2011** (● 26,000 bt), which is slightly below par, has blossomy, fruity breadth and a soft, succulent palate which, alas, is dried somewhat by the tannins and tightens on the finish. The effective, full-flavored **Lacrima di Morro d'Alba Rubico 2012** (● 60,000 bt), is refreshing ad pleasantly fruity. We were alos taken by the character-packed, Bordeaux-style **Donderè 2009** (● petit verdot, cabernet, montepulciano; 5,000 bt) and its lively tannins.

PEOPLE - Massimo Bernetti laid the foundations, his son Michele is the "architect" who designed and developed the young, dynamic, harmonious structure. Michele, the star of the winery's generational turnover, is backed by a pool of competent, well-trained collaborators, all ambitious and all sharing the same objectives, who work in the vineyard, in the cellar and in the sales department with capability and passion. These are the values behind the success of Umani Ronchi.

VINEYARDS - The big news is that the Serra de Conti, Montecarotto and Busche vineyards are converting to organics. It's a step that has been carefully prepared in the last few years, gradually enriching the soil with organic substances and reducing the use of plant protection products to accustom the vines to react autonomously without having to depend on "medicines". The cellar has reached this goal not for reasons of ideology but out of conviction under the proficient direction of the agronomist Luigi Piersanti.

WINES - The range has its usual uniform quality, land-rootedness and varietal identity. The excellent **Castelli di Jesi Ris. Cl. Plenio 2010** (O 21,000 bt) has assertive spices that do not, however, overwhelm the sweetness of the fruit, while the palate is soft and all-embracing, deep but somewhat lacking in suppleness. With its well-tapered, delicately salty body and broad, fresh hints of aniseed and fruit, *Verdicchio dei Castelli di Jesi Cl. Sup. Casal di Serra 2012* (O 90,000 bt) is an excellent Everyday Wine. The warm growing year didn't favor **Verdicchio dei Castelli di Jesi Cl. Sup. Vecchie Vigne 2011** (O 16,000 bt), which is slow to express itself, rich but devoid of its customary dynamism. **Rosso Conero San Lorenzo 2011** (● 75,000 bt) is very good indeed, with tannins that leave their mark on the finish. The flagship red, Pelago and Cumaro, will age another year.

FERTILIZERS organic-mineral
PLANT PROTECTION chemical, copper and sulphur
WEED CONTROL chemical, mechanical
YEASTS selected
GRAPES 100% estate-grown
CERTIFICATION none

FERTILIZERS manure pellets, natural manure
PLANT PROTECTION chemical, copper and sulphur, organic
WEED CONTROL chemical, mechanical
YEASTS selected, native
GRAPES 20% bought in
CERTIFICATION organic for some vineyards

OSTRA VETERE (AN)

Bucci

Località Pongelli
Via Cona, 30
tel. 071 964179
www.villabucci.com
bucciwines@villabucci.com

31 ha - 120,000 bt

66 Bucci is tradition, a cellar with a productive philosophy of its own and a natural vision of viticulture. The eloquent simplicity is the force that makes it modern. 99

PEOPLE - Bucci is an old farm with 400 hectares of land which only 31 are cultivated with vines. The fact is a good advertisement for a place where wine is a component of a broader, comprehensive agricultural supply chain. This is the production philosophy Ampelio has given to the family business. The watchword is "equilibrium", in the fields, in the vineyards, in the cellar.

VINEYARDS - The vineyard management holds no secrets, other than the desire to apply contemporary know-how to the work of the past. Hence vegetative competition to create biodiversity, little under-vine soil working, polyclonal massal selections during replanting, organic treaments. Everything appears to be simple and spontaneous, but it is precisely care and attention in maintaining this small ecosystem that is Bucci's strong point.

WINES - The excellence of Bucci lies in the delicate, unassuming aromas that make its wines unique and impossible to replicate. Every year one wonders how they will evolve and how long they will live. One thing is certain and that is that **Castelli di Jesi Verdicchio Ris. Cl. Villa Bucci 2010** (○ 20,000 bt) is a Great Wine, one of the most elegant ever produced. In it a delicate touch of fruitiness caresses the nose and palate, braced by vibrant acidity and a savory hint which makes it lively and long — a wine that whispers everlasting harmony. Verdicchio dei **Castelli di Jesi Cl. Sup. Bucci 2011** (○ 80,000 bt) is another jewel, a refreshing wine from a warm year that exudes complexity over a pervasive, delicately salty palate. **Rosso Piceno Pongelli 2010** (● 13,000 bt) is a blend of fruit and crispness.

FERTILIZERS manure pellets, biodynamic preparations, green manure, none
PLANT PROTECTION copper and sulphur, organic
WEED CONTROL mechanical
YEASTS selected, native
GRAPES 100% estate-grown
CERTIFICATION organic

SAN MARCELLO (AN)

Tenuta San Marcello

Via Melano, 30
tel. 0731 831008
www.tenutasanmarcello.net
info@tenutasanmarcello.net

3,6 ha - 11,000 bt

PEOPLE - Massimo Palmieri and his wife Pascale Marquet were once business people with careers ahead of them in Milan. Then, in 2007, they bought an abandoned farmhouse in the Marche region and turned it into an agriturismo. "Our goal is self-sufficiency for the family," says Massimo. "Six years ago, our reasoning was that by leaving the frenetic life of the city to come to live in the country, we would live a better life with a sixth of what we earned there, that we would have more quality time again and rediscover the natural rhythm of the days going by."

VINEYARDS - The vineyard is simply an added value for our agriturismo and we don't hold out great economic objectives for it." This is how Massimo explains the planting of about four hectares of verdicchio and lacrima grapes. "We set out with organics and biodynamics in mind, but we had to guarantee a minimum level of production. We thus opted for low impact with as few interventions as possible." Work in the vineyard is thus based round grassing, grubbing, organic fertilization and mowing, with a very limited use of chemicals.

WINES - Forthright wines crafted on steel without forcing and with minimal technique. Lacrima di Morro d'Alba Bastaro 2012 (● 2,800 bt) was on top form, an impeccable Everyday Wine that releases clear-cut blossomy aromas with munchy, fleshy fruit and a juiciness and balance in the mouth that makes for a long, delicate finish. **Lacrima di Morro d'Alba Sup. Melano 2011** (● 1,300 bt) has a very intense nose, a palate of all-over softness and a finish that veers between alcohol and tannin. Of the whites, though its aromas are somewhat static, **Verdicchio dei Castelli di Jesi Cl. Sup. Cipriani 2011** (○ 2,800 bt) is well-mouthed, mouthfilling and nicely salty. **Verdicchio dei Castelli di Jesi Cl. Buca della Marcona 2011** (○ 2,400 bt) has fruity aromas but a certain lack of thrust on the palate.

FERTILIZERS manure pellets, compost
PLANT PROTECTION chemical, copper and sulphur
WEED CONTROL mechanical
YEASTS selected
GRAPES wine bought in
CERTIFICATION none

Colline Maceratesi e Piceno

ASCOLI PICENO

Velenosi

Via dei Biancospini, 11
tel. 0736 341218
www.velenosivini.com
info@velenosivini.com

104 ha - 2,500,000 bt

PEOPLE - Velenosi released its first bottles in 1985. Angela and Ercole were setting out on a journey strewn with pitfalls, though maybe they weren't aware of the fact at the time. Today Velenosi is one of the pillars of the Marche region in general and the Piceno district in particular, an unstoppable driving force. The wines are beautifully crafted, they express grape varieties well, they satisfy the taste of customers, they combine drinkability and modernity. Which explains their success and the number of bottles produced.

VINEYARDS - The vineyards, which cover a total area of 104 hectares, are situated on some of the best hillsides of the Piceno, grow local and international grapes. On the sunny hilltops of Castel di Lama and Castorano, on land with different types of soil composition, modern, sometimes renovated plantings stand alongside fully mature 20-year-old vineyards. The Apennines further inland and the sea, visible not far below, produce plenty of air exchange and a considerable temperature range.

WINES - It's becoming increasingly difficult to choose which wines to mention and which to leave out. **Offida Pecorino Villa Angela 2012** (○ 120,000 bt) is once more a Great Wine for the aromatic sophistication with which it interprets a warm growing year and the sinuous silhouette with which it produces an intriguing, tangy palate. **Rosso Piceno Sup. Roggio del Filare 2009** (● 45,000 bt), austere and majestic, is smooth and dignified with just the right amount of tannins and a long, flavor-impregnated finish. Of the two metodo classico Bruts, we prefer the enticing **The Rose 2008** (◉ 26,000 bt), the best version produced to date, delicate and balanced, enjoyably mineral. Rosso Piceno Sup. Brecciarolo 2010 (● 450,000 bt) is an Everyday Wine that combines aromatic modernity with an assertive, uniform body to ensure huge drinkability.

FERTILIZERS organic-mineral, natural manure, green manure
PLANT PROTECTION copper and sulphur
WEED CONTROL mechanical
YEASTS selected, native
GRAPES 40% bought in, wine bought in
CERTIFICATION none

CASTEL DI LAMA (AP)

De Angelis

€

Via San Francesco, 10
tel. 0736 87429
www.tenutadeangelis.it
info@tenutadeangelis.it

50 ha - 500,000 bt   **10% discount**

PEOPLE - De Angelis is the emblem of the Piceno winemaking tradition. In the 1950s, Alighiero De Angelis began buying grapes and selling the wine he made with them unbottled in vats. In 1985, under his son-in-law Quinto Fausti, the company moved from Cossignano to Castel di Lama and began to plant vineyards. In the early 1990s the cellar expanded and the amount of wine produced increased. It was thus that bottling began and now predominates.

VINEYARDS - The main plot has an area of 40 hectares and was bought in the 1990s. It is situated near Offida in an open, sunny valley. White grapes grow on the valley floor, native and international red grapes higher up where the climate is warmer. The soil is never worked and the vines stand in grass that is periodically mowed. The other vineyards are situated by the company headquarters at Castel di Lama. Conversion has been completed and all the vineyards are now organic.

WINES - Coherent style, reliability and quality, affordability — these are the qualities of Quinto Fausti, produced in copious quantities in every range. **Anghelos 2009** (● 25,000 bt) is a blend of montepulciano, sangiovese and cabernet. The palate is assertive, crisp and delightful, well-balanced with close-knit tannins. The impeccable **Rosso Piceno Sup. 2009** (● 150,000 bt) is an Everyday Wine that appeals for the crunchiness of its fruit and supple, smooth, clear-cut palate, enriched by a slight hint of spiciness. **Rosso Piceno 2011** (● 120,000 bt) is juicy and fragrant. Moving on to the whites, **Offida Pecorino 2011** (○ 30,000 bt) has very sweet fruit refreshed by citrussy tones, a rich palate and a nicely tangy finish. **Offida Passerina 2011** (○ 13,000 bt) is fruity and fluent.

FERTILIZERS manure pellets
PLANT PROTECTION copper and sulphur
WEED CONTROL mechanical
YEASTS selected
GRAPES 100% estate-grown
CERTIFICATION organic

Sant'Isidoro

Frazione Colbuccaro
Contrada Colle Sant'Isidoro, 5
tel. 0733 201283
www.cantinasantisidoro.it
info@cantinasantisidoro.it
🐌—o

13 ha - 70,000 bt

PEOPLE - This young company has crowned the wine dream of the Foresi family. After working in the prefab sector for many years, they decided to set up a winery by planting part of their land with vines. Work is still under way on the underground cellar which blends in perfectly with the landscape. The old building which stands alongside it has been restructured and converted into a relais. The consultant enologist Roberto Potentini is helped in the cellar by Simone Colombo.

VINEYARDS - The 13 hectares planted with vines are just a small part of a 60-hectare property which also includes woodland and olive groves. Most of the vines were planted in 2005 and 2006 and a small portion was added in 2009. The vineyards are equally divided between white and red grapes and grow on clayey and partly sandy soil. The largest vineyard has an area of about eight hectares, faces south and has good air circulation. Some of the maceratino and pinot nero grapes grow in a cooler east-facing position.

WINES - After pressing and reduction, the white grapes ferment at a low temperature to raise aromatic intensity, whereas the red grapes are vinified traditionally. The impressive **Isidoro 2012** (○ 10,000 bt) is a spacious Pecorino with close-focused aromas of peach and tropical fruit; despite hefty alcohol, it is full-bodied with saline assertiveness. **Colli Maceratesi Ribona Pausula 2012** (○ 10.000 bt) convinces more for its expansion and crispness of its palate than for its sweet, intense aromas, which tend to become cloying in the glass. **Rosso Piceno Pinto 2011** (● 6,000 bt) is admirable for its supple palate and aromatic fragrance. **Montolmo 2011** (● 6,000 bt), made with sangiovese grapes topped up with montepulciano, has nice body and fruity juiciness.

FERTILIZERS	organic-mineral, compost
PLANT PROTECTION	chemical, copper and sulphur, organic
WEED CONTROL	chemical, mechanical
YEASTS	selected
GRAPES	100% estate-grown
CERTIFICATION	none

Le Vigne di Franca ⓔ

Contrada Santa Petronilla, 69
tel. 335 6512938
www.levignedifranca.it
info@levignedifranca.it

1.6 ha - 20,000 bt

PEOPLE - Majestic secular olive trees surround the farmhouse-cum-wine cellar just outside Fermo that Claudio Paulich bought in 1998. Claudio had originally come to the Marche region to manage a series of major shoe factories, but he and his wife Franca, for whom the company is named, subsequently decided to cultivate the passion for the land inculcated in him by his father. Paulich is a farmer, cellarman and salesman rolled up in one and he follows every aspect of the short production chain with great attention to detail. The results are there for all to see.

VINEYARDS - Three hectares of land on mixed clayey and sandy soil, 1.6 of which planted which vines, are situated, protected from the cold north winds, on a slight southeast facing slope. The montepulciano, merlot and cabernet vineyards were planted in the year 2000 with a density of 7,000 plants per hectare and are cordon-trained. Field beans and clover grow in the vineyard which is managed entirely by hand. Only the under-vine soil is worked. Given the limited area, treatments can be carried out promptly and grapes transported quickly.

WINES - Last year's excellent results were no freak, as Claudio Paulich, a hard worker with clear ideas, proves again this year with a repeat performance. Far from weighing down the wines, 12 months of barrel- and bottle-aging make them balanced and supple. **Crismon 2011** (● 2,200 bt) is a delightful montepulciano and just misses out on a symbol. It's a concentrate of brambles and blackcurrant syrup with faint vegetal and spicy nuances that create complexity without being cloying. The robust palate, in no way over-extracted, is vigorous and grows in the glass. The finish is uniform with close-knit tannins. **Rubrum 2011** (● 10,000 bt) is a blend of montepulciano and merlot with fruit that is rich but never heavy. Juicy and dynamic, it has staying power and tannic finesse.

FERTILIZERS	green manure
PLANT PROTECTION	chemical, copper and sulphur
WEED CONTROL	mechanical
YEASTS	selected
GRAPES	100% estate-grown
CERTIFICATION	none

Aurora

OFFIDA (AP)

Località Santa Maria in Carro
Contrada Ciafone, 98
tel. 0736 810007
www.viniaurora.it
enrico@viniaurora.it

9.5 ha - 50,000 bt | **10% discount**

66 Aurora is a self-contained good, clean and fair project that offers wines of character and personality all made with respect for the environment by a community with a social, anticonformist spirit. 99

PEOPLE - Aurora is a multiform winery that has been living and thinking organic since 1980. The original founders are all around 60 years of age and the second generation is now starting to work with them. After various outside experiences, Francesco Pignati is back to lend a hand in the vineyard and the cellar. The many plaudits the winery has received have not undermined the integrity of its approach to farming and desire to put itself on the line.

VINEYARDS - A magnificent oak tree towers over the lovely pecorino vineyard in the coolest part of the estate, two hectares, a third of which date from 1996, the rest from 2006, facing north at the foot of the Monti Sibillini. In this oasis of biodiversity, six hectares are also given over to red grapes. Worthy of mention are a 150,000 square-meter vineyard, over 25 years old, that grows montepulciano, the soul of the Barricadiero wine, and a half-hectare plot of morettone, a local grape variety in which the "old boys" are now investing.

WINES - Aurora wines are marked by flavor and freedom of expression. The reds, Barricadiero and Rosso Piceno Sup. 2011, still are aging in the bottle. Moving on to the whites, Offida Pecorino Fiobbo 2011 (O 8,000 bt) is again an Everyday Wine. It veers between chamomile, sweet fruit and a slight spiciness that enhances the zippy yet reactive, salty palate. A round of applause for **Falerio 2012** (O trebbiano, passerina, pecorino; 10,000 bt), an enjoyable blend with hints of fruit and garden vegetables and an agreeable supporting acidity. **Passerina 2012** (O 4,000 bt) is tonic and tangy and closes on notes of ripe fruit. **Rosso Piceno 2012** (● 16,000 bt) is a simple succulent table wine.

FERTILIZERS biodynamic preparations, green manure
PLANT PROTECTION copper and sulphur, organic
WEED CONTROL mechanical
YEASTS native
GRAPES 100% estate-grown
CERTIFICATION organic

Fattoria Dezi

SERVIGLIANO (FM)

Contrada Fontemaggio,14
tel. 0734 710090
fattoriadezi@hotmail.com

15 ha - 42,000 bt | **10% discount**

66 The Dezi brothers have raised the profile of the terroir adding luster to their winemaking, which has been supporting the family for decades. 99

PEOPLE - Servigliano in an unspoiled oasis, neither polluted by industry nor invaded by mass tourism, much frequented by nature lovers. The fields are washed by the colors of the seasonal crops, while the value of the arable land, olive groves and vineyards is more of agricultural than of economic value. Here the Dezi brothers work in the furrow of the family tradition by drawubg the best out of the fruits of the earth.

VINEYARDS - The steep terrains of the Fontemaggio district are grassed or worked according to the season. The southern location and the breezes that blow down the Tenna river facilitate the ripening and ensure the good health of the grapes. It is in this context that Davide works, without following protocols, intervening when necessary and seeking to be as non-invasive as possible. The result is balanced soil and vineyards which enable the over 40-year-old montepulciano vines to produce excellent clusters.

WINES - The Dezi wines are once more a model of consistency. **Regina del Bosco 2010** (● montepulciano; 6,000 bt) has a palate combining density with suppleness and broad, fine aromas whose spicy notes will be amalgamated with bottle-aging. Somewhat clenched, **Dezio 2011** (● montepulciano, sangiovese; 18,000 bt) has a mature nose and a palate that fills out on the finish. The word to describe **Servigliano P 2011** (O pecorino; 4,500 bt) is robust.

vino slow **SOLO 2011** (● sangiovese; 6,000 bt) A wine that develops slowly but effectively. A blend of crushed red berries and sweet spices, on the palate it is vigorous, in no way sluggish, with a fleshy, long, vivacious finish.

FERTILIZERS natural manure, green manure
PLANT PROTECTION copper and sulphur, organic
WEED CONTROL mechanical
YEASTS native
GRAPES 100% estate-grown
CERTIFICATION none

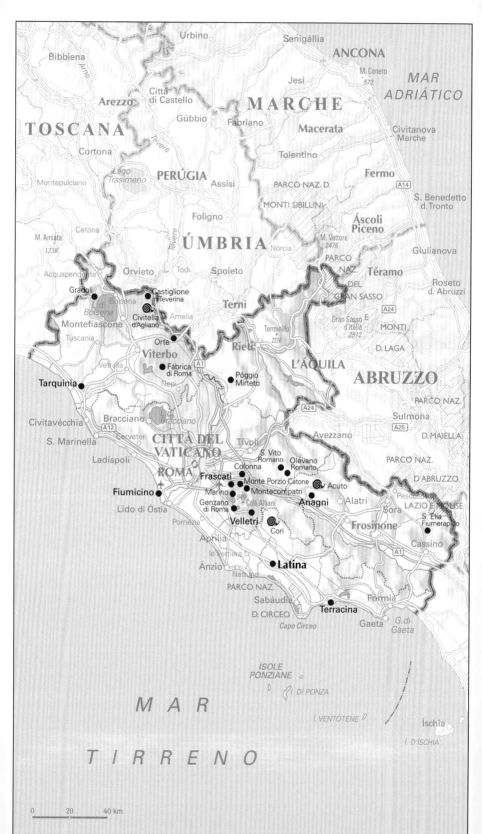

LAZIO

It's just not good enough. That may sound like a damning comment on the wine situation in Lazio, but the fact is that sweeping problems under the carpet and rambling on about potential, purposeful signs, urge to act, mistakes at the correction stage and other platitudes may be justifiable when discussing new terroirs with climates and microclimates still to be discovered, where experiments and insights are harnessed to achieving new results and raising expectations. In the case of Lazio it's no longer worth the effort. No way! After paying for its many past errors — quantity as opposed to quality, markets that absorbed oxidization, acetic acid, second-fermentations and all the other usual suspects — and showing signs of good intentions in recent years, what is arguably one of the best winegrowing regions in the world has given up the ghost again, virtually all over. That's the way it is, alas. Outside the region the market has still to fully assimilate Lazio's "new deal" and the agronomic and productive fabric continues to fray. 2012 was nothing to write home about white wine-wise, some producers investing badly, others biting off more than they could chew, others still sensing once and for all that the game is no longer worth the candle. Compared with what the Castelli Romani zones is capable of attaining, and excepting a few interesting names, some of them new, the reality is at best one of productive honesty and cleanness — nothing more. Cori is the last life belt (what the nero buono grape can achieve remains to be seen) in the Agro Pontino zone, where standardization reigns from the coastal strip on the outskirts of Rome down to Terracina, with odd surprises casting rays of light here and there. Rieti still sees oil as its cure-all, especially (it hopes) from an economic view, whereas a grape like cesanese (especially that of Affile), which wouldn't be out of place even in the most distinguished winemaking contexts, continues to be used always by the same old wineries. The fact that a few do turn it into good wines only goes to show how wobbly the situation is. Awaiting a great red from the coast between Cerveteri and the Tuscan border, the most dynamic zone continues to be the northern part of the province of Viterbo where, despite ups and downs this year, a few satisfactory results were achieved with mostly consistent Grechettos and Aleaticos, at long last produced with a modicum of gumption. The average performance of reds wasn't particularly exciting and we are curious to see if recently established wineries, some vinifying for the first time, can show the freshness and purpose needed to bring about important changes, even among the names listed in this guide. A turnover would be natural, not to say necessary. Once achieved, things might take a turn for the better.

snails 🐌

182 CASALE DELLA IORIA
SERGIO MOTTURA
MARCO CARPINETI

bottles 🍾

183 L'OLIVELLA

coins €

182 TRAPPOLINI

ACUTO (FR)

Casale della Ioria

Località Agnani
Strada Provinciale 118
Anagni-Paliano km. 4,200
tel. 0775 56031
www.casaledellaioria.com
info@casaledellaioria.com

38 ha - 65,000 bt

66 Clean agriculture, intelligent interpretation of a difficult grape but with great potential like cesanese, competitive prices — that's Casale della Ioria in a nutshell. 99

PEOPLE - With the help of skilled professionals, Paolo Perinelli has been cultivating local grapes since the 1970s. Even his new fermentation cellar is part of a precise project. He'll explain it to you under the century-old oak tree that is also the symbol of the cellar.

VINEYARDS - Situated in the communes of Anagni and Acuto, surrounded by splendid woodland and breathtaking scenery, the vineyards are Guyot- and spurred cordon-trained at an altitude of 300-400 meters. The main grape variety used is cesanese di Affile, which ripens in October. Then comes olivella, so-called for its olive-shaped berry, recovered some years ago in an orchard in Monticelli d'Esperia, near Cassino, where it was growing ungrafted on its own root.

WINES - **Olivella 2011** (● 5,000), made with the grape of the same name from vines planted ten years ago, is a singular wine, well-balanced and alluring. **Cesanese del Piglio Camponovo 2012** (● 25,000 bt), the first and so far the only wine to be produced by the cellar with native yeasts (following lengthy experimentation with the most promising vines), is characterized by intense fruitiness with a prevalence of wild cherry. **Cesanese del Piglio Sup. Torre del Piano 2011** (● 5,000 bt) is made with grapes from the oldest vineyard and aged half in barriques and half in mid-sized casks, while the magnificent **Cesanese del Piglio Tenuta della Ioria 2011** (● 35,000 bt) is aged in large barrels: it has potent fruit and hefty structure. Lazio's red of the year and a Great Wine.

CASTIGLIONE IN TEVERINA (VT)

Trappolini €

Via del Rivellino, 65
tel. 0761 948381
www.trappolini.com
info@trappolini.com

23 ha - 200000 bt

PEOPLE - Brothers Roberto and Paolo Trappolini form a well-knit tandem. Today they successfully run the company their grandfather Giovanni and father Mario founded 60 years ago, first selling unbottled wine, then bottling quality local labels produced with respect for the environment. All the company's wines stand out for their excellent value for money.

VINEYARDS - The company owns over 20 hectares of vineyards situated in favorable positions, almost all planted with typical local grape varieties: the white grechetto, malvasia, trebbiano, drupeggio, verdello and rossetto and the red sangiovese, montepulciano and aleatico. Albeit not yet organically certified, work in the vineyard and the cellar sees to it that the wines are authentically terroir-dedicated.

WINES - Aromatic with characteristically bitter notes, **Orvieto 2012** (O 30,000 bt) is a sound interpretation of a DOC with great potential. The steel-fermented **Grechetto 2012** (O 8,000 bt), is fresh, fruity and quaffable. More complex and improved by aging in wood casks, **Brecceto 2011** (O grechetto, chardonnay; 6.000 bt) is already good when young and will age well in the bottle. As every year, Cenereto 2012 (● sangiovese, montepulciano; 70,000 bt) is fruity and smooth and comes at a bargain price: it's a perfect Everyday Wine. **Paterno 2011** (● sangiovese; 15.000 bt) is a complex wine packed with red berries, spicy notes and soft tannins. Last but not least, **Idea 2012** (● aleatico; 6,000 bt) is a soft passito that goes well with every dessert imaginable.

| FERTILIZERS manure pellets, green manure |
| PLANT PROTECTION copper and sulphur |
| WEED CONTROL mechanical |
| YEASTS selected |
| GRAPES 100% estate-grown |
| CERTIFICATION none |

| FERTILIZERS natural manure, green manure |
| PLANT PROTECTION copper and sulphur |
| WEED CONTROL mechanical |
| YEASTS selected |
| GRAPES 100% estate-grown |
| CERTIFICATION none |

Sergio Mottura

Via Poggio della Costa, 1
tel. 0761 914533
www.motturasergio.it
vini@motturasergio.it

37 ha - 95,000 bt **10% discount**

66 Sergio and Giuseppe Mottura's splendid winery is one of the most successful in Central Italy. Promotion of native vines, especially grechetto, respect for the environment (hence organic certification) and clean, elegant wines — these are its distinctive features. 99

PEOPLE - The production facilities are worth a visit for the spectacular tufa caves in which the spumante matures.

VINEYARDS - The vineyards are situated in a good growing district conducive to long-living wines of great character. Tastings of the old vintages of Grechetto and Orvieto confirmed the durability of the two wines, both highly nuanced. The cellar grows mainly white grapes, but also native red and international ones.

WINES - No Latour at Civitella this year: the 2011 version of the cellar's flagship wine will be released later to let it evolve well. Some consolation comes from **Orvieto 2012** (O 20,000 bt), fragrant with a bitterish finish. The same characteristics recur in **Orvieto Tragugnano 2012** (O 12,000 bt). The excellent **Muffo 2010** (O 3,300 bt) is a monovarietal passito from grechetto grapes, elegant and leisurely, uncloying with a very long finish. Standing out among the reds are **Magone 2011** (● 2,500 bt) and **Nenfro 2010** (● 4,000 bt), both worthy interpretations of the pinot nero and montepulciano grapes.

vino slow **POGGIO DELLA COSTA 2012** (O 30,000 bt) The right price, great character, clean agriculture, perfect slow spirit — a white to which the grechetto grape confers huge fruitiness and a typical slightly astringent finish.

FERTILIZERS none
PLANT PROTECTION copper and sulphur
WEED CONTROL mechanical
YEASTS selected
GRAPES 100% estate-grown
CERTIFICATION organic

L'Olivella

Via Colle Pisano, 5
tel. 06 9424527
www.racemo.it
info@racemo.it

14 ha - 68,000 bt **10% discount**

PEOPLE - For some years now, like other wineries, L'Olivella has been committed to relaunching Frascati. This has led to the drawing up of a new discipline more conducive to the use of the native malvasia puntinata grape, to the detriment of trebbiano. Umberto Notarnicola and Bruno Violo have handed down to their sons Danilo and Pietro a new vineyard management philosophy that has earned the winery organic certification.

VINEYARDS - The vineyards were all replanted in 1980s. They are double Guyot-trained and situated at an altitude of 350 meters on the volcanic hill known as Colle Pisano. Since the winery specializes in Frascati, the most grown grape variety is malvasia puntinata, followed by trebbiano, bellone and grechetto, plus the red grapes cesanese, sangiovese, syrah and malvasia rossa (just a few vines).

WINES - Frascati Sup. Racemo 2012 (O 28,000 bt), the fruit of cold maceration, tempts with scents of spring flowers and an after-aroma of toasted almonds thanks to a sizable percentage of malvasia puntinata. Grapefruit prevails in the decently priced **Bombino 2012** (O 4,000 bt). Of the reds we recommend **Quaranta Sessanta 2012** (● syrah, cesanese; 14,000 bt), it has fruity, fleshy notes and a spicy finish. **Maggiore 2009** (● cesanese; 6,000 bt) has a structure that is simultaneously powerful and stylish. The late harvest and proper use of wood add structure and great elegance to **Tre Grome 2012** (● malvasia puntinata, mavasia rossa, bellone; 4,000 bt).

vino slow **TRE GROME PASSITO 2012** (O malvasia puntinata, malvasia rossa, bellone; 1,800 bt) A wine with rich, varietal aromas, one of the best in its typology. It possesses all the character of the terroir with stupendous saltiness and a finish of bitter almonds.

FERTILIZERS organic-mineral, green manure
PLANT PROTECTION copper and sulphur
WEED CONTROL mechanical
YEASTS selected
GRAPES 100% estate-grown
CERTIFICATION organic

ABRUZZO AND MOLISE

It's a mistake to speak about the Abruzzo as an emerging winegrowing region. Consistent quality has now become general, no longer the prerogative of a handful of historic cellars plowing the furrow of tradition, but also a characteristic of the work of both small wineries and large cooperatives.

There are many reasons for this success. They include soil and climate conditions and determined efforts to promote the region and its most important grapes, from montepulciano and trebbiano to minor varieties such as passerina and pecorino (in other regions the onus has been placed on international grapes). Other factors — such as updated cellar technology, improved, less invasive vineyard management and the presence of better qualified enologists, with the young generation of Abruzzese winemakers often counting upon the guidance of experts of national and international fame — have also been influential.

After two vintages in which white wines shone — not that they haven't performed at top level this year too — we are delighted to report the brilliant displays of a number of Montepulciano d'Abruzzos. The excellent results are all the more conspicuous for being spread over the region's various productive areas, vintages and typologies, wines being lifted to high levels of drinkability and freshness by not over-invasive vinification techniques. As a result of above-average temperatures in 2012, white wines matured a little too rapidly and lost some of their acid vigor. Having said that, many producers managed to limit the damage with meticulous care for their vineyards and produced wines — especially Trebbiano d'Abruzzos and Pecorinos — of great depth. Likewise for the Cerasuolo d'Abruzzos, which pull off an amazing balancing act between freshness and structure and are again a joy to drink. These really are wines to accompany the entire meal.

All in all, the Abruzzo wine world is in good health, working the land more sustainably than in the past and affording consumer enjoyment with very reasonably priced labels.

The quality of Molise wines is also improving year by year and hopes are high for the future. A leading role in all this is being played by the tintilia grape, in which producers are investing heavily and intelligently.

snails 🐌

187	TORRE DEI BEATI
188	VALENTINI
188	CATALDI MADONNA
189	EMIDIO PEPE

bottles 🍾

186	PASETTI
189	VALLE REALE
190	FEUDO ANTICO

coins €

186	SAN LORENZO
187	COLLEFRISIO
189	CANTINA FRENTANA
190	TENUTA TERRAVIVA

CASTILENTI (TE)
San Lorenzo   €

Contrada Plavignano, 2
tel. 0861 999325
www.sanlorenzovini.com
info@sanlorenzovini.com

FRANCAVILLA AL MARE (CH)
Pasetti

Contrada Petravo
Via San Paolo, 21
tel. 085 61875
www.pasettivini.it
info@pasettivini.it

---

150 ha - 800,000 bt

60 ha - 600,000 bt

PEOPLE - The Galasso and Barbone families have been farming for generations. Gianluca, who has been helped by his brother Fabrizio for some years now, has learned their lessons and put into practice. The winery came into being in 1998 and, with the collaboration of the brothers' uncle Gianfranco Barbone, who oversees the vineyards, and enologist Riccardo Brighigna, has always banked on quality.

VINEYARDS - From the cellar one sees only a small portion of the company's vast properties — 150 hectares, partly arbourtrained, partly double Guyot-trained. For some years now its agricultural practices have moved towards greater respect for the environment, hence solely mechanical weed control and a minimal use of pesticides.

WINES - The consistency, quality and reliability of the wines improve by the year. **Montepulciano d'Abruzzo Colline Teramane Escol 2009 (●**22,000 bt) has a complex nose of ripe fruit, well-amalgamated with oaky notes and a rich-textured, tannic, leisurely palate. The more approachable **Montepulciano d'Abruzzo Colline Teramane Oinos 2010 (●** 30,000 bt) has bundles of fruit and spices on the nose and mouthfilling flavor. **Pecorino 2012 (**○ 60,000 bt) has a deep nose of fruit and aromatic herbs. **Trebbiano d'Abruzzo Casabianca 2012 (**○ trebbiano, malvasia; 100,000 bt), the fruit of spontaneous fermentation, has a citrussy, blossomy tone. Long maceration on the skins gives **Trebbiano d'Abruzzo Zerosolfiti 2012 (**○ 8,000 bt) aromatic intensity and character. **Montepulciano d'Abruzzo Casabianca 2011 (●** 20,000 bt) is enjoyable too.

PEOPLE - The Pasetti cellar plays a starring role on the regional wine scene thanks to the authoritativeness it has acquired. The family's pride in their work is that typical of people with inbred knowledge of farming. Domenico Pasetti is the leader of a project that is growing increasingly ambitious, hence raising the expectations of enthusiasts. The consultant enologist is Romeo Taraborrelli.

VINEYARDS - The vineyards are split into two plots, one at Pescosansonesco, where a beautiful farmhouse receives guests, the other at Capestrano, where new vines were recently planted. The high-trained, Guyotpruned vines grow on skeleton-grain soil composed of a mixture of clay and pebbles. Common sense governs work in the vineyard, where interventions are measured and only made when necessary.

WINES - A truly impressive range dominated by **Montepulciano d'Abruzzo Testarossa 2009 (●** 90,000 bt), a perfect Great Wine which flaunts full, robust fruit, well-integrated with spices and a palate that is supple despite its hefty structure and alcohol. Far from holding the wine back, the gusty tannins make it all the deeper. The excellent **Pecorino Colle Civetta 2011 (**○ 5,000 bt), which rests for two months on fine lees, has a complex nose with aromas that range from fruit to aromatic herbs and a juicy, dynamic palate with a nice citrussy finish. **Montepulciano d'Abruzzo Harimann 2007 (●** 5,000 bt) has a bouquet of dense fruit backed up by sweet spices and a soft, slightly clinched palate. **Cerasuolo d'Abruzzo 2012 (**⊙ 3,200 bt) is an easy-drinking wine, while **Abruzzo Passito 2011 (**○ moscatello; 3,000 bt) is definitely worth a taste.

FERTILIZERS organic-mineral, manure pellets, green manure
PLANT PROTECTION copper and sulphur
WEED CONTROL mechanical
YEASTS selected, native
GRAPES 100% estate-grown
CERTIFICATION none

FERTILIZERS organic-mineral, natural manure
PLANT PROTECTION copper and sulphur
WEED CONTROL mechanical
YEASTS selected
GRAPES 100% estate-grown
CERTIFICATION none

Collefrisio €

Località Piane di Maggio
tel. 085 9039074
www.collefrisio.it
info@collefrisio.it

36 ha - 350,000 bt

PEOPLE - Amedeo De Luca, Katiuscia Di Ciano and Antonio Patricelli form the third generation of this family of winegrowers and were the first to bottle directly. They took the decision in 2004 and it immediately proved the right one, thanks mainly to the consistent quality of their wine, made with the principal Abruzzo grape varieties. Part of the credit must also go to enologist Romeo Taraborrelli, who has followed work in the cellar right from the outset.

VINEYARDS - The company's 36 hectares are split up into three properties: Valle del Moro, Morrecine and Giuliano Teatino. All are excellently located with good air circulation. They grow mainly montepulciano, trebbiano, pecorino and, for a few years now, passerina grapes. The vines are mostly arbor-trained and managed using organic methods.

WINES - Collefrisio's wines are approachable, clean and meticulously interpreted. They are also extremely good value for money. A good example is Trebbiano d'Abruzzo Zero 2012 (○ 65,000 bt), a fragrant Everyday Wine with distinct notes of citrus fruit and aromatic herbs and fresh, lingering flavor. Another is **Montepulciano d'Abruzzo Morrecine 2011 (●** 13,000 bt) with its nose of crisp fruit and spices, followed up by a pleasant grassy note and a no-nonsense, juicy palate. **Cerasuolo d'Abruzzo 2012 (⊙** 20,000 bt) is very enjoyable. **Montepulciano d'Abruzzo Collefrisio di Collefrisio 2009 (●** 21,000 bt) has a suite of aromas redolent of ripe fruit and a rich, concentrated palate. The fresh and fruity **Passerina 2012 (○** 21,000 bt) and **Falanghina 2012 (○** 13,000 bt) are both interesting.

FERTILIZERS organic-mineral, natural manure, green manure
PLANT PROTECTION copper and sulphur, organic
WEED CONTROL mechanical
YEASTS selected
GRAPES 100% estate-grown
CERTIFICATION organic

Torre dei Beati

Contrada Poggioragone, 56
tel. 333 3832344
www.torredeibeati.it
info@torredeibeati.it

17 ha - 100,000 bt

❝ Adriana Galasso and Fausto Albanesi were absolute beginners when they started making wine. But they've always been convinced about one thing: if you respect the land, it will reward you handsomely. ❞

PEOPLE - Adriana and Fausto, partners in business and in life, are the driving force behind this wonderful little winery, which they opened in 1999. Since then the quality of their wines has never ceased to improve and their sense of purpose has increased accordingly. The secret of their success is meticulous hard work, from the vineyard through selective multi-pass harvesting to, in the case of the two crus, aging in small wood casks.

VINEYARDS - The montepulciano grape represents the winery's enduring bond with the land. All the vineyards but one surround the cellar and grow on clayey soil. Most are still pergola-trained and some vines are 40 years old. The estate is managed to organic criteria.

WINES - The winery interprets the terroir with a modern style, producing very severe fleshy, fruity wines with somewhat austere tannins. **Montepulciano d'Abruzzo Mazzamurello 2010 (●** 5,000 bt) is full-bodied, juicy and also a tad austere, coaxing out the grape's vigor without overwhelming the palate. Full-bodied and dryish but coherent, **Montepulciano d'Abruzzo Cocciapazza 2010 (●** 10,000 bt) is more modern. **Montepulciano d'Abruzzo 2011 (●** 35,000 bt) has notes of blackcurrant and rich flavor. The excellent **Pecorino Giocheremo con i Fiori 2012 (○** 25,000 bt), is fruity with nicely acid, tangy texture. **Cerasuolo d'Abruzzo Rosaae 2012 (⊙** 25,000 bt) is also commendable.

FERTILIZERS manure pellets, natural manure
PLANT PROTECTION copper and sulphur, organic
WEED CONTROL mechanical
YEASTS selected
GRAPES 100% estate-grown
CERTIFICATION organic

Valentini

Via del Baio, 2
tel. 085 8291138

OFENA (AQ)

Cataldi Madonna

Località Piano
tel. 0862 954252
www.cataldimadonna.it
cataldimadonna@virgilio.it

---

66 ha - 50,000 bt

28 ha - 240,000 bt | **10% discount**

" It's rare to meet a wine producer so attentive to the agronomic management of his vineyards, so careful to take note of any event that might somehow affect his vines and wines. "

PEOPLE - Francesco Valentini is all this and much more, an artisan winemaker who follows the family tradition by producing uniquely complex, long-lasting wines. With him work his wife Elena and his son Gabriele.

VINEYARDS - The trebbiano and montepulciano vineyards are trained with the traditional pergola system, never questioned by the Valentini family even when it was deemed unsuitable for quality wine production. As anyone acquainted with the area knows fine and well, properly tended, the pergola creates a perfect leaf canopy to protect the grapes from the sun's rays in the summer.

WINES - Work in the cellar, always selective and precise, envisages spontaneous fermentation, no temperature control or filtration and minimal use of sulphur. On account of a series of hot summers and unsatisfactory phenolic ripening, Montepulciano was again conspicuous by its absence, so we had to draw consolation from the following two Slow Wines, both splendid.

vino slow **CERASUOLO D'ABRUZZO 2012** (⊙ 6,000 bt) Hints of fruit and delicate blossomy nuances make the initial impact remarkably complex, while the palate is well-structured, braced by enviably lively acidity.

vino slow **TREBBIANO D'ABRUZZO 2011** (○ 16,000 bt) Complex, elegant mineral notes usher in fruit with customary balsamic overtones. The palate is, as ever, extraordinarily delicate and rich.

" Luigi Cataldi Madonna is a unique character on the Abruzzo wine scene. A tour of the cellar in his company is an experience we recommend to any wine lover, if only for the energy Luigi exudes in his brilliant exposition of his work and the local area. "

PEOPLE - The Cataldi Madonna family has been making wine in the Ofena district for almost a century. Which is probably why Luigi has stubbornly continued to soldier on, making wine as it should be made, despite the present-day air of abandonment.

VINEYARDS - "I believe that awareness of the environment is a duty," says Luigi to explain why this year he as decided to convert to organics. His vineyards are mostly bilateral cordon-trained on gravelly limestone soil. Despite climate change, the phenolic ripening of the grapes is ensured by the copious number of leaves left on the vine and the considerable temperature range.

WINES - All the wines possess character, complexity and depth. **Montepulciano d'Abruzzo Tonì 2010** (● 3,000 bt) is a refined, full-bodied yet energy-filled Great Wine, every sip of which is a delight for the palate. Truly excellent too is **Montepulciano d'Abruzzo Malandrino 2011** (● 6,000 bt): pervasive and complex, it has a hefty, lingering palate. **Pecorino Giulia 2012** (○ 35,000 bt), vegetal on the nose and tangy on the palate, and the fragrant, juicy **Cerasuolo d'Abruzzo 2012** (⊙ 35,000 bt) never fail to impress either.

vino slow **PECORINO 2011** (○ 3,000 bt) A pedigree wine that stands out for its aroma and sinew, backed up by a taut and tantalizing palate. It was a great notion to cultivate the pecorino variety, once virtually unknown, on the plain of Ofena, as this label proves.

FERTILIZERS none
PLANT PROTECTION copper and sulphur
WEED CONTROL mechanical
YEASTS native
GRAPES 100% estate-grown
CERTIFICATION none

FERTILIZERS natural manure
PLANT PROTECTION copper and sulphur
WEED CONTROL mechanical
YEASTS selected
GRAPES 100% estate-grown
CERTIFICATION converting to organics

POPOLI (PE)

Valle Reale

Località San Calisto
tel. 085 9871039
www.vallereale.it
info@vallereale.it

ROCCA SAN GIOVANNI (CH)

Cantina Frentana ⓔ

Via Perazza, 32
tel. 0872 60152
www.cantinafrentana.it
info@cantinafrentana.it

---

49 ha - 330,000 bt

650 ha - 650,000 bt   **10% discount**

PEOPLE - In just over ten years, Leonardo Pizzol, born in Veneto but Abruzzese by adoption, has managed to create a model winery. Convinced of the potential of piedmont viticulture, lately enhanced by sustainable agronomic techniques, he has shown and continues to show courage, ambition and passion.

VINEYARDS - Half the property stretches into the short Valle Reale, at an altitude of 350 meters on a hill north of the River Aterno-Pescara; here it's as if the vineyards are holding the cellar in an embrace. The rest are situated at Capestrano, in the mountain area where the Gran Sasso massif creates a special microclimate with high temperatures by day and much lower ones by night.

WINES - Thanks to continuous experimentation, the wines are gaining identity year by year and more surprises are in store in the future. **Montepulciano d'Abruzzo Sant'Eusanio 2012** (● 15,000 bt) has notes of blackcurrant and spices and makes for addictive drinking. In the more stylish **Montepulciano d'Abruzzo San Calisto 2010** (● 8,000 bt), oak-aging buttresses rich, silky fruit. Pleasing and delicate with notes of citrus fruit and apple, Trebbiano d'Abruzzo Valle Reale 2012 (○ 15,000 bt) is fermented spontaneously without selected yeasts and bottled without filtration, as are the two Slow Wines. It's a great Everyday Wine.

> **vino slow** TREBBIANO D'ABRUZZO VIGNETO DI POPOLI 2011 (○ 5,000 bt) A blossomy nose preludes fruit with grassy nuances and a note of spice. The palate is well-rounded with impressive mineral grip.

> **vino slow** TREBBIANO D'ABRUZZO VIGNA DI CAPESTRANO 2011 (○ 2,700 bt) A wine of great nose-palate complexity in which meadow flowers and wild herbs melt into ripe oranges and lemons and exotic fruit whose encore is accompanied by a chorus of pronounced piquancy.

FERTILIZERS natural manure, biodynamic preparations, green manure
PLANT PROTECTION copper and sulphur, organic
WEED CONTROL mechanical
YEASTS native
GRAPES 100% estate-grown
CERTIFICATION organic

PEOPLE - Today Cantina Frentana is a solid cooperative with a strong project, which resilient, pragmatic administrators, from president Carlo Romanelli to sales manager Felice Di Biase, are implementing with the vital support of 400 members. Enologist Gianni Pasquale and agronomists Maurizio Piucci and Maurizio Gily enjoy the stimulating ongoing task of creating prime-quality, value-for-money wines.

VINEYARDS - The vineyards, trained with the local "pergoletta abruzzese", arbour and Guyot systems, are situated in the alluvial valleys that run down towards the Adriatic. The soil varies from sandy to moderately clayey. Besides the classic Abruzzo grapes, in the San Giacomo zone at Rocca San Giovanni, the cellar also grows about 80 hectares of cocicciola, a white grape typical of this corner of the province of Chieti.

WINES - A beautiful wine tower has watched over the cellar's 55 harvests, all impeccable seeing the elegance and harmony of the wine they have produced. As impressive as ever — hence deserving of another Every Day wine symbol — Cococciola Costa del Mulino 2012 (○ 20,000 bt), also contains a small percentage of pecorino: it's alluring on the nose, deliciously juicy in the mouth. The more complex **Pecorino 2012** (○ 12,000 bt), an organic, spontaneously fermented wine, has delightful notes of citrus fruit and very full flavor. We enjoyed **Montepulciano d'Abruzzo 2011** (● 10,000 bt) for its typical "sauvageness" and uncompromising tannins. **Montepulciano d'Abruzzo Panarda 2010** (● 5,600 bt) is complex and well-structured.

> **vino slow** PECORINO DONNA GRETA 2011 (○ 6,500 bt) As always, a white of great texture. Brief maceration on the skins and long aging on yeasts make it deep, delicious and long.

FERTILIZERS organic-mineral, mineral, manure pellets, green manure
PLANT PROTECTION chemical, copper and sulphur, organic
WEED CONTROL chemical, mechanical
YEASTS selected, native
GRAPES 100% estate-grown
CERTIFICATION organic for some vineyards

Valori

Via Torquato al Salinello, 8
tel. 0861 88461
luigivalori@hotmail.it

Feudo Antico

Via Perruna, 35
tel. 0871 969128
www.feudoantico.it
info@feudoantico.it

---

20 ha - 70,000 bt

PEOPLE - Everything revolves around Luigi Valori in this wine company — a little "temple" in which he has realized himself and his dream — established in 1997. He sees himself as a biologist: "I live in symbiosis with the vines and the naturalness of things," he says. Here one senses love among the vineyards, as well as respect, enthusiasm and harmony with the land. A curious, many-talented producer, Luigi is the company's agronomist, pruner and enologist all rolled into one.

VINEYARDS - The vineyards are all arranged in rows and the vines are Guyot-trained, even the oldest, planted 50 years at a time, when most in the area adopted the typical "tendone abruzzese" system. The truth is that Luigi's uncle, the previous owner, had shoulder problems at the time and for him it was more convenient to do things that way! The soil is sandy, of poor quality, and the methods adopted are spartan: no fertilization, no watering, no working of the soil, only mowing and inter-row grassing to avoid erosion when it rains.

WINES - Organic certification was an obvious step for wines that reflect the spirit of their maker. They are full-bodied and exciting, amazingly land-rooted. We liked Montepulciano d'Abruzzo 2012 (● 50,000 bt) for its length and warmth, its even fruity palate and its enjoyable tannins — an excellent Everyday Wine. Aged for 18 months in barriques, Merlot Inkiostro 2009 (● 3,000 bt) has ripe fruit with fine progression accompanied by hints of pepper and vanilla. The deliciously mineral, fresh and fragrant Pecorino 2012 (○ 13,500 bt) has a nose with faint hints of fruit. The easy-drinking Trebbiano d'Abruzzo 2012 (○ 30,000 bt) has a citrussy, balsamic nose and is as reliable as ever. The value-for-money Cerasuolo d'Abruzzo 2012 (◉ 6,600 bt) strikes a nice balance between soft and acid notes.

---

14 ha - 80,000 bt   10% discount

PEOPLE - Feudo Antico is the flagship winery of the Tullum DOC. It's run by Andrea Di Fabio, a capable, dynamic young man who, with support of the two large Tollo co-operatives, is already receiving critical acclaim and achieving success on the market. His agonomist Antonio Sitti oversees every phase of work in the vineyard, from the pruning to the harvesting. Enologist Riccardo Brighigna follows cellar operations.

VINEYARDS - The company controls about 14 hectares of land in the commune of Tollo. All activities are based on respect for the vineyards in order to give the wines a greater sense of terroir. Attention is focused on the main native Abruzzo grapes, pecorino and passerina first and foremost. Agronomic management is eco-friendly: some of the vineyards are already organic, the rest are in the process of being converted.

WINES - The practices adopted in the cellar are relatively non-invasive. Preference is given to acidity and minerality over concentration and alcohol. Hence the success of spontaneous fermentation wines such as Rosato 2012 (◉ montepulciano; 10,000 bt). It has balsamic, floral notes on the nose and a deliciously full mouth of munchy cherries. Also fermented on natural yeasts, Bianco 2012 (○ trebbiano, passerina; 8,000 bt) has a fruity bouquet with a faint hint of blossom. The tonic, dynamic palate is satisfyingly balanced and fresh. Tullum Passerina 2012 (○ 12,000 bt) unbends beautifully over the palate. Tullum Rosso 2010 (● montepulciano; 20,000 bt) has notes of ripe fruit and spices. Pecorino 2012 (○ 3,000 bt) is well-crafted.

FERTILIZERS organic-mineral, natural manure, humus
PLANT PROTECTION copper and sulphur, organic
WEED CONTROL mechanical
YEASTS selected, native
GRAPES 100% estate-grown
CERTIFICATION organic

FERTILIZERS organic-mineral, manure pellets, natural manure, green manure
PLANT PROTECTION copper and sulphur, organic
WEED CONTROL mechanical
YEASTS selected
GRAPES 100% estate-grown
CERTIFICATION organic for some vineyards

TORANO NUOVO (TE)

Emidio Pepe

Via Chiesi, 10
tel. 086 1856493
www.emidiopepe.com
info@emidiopepe.com

17 ha - 75,000 bt

66 Emidio Pepe has always believed that good wine results from experience of working in the vineyard. After half a century doing precisely that, he hasn't changed his mind and is still to be found out in the fields every day. 99

PEOPLE - It was in 1964 that Emidio Pepe set up a cellar that has written a whole chapter in the history of quality Abruzzo winemaking. Today he is helped by his daughters — Sofia, who divides her time between vineyard and cellar, and Daniela, who deals with the administrative side of the business — and his granddaughter Chiara De Julis, who organizes events and oversees overseas affairs.

VINEYARDS - The gradual switch from organics to biodynamics has been smooth as far as vineyard management is concerned. The vines, all 10 to 40 years old, are planted on gentle slopes. The soil is medium-textured with a prevalence of clay and limestone. The oldest vineyards are overhead-trained and the most recent are planted in rows. The nearby Gran Sasso massif ensures good circulation of air and temperature ranges.

WINES - Processing and enological practices have always been established by Emidio and Sofia. Not that there are many of them to follow, given that the cellar's philosophy is to let wine develop naturally. Bottle-aging makes for long-lasting, unique wines. **Trebbiano d'Abruzzo 2011** (○ 25,000 bt) has a nose of ripe apples and pears rounded off by a leisurely, lingering palate. **Pecorino 2011** (○ 3,000 bt) is well-textured in the mouth and is certain to age well. The splendid **Cerasuolo d'Abruzzo 2012** (◉ 8,000 bt) is succulent with a long fruity finish. With its full fruit, vegetal hints and vigorous acid-tannic texture, the austere, dry and typical **Montepulciano d'Abruzzo 2010** (● 35,000 bt) is no less impressive.

FERTILIZERS natural manure, biodynamic preparations, green manure
PLANT PROTECTION copper and sulphur
WEED CONTROL mechanical
YEASTS native
GRAPES 100% estate-grown
CERTIFICATION biodynamic, organic

TORTORETO (TE)

Tenuta Terraviva   €

Via del Lago, 19
tel. 0861 786056
www.tenutaterraviva.it
info@tenutaterraviva.it

18 ha - 35,000 bt

PEOPLE - Terraviva is the business venture Pietro Topi and Martino Taraschi embarked upon in 2006 when they joined forces to produce terroir-dedicated wines at reasonable prices adopting a sustainable agricultural approach self-sufficient in terms of its energy requirement — hence organic certification and the installation of a photovoltaic plant. In the spirit of the winery, the young enologist Claudia Galterio simply coaxes along the vinification and aging in the cellar.

VINEYARDS - The vineyards are situated on hillsides at an altitude of about 180 meters where the soil is generally clayey with veins of limestone. The vines are spur cordon-trained and grow in rows. Only the Mario's cru is produced with trebbiano grapes from traditionally arbor-trained vines with an average age of about 43 years. Here the sweltering summer heat is mitigated, in part, by the breeze from the nearby Adriatic.

WINES - The company's wines are always very distinctive and terroir-dedicated, each vineyard adding unique characteristics of its own. All are notably minerally and pleasantly drinkable. **Trebbiano d'Abruzzo Mario's 39 2011** (○ 5,000 bt) has a rich nose of spices, aromatic herbs and ripe fruit, followed by a well-balanced, deep palate with a clearcut finish. The impressive Montepulciano d'Abruzzo Luì 2010 (● 10,000 bt) with its nicely ripe fruit, vigorous tannins and extracts amply deserves the Everyday Wine symbol. **Pecorino Ekwo 2012** (○ 3,500 bt) — hints of peaches and apricots with balsamic notes on the nose, complexity and flavor on the palate — is packed with personality. **Solobianco 2012** (○ trebbiano, malvasia, chardonnay; 4,000 bt) has a bouquet of sweet fruit, racy, rich progression and a gratifying finish.

FERTILIZERS natural manure
PLANT PROTECTION copper and sulphur
WEED CONTROL mechanical
YEASTS native
GRAPES 100% estate-grown
CERTIFICATION organic

CAMPANIA

White, white and more white — Campania is whiter than ever this year! The decision of a dozen or so cellars to delay the presentation of Fiano di Avellino by at least a year evidenced the great qualities of this extraordinary grape variety. If our tastings are anything to go by, the resulting wines are among the finest in Italy. In a more general context, besides the excellent performance of the 2012 vintage in Irpinia, points of excellence are also emerging in the Cilento, Colline Salernitane and Sannio zones. In parallel, Greco di Tufo, concrete and typical, is as reliable as ever, while Falanghina has exploded in the Sannio and Campi Flegrei zones. Both are wines that are (luckily) never cloying but always fresh, rarely aged on wood and, when they are, in a very measured fashion. Above all, they are capable of evolving in time.

Whites also shine on the islands and along the the Costiera Amalfitana and on Vesuvius, along with some Lacryma Christis and wines made with the newly rediscovered catalanesca grape.

The region produced one and a half million hectoliters of wine, a decrease of 9 per cent with respect to 2011, though certified production continues to grow and has now reached 263,000 hectoliters (17 per cent of the total). The four DOCGs (Fiano, Greco, Taurasi and Aglianico del Taburno) and 15 DOCs, all made exclusively with native grapes, and the IGTs provide an excellent normative framework for a well-characterized productive platform: they occupy 4,000 hectares in the mountains with vineyards at altitudes of up to 700 meters, 18,000 in the hills and only 800 on flat land.

Moving on to reds, Piedirosso has improved constantly in the Sannio zone and in the province of Naples, where it has become something of a cult. It was good to see Tintore consolidate its position on the Costiera Amalfitana, but the 2009 harvest was fraught with difficulties for Taurasi.

Irpinia's primacy in terms of quality is firmly established, but the Benevento area is also making impressive progress with both whites and reds. This sleeping giant, where over half of the region's production is concentrated, has at last woken up thanks to the work of the local Consorzio. The typicalization of wines in the provinces of Naples, some of which are now very exciting, and Salerno is proving successful. For the second year running, the province of Caserta showed great difficulty in defining the style of its reds, remaining anchored to alcoholic, over-powerful often cloying wines.

In conclusion, Campania may be a niche region, but it does have a distinct style with wines that offer a broad and varied sense of place, wines that stand out for minerality and freshness. Keep up the good work!

BACOLI (NA)

La Sibilla

Via Ottaviano Augusto, 19
tel. 081 8688778
www.sibillavini.it
info@sibillavini.it

9.5 ha - 65,000 bt   **10% discount**

PEOPLE - The Di Meos form a team that works in harmony to coax the best out of their land. Luigi's efforts in the vineyard, his wife Tina's in the office and son Vincenzo's in the cellar are producing a crescendo of satisfactions for a winery that is part of a Terra Madre "food community". Now with the return to the business of their other son Salvatore, a trained sommelier, the Di Meos will add luster to their cellar tastings.

VINEYARDS - A vegetable garden, vineyards and archaeological remains — all within the farm's perimeter. The vineyards are perfectly kept on terraces of volcanic and sandy-silty soil to the rear of the cellar. From here the view extends across Lake Fusaro down to the sea. Some of the vines are ungrafted and reach 100 years of age. They are situated at altitudes of up to 100 meters.

WINES - Consistency is the word to define the production style. The linear **Cruna Delago 2011** (O falanghina; 3,000 bt) is a thrill to drink with its citrus, mineral tones. **Pedirosa 2012** (⊙ piedirosso; 2,000 bt) expresses racy minerality and sour, juicy berries. **Campi Flegrei Falanghina 2012** (O 35,000 bt) is impressively simple and drinkable. **Passio 2008** (O falanghina; 1,000 bt) is the excitingly styled fruit of a great vintage.

vino slow **CAMPI FLEGREI PIEDIROSSO VIGNE STORICHE 2011** (● 2,400 bt) The rare, elegant representation of a difficult, traditional grape variety: hence the deep, eloquent nose and the juicy, heavyset palate with its encore of leafy flowers. A charismatic red made possible by attentive, eco-friendly farming.

FERTILIZERS natural manure, green manure
PLANT PROTECTION copper and sulphur
WEED CONTROL mechanical
YEASTS selected
GRAPES 30% bought in
CERTIFICATION none

CASTELLABATE (SA)

Maffini

Località Cenito
tel. 0974.966345
www.luigimaffini.it
info@luigimaffini.it

11 ha - 100,000 bt

66 Wine as a coherent life choice. Raffaella and Luigi Maffini are raising their kids in the hills near Giungano, where they grow vines with respect for the environment and produce wines of great quality and durability. Above all, they invest in the land, gritting their teeth in a tough environment. 99

PEOPLE - They have been growing vines for 40 years and making wine for 20. Luigi Maffini and Raffaella Gallo have thus closed the circle opened by his parents in the best possible manner. Their style is as inimitable as ever and they boast a number of consolidated labels. They are supported in their life project by enologist Luigi Moio.

VINEYARDS - The Giungano property — seven hectares at an altitude of 350 meters on a favorably located hilltop with plenty of air ciruclation — takes up most of Luigi's time day after day. Here the soil is pebbly whereas, in the historic vineyard of Castellabate, a stone's throw from the sea, it is sandy. All the vineyards are being converted to organics.

WINES - **Kratos 2012** (O fiano; 40,000 bt) has always been matured in steel vats. It opens on the nose with definite hints of Mediterranean scrub, followed by white fruit. Immediate acidity on the palate makes for refreshing, dynamic drinkability. Then the fruit returns and the wine finishes crisply without gratuitous sweetness. **Pietraincatenata 2011** (O fiano; 8,000 bt) has great prospects ahead of it with wood and fruit well fused from the outset and sweet spices on the nose countervailed by an elegant palate. **Cilento Aglianico Cenito 2009** (● 5,000 bt) shows modern freshness, balanced as opposed to concentrated.

vino slow **KLEOS 2011** (● 35,000 bt) A monovarietal aglianico aged in steel vats. It has succulence, power, harmony, sense of place and character — all at the right price.

FERTILIZERS natural manure, green manure
PLANT PROTECTION copper and sulphur
WEED CONTROL mechanical
YEASTS selected
GRAPES 100% estate-grown
CERTIFICATION converting to organics

CASTELLABATE (SA)

San Giovanni 🐌

Località Punto Tresino
Parco Nazionale del Cilento
tel. 0974 965136
www.agricolasangiovanni.it
info@agricolasangiovanni.it
🍴—o

4 ha - 25,000 bt

66 Ida and Mario Corrado are reaping the fruits of the gamble of their lives. In the protected area of Punta Tresino they took their chance with great determination and resolve, in the early days without electricity and links with the outside world. Today people throng to visit but Mario and Ida remain true to themselves, he working in the vineyard with enologist Michele D'Argenio, she welcoming guests to the little corner of paradise they have created. 99

PEOPLE - One of the most spectacular cellars in Italy. Set up relatively recently, it turns out wines with a pronounced sense of place at competitive prices.

VINEYARDS - Surrounded by Mediterranean scrub, perched on a steep cliff over the sea, the fiano, aglianico and piedirosso vineyards are high-trained in accordance with the certified organic method. The 30-year-old vines receive plenty of sun and wind and yield clean fruit. The cellar, now well organized, is managed by the young enologist Michele D'Argenio.

WINES - The eminently affordable whites always win us over, one by one, year by year. This time round we took to the ready-to-drink Tresinus 2012 (O fiano; 4,000 bt), which has a complex nose of fruit and Mediterranean maquis, freshness and zest on the palate and good structure: it's a perfect Everyday Wine. **Fiano 2012** (O 10,000 bt), which Mario regards has his base wine, has pleasant, very pronounced hints of citrus fruit, welcome acidity and tanginess on the palate and a clean, clear-cut finish. The debut wine **Ficonera 2011** (● 1,000 bt) is an ultra-concentrated monovarietal piedirosso with an unmistakable whiff of geraniums underpinned by acidity on the palate, which follows through with soft, mellow tannins. Given the limited number of bottles available, it will be a treat for only a few lucky wine lovers.

FERTILIZERS natural manure
PLANT PROTECTION copper and sulphur
WEED CONTROL mechanical
YEASTS selected
GRAPES 100% estate-grown
CERTIFICATION organic

CASTELVENERE (BN)

Antica Masseria Venditti 🐌

Via Sannitica, 120/122
tel. 0824 940306
www.venditti.it
masseria@venditti.it
🍴—o

11 ha - 70,000 bt

66 One man at the helm — Nicola Venditti is the only winemaker left who works with organically grown grapes without recourse to wood. His vision made him come across first as backward-looking, now as fashionable. In reality, he has simply been consistent, which is how and why his wines capture the essence of the Sannio terroir every year. 99

PEOPLE - Every time is like the first. Nicola Venditti manages to attract the attention of guests even when it isn't their first visit. It's not only a matter of details; the latest novelty is the addition of an agriturismo to complete Nicola's wine "island of culture" project, the strong point of which is an educational vineyard where grapes are harvested by night.

VINEYARDS - Vines have been growing on the land on which the cellar's vineyards are situated for centuries, as a grape press dating back to 1595 in the cellar testifies. The aim is to bring home healthy fruit with a minimum amount of intervention. Nicola achieves it partly thanks to the curtain training system, partly to his experience in the field.

WINES - The end-result is a series of particularly approachable wines such as **Sannio Barbera Barbetta 2010** (O 9,000 bt), packed with red berries and bracing freshness, and **Sannio Aglianico Marraioli 2008** (● 8,000 bt) in which the fruit is intact and the tannins beautifully smooth. With its elegant, peppy, by no means unoriginal drinkability, **Sannio Bosco Caldaia 2007** (● aglianico, montepulciano, piedirosso; 4,000 bt) is a total success. Moving on to the whites, **Sannio Bacalat 2012** (O falanghina, grieco di Castelvenere, cerreto; 1,300 bt) is rounded and fresh, while **Falanghina del Sannio Vàndari 2012** (O 15,000 bt) is typical.

FERTILIZERS organic-mineral, green manure
PLANT PROTECTION copper and sulphur
WEED CONTROL mechanical
YEASTS selected
GRAPES 100% estate-grown
CERTIFICATION organic

Agnanum Raffaele Moccia €

Via Vicinale Abbandonata agli Astroni, 3
tel. 081 2303507 - 338 5315272
www.agnanum.it
info@agnanum.it

4 ha - 13,000 bt | 10% discount

PEOPLE - With the help of his elderly father Gennaro, Raffaele Moccia strenuously defends his own identity as a farmer and the land of his forefathers. "If this land has come down to us in this condition, it's because it hasn't gone a day without being cared for." Wise words! Assisted by Gianluca Nicoletti he oversees the vineyard, the wine cellar and a rabbit farm. His young son Gennaro is now starting to give him a hand with the administrative side of the business.

VINEYARDS - Moccia's vineyards run from the town of Agnano to Pozzuoli. Some of them have vines planted from 30 to more than 100 years ago and they grow on volcanic sand, in some tracts "dust", on half-moon-shaped terraces. Ongoing erosion and the risk of summer fires mean that they have to be constantly monitored. The falanghina and piedirosso grapes struggle to grow on these terrains, some of which reach an altitude of 250 meters, and have poor yields: if achieved, 30 quintals per hectare would be a record result.

WINES - Bottles, produced in limited quantities, are all numbered. With all the difficulties involved in growing vines on this ridge alongside the Astroni Reserve, from which foxes roam, Raffaele Moccia couldn't do more even if he wanted to. The inebriating **Campi Flegrei Falanghina 2011** (O 9,000 bt) is a pearl of simplicity. Typical, juicy and enjoyable, Campi Flegrei Piedirosso 2012 (● 2,200 bt), is again an Everyday Wine, ideal for the table. Our sneak preview of **Campi Flegrei Piedirosso Vigna delle Volpi 2011** (● piedirosso; 600 bt) revealed a touch of sober elegance from aging on wood. The few bottles produced in the 2010 vintage have already been sold out. **Vigna del Pino 2010** (O falanghina; 600 bt) has rich flavorful notes of Mediterranean scrub.

FERTILIZERS natural manure, green manure
PLANT PROTECTION chemical, copper and sulphur
WEED CONTROL mechanical
YEASTS selected
GRAPES 100% estate-grown
CERTIFICATION none

Contrada Salandra

Via Tre Piccioni, 40
tel. 0815265258
www.dolciqualita.com
dolciqualita@libero.it

4 ha - 15,000 bt | 10% discount

66 In the conundrum of the Campi Flegrei zone, where the fury of the volcanoes is matched by that of property speculation, Peppino Fortunato is a watchful steward of agricultural practices and a meticulous artisan interpreter of the falanghina and piedirosso grapes. Every year the wines he comes up with are exciting and full of character. 99

PEOPLE - After graduating respectively in engineering and economics, Giuseppe Fortunato and his wife Sandra Castaldo have found their raison d'être in their family land. After starting out as beekeepers, they have translated their thirst for greater equilibrium between humans and nature into wine. Giuseppe tends to the vineyards (and the bees), while Sandra takes care of the administrative side of the business and runs a point of sale in the center of Pozzuoli.

VINEYARDS - After long days out in the country, Giuseppe Fortunato goes back to the cellar to do even more work. Besides overseeing the beehives, his job consists of pruning, grubbing, cutting, mowing and binding the vine rows on the company's four hectares of vineyards, all round and some of them very close to the cellar. The landscape here in the Coste di Cuma district is halfway between coastal and urban. The soil is volcanic, very loose, with low percentages of clay. In the three vineyards the average age of the vines is 40.

WINES - The cellar's wines are "physical" and alive, like the bees that, as of this year, will be gracing both its labels. **Campi Flegrei Falanghina 2011** (O 8,500 bt) combines drinkability with richness and shows off enviable equilibrium, built round tangy, Mediterranean notes. Though it has to be made with care to avoid the grape's characteristic reduction tendency, Campi Flegrei Piedirosso 2011 (● 6,500 bt) is disarmingly linear and clear-cut, enjoyably juicy with lingering hints of fruit. An exemplary Everyday Wine.

FERTILIZERS natural manure, green manure
PLANT PROTECTION copper and sulphur
WEED CONTROL mechanical
YEASTS selected
GRAPES 100% estate-grown
CERTIFICATION none

Villa Dora

Via Bosco Mauro, 1
tel. 081 5295016
www.cantinevilladora.it
info@cantinevilladora.it

Tenuta San Francesco

Via Solficiano, 18
tel. 089 876748 - 856190
www.vinitenutasanfrancesco.it
aziendasanfrancesco@libero.it

---

13 ha - 60,000 bt   **10% discount**

❝ The switch from organic olive growing to wine is virtually automatic on Vesuvius. Which is why, helped by his children, Vincenzo Ambrosio set up his cellar. His aim is to interpret the volcano's Lacryma Rosso and Bianco, wines capable of lasting and evolving, as simply as possible and better than anyone has ever done before. ❞

PEOPLE - The Ambrosio family had always produced extra virgin olive oil on the slopes of the volcano. Their new passion for wine-growing began when they bought an old property and converted the main villa into a cellar.

VINEYARDS - In this heavily built-up area, Villa Dora is an oasis of beauty and quiet. Its old Vesuvius pergola-trained vineyards, planted after the eruption of 1942, create an enchanting landscape at the foot of the volcano and in the Valle dell'Inferno. The estate is surrounded by the vast secular pine forest of the Vesuvius National Park.

WINES - The enologist is Fabio Mecca. Vesuvio Bianco 2012 (○ coda di volpe, falanghina; 8,000 bt) is an honest bianco del Vesuvio at an honest price and its blossomy, fruity aromas make it an excellent Everyday Wine. The complex **Lacryma Christi Bianco Vigna del Vulcano 2011** (○ coda di volpe, falanghina; 15,000 bt) is mineral and fruity with a zesty, rich mouthfeel. It needs to be tasted again in the future. **Vesuvio Rosso 2011** (● piedirosso, aglianico; 10,000 bt) is a typical, well-crafted Vesuvius red. **Lacryma Christi Rosso Gelso Nero 2011** (● piedirosso, aglianico; 15,000 bt) comes from an old vineyard and reveals greater structure and aromatic intensity. **Lacryma Christi Forgiato 2011** (● piedirosso, aglianico; 8,000 bt), made from very low-yield grapes, is full of fruit on the nose with stylish notes of iodine and spices.

FERTILIZERS green manure
PLANT PROTECTION copper and sulphur
WEED CONTROL mechanical
YEASTS selected
GRAPES 100% estate-grown
CERTIFICATION organic

---

10 ha - 60,000 bt

❝ Gaetano and Generoso Bove, Vincenzo D'Avino and Luigi Giordano are companions on an adventure that began almost by chance, ten years ago among the woods of Tramonti. In the cellar, surrounded by century-old ungrafted vineyards, crystalline whites, long-lasting reds and wonderfully drinkable rosés see the light. ❞

PEOPLE - Thanks to foreign tourists and a growing number of Italian enthusiasts, the business set into motion by Gaetano Bove, a vet, in partnership with his brother and a couple of farmer friends, is consolidating its success.

VINEYARDS - To understand how the winery works you only have to take a stroll outside the cellar. You'll find yourself in a "wood of vines", all over a hundred years old, all gigantic, all ungrafted — a genetic pool unique in Campania, and maybe in the rest of Italy too. The grape selection for the white wine comes from a vineyard at an altitude of 600 meters. The area is swept by the wind and experiences sharp drops in temperature from day to night. This is cold weather wine-making but it produces exciting results.

WINES - Costa d'Amalfi Tramonti Rosso 2012 (● aglianico, piedirosso, tintore; 13,000 bt) is a snappy wine that goes well with food. Above all, it's full of flavor, which is why we regard it as a great Everyday Wine. **Costa d'Amalfi Bianco 2012** (○ falanghina, biancolella, pepella; 18,000 bt) is stunningly bright and breezy with delicate blossomy aromas and a pleasing palate. On its debut, the other white, **Costa d'Amalfi PerEva 2011** (○ fenile, pepella, ginestra; 6,500 bt) is animated by vibrant acidity and crunchy white fruit: the jury's now out for the final verdict. **E' Iss Prefillossera 2010** (● tintore; 4,500 bt) is husky, very rich and refreshing. **Costa d'Amalfi 4 Spine Ris. 2009** (● aglianico, piedirosso, tintore; 6,500 bt) has beautifully fused fruit and wood and shows great balance and elegance.

FERTILIZERS green manure
PLANT PROTECTION copper and sulphur
WEED CONTROL mechanical
YEASTS selected
GRAPES 5% bought in
CERTIFICATION none

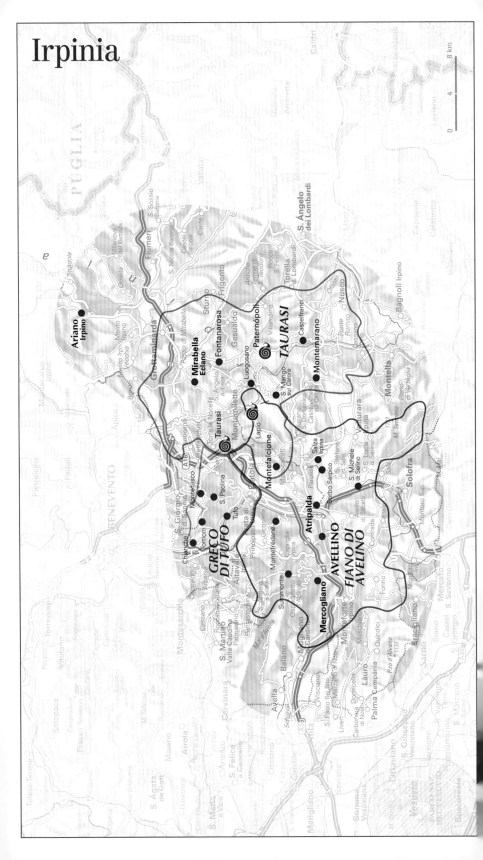

Irpinia

LAPIO (AV)

Colli di Lapio

Via Arianiello
tel. 0825 982184
www.collidilapio.it
info@collidilapio.it

6 ha - 50,000 bt

66 The meeting of Clelia Romano and Angelo Pizzi has changed the history of winegrowing in Lapio. In these silent hills, year after year, earnestly and without show, they have produced a Fiano that invariably displays strength and the capacity to evolve in the course of time. 99

PEOPLE - The family of Clelia Romano, her husband Angelo and their children Federico and Carmela, extraordinary terrain, the vast experience of enologist Angelo Pizzi — put them together and you have an unrepeatable magic formula, a sort of Fiano dolmen, the first cellar to make the most of the spectacular Lapio area and spread its fame in Italy.

VINEYARDS - Straight after Lapio became famous, so did the Arianello contrada, where the vineyards are, where a small cellar was built, where lovers of the great white wine come in their droves. Here the altitude exceeds 500 meters, the soil is composed of clay and limestone and cool winds from the Terminio massif create a good temperature range.

WINES - The style of Clelia Romano's wines — the result of fermentation in stainless steel vats and a minimum amount of intervention in the cellar — is very simple indeed. It has given rise to masterpieces that challenge time beyond imagination. After wisely passing on the Taurasi 2009, we tried **Campi Taurasini 2011** (● 4,000 bt), elegant on nose and palate, and **Greco di Tufo 2012** (○ 4,000 bt), made with bought-in grapes.

> **vino slow** Fiano di Avellino 2012 (○ 40,000 bt) This wine starts with a nose of citrus and white fruit with hints of Mediterranean scrub. On the palate it has masses of body braced by vibrant acidity, not as yet full integrated, as was the case in previous vintages. The wine is long and dry with a pleasant, slightly bitter finish.

FERTILIZERS green manure
PLANT PROTECTION chemical, copper and sulphur
WEED CONTROL mechanical
YEASTS selected
GRAPES 10% bought in
CERTIFICATION none

LAPIO (AV)

Rocca del Principe

Contrada Arianiello, 9
tel. 0825 982435
www.roccadelprincipe.it
info@roccadelprincipe.it

5 ha - 25000 bt   `10% discount`

PEOPLE - The trials of Hercules, alias Ettore Zarrella, aren't over but the first results are there for all to see. Extension work on the cellar has been completed, a decisive step for improved work and storage space. The aglianico vineyards bought at Lapio are now at their second harvest and Ettore has decided to wait another year before releasing the Fiano. The winery, which Ettore runs with his wife Aurelia and brother-in-law Antonio Fabrizisi, is thus completing its efforts to achieve absolute quality.

VINEYARDS - The vineyards are split into five plots in the country districts of Arianello, the largest, Lenze and Tognano, where the aglianico vines have started to yield. Lapio, which stands at an altitude of about 500 meters and where the soil is clayey, is the only commune in which the Taurasi and Fiano DOCGs converge. The agriculture is conventional, but we hope Ettore will think about converting it soon.

WINES - The interesting **Taurasi Mater Domini 2009** (● 2,500 bt) is made with grapes bought at Paternopoli and Taurasi; it has a fruity, delicately salty nose with mineral notes and a beautifully fresh palate. Both the red and the white promise to age well. The overall range was superlative, which is why we decided to assign this admirable cellar the Bottle symbol.

> **vino slow** Fiano di Avellino 2011 (○ 20,000 bt) We've always argued that Fiano should be released at least 12 months after the grape harvest. Ercole waited almost a year and a half, but the decision has paid off. His entirely steel-fermented Fiano is a splendid fusion of citrus fruits, apples and pears and meadow herbs with a faint toasted note. In the mouth, it is packed with energy, drinkable, full-bodied with fruity encores, uncloying and flavorsome with a palate-cleansing bitter finish. A class act.

FERTILIZERS organic-mineral
PLANT PROTECTION chemical, copper and sulphur
WEED CONTROL mechanical
YEASTS selected
GRAPES 100% estate-grown
CERTIFICATION none

MONTEFREDANE (AV)

Pietracupa 🍾

Contrada Vadiaperti, 17
tel. 0825 607418
pietracupa@email.it

MONTEFREDANE (AV)

Villa Diamante 🍾

Via Toppole, 16
tel. 0825 670014
www.villadiamante.eu
villadiamante1996@gmail.com

7.5 ha - 45,000 bt

4 ha - 10,000 bt

PEOPLE - Pietracupa was bought by Sabino Loffredo's father in the 1970s. Here, over the years, Sabino has become one of the great interpreters of the white grapes of Irpinia. Thanks to the fantastic Montefredane terroir, the experience picked up on his travels round the world (before deciding to come home and settle down for good) and sensitivity accumulated in the wine cellar, his wines are invariably impressive.

VINEYARDS - The vineyards are managed conventionally with high-trained vines, but the weather and soil conditions permit non-invasive, eco-friendly practices. The fiano vineyard stands on volcanic soil is beside the cellar at Montefredane. The grapes for the Greco come from nearby Santa Paolina, a historic growing area.

WINES - Again this year this talented Irpinian vigneron has come up with two sensational wines. **Greco di Tufo 2012** (O 16,000 bt) releases no-nonsense minerality and citrus fruits on the nose, while the full-bodied palate is fresh, long and gratifying with a pleasingly clean finish. At least for the time being, though, **Fiano di Avellino 2012** (O 16,000 bt) seems to have something extra: the wonderfully spacious aromas are precise and convincing and the palate is amply with just the right balance between body and freshness. Both wines are sure to evolve well, as previous vintages have already done. The Fiano is a Great Wine, one of Italy's finest whites. If Sabino gets the chance to hold back its release by a year in the future, we're confident it will reach the very top of the tree.

PEOPLE - Antoine Gaita is a cultured, determined wine maker, who leaves his own personal stamp on his Fiano without detracting anything from the diverse expressions of each single vintage. He manages his vineyards with his wife Diamante, accumulating experience as he goes along, and now acts as a focus for the local area. The latest news is that he has now undertaken an external consultancy working with the aglianico grapes of Guastaferro at Taurasi, their prime growing area.

VINEYARDS - The hill of Montefredane — with well-positioned vineyards planted on volcanic, clayey soil, immersed in chestnut woods at an altitude of 400 meters — is one of the best fiano growing areas. The new vines are spurred cordon-trained, the old ones Guyot-trained. Here the microclimatic conditions, with sharp day-to-night temperature swings and constant air circulation, favor organic cultivation.

WINES - Ever since his first grape harvest in 1997, now something of a legend, Antoine Gaita has always waited a year before releasing his wines.

> **vino slow** FIANO DI AVELLINO VIGNA DELLA CONGREGAZIONE 2011 (O 8,000 bt) A wine which made its debut, as always, at the Vinitaly show in Verona. Our first tastings vouch for the work Gaita has put into it. On the nose blossom and apples and pears are tinged with pleasant hints of Mediterranean scrub. Its impact on the palate is immediate, its customarily weighty matière thrust forward by acidity. A full-bodied, full-flavored white, lean and thirst-quenching: bottle-aging will not only favor its evolution but also allow it to find better balance. As we have had the opportunity to verify in many a vertical tasting, Antoine's whites invariably improve with age, preserving all their freshness while acquiring complexity.

FERTILIZERS natural manure, green manure
PLANT PROTECTION chemical, copper and sulphur
WEED CONTROL mechanical
YEASTS selected
GRAPES 100% estate-grown
CERTIFICATION none

FERTILIZERS mineral
PLANT PROTECTION copper and sulphur
WEED CONTROL mechanical
YEASTS selected
GRAPES 3% bought in
CERTIFICATION organic

Montesole

Via Serra
tel. 0825 963972
www.montesole.it
info@montesole.it

30 ha - 1,200,000 bt

PEOPLE - This winemaking cellar came into being almost 20 years ago as a result of the law on female entrepreneurship. With the purchase of land and the creation of crus, it is now at a turning point in its history. According to administrator Giovanni De Santis, this is a necessary step to counter the phenomenon of the abandonment of the land. The revolution is the continuation of the serious, concrete work carried out since 1995.

VINEYARDS - The cellar in Montefusco is at the baricenter of a number of grape-growing areas. The most prominent variety is greco, which the company cultivates in a vertiginously steep vineyard at an altitude of 600 meters. Fiano, instead, is grown at San Michele di Pratola, aglianico at Montemiletto. Falanghina, finally, grows in the Sannio district, not many kilometers away. The viticulture is conventional and is supervised by Rosa Pesa, an agronomist and partner in the company.

WINES - The two principal whites were well to the fore. **Greco di Tufo Vigna Breccia 2011** (O 10,000 bt) is full of personality, with a citrussy, very minerally nose, a full-flavored, still fresh palate and a long, confident finish. **Fiano di Avellino Vigna Acquaviva 2011** (O 10,000 bt) is a rung higher up the ladder: it offers the nose apples and pears with hints of toast, while on the palate it has good body and balance segued by length. It's a Great Wine. Both the above are steel-fermented, as is the thirst-quenching **Sannio Falanghina Vigna Zampino 2012** (O 7,000 bt). Too much fruit on the nose overwhelms the minerality of **Taurasi Vigna Vinieri 2007** (● 5,000 bt). The other two labels — the Charmat-method **Spumante Griaè 2012** (O greco; 50,000 bt) and **Aglianico Sairus 2008** (● 7,000 bt) — are both enjoyable.

FERTILIZERS mineral, green manure
PLANT PROTECTION chemical, copper and sulphur
WEED CONTROL chemical, mechanical
YEASTS selected
GRAPES 60% bought in
CERTIFICATION none

Luigi Tecce

Via Trinità, 6
tel. 0827 71375
lteccel@libero.it

4 ha - 9,700 bt

66 Every vintage is different. If that weren't so, we'd be disappointed insofar as the greatness of this high-altitude winemaker lies precisely in his craftsmanship. His bottles travel and relate stories and suggestions. His is a timeless wine, coherently produced, full of character and promises kept. 99

PEOPLE - The premature death of his father changed Luigi Tecce's life, inducing him to return to the family wine business and making it one of the ablest, most sensitive interpreters of the aglianico grape. While building work proceeds on his new cellar, closer to the vineyards, he continues to receive visitors in the old farmhouse, where he enjoys experimenting with long macerations for whites and amphora-aging for reds.

VINEYARDS - The soil is rich in limestone and ash and the four hectares of vineyard are scattered in small plots round the house and the cellar. Here, at an altitude of 500-600 meters, the aglianico grape, the only one grown by Luigi, matures slowly and is harvested in late October and early November. The vines face southwards and are always well ventilated by the breezes that come up from the valley to ensure healthy grapes.

WINES - **Taurasi Poliphemo 2009** (● 4,500 bt) is the fruit of a harvest that went on for 25 days under a constant threat of rain. The grapes were picked in four batches from the middle of October until November 10 and aged in large 50-hectoliter barrels (a radical turnaround from the chestnut casks of the past). Fruitiness has been supplanted by darker notes of liquorice, camphor, orange zest, mushrooms and, as always, ash on the finish. **Campi Taurasini Satyricon 2010** (● 5,200 bt) expresses energy through a racy palate and uncompromising, thirst-quenching acidity.

FERTILIZERS green manure
PLANT PROTECTION copper and sulphur
WEED CONTROL mechanical
YEASTS native
GRAPES 100% estate-grown
CERTIFICATION none

SAN MICHELE DI SERINO (AV)

Villa Raiano

Località Cerreto
Via Bosco Satrano, 1
tel. 0825 495663
www.villaraiano.com
info@villaraiano.com

20 ha - 300,000 bt | **10% discount**

PEOPLE - Sabino and Simone Basso and their brother-in-law Paolo Sibillo are increasingly at the forefront. Their collaboration with enologist Fortunato Sebastiano is shifting their focus to vineyard management. The line of their wines is precise with a distinctly terroir-dedicated style. Their total output is increasing and their investment in the vineyards is proceeding apace.

VINEYARDS - The company's main property is a 10-hectare vineyard on clayey, marbly soil at Castelfranci, at an altitude of 500 meters one of the highest points in the Taurasi zone. It also owns four hectares of greco at Montefusco, in the Marotta area, and three of fiano in the hills of Montefredane. Fiano also grows in the lovely vineyards that surround the modern cellar.

WINES - Looking forward to the reds, this year we tasted mostly whites and were suitably impressed with the base line. **Fiano di Avellino 2012** (O 50,000 bt) brims with blossomy scents, **Greco di Tufo 2012** (O 90,000 bt) is minerally and refreshing, and **Falanghina 2012** (O 90,000 bt) is rich and aromatic with decent body. All promise to evolve well, like Fiano 2011, which we tasted for a second time and found simply perfect. **Greco di Tufo Contrada Marotta 2012** (O 3,000 bt), the result of a good growing year is a powerhouse of a wine with hints of minerals and a well-balanced palate. **Fiano di Avellino Alimata 2012** (O 3,000 bt) is also excellent. We were favorably impressed by **Taurasi Raiano 2009** (● 15,000 bt), which has austere fruit fused with wood and a fresh, racy palate. Despite the relatively unfavorable growing year, we have to acknowledge that Villa Raiano has performed a miracle by bottling this Taurasi. It's very good indeed, for us a Great Wine.

FERTILIZERS natural manure, green manure
PLANT PROTECTION copper and sulphur
WEED CONTROL mechanical
YEASTS selected
GRAPES 20% bought in
CERTIFICATION converting to organics

SUMMONTE (AV)

Ciro Picariello €

Località Acqua della Festa
Via Marroni
tel. 0825 702516
www.ciropicariello.com
info@ciropicariello.com

7 ha - 21,000 bt | **10% discount**

PEOPLE - The years fly by. Helped by their children, Ciro Picariello and Rita Guerriero have built up an admirable winery that is now celebrating the tenth anniversary of its first label. Extension work on the cellar is now close to completion, and another hectare of fiano for the Irpinia Doc is being rented at nearby Grottolelle.

VINEYARDS - The vineyards at Montefredane and Summonte, situated at an altitude of 600 meters, enjoy sharp day-to-night temperature swings. Besides fiano, aglianico is also traditionally cultivated on a parcel of 1.5 hectares. The soil is clayey and pebbly and coated by debris from the last eruption of Vesuvius in 1944. Though the viticulture is conventional, the management of the vineyards and the soil and weather conditions make chemical products virtually superfluous.

WINES - Numerous vertical tastings confirmed the vitality of Ciro Picariello's marquee white: the 2004, for example, is in a perfect state of grace. Ciro's little big secret is to make it wait a year before bottling. **Irpinia Fiano 2012** (O 10,000 bt) is also valid. The range is rounded off by **Greco di Tufo 2012** (O 6,500 bt), made with bought-in grapes, and two approachable red wines — **Campania Rosso 2011** (● aglianico, piedirosso, sciascinoso; 10,000 bt) and **Irpinia Aglianico Zi Felicella 2011** (● 6,500 bt) — both with character to spare thanks to the freshness of their fruit and pronounced flavor.

vino slow **FIANO DI AVELLINO 2011** (O 25,000 bt) The nose is complex, all apples and pears with an oaky note and hints of undergrowth and Mediterranean scrub. Delicate and stylish, it oozes energy in the mouth. Here Ciro has treated us to a bargain-price wine, the fruit of old country practices and filled with a farmer's love of the land.

FERTILIZERS green manure
PLANT PROTECTION copper and sulphur
WEED CONTROL mechanical
YEASTS selected
GRAPES 10% bought in
CERTIFICATION none

Antonio Caggiano

Contrada Sala
tel. 0827 74723
www.cantinecaggiano.it
info@cantinecaggiano.it

28 ha - 150,000 bt

66 Before him was the wine, not the village. It was in 1994 that everything changed after his meeting with Luigi Moio and the opening of the first cellar to visitors. That was the moment at which Aglianico became modern without losing its roots. In the 20 years since then, Caggiano has given a terroir of huge unexpressed potential the drive it needed. 99

PEOPLE - The twentieth anniversary of the first harvest under the Caggiano label is approaching and Antonio has already handed the baton to his son Pino.

VINEYARDS - The grapes for the two best-known wines are grown just a few meters from the cellar in the historic vineyards they are named for: Salae Domini, with vines that go back 30 years, and Vigna Macchia dei Goti, planted in the early 1990s. Both are well located at an altitude of about 300 meters. Methods are conventional, the density is 5,000 plants per hectare and the yield is lower than 50 quintals.

WINES - This year Salae Domini wasn't produced, while the two reds made with aglianico are at the top of their form. **Irpinia Aglianico Taurì 2012** (● 35,000 bt) is refreshing, fruity and quaffable. **Taurasi Vigna Macchia dei Goti 2009** (● 13,000 bt), which is still feeling its way, reflects the cellar's style: fine and stylish on the nose, in which the fruit is supplemented by pleasant balsamic, fresh-tasting and long on the palate with velvety tannins. Like previous vintages, it promises to evolve magnificently. The whites are made with grapes that are bought in and fermented in steel vats. **Fiagre 2012** (○ fiano, greco; 25,000 bt) denotes awesome minerality and is already well-balanced and full-flavored with plenty of body. **Fiano di Avellino Bechar 2012** (○ 25,000 bt) and **Greco di Tufo Devon 2012** (○ 25,000 bt) are both pleasant to drink.

FERTILIZERS organic-mineral, natural manure, green manure
PLANT PROTECTION chemical, copper and sulphur
WEED CONTROL mechanical
YEASTS selected
GRAPES 25% bought in
CERTIFICATION none

Contrade di Taurasi

Via Municipio, 39
tel. 0827 74483
www.contradeditaurasi.it
info@cantinelonardo.it

5 ha - 20,000 bt · **10% discount**

66 The tradition defended by Sandro Lonardo, the commitment of his daughter Antonella and her husband Flavio Castaldo, the science of enthusiast Professor Moschetti — plus Aglianico, vinified in large barrels. It is in this context that two great crus, wines of immense substance, are born. 99

PEOPLE - Partly thanks to the collaboration of Professor Giancarlo Moschetti, the Lonardo family cellar has at last reached the perfect solution: a base Taurasi and two crus. Now that the cellar has the grapes to make two wines, novelties are in store on the white wine front.

VINEYARDS - At Case d'Alto, near the cellar, the soil is loose, at Coste, a little lower down, it is composed of limestone and clay. The decision to produce the two crus was dictated by the difference. Another property of a hectare and a half is to be found at Macchia dei Goti. The vineyard is managed organically, the vines are starsete- and high-trained. The grapes used to make Grecomusc' are grown round about on small plots of land.

WINES - The range impresses for quality and strength of depth in this, enologist Vincenzo Mercurio's second year at the cellar. **Grecomusc' 2011** (○ roviello; 2,500 bt) has a deep nose which is a fusion of fruit, undergrowth and fumé notes. The excellent **Taurasi 2008** (● 3,000 bt) is rich on nose and palate but needs more time to improve. As ever, the two crus, both of great substance, are dividing wine lovers. In our opinion, albeit offering a spacious, rich nose and a juicy, concentrated, zesty palate with a beautifully fine finish, **Taurasi Coste 2008** (● 1,300 bt) has gone half a step backwards. We prefer **Taurasi Vigne d'Alto 2008** (● 1,300 bt), which has a fine, pleasant nose and a full-bodied, refreshing palate with fine tannins.

FERTILIZERS none
PLANT PROTECTION copper and sulphur
WEED CONTROL mechanical
YEASTS native
GRAPES 100% estate-grown
CERTIFICATION organic

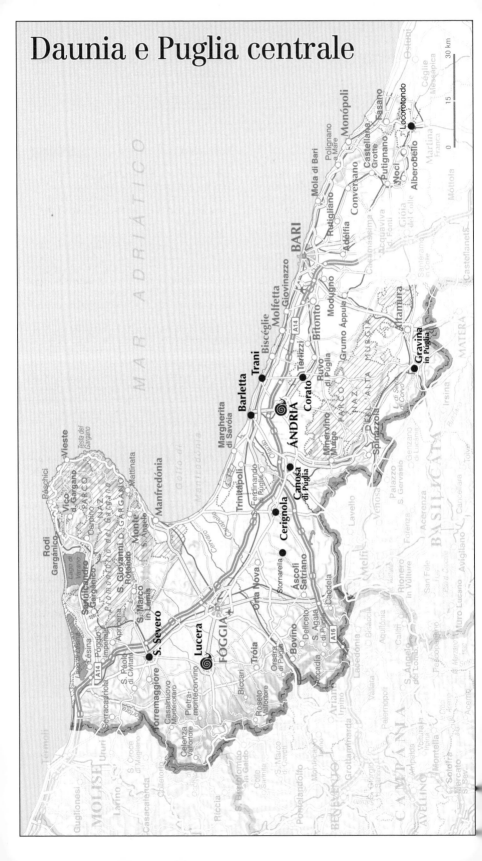

Daunia e Puglia centrale

Botromagno

Via Archimede, 22
tel. 080 3265865
www.botromagno.it
info@botromagno.it

45 ha - 300,000 bt

PEOPLE - In 1991 Beniamino D'Agostino was a young lawyer when his father told him that the Gravina wine cooperative risked going bust. All it took to save the place was a phone call to Severino Garofano. Today Beniamino and his brother run the winery, named for the hill that overlooks it, with a confident touch. Helping them in the job are enologists Alberto Antonini, Goffredo Agostini and Matteo De Rosa and agronomist Stefano Dini.

VINEYARDS - The winery's properties are spread across the commune of Gravina on land typical of the Murge district with altitudes of 400 to 600, sometimes very steep and hard to cultivate. The soil is karstic, alluvial and clayey, interspersed with boulders, in some places sandy, all characteristics that give wines pronounced flavor and make the place ideal for the production of whites. The viticultural methods used are certified organic.

WINES - Flavor and freshness are the thread that sews the wines together. They are divided into two lines, one certified organic, the other traditional. The flagship label is the floral, refreshing, tangy **Gravina 2012** (O greco, malvasia bianca; 100,000 bt). Made with the same blend of grapes, **Gravina Poggio al Bosco 2012** (O 2,500 bt) has more spacious aromas and an impressively dynamic palate. We liked the blossomy, balsamic, spicy, long Nero di Troia 2012 (● 12,000 bt) so much we decided to award it the Everyday Wine symbol. **Pier delle Vigne 2008** (● aglianico, montepulciano; 18,000 bt), elegant and balsamic with notes of undergrowth, is the winery's historic red. **Gravisano Passito 2007** (O malvasia bianca; 5,000 bt) is all-embracing and soft with a lingering palate-cleansing finish.

FERTILIZERS manure pellets, natural manure
PLANT PROTECTION copper and sulphur
WEED CONTROL mechanical
YEASTS selected
GRAPES 100% estate-grown
CERTIFICATION organic

Paolo Petrilli

Località Motta Caropresa
tel. 0881 523982
www.lamotticella.com
lamotticella@libero.it

11 ha - 24,000 bt

66 Paolo Petrilli has applied to viticulture the same professionalism, skill and passion that made the tomatoes he used to grow on his farm among the best and most natural in the whole Foggia area. 99

PEOPLE - Meeting and talking with Paolo Petrilli is never a dull experience. When we visit every year we always discover new sides to his wine company. His aim is always the same: to reduce bottles and achieve pinnacles of quality without compromise.

VINEYARDS - The grapes from the 11 hectares managed organically achieved good ripeness and the soil was worked for the first time, much to the benefit of the vines. The varieties cultivated are either native or well-rooted locally. The limestone terrain is on a slight slope at an altitude of 300 meters with a good day-to-night temperature range and air circulation that exploits the influence of the sea round the Gargano promontory.

WINES - Like other producers in the area, Paolo has come to the conclusion that Nero di Troia needs to age more after the grape harvest. He has thus delayed the release of his two most important wines. The grapes are fermented in wood as opposed to steel vats. Even in the least ambitious wines, we noted balance and elegance. Fortuita 2011 (● sangiovese, montepulciano, aglianico, uva di Troia; 6,500 bt) has soft tannins and complex balsamic, floral and fruity notes with a long finish of lavender and spices. It's a fantastic Everyday Wine. Also excellent was **Cacc'e Mmitte di Lucera Agramante 2011** (● uva di troia, sangiovese, montepulciano, bombino bianco; 13,000 bt), which has spices and aromatic herbs, pronounced acidity and stylish tannins.

FERTILIZERS none
PLANT PROTECTION copper and sulphur
WEED CONTROL mechanical
YEASTS selected
GRAPES 100% estate-grown
CERTIFICATION biodynamic

Grande Salento

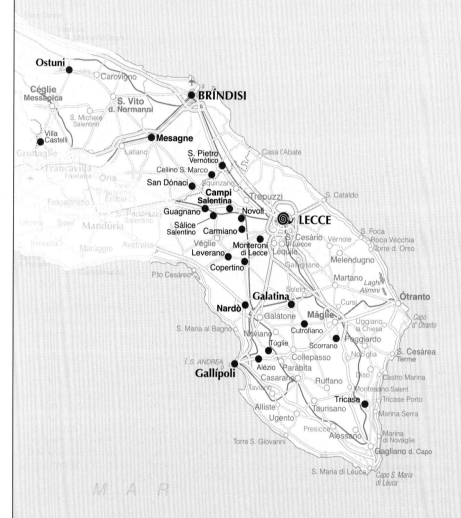

Sergio Botrugno €

Via Arcione, 1
tel. 0831 555587
www.vinisalento.it
sergiobotrugno@virgilio.it

33 ha - 80,000 bt `10% discount`

PEOPLE - Sergio Botrugno, a qualified agronomist and a born farmer, spends his time in the vineyard, but also manages the provincial farmers' association. His passion is born of a long family tradition and maybe owes something too to the etymology of his surname — "botrus" in Latino means "bunch". His brother Antonio lends a helping hand with the administrative side of the business and the consultant enologist is Cosimo Spina. This year Sergio was proud to introduce us to his new cellarman Steven Erebor, a Nigerian.

VINEYARDS - The company owns 33 hectares of land in the countryside north of Brindisi. The soil is sandy along the coast, mixed and calcareous inland. The vines are trained using the bilateral spurred cordon system. Some of them, the ones that had just been planted when we visited for the first edition of this guide, are still very young, the rest go back from 15 to 50 years. The vineyards are managed painstakingly and thriftily using conventional methods. "The best treatment comes from nature itself," said Sergio. We agree.

WINES - The wines are terroir-dedicated and approachable. We liked the refreshing, flavorful Passito Botrus 2012 (● malvasia nera; 8,000 bt) a lot for its balance and measured sweetness. In view of its price, it deserves the Everyday Wine symbol. **Patrunu Rò 2012** (● negroamaro; 20,000 bt) is pleasantly fruity and moreish. **Malvasia Nera 2012** (● 8,000 bt) is aromatic and caressing. **Patrunu Rò 2012** (● primitivo; 10,000 bt) is soft and fruity and refreshing. Aged on wood, the spicy, balsamic **Vigna Lobìa 2011** (● negroamaro; 10,000 bt) is austere and promises to evolve well. **Pinea 2012** (○ malvasia bianca; 5,000 bt) is full-flavored and firmly structured. The company also sells top quality unbottled wine directly at the cellar.

FERTILIZERS organic-mineral, green manure
PLANT PROTECTION chemical, copper and sulphur
WEED CONTROL chemical, mechanical
YEASTS selected
GRAPES 100% estate-grown
CERTIFICATION none

Severino Garofano Vigneti e Cantine

Località Tenuta Monaci
tel. 0832 947512
www.aziendamonaci.com
vini@aziendamonaci.com

36 ha - 220,000 bt `10% discount`

PEOPLE - The winery was formed in the mid 1990s and named for the masseria, or farmhouse, Monaci, in which it was based. This year it has been renamed for its founder, Severino Garofano, an enologist from Irpinia who has made the potential of the negroamaro grape know the world over. Today the business is run with passion, nous and dedication by Severino's son and daughter, Stefano and Renata, who continue to heed his lessons and advice.

VINEYARDS - The company owns 16 hectares of vineyards and rents 20, all bush- and spurred cordon-trained. It cultivates almost exclusively negroamaro grapes, seven hectares of which were recently replanted. Plant protection treatments are limited to a bare minimum and work in the fields is overseen by the agronomist Antonio Protezione.

WINES - The wines evoke the negroamaro in its myriad nuances. Topping the bill is Girofle 2012 (☉ 35,000 bt), once more an Everyday Wine. A top-notch rosé, it has all the typology's characteristic intensity, fruitiness, flavor, freshness and length. **Copertino Eloquentia 2010** (● 100,000 bt) is delicate with a bouquet of berries and Mediterranean scrub and soft tannins on the palate. **I Censi 2011** (● negroamaro, malvasia; 20,000 bt) has been given warmth and spiciness by six months' aging in oak casks. **Simpotica 2007** (● negroamaro, montepulciano; 20,000 bt) has a generous jammy nose and warm, complex, lingering flavor. We'll have to wait a little longer to taste the flagship Braci label, but retasting previous versions we realized how well it's going to age.

FERTILIZERS green manure
PLANT PROTECTION copper and sulphur
WEED CONTROL mechanical
YEASTS selected
GRAPES 100% estate-grown
CERTIFICATION none

CUTROFIANO (LE)

L'Astore Masseria

Località L'Astore
Via Giuseppe di Vittorio, 1
tel. 0836 542020
www.lastoremasseria.it
info@lastoremasseria.it

20 ha - 90,000 bt | **10% discount**

PEOPLE - In the mid 1990s, the Benegiamo farm resumed producing wine and became completely operational again in 2004. This was thanks to the passion of Achille and his children who, with Paolo at the forefront, now conduct the enterprise. After various ups and downs, L'Astore has now settled into a rhythm and established a personality of its own — firmly rooted in the local area with great respect for its history and environment.

VINEYARDS - Vineyards occupy 20 of the farm's 85 hectares. After initial infatuation with international grapes such as cabernet, merlot and others, the owners replanted all the vineyards with native varieties. Great efforts have been made to revive an old bush-trained negroamaro vineyard first planted in 1947. Work in the fields is coordinated by the agronomist Pietro Mandurino.

WINES - Massaro Rosa 2012 (⊙ negroamaro; 6,000 bt), an exemplary Salento rosé, is fruity, flavorsome and fresh with a deft and pleasing almondy aftertaste; it's an excellent Everyday Wine. **Filimei 2011** (● negroamaro; 20,000 bt) is intense and delicately balsamic with dry, full, pervasive flavor. **Jema 2011** (● primitivo; 20,000 bt) offers unusual notes of minerality and freshness. On the nose, **Alberelli 2009** (● negroamaro; 4,000 bt) is broad and ethereal with effective equilibrium between fruit and spices, and dry and lingering in the glass. **Astore 2011** (● aglianico; 5,000 bt) is complex and well-structured and promises to develop well. **Krita 2012** (○ malvasia; 10,000 bt) scores marks for freshness and flavor.

LECCE

Agricole Vallone

Via XXV Luglio, 7
tel. 0832 308041
www.agricolevallone.it
info@agricolevallone.it

161 ha - 400,000 bt

66 Vittoria and Maria Teresa Vallone's old winery has always been managed by Donato Lazzari. It is distinguished by the exactness of its wines, their adherence to the terroir and its bond with tradition. But it is also open to novelties and environmental sustainability. 99

PEOPLE - The Vallone sisters' trusted collaborators are Oronzo Lazzari, who supervises the growers, one for each of the three estates, and sales manager Giuseppe Malazzini.

VINEYARDS - The vineyards are spread over three areas: the historic Vigna Flaminio estate, where the cellar and a new modern production plant, operational from this year, are situated; a bush-trained vineyard in the countryside at San Pancrazio, with six hectares of wines planted over 80 years ago in the Caragnuli district; and Castelserranova, which rims the Torre Guaceto nature reserve. All the properties are managed with integrated farming methods and cover-cropped with field beans.

WINES - Vallone wines are of a consistently high standard. **Brindisi Rosato Vigna Flaminio 2012** (⊙ negroamaro, montepulciano; 18,000 bt) is fruity, fine and flavorful. Just as good is the seductive, velvety **Salice Salentino Vereto Ris. 2009** (● negroamaro; 6,000 bt). We were also impressed by **Fiano Tenuta Serranova 2012** (○ 5,000 bt), with its clear-cut, savory finish. **Brindisi Rosso Vigna Flaminio 2011** (● negroamaro, montepulciano; 125,000 bt) is distinctly terroir-dedicated, **Passo delle Viscarde 2012** (○ sauvignon, malvasia bianca; 6,000 bt) is well-balanced.

vino slow GRATICCIAIA 2009 (● 15,000 bt) One of the finest examples, once again, of the great Puglia tradition of raisining negroamaro grapes. It has magnificently spacious aromas with spicy, balsamic notes and an opulent soft but austere palate with a very long finish.

FERTILIZERS manure pellets, green manure
PLANT PROTECTION copper and sulphur
WEED CONTROL mechanical
YEASTS selected
GRAPES 100% estate-grown
CERTIFICATION organic

FERTILIZERS green manure
PLANT PROTECTION copper and sulphur
WEED CONTROL mechanical
YEASTS selected
GRAPES 100% estate-grown
CERTIFICATION none

Alessandro Bonsegna €

Via Volta, 17
tel. 0833 561483
www.vinibonsegna.it
vinibonsegna@vinibonsegna.it

Francesco Candido

Via Diaz, 46
tel. 0831 635674
www.candidowines.it
candido@candidowines.it

18 ha - 100,000 bt   **10% discount**

PEOPLE - Like so many others in Southern Italy, the company, founded in the 1960s by Primo Bonsegna, initially produced and sold unbottled wine. It was only in 1993, when Primo's son Alessandro took over the management, that bottling began. Alessandro monitors the entire productive process and, thanks to his passion, the company has made constant steps forward over the years.

VINEYARDS - Most of the vineyards are in the countryside round Nardò, though a few residual parcels are also to be found in the Portoselvaggio Nature Reserve. They are all trained using the spurred cordon system and grow mostly native grape varieties. They are managed with great environmental awareness: only a bare minimum of interventions is carried out and weed control is performed with a special machine designed by Alessandro himself.

WINES - The wines offer excellent value for money. This is the case of the splendid Everyday Wine, Nardò Rosso Danze Della Contessa 2011 (● negroamaro, malvasia; 8,000 bt), which has complex, intense aromas and a warm, leisurely palate. Nardò Rosso Danze della Contessa Barricato 2010 (● negroamaro, malvasia; 10,000 bt) is similar but somewhat spicier. Nardò Rosato Danze della Contessa 2012 (☉ negroamaro, malvasia; 10,000 bt) is a typically enjoyable Salento rosé. Cenate Vecchie 2012 (○ malvasia bianca, garganega; 15,000 bt) and the intensely scented Primitivo Baia di Uluzzo 2011 (● 12,000 bt) are both enjoyable easy-drinking wines. Primo 2010 (● negroamaro, primitivo; 5,200 bt) opens on aromas of jam and spices and has fresh, mouthfilling flavor.

140 ha - 1,800,000 bt   **10% discount**

PEOPLE - Without doubt one of the most important cellars in the region, it exports about two third of its output and has made the wines of Salento known and admired throughout the world. It owes its ongoing success to the experience and attentive guidance of Alessandro Candido, who is helped by enologist Donato Lanati, and a dynamic team of local youngsters.

VINEYARDS - Candido attaches huge attention to agronomic practices which he has converted to organic and limits treatments to a minimum. He has also passed these precepts on to the growers he buys his grapes from to ensure they characterize the entire production range. Most of the vineyards are situated in the Salice Salentino zone, of which he is a stalwart defender.

WINES - Quality and style, modern enological techniques with an eye to tradition, respect for local identity — these are the distinctive features of the cellar's wines. It's hard to find examples of top-quality mass-produced wines comparable to **Cappello di Prete 2008** (● negroamaro; 400,000 bt), **Salice Salentino Ris. La Carta 2008** (● negroamaro, malvasia nera; 1,000,000 bt) and **Salice Salentino Le Pozzelle 2012** (● negroamaro, malvasia; 150,000 bt). **Salice Salentino Ris. I Satiri 2008** (● negroamaro; 10,000 bt) and **Tenuta Marini 2012** (○ fiano; 12,000 bt) are also well-crafted.

> **vino slow** DUCA D'ARAGONA 2007 (● negroamaro, montepulciano; 65,000 bt) Again one of the most reliable Salento wines for typicality and consistent quality. Its stylish balsamic, soft, pervasive aromas are backed up by tannins made silky by long bottle-aging prior to commercial release.

FERTILIZERS manure pellets
PLANT PROTECTION chemical, copper and sulphur
WEED CONTROL mechanical
YEASTS selected
GRAPES 100% estate-grown
CERTIFICATION none

FERTILIZERS none
PLANT PROTECTION copper and sulphur
WEED CONTROL mechanical
YEASTS selected
GRAPES 40% bought in
CERTIFICATION converting to organics

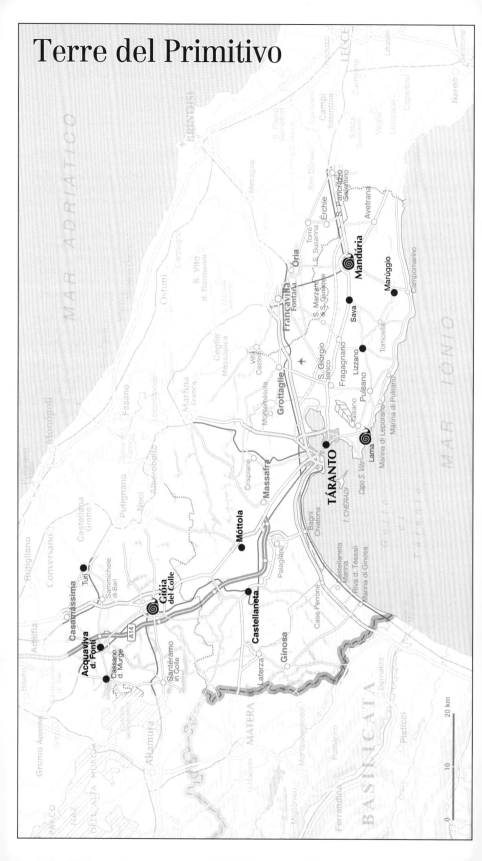

Terre del Primitivo

Pietraventosa

Contrada Parco Largo
tel. 335 5730274
www.pietraventosa.it
info@pietraventosa.it

Polvanera

Strada Vicinale Lamie Marchesana, 601
tel. 080 758900
www.cantinepolvanera.com
info@cantinepolvanera.it

5.9 ha - 12,000 bt

PEOPLE - Marianna Annio and Raffaele Leo are a lovely couple. Young and dynamic, they only embarked on their adventure in the wine world eight years ago. They haven't got special family stories to tell; all they have to declare is their passion and eagerness to invest in agriculture. Raffaele's know-how as an engineer and designer of enological machinery has, of course, come in handy, but the real driving force behind the company is Marianna's dynamism. Their enologist is Oronzo Alò, their grower Angelo Capurso.

VINEYARDS - A vineyard of slightly more than five hectares, at an altitude of 350 meters and surrounded by olive trees and holm oaks, constitutes the heart of the property, and it is here that the cellar is situated. The soil — a stratum of no great depth with limestone and pebbles covering the rock below — is typical of Gioia del Colle. At the center of the estate, the otherwise thriving plants become oddly scrubby. The top wine is made with grapes from a small, half-hectare, bush-trained vineyard.

WINES - It is the cellar's policy, out of respect for the primitivo grape and the terroir, to leave wines to mature, hence enabling to express all their potential. **Gioia del Colle Primitivo Allegoria 2012** (● 3,500 bt) comes from young vineyards and is aged exclusively in steel vats: mineral and balsamic, it's a joy to drink. The softness of the grape is counteracted by a small percentage of aglianico in **Ossimoro 2011** (● 3,500 bt), a wine of great tannic and acid structure, rounded and spiced by the wood. This year's new arrival, **Estrosa 2012** (⊙ 1,500 bt), impressed for its fruity, tangy freshness.

> **vino slow** GIOIA DEL COLLE PRIMITIVO RIS. 2010 (● 1,500 bt) This stylish, potent Primitivo stood out for its charisma and quality. Spicy and crisply fruity, mineral and balsamic, it's a great modern wine that smacks, positively, of the past.

---

70 ha - 200,000 bt

❝ Determination and great professionalism plus personableness —you admire the man for his wine and the wine for the man who makes it. ❞

PEOPLE - Filippo Cassano wasn't the first or only person to grasp the potential of primitivo di Gioia del Colle which, after being discovered locally, fell into a long period of oblivion. What he has done is to spread the word right from his earliest bottles, giving recognizability to both grape and terroir.

VINEYARDS - The vineyards cover an area of 70 hectares, 30 of which new plantings, and they don't grow primitivo alone . Filippo hasn't forgotten other traditional grape varieties and has also rescued some bush-trained vines for the most important wines. The youngest vineyards have lean, pebbly soil of little depth, the bush-trained ones have deep soil composed of clay and ferrous limestone. The vineyard management is certified organic.

WINES - All wines are aged in steel vats only and are characterized by a style based on drinkability with mineral connotations. **Gioia del Colle Primitivo 17 2010** (● 20,000 bt) is meaty, crisp and heavyset. The enjoyable **Gioia del Colle Primitivo 14 2010** (● 60,000 bt) offers the same style and the same emotions at a lower price. The blossomy, tangy **Minutolo senza solfiti 2012** (○ 6,000 bt) and the more aromatic, unctuous **Minutolo 2012** (○ 40,000 bt) are both excellent. The enjoyable **Rosato 2012** (⊙ aleatico, primitivo, aglianico; 20,000 bt) has blossomy, fruity notes.

> **vino slow** GIOIA DEL COLLE PRIMITIVO **16 2010** Gioia del Colle Primitivo 16 2010 (● 20,000 bt) It's hard to choose between the various versions of primitivo, which differ by alcohol proof. In the end we plumped for 16, a delicate crisp, long wine subtly poised between elegance and body, slightly less potent hence better-balanced.

FERTILIZERS natural manure, green manure
PLANT PROTECTION copper and sulphur
WEED CONTROL mechanical
YEASTS selected
GRAPES 100% estate-grown
CERTIFICATION organic

FERTILIZERS none
PLANT PROTECTION copper and sulphur
WEED CONTROL mechanical
YEASTS selected
GRAPES 100% estate-grown
CERTIFICATION organic

LAMA (TA)

Gianfranco Fino

Via Fior di Salvia, 8
tel. 099 7773970
www.gianfrancofino.it
gianfrancofino@libero.it

8 ha - 18,000 bt   **10% discount**

❝ Innovation and tradition, scientific research and ancient peasant wisdom — this is the dichotomy that Gianfranco Fino and his wife Simona Natale address with intelligence and determination. Though they are well aware, of course, that the third ingredient for the right recipe for success is time. ❞

PEOPLE - After studying enology and completing important experiences at some of the great wineries, Gianfranco began, with Simona at his side, to rescue semi-abandoned old vineyards and realize his dream of becoming a winemaker in the marvelous land of his birth.

VINEYARDS - Over the years Gianfranco and Simona patiently and stubbornly "conquered" 12 parcels. In them grow exclusively old vines planted 60-90 years ago. These spectacular plants are interpreted one by one, especially at the pruning stage, which Gianfranco supervises personally. In the Li Reni district, east of Manduria, new vineyards were planted two and three years ago with four clones selected in collaboration with the Caramia Institute in Locorotondo and trained with the classic "hare's ear" system.

WINES - On more than one occasion we have defined Gianfranco and Simona's wine as "neoclassical", and this year has once more confirmed that we are right. **Primitivo di Manduria Es 2011** (● 15,000 bt) is a Great Wine that combines the power and body typical of the grape variety and aromas of great finesse and complexity. The perfect balance comes out to the full on the palate, where freshness and tanginess enhance the flavor and prolong it deeply and crisply and evenly, thereby ensuring its longevity. With the passing of the vintages, though, it maintains its characteristic opulence. In short, Es is becoming increasingly subtle and stylish.

FERTILIZERS none	
PLANT PROTECTION copper and sulphur	
WEED CONTROL mechanical	
YEASTS selected	
GRAPES 100% estate-grown	
CERTIFICATION none	

MANDURIA (TA)

Attanasio

Via per Oria, 13
tel. 099 9737121
www.primitivo-attanasio.com
info@primitivo-attanasio.com

7.2 ha - 14,000 bt

❝ It's partly thanks to Luca Attanasio's example that so much is changing on the wine scene in one of Puglia's most prestigious terroirs, Manduria ❞

PEOPLE - This committed young winemaker, heir to the peasant tradition of Manduria, is totally dedicated to his craft. Helped by advice from his father and brother and supported by his wife, who recently gave him a son, Luca has now reached a maturity that is reflected, year by year, in his wines.

VINEYARDS - Luca's vines are all bush-trained. He spends most of the day in the vineyards and it's easier to find him on his tractor than in the office. Careful work with a bare minimum of intervention makes for high-quality grapes. The soil varies from red to black.

WINES - The new vintages of the dry wines — which on second tasting excited us for their aging capacity — aren't ready yet. We thus had the pleasure — and what a pleasure it was — to try the new versions of the two white wines, Luca's specialty. The refined, well-crafted **Primitivo di Manduria Dolce Naturale 2010** (● 800 bt) has pronounced supporting acidity, which tempers the sweet notes of the sugars and makes the wine supremely drinkable.

> **vino slow** **PRIMITIVO DI MANDURIA DOLCE NATURALE PASSITO 2009** (● 900 bt) An exciting wine, made with grapes dried in the fruit room, which pervades and caresses the nose with hints of ripe fruit, spices and sweet tobacco. Poised between softness and freshness, it has a long, dense finish.

FERTILIZERS green manure	
PLANT PROTECTION copper and sulphur	
WEED CONTROL mechanical	
YEASTS selected	
GRAPES 100% estate-grown	
CERTIFICATION none	

MANDURIA (TA)

Morella

Via per Uggiano 147
tel. 099 9791482
www.morellavini.com
info@morellavini.it

16.5 ha - 20,000 bt

❝ A project born of love for an old bush-trained vineyard. This, thought Lisa Gilbee, is where I want to put down roots. Lisa has had a set idea right from outset: to make wine with local personal and identity with total respect for nature. ❞

PEOPLE - The fantastic story of the Australian enologist Lisa Gilbee reads like a novel. She has named the winery for her lifelong partner, Gaetano Morella.

VINEYARDS - There are two plots of vineyards, both gorgeously bush-trained, both rescued from the explanation that has ravaged the landscape round Manduria: old vines, some planted 80 years ago, now revived and lovingly tended. Lisa has selected and recovered the biotypes most suitable for the gradual replanting of the vines and manages them using biodynamic practices.

WINES - Modernity and tradition combine to perfection in Lisa's clean, wonderfully complex wines. Produced with grapes from the oldest vines, **Primitivo Old Vines 2010** (● 4,500 bt) seduces the palate with iodine notes and bundles of minerality. **Mezzanotte 2012** (● 3,000 bt) is an easy-drinking wine that has changed its grape mix vintage by vintage, and is now made only with primitivo. **Primitivo Negroamaro 2010** (● 4,000 bt) is all structure and flavor, with the blend evidencing the freshness and potency of the two grapes. Already good and impressive but still capable of evolving, **Primitivo Malbek 2010** (● 6,500 bt) has stylish extracts.

vino slow LA SIGNORA 2010 (● 3,000 bt) A Primitivo of rare elegance and personality, braced by zesty freshness and ample length, perfectly poised between weight and lightness.

FERTILIZERS biodynamic preparations, green manure
PLANT PROTECTION copper and sulphur, organic
WEED CONTROL mechanical
YEASTS native
GRAPES 100% estate-grown
CERTIFICATION none

SAVA (TA)

Vinicola Savese

S.S.7 TER Km 27,790
tel. 099 9726232
www.vinipichierri.com
vinicolasavese@vinipichierri.com

18 ha - 180,000 bt   **10% discount**

PEOPLE - Vinicola Savese, a winemaking institution in the province of Taranto, has now moved to its new headquarters. Brothers Vittorio, Roberto and Aldo Picherri continue to teach the ropes to the new generation, represented Mara and Massimiliano, while Francesco Pezzarossa has come in as marketing manager, bringing new ideas with him.

VINEYARDS - The spurred cordon-trained vineyards grow on calcareous-clayey soil which add power and structure to the grapes, hence to the wines. The Pichirri family is showing increasing concern for agronomic practices, with Vittorio overseeing vineyard operations and helping his nephew Massimiliano t select the grapes.

WINES - It's not hard in a blind tasting to recognize the aromas and technical precision of Savese wines. The excellent **Gocce di Giada 2012** (☉ primitivo; 2,500 bt) is a firmly structured rosé with good acidity. **Vittoria 2012** (● 10.000 bt), a well-balanced Negroamaro with silky tannins, and the pleasingly fruity **Novantino 2011** (● primitivo; 8,000 bt) both offer fantastic value for money. **Ajanoa 2009** (● primitivo; 6,000 bt) offers all the richness of ripe fruit and good length.

vino slow CAPASONATO 1985 (● primitivo; 1.850 bt) No, the vintage isn't a printing error! Aged in capasoni, large traditional terracotta pitchers, this is an alluring wine. Its aromatic impact is outstandingly complex with the terroir very much to the fore. A wonderfully enthralling sipping dinner wine that grows on the drinker.

FERTILIZERS natural manure
PLANT PROTECTION copper and sulphur
WEED CONTROL mechanical
YEASTS native
GRAPES 100% estate-grown
CERTIFICATION none

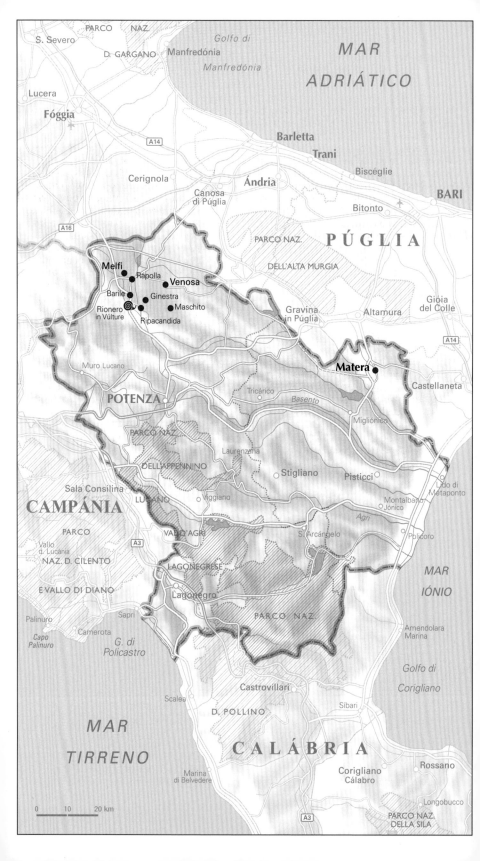

BASILICATA

In the space of just a few years wine production in Basilicata has dropped by virtually half, from 208,000 hectoliters in 2008 to 110,000 last year, of which only 10 per cent were DOC or IGT wines. The area of land given over to winegrowing has also decreased by a two-zero figure. The stats spell structural crisis and the region's great winegrowing tradition risks becoming nothing more than a memory. Alas, our visits to wineries confirmed the existence of an air of something approaching resignation. We believe two factors have reinforced the trend. The first was the decision to allow DOC production outside the original areas which, ostensibly taken to make money, has, de facto, lowered prices and, as a consequence, the income of farmers (which is how Aglianico has ended up being sold off at cut prices to bottling companies outside the region). The second is the now consolidated inability of winemakers to organize themselves and stick together. In the past, when conditions were more favorable, they preferred to turn to advertising companies for promotion, a choice that failed to bear fruits. There are also positive pointers, however, that leave room for hope. The first of these is the change in style, now more focused on drinkability and sense of place, evident since the 2009 vintage: hence fewer special effects and more faith in Aglianico's ability to improve with age. The second is economic and the investments made by major companies like Giv and Feudi di San Gregorio in clean vine growing and in improving their best vineyards have not gone unobserved. There is no shortage of small wineries committed to quality and capable of coming up with interesting bottles. Lastly, we were pleased with the growth of well-organized wineries in the province of Matera, easily the most dynamic, lively area in the region.

Breathtaking landscapes, picturesque villages, magnificent castles, tourist attractions, from wonderful beaches to the city of Matera, the quality of the volcanic soil of Mount Vulture — Basilicata is the great green lung of the South, a region in which the development of a comprehensive winegrowing project would be feasible. A number of vertical tastings showed how, albeit susceptible to different interpretations, Aglianico is a wine capable of conveying emotion as time goes by. More, in the Matera area the fruit in Primitivo has lost the cooked taste that had become the standard over previous years, replacing it with freshness and drinkability. Of the white wines, the ones made with fiano and moscato grapes in particular continued to amaze. In conclusion, we are impatient to experience new emotions and witness new adventures in the future.

snails	bottles 🍾	coins €
217 Cantine del Notaio	216 Basilisco	217 Grifalco
	216 Carbone	

BARILE (PZ)

Basilisco

Via delle Cantine, 22
tel. 0972 771033
www.basiliscovini.it
basiliscovini@gmail.com

24 ha - 55,000 bt | **10% discount**

PEOPLE - Viviana Malafarina, general manager of the Basilisco farm, now owned by Feudi di San Gregorio, is completely dedicated to her job. Alongside her works the agronomist and production consultant Pier Paolo Sirch. Under the new team, this historic cellar in Barile, at the heart of the Vulture zone, maintains a close bond with the terroir and benefits from their fresh energy and solid global vision.

VINEYARDS - When Viviana takes us round the vineyards we begin to understand why she's so in love with this unique area. The farm grows 24 hectares of vines at an altitude of 480-580 meters. The oldest vines in the historic vineyard are 45 years old and ungrafted. The most recent aglianico plantings date from 2001-2004. The soil is mainly volcanic and work on organic conversion began two years ago.

WINES - The Basilisco buildings stand in an old area of tufa caves, known as shesh, which date back to the 15th century, when Albanians first came to settle here. The vertical barrel room remains as a testimony of that tradition. The whole wine range is of the highest quality. The white **Sofia 2012** (O fiano, traminer; 8,000 bt) is peppy and breezy, intense and long. **Aglianico del Vulture Basilisco 2010** (● 14,000 bt), which spends a year on new and second-fill wood, is full of substance, minerally, ageworthy and well-rounded.

vino slow AGLIANICO DEL VULTURE TEODOSIO 2011 (● 27.000 bt) A wine aged for a year or so in second- and third-use barriques, well-balanced, delicate and intense with plenty of acidity and flavor and perfect, well-amalgamated tannins. The product of clean agriculture and reasonably priced — a perfect Slow Wine.

FERTILIZERS natural manure, green manure
PLANT PROTECTION copper and sulphur
WEED CONTROL mechanical
YEASTS selected
GRAPES 100% estate-grown
CERTIFICATION converting to organics

MELFI (PZ)

Carbone

Via Nitti, 48
tel. 0972 237866
www.carbonevini.it
info@carbonevini.it

18 ha - 40,000 bt | **10% discount**

PEOPLE - In this evocative old cellar in the heart of Melfi, a warren of caves cut into the tufa rock, you'll be welcomed by Sara Carbone and her brother Luca. Their family's vineyards, planted in the 1970s, provided the springboard for them to start making wine in 2005. Today the company is still "all in the family" and it was no coincidence that we should bump into Luca's father-in-law Michele Lafelice out among the vineyards, for example. Luca and Sara have entrusted the enological side of the business to Sergio Paternoster.

VINEYARDS - The Vulture, an extinct volcano, towers over the vineyards. The oldest plot occupies 10 hectares and grows mainly aglianico and fiano vines, all 25 to 45 years old. The soil is medium-textured and volcanic in origin, and the vineyards stand at an altitude of about 550 meters. At the same altitude at Braide, new vines were planted about five years ago and will be fully productive from next year.

WINES - **Fiano 2012** (O 3,500 bt) is a white wine with a rich aroma of flowers and herbs, fresh and well-structured with a long finish. This is the first vintage in which **Rosa Carbone 2012** (⊙ aglianico; 3,500 bt) has been bottled. Quaffable, with good supporting acidity, whiffs of minerality, excellent flavor and delicious fruit, it gave a good account of itself. The exquisite **Aglianico del Vulture Terra dei Fuochi 2011** (● 10,000 bt) is aged in steel vats only. It isn't intended as a flagship wine exactly but it does capture the essence of the typology and terroir very well. **Aglianico del Vulture Stupor Mundi 2011** (● 8,000 bt) displays notes of fruit well fused with the wood. The superlative **Aglianico del Vulture 400 Some 2011** (● 10,000 bt) is aged in wood casks and has a soft, sweet palate with pleasing tannins and fine graphite notes. It's a Great Wine that ennobles the whole denomination.

FERTILIZERS green manure
PLANT PROTECTION chemical, copper and sulphur
WEED CONTROL mechanical
YEASTS selected
GRAPES 100% estate-grown
CERTIFICATION none

Cantine del Notaio 🌀

Via Roma, 159
tel. 0972 723689
www.cantinedelnotaio.it
info@cantinedelnotaio.it

Grifalco €

Località Pian di Camera
tel. 0972 31002
www.grifalco.com
grifalcodellalucania@email.it

---

30 ha - 230,000 bt **10% discount**

❝ No one has changed the world of Aglianico del Vulture more than Gerardo Giuratrabocchetti. From his sustainable vine dressing to the warm welcome he extends to his cellars, to his never overblown communication, he represents the South of Italy's virtuous, unrelenting side. And he's even improved his use of wood, now more careful and measured than in the past. ❞

PEOPLE - Gerardo Giuratrabocchetti is at the helm of Basilicata winemaking and promotes wine tourism in the region. His wines are elegant, clean and modern in style, thanks partly to the advice of enologist Luigi Moio.

VINEYARDS - The vineyards cover an area of 30 hectares and are divided between aglianico, moscato, malvasia and fiano. The oldest go back over a century and rest on volcanic soil in some of the most favorable parts of the Vulture zone. A project is currently under way in conjunction with the University of Basilicata to study old varieties of local grapes.

WINES - The early-drinking, reasonably priced L'Atto 2011 (● 85,000 bt) is an elegant, crisp aglianico with clear-cut hints of cherry, redcurrant and spices — a fine Everyday Wine. Complex, well-rounded with precise notes of dried fruit, **Aglianico del Vulture La Firma 2010** (● 20,000 bt) can either be enjoyed today or set aside for tomorrow. **Aglianico del Vulture Il Sigillo 2009** (● 15,000 bt) is made with late-harvested grapes and offers a chewy, rounded palate. Fine and soft with crunchy cherries, **Rogito 2011** (☉ aglianico; 25,000 bt) is a pleasure to drink.

> **vino slow** AGLIANICO DEL VULTURE IL REPERTORIO 2010 (● 20,000 bt) Tangy, vibrant, long, balsamic — a superb example of the massive potential of the grape when a producer decides against concentration and wood-induced spiciness at all costs.

---

14 ha - 70,000 bt **10% discount**

PEOPLE - The agronomist and enologist Fabrizio Piccini is a native of Tuscany. He embarked on his adventure in Basilicata ten years ago when he bought the aglianico vineyards and built the cellar. In view of the flattering results, Fabrizio decided to involve the whole family. Now his wife Cecilia Naldoni is in charge of sales and his son Lorenzo, soon to graduate in enology, works fulltime at the winery. Venosa-born Maria Madio also lends a hand.

VINEYARDS - The vineyards cover close on ten hectares in the hills of the communes of Rapolla, Ginestra and Maschito at an altitude of about 500 meters. These are good growing areas where the soil is rich in lava and the some of the vineyards are 60 years old. Judging from initial barrique tastings, in which we had the pleasure to take part, the 2012 harvest promise to be exceptional. Other 10-year-old vineyards bound the cellar at Pian di Camera di Venosa.

WINES - Four wines are produced, all with the aglianico grape. The company's top wine, Bosco del Falco, wasn't released in 20008, while the oldest vineyards have regaled us with **Aglianico del Vulture Damaschito 2009** (● 5,000 bt), which offers bosky notes of undergrowth, mushrooms, truffles and ripe cherries and a full-bodied, wellrounded palate with unobtrusive tannins. The other labels are also top-notch, first and foremost Aglianico del Vulture Grifalco 2011 (● 20,000 bt), redolent of black cherry, ripe fruit and redcurrants. Given its quality, its value for money and its versatility with food, it's a perfect example of an Everyday Wine. **Aglianico del Vulture Gricos 2011** (● 35,000 bt) releases distinct and pleasing notes of aromatic herbs.

FERTILIZERS organic-mineral, natural manure, green manure
PLANT PROTECTION copper and sulphur
WEED CONTROL mechanical
YEASTS selected
GRAPES 25% bought in
CERTIFICATION biodynamic, organic

FERTILIZERS natural manure, green manure
PLANT PROTECTION copper and sulphur
WEED CONTROL mechanical
YEASTS native
GRAPES 100% estate-grown
CERTIFICATION organic, converting to biodynamics

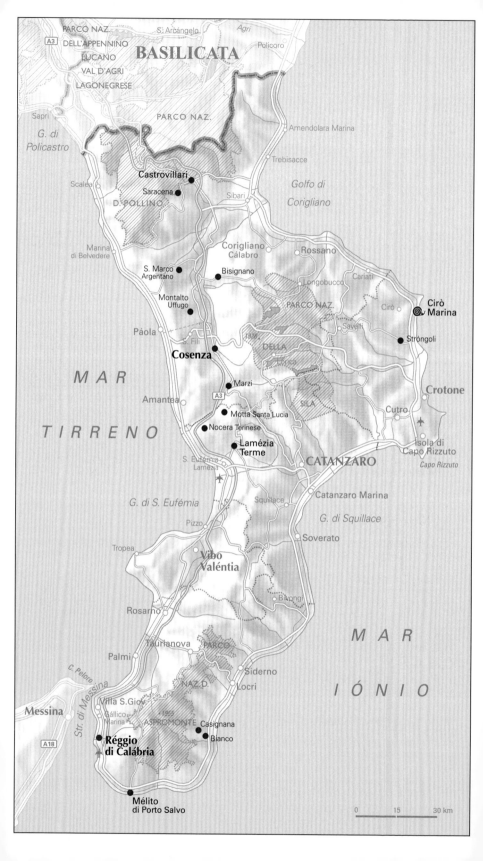

CALABRIA

The top bottles are sweet without being cloying. Producers in Saracena and Bianco are currently releasing exciting, technically flawless wines of massive personality, complexity and ageability, wines that recapture the great peasant tradition by removing all traces of syrupiness. It's small artisans we are speaking of here and it's a joy for us to record and support a trend that is growing more interesting year by year.

This isn't the only positive note to emerge from this year's tastings. The crisis that hit winegrowing round Crotone now seems to have been overcome — at one stage the Cirò DOC had to "surrender" to international grape varieties — and the new wave of young Cirò lions has continued on its way, with Librandi playing a supporting role in the background, despite the death unforgettable Antonio. The Frankentein reds, concentrated and black as pitch, are being countervailed by authentic renderings of Gaglioppo, with transparency, freshness, minerality and flavor now dominating the palate.

A third reason to be enthusiastic is Magliocco, arguably the most rounded expression of the fortunate moment being lived by the province of Cosenza. Not surprisingly, production is stable, with reds that are nicely drinkable yet amazingly simple, perfect with any kind of cooking.

All things considered, after an awful decade in which the area of land on which wines were grown plummeted by 35 per cent from 13,800 hectares to 9,100, Calabrian winemaking would appear to have emerged from the tunnel. It's no coincidence that production is down in the non-certified segment of the region, whereas in Cosenza, now the most important winegrowing province, production it has remained virtually unvaried at 126,000 hectoliters. Table wines are down from 72 to 69 per cent, DOCs are up from 17 to 19 per cent, IGTs exceed 12 per cent. The shortcomings that are slowing down production and the revival of overall regional production are two fold: the insistence of some large companies on producing international wines that stand out like a sore thumb in a region that boasts the highest number of native grapes, some of which highly prized; lack of faith in the potential of white wines, especially in areas like the Sila plateau, where great results could be achieved thanks to the cool climate and day-to-night temperature swings.

snails 🐌

220 SERGIO ARCURI
220 'A VITA

coins €

221 LIBRANDI

CIRÒ MARINA (KR)

Sergio Arcuri

Via Roma Vico III, 3
tel. 0962 31723
www.vinicirosergioarcuri.it
info@vinicirosergioarcuri.it

4 ha - 10,000 bt

❝ Right in the heart of the town of Cirò Marina there's a cellar where they age wine made with grapes grown organically in country vineyards in cement vats. The result is a rendering of the gaglioppo variety that proves that often, to be ahead of the field, all it takes is consistency. ❞

PEOPLE - Giuseppe Arcuri bought the cellar in 1973 and over the last few years he has been helped by his sons Sergio and Francesco.

VINEYARDS - Red sand and clay characterize the soil on which the bush-trained vines were planted in 1945. Thirty-year-old vines are planted on similar land and the most recent vertical-trellised vineyard was planted in 2005. Arcuri and his two sons work gaglioppo with traditional methods, enhanced by pronounced temperature ranges and good air circulation. The cellar is certified organic.

WINES - The prevalent style is one of elegance. The balance of the wines is heralded by their color, not concentrated but bright, itself a promise of longevity. This is true of both the selections submitted. Cirò Rosso Cl. Sup. Aris 2010 (● 7,500 bt) repeats last year's splendid performance with a nose of rose and cherry blossom, a zesty, fresh, crisp palate and a finish entirely devoid of sweetness. Fine yet at once full of distinctive character, it's a magnificent Everyday Wine and a credit to the whole category. **Marinaretto 2010** (● gaglioppo; 5,000 bt) is arguably even fresher and refined on the nose, which is characterized by pleasant sensations of blossom and peaches and apricots. In the mouth it releases softness, a touch of mid-palate huskiness and a finish in which the fruit makes its final encore.

FERTILIZERS green manure
PLANT PROTECTION copper and sulphur
WEED CONTROL mechanical
YEASTS native
GRAPES 100% estate-grown
CERTIFICATION organic

CIRÒ MARINA (KR)

'A Vita

S.S. 106, km 279,800
tel. 0962 31044
www.avitavini.it
avita.info@gmail.com

8 ha - 15,000 bt

❝ Francesco De Franco is the pioneer of a new trend in Calabria: following tradition not the latest fashion trends, while at the same time keeping up to date with a global vision. His is a charismatic style of winegrowing that respects the grape and the soil. ❞

PEOPLE - In his cellar under the family shop, Francesco De Franco carries forward the fantastic project he embarked upon in 2004.

VINEYARDS - Francesco has an architecture degree in his drawer, but also one in enology. The second is much handier when it comes to managing his family's four vineyards between Sant'Anastasia, Muzzunetto, Frassà and Fego. All are situated in the hills on clayey limestone soil and all face south. The agricultural methods adopted are certified organic.

WINES - We look forward to tasting 'A Vita, the label which made Francesco's name in 2008. In the meantime, we tasted **Rosato 2012** (☉ 2,800 bt), a well-crafted wine whose declared objective is easy drinking, especially with seafood. We were impressed by the austerity of this rosé, free of any cloying effects and full of minerality with a precise, crystal-glass finish. In both wines we noted a rendering of the gaglioppo grape that countervails the concentration, alcohol, sweetness cliché.

> **vino slow** CIRÒ ROSSO CLASSICO F36 P27 2009 (● 6.000 bt) Named for the land registry unit on which its grapes are grown, this wine has a style that has impressed us ever since its first release. It has non-concentrated color, a nose of cherries followed by a very lean, fine palate devoid of sweetness and rounded off by a clean finish. A gaglioppo that's a joy to drink.

FERTILIZERS green manure
PLANT PROTECTION copper and sulphur
WEED CONTROL mechanical
YEASTS native
GRAPES 100% estate-grown
CERTIFICATION organic

CIRÒ MARINA (KR)

Librandi €

Contrada San Gennaro
S.S. 106
tel. 0962 31518
www.librandi.it
librandi@librandi.it

260 ha - 2,500,000 bt

PEOPLE - This is a tough moment of transition for the cellar that modernized the image of Calabrian wine and all the agricultural work that goes into it. The 50-year partnership between brothers Nicodemo and Antonio has come to an end with the latter's death and a generational turnover is now under way. Despite this body blow, research projects with Donato Lanati are proceeding as planned and Cirò vine dressers are still supporting the company in its efforts to defend local biodiversity.

VINEYARDS - The company's 260 hectares are spread out over numerous properties in various parts of the regions. The three main plots are: in Cirò Marina, where the company's grape suppliers also have their vineyards; on the spectacular Rosaneti estate, where most of the vineyards are concentrated; in Melissa, in the DOC zone of the same name, relaunched in the mid 1990s. International and native grapes are cultivated using conventional agricultural methods.

WINES - Cirò Rosso 2012 (● 300,000 bt) has an approachable, refreshing mouthfeel braced by rich flavor. It's a perfect Everyday Wine. In these early stages of its life, **Cirò Rosso Cl. Duca San Felice Ris. 2011** (● 120,000 bt) is already excellent but has even greater prospects ahead of it. The aroma offers notes of citrus fruit and red berries, the palate is long and enjoyable. At present **Magno Megonio 2011** (● magliocco; 30,000 bt) is over-rich and over-concentrated but, like previous versions, it will settle with time. The excellent **Gravello 2011** (● gaglioppo, cabernet sauvignon; 70,000 bt) rounds off the range of red wines. The two whites are refreshing and enjoyable: **Melissa Asylia 2012** (○ greco; 60,000 bt) is approachable and agreeable, **Efeso 2012** (○ mantonico; 12,000 bt) is very rich and needs time to develop.

FERTILIZERS organic-mineral, green manure
PLANT PROTECTION chemical, copper and sulphur
WEED CONTROL mechanical
YEASTS selected
GRAPES 30% bought in
CERTIFICATION none

SAN MARCO ARGENTANO (CS)

L'Acino

Via XX Settembre, 98
tel. 0984 512095
www.acinovini.com
info@acinovini.com

8.5 ha - 18,000 bt

PEOPLE - The adventure Antonello Canonico, Emilio Di Cianni e Dino Briglio embarked upon in 2006 is speeing ahead at a rate of knots. After performing trials at an outside cellar, since 2010 they have been vinifying their own grapes and the results are there for all to see. The basic idea is not only to squeeze the best out of local native grapes, but also to bank on biodynamics as a definitive life and professional choice.

VINEYARDS - The winery's properties don't form a single plot but stand very close together in the Tocco district in the commune of Cervicati and in theValle delle Pietre near Mongrassano. The first, already productive, is home to the magliocco dolce and guarnaccia grapes, the second is planted with mantonico pinto and pecorello. The company also rents a three-hectare vineyard in a particularly good winegrowing area in the commune of Frascineto.

WINES - **Mantonicoz 2010** (○ mantonico pinto; 2,000 bt) has a pleasant suite of fruity aromas with blossomy notes and a nicely soft, long palate. **Chora Rosso 2012** (● magliocco, guarnaccia nera; 6,000 bt) is a quaffable wine that brims over with ripe fruit. **Chora Bianco 2012** (○ mantonico, guarnaccia bianca, pecorello; 4,000 bt) is a felicitous blend with a delightful citrussy bouquet and nicely expressed balance on the palate. The four wines are different but sewn together by a common thread: namely the desire never to overdo things and to avoid "special effects".

> **vino slow** **TOCCOMAGLIOCCO 2009** (● magliocco; 6,000 bt) The result of long maceration and aging on wood, a wine that exudes scents of red berries which fuse into the palate with pervasive freshness. A magnificent label that reveals all the potential of the grape and, we feel certain, will be the source of great satisfaction in the near future.

FERTILIZERS natural manure, biodynamic preparations, green manure
PLANT PROTECTION copper and sulphur, organic
WEED CONTROL mechanical
YEASTS native
GRAPES 30% bought in
CERTIFICATION none

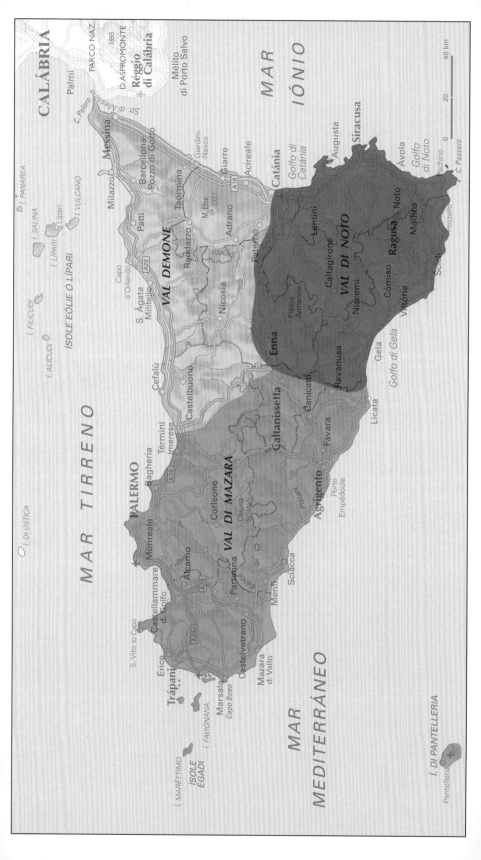

SICILY

In 2012 Sicilian wine production returned to its 2010 growth levels, an inversion in trend with respect to the two previous years, when a drastic drop was recorded, presumably the consequence of the uprooting of vineyards. The new increase stems from a decrease in the number of areas subjected to green harvesting and a growth in productivity of vineyards in the most fertile areas. In 2012, which saw the entry into force of the Sicilia DOC, exaggerated use seems to have been made of the IGT, which accounted for a 59 per cent share of total regional production, against 22 per cent nationally. The phenomenon, which was set into motion in 2007, is eroding the production of denomination wine which, according to ISTAT, the Italian National Statistics Institute, is still pegged below 200,000 hectoliters. As we have said, 2012 was the year in which the first labels of the Sicilia DOC, the twenty-third on the island, were released. According to the harvest and production declarations of the National Agricultural Computer Data Service, production amounted to 520,000 hectoliters, hence about 70 million bottles. The figures were awaited with bated breath by the regional supply chain, in particular by the nascent Consorzio Doc Sicilia chaired by Antonio Rallo, who will at last have a base to build on when it comes to restructuring the protection body itself.

The wines reviewed in the 2014 edition of the guide failed to show any significant change in direction in taste. Beyond increased income for grape suppliers' cooperatives, the local effects of the Sicilia DOC will be relatively negligible.

Follow any road in Sicily and you'll find pretty, sometimes breathtaking lanscapes, with hills rising in succession up to altitudes of sometimes 1,000 meters. There is no corner of the region, minor islands included, where vines aren't being cultivated with methods and techniques whose origins are lost in time.

Our visits to the wineries showed us a face of Sicily increasingly different and distant from the stereotype. It's a face that is simply asking to be listened to and described.

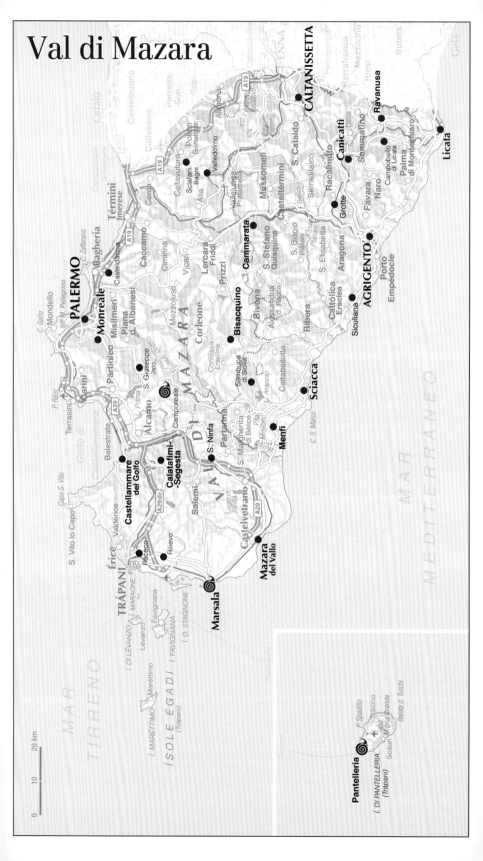

CAMPOREALE (PA)

Valdibella

Via Belvedere, 91
tel. 0924 582021
www.valdibella.com
info@valdibella.com

MARSALA (TP)

Cantine Rallo

Via Vincenzo Florio, 2
tel. 0923 721633
www.cantinerallo.it
info@cantinerallo.it

42 ha - 80,000 bt   **10% discount**

90 ha - 340,000 bt

66 Moving obstinately against the tide, notwithstanding a host of difficulties, Valdibella has managed to inject new lifeblood into the cooperative model, historically unsuccessful in Sicily. With two great Everyday Wines under its belt, this is the only Sicilian cellar that really does distil into its labels the essence of our accolades. 99

PEOPLE - This Salesian-inspired project, which extends beyond wine alone, involves ten members who, animated by a very strong spirit of solidarity have given life, one step at a time, to an example that deserves to be imitated. In charge of the cellar is Pietro Vaccaro with Vincenzo Drago and, since 2012, Benoit De Coster as his external consultants.

VINEYARDS - Biodiversity and improvement of the vineyards are the fil rouge that sews the whole project together. The aim is to restore dignity to generous soil too often mortified by the work of nearby wine cooperatives. The vineyards vary for location, structure and cultivars. All organically managed, they are peppered across the area between Camporeale and Monreale.

WINES - Valdibella wines never fail to amaze. After leaving them for a few minutes in the glass, one is struck by their depth of character and outstanding personality. Fermented with native yeasts, **Isolano 2012** (O catarratto; 3,000 bt) is juicy and corpulent, gutsy and enjoyable. The Two Everyday Wines are: Munir 2012 (O catarratto; 15,000 bt), intense and varietal, and Ariddu 2012 (O grillo; 9,000 bt), which has close-focused aromas. Both have fresh palates and pleasing acid sinew. The complex **Ninfa 2012** (O catarratto; 3,000 bt) has no added sulphites and is dynamic and pleasing on the palate. **Kerasos 2012** (● nero d'Avola; 30,000 bt) is very expressive and varietal. **Respiro 2012** (● nero d'Avola; 12,000 bt) is close-focused and forthright.

PEOPLE - The company's vineyards are situated at altitudes of 200 to 600 meters in the hills of the rural district of Patti Piccolo, between Alcamo and Camporeale. The estate has been owned by the Vesco family since 1920 and is run today by Andrea, a dynamic entrepreneur with a sound business curriculum under his belt. The lovely 19th-century wine cellar is in Marsala. From this year the company is employing Carlo Ferrini as its consultant.

VINEYARDS - Eighty hectares of organically certified vineyards are situated in the Alcamo DOC zone. Among the parcels numerous "islands" of spontaneous biodiversity have been preserved with beneficial effects for the health of the vines. Another ten hectares of bush-trained grillo vineyards are to be found in the countryside inland from Marsala, while two hectares of zibibbo for passito are cultivated in the Bugeber district on the island of Pantelleria.

WINES - **Carta d'Oro 2012** (O catarratto; 120,000 bt) is fresher than in previous years with less pronounced exotic notes, tangy and very citrussy. Made from select grapes, **Beleda 2012** (O catarratto; 6.000 bt) has marked acidity and scents of citrus fruit that capture the variety and the terroir well. **Bianco Maggiore 2012** (O grillo; 40,000 bt) conveys mineral sensations with the freshness characteristic of its terroir and vintage. Principe 2012 (● nero d'Avola; 140,000 bt) has crisp cherries and lively but intact tannins. Congratulations: it's a top class Everyday Wine. **Passito di Pantelleria 2010** (O 10,000 bt) offers nice impressions of honey, sweetness and the minerality typical of Pantelleria.

FERTILIZERS green manure
PLANT PROTECTION copper and sulphur
WEED CONTROL mechanical
YEASTS native
GRAPES 100% estate-grown
CERTIFICATION organic

FERTILIZERS natural manure
PLANT PROTECTION copper and sulphur
WEED CONTROL mechanical
YEASTS selected
GRAPES 100% estate-grown
CERTIFICATION organic

MARSALA (TP)

Marco De Bartoli ◎

Contrada Fornaia Samperi, 292
tel. 0923 962093
www.marcodebartoli.com
info@marcodebartoli.com

20 ha - 90,000 bt

66 De Bartoli never fails to amaze us. The wines we tasted were simply incredible. Every time round it's as if we we're catching up with a sort of "taste film" we stopped watching the year before — but with wines with something extra. 99

PEOPLE - Accustomed to seeing Marco, going back to Samperi after his death was a painful assignment. Everything there reminds one of him but this year we also felt the personal touch his son Renato has, with some authoritativeness, given to what have now become "his" wines.

VINEYARDS - The company has two estates: Samperi in the commune of Marsala and Bukkuram on the island of Pantelleria. The artisan agricultural methods adopted show respect for the environment and are practiced with impeccable care.

WINES - M. Cl. Brut Nature Terzavia (○ grillo; 7,000 bt) and Cuvée Campagne di Samperi Terzavia Ris. (○ grillo; 1,200 bt), made from the old Samperi Ventennale, are both very good indeed. The delicate, complex Grappoli del Grillo 2011 (○ 10,000 bt) has assertive acid texture and coaxes out the best from the grillo grape. Lucido 2012 (○ catarratto; 10,000 bt) is elegant on the nose with marine notes to the fore. Deep and rich, Vecchio Samperi Ventennale (○ 6,000 bt) has engrossing complexity and, with flavor and freshness, reveals all the nuances generated by bottle-aging. Marsala Sup. Oro Vigna La Miccia (○ 7,000 bt) appears essential, almost minimalist.

> **vino slow** MARSALA SUP. RIS. 10 ANNI 2004 (○ 8,000 bt) Aromas of disarming complexity — walnut, hazelnut, iodine, saltiness, Mediterranean scrub —followed up by a palate that starts sweet and never ends.

MARSALA (TP)

Florio

Via Florio, 1
tel. 0923 781306
www.cantineflorio.it
info@cantineflorio.it

0 ha - 3,500,000 bt   **10% discount**

PEOPLE - For almost two centuries the name Florio has evoked taste, elegance and refinement. After a brief period out of the picture, the historic Marsala company is now becoming a synonym of these three virtues once more. Alongside its wonderful old cellars, the owners, the Ilva group of Saronno has radically renewed the company image by restoring other spaces and setting up a multi-sensory tasting room. A visit is de rigueur.

VINEYARDS - A great deal of work goes into the selection of the finest grapes, bought in from tried-and-tested grillo and catarratto growers across a vast area near the sea between Marsala and Mazara del Vallo. This is the best land for producing the golden, fleshy grapes that go into Marsala production.

WINES - Drinking Florio's Marsalas is like making a journey through the history of the wine and its area of origin. Marsala Vergine Baglio Florio 2000 (○ 7,000 bt) is complex and rich in the aromas generated by the passing of time, hence dried and candied fruit and almond paste, with a delicately salty, savory palate and a dry, refreshing finish; it's a Great Wine. Elegant, proud and enjoyable, Marsala Vergine Terre Arse 2002 (○ 35,000 bt), plows a classical furrow. With its 90 per cent of residual sugar, Marsala Sup. Semisecco Ambra Ris. Donna Franca (○ 4,000 bt) is well-poised between acidity and softness. Marsala Sup. Semisecco Ambra Targa Ris. 2002 (○ 40,000 bt) is intense and emphatic on the nose.

FERTILIZERS none	FERTILIZERS na
PLANT PROTECTION copper and sulphur	PLANT PROTECTION na
WEED CONTROL mechanical	WEED CONTROL na
YEASTS native	YEASTS selected
GRAPES 10% bought in	GRAPES 100% bought in
CERTIFICATION none	CERTIFICATION none

MENFI (AG)

Planeta

Contrada Dispensa
tel. 091 327965
www.planeta.it
planeta@planeta.it

367 ha - 2,000,000 bt

PEOPLE - Last year we said that in rediscovering the authenticity of single terroirs, Planeta has turned Sicily from "Neverland" to "Everland". This year, partly thanks to new, interesting wines from Etna, we can affirm that Sicily is now "Evermoreland"! For their constant, restless, untiring work, we have to say thanks to Alessio, Santi and Francesca Planeta.

VINEYARDS - Six estates and five wine cellars. The pieces in the puzzle are: Ulmo at Sambuca di Sicilia, Dispensa at Menfi, Buonivini at Noto, Dorilli at Vittoria, Feudo di Mezzo on Etna, and La Baronia at Capo Milazzo. Plus Vittoria, where the sandy soil rests on a stratum of tufa and produces the grapes for Cerasuolo. The head enologist is Patricia Töth.

WINES - All the wines are very good, as usual. The blossomy, delicate Sicilia Alastro 2012 (O grecanico; 100,000 bt) combines a fresh bouquet with grip. We liked the label so much we awarded it the Everyday Wine symbol. **Chardonnay 2011** (O 160,000 bt) happily marries terroir and international style. The inevitable comparison between **Cerasuolo di Vittoria 2011** (● 80,000 bt) and **Cerasuolo di Vittoria Cl. Dorilli 2011** (● 14,000 bt) revealed two wines of great body, a synopsis of the dialogue between soil and grape. Both are magnificent but we prefer the second, which we consider a Great Wine. Etna gave us **Sicilia Eruzione 1614 Carricante 2012** (O 23,000 bt) and **Sicilia Eruzione 1614 Nerello Mascalese 2011** (● 20,000 bt), both minerally, deep and varietal, while from the area of Sicilian baroque came the rich and pleasing **Passito di Noto 2011** (O 21,000 bt) and the juicy **Noto Nero d'Avola Santa Cecilia 2010** (● 50,000 bt).

FERTILIZERS organic-mineral, green manure
PLANT PROTECTION chemical, copper and sulphur
WEED CONTROL mechanical
YEASTS selected
GRAPES 100% estate-grown
CERTIFICATION none

PANTELLERIA (TP)

Ferrandes

Contrada Tracino Kamma
Via del Fante, 8
tel. 0923 915475
www.passitodipantelleriaferrandes.com
dsferrandes@meditel.it

2 ha - 3,000 bt   **10% discount**

❝ Salvatore is the quintessence of the Pantelleria farmer, at home only in his vineyard and in his cellar, converted from a dammuso, a typical stone island dwelling. The place is situated at Mueggen, which can be reached only by secondary, impassable roads. Like his Passito. ❞

PEOPLE - Apparently and to the less attentive observers, Salvatore Ferrandes is the archetype of the island's almost ataraxic immutability. The purity and intelligence of his blue eyes suggest otherwise.

VINEYARDS - The three vineyards are situated in the districts of Mueggen (east-facing at an altitude of 350 meters), Dietro l'isola and Acquedolci (a south-facing vineyard overlooking the sea, planted in 1965). They are trained in traditional lava hollows on sandstone, tufa and pumice. The last two years have been dedicated to the tough job of restructuring the cellar.

WINES - Let's hear what Salvatore has to say. "Of all the phases in the production of Passito two are crucial. The first is the raisining and dehydration of the grapes, which is performed in the open air. Here it's important to prevent the grape from caramelizing. The second involves processes of fermentation. It takes a lot of experience to understand how many grapes to add and when. From raisined to dry, they have to go in in a natural sequence." The release of Del Passito di Pantelleria 2009 (11 hectoliters) has been held back. We consoled ourselves with a second tasting of the 2008, still on the market, and the 2006. Both are richly textured with all the aromas of the raisins on the nose and tactile, almost monumental palates. Their fresh, deep, intriguing complexity come to the surface in the space of seconds — sincere dialog between vineyard, terroir and wine.

FERTILIZERS none
PLANT PROTECTION copper and sulphur
WEED CONTROL mechanical
YEASTS native
GRAPES 100% estate-grown
CERTIFICATION organic

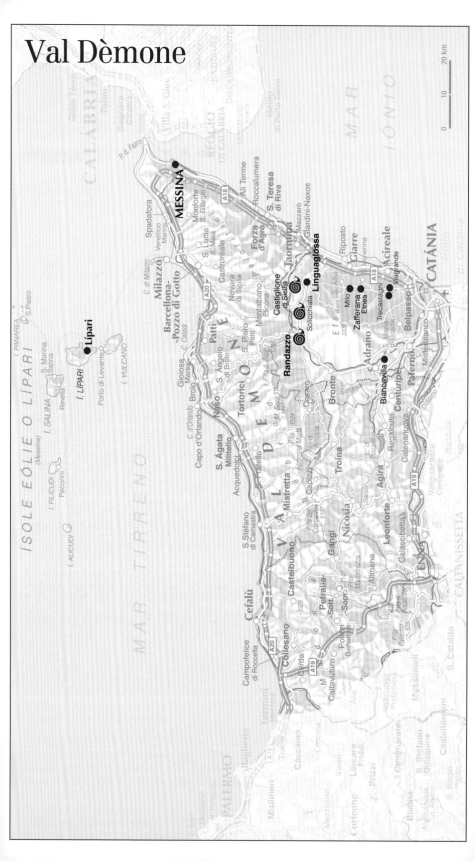

Val Dèmone

CALTAGIRONE (CT)

Gianfranco Daino

Via Croce del Vicario, 115
tel. 0933 58226 - 335 5243345
www.vinidaino.it
info@vinidaino.it

CASTIGLIONE DI SICILIA (CT)

Graci

Contrada Arcuria Passopisciaro
tel. 348 7016773
www.graci.eu
info@graci.eu

---

3 ha - 13,000 bt

PEOPLE - Gianfranco Daino used to do and still does a different job, but his great passion for wine made him dream of having a vineyard all of his own. His adventure began in 2006 when he met Salvo Foti. Gianfranco isn't just another one of the many who have bought a winery as a pastime. On the contrary, courageously and making sacrifices — and with the help of I Vigneri — he has set up an admirably terroir-dedicated company.

VINEYARDS - The vineyard is immersed in the breathtaking Bosco di San Pietro nature reserve, a wild, rugged area with a wealth of biodiversity, one example of which is the famous cork oak (Quercus suber). Fewer than three hectares are planted with bush-trained nero d'Avola, frappato and alicante vines with a density of 9,000 per hectare. The climate is characterized by good air circulation and the altitude, 325 meters above sea level, ensures a considerable temperature range.

WINES - Efforts are concentrated on a single label vinified with a non-interventionist approach to coax out its sense of place. The wine ferments in steel vats with a small amount of unstemmed grapes and ages in old and new barriques and mid-sized casks.

> **vino slow** **SUBER 2011** (● nero d'Avola, frappato, alicante; 6,800 bt) Generous and deep-reaching on the nose, it offers sweet, pervasive notes of black berries and Mediterranean maquis with faint hints of peach and deliciously spicy notes. The palate is full-bodied, flavorsome and juicy, braced by compact tanginess and acidity to prolong the finish. From this year the bottle is stopped with cork from the surrounding woodland of Bosco di San Pietro. Talk about zero food (and drink) miles!

---

18 ha - 55,000 bt   `10% discount`

❝ The idea that by taking something away from the traditional vinification process it's possible to add value by representing the characteristics of the terroir has produced wines of excellence. **❞**

PEOPLE - Owner Alberto Aiello Graci knows what he expects from his wine and now he feels he is getting closer to his objective. His passion is so strong it fuses together his private life and his work in the vineyard. It translates into personified wines that increasingly reflect his own character: young and determined, happy with what he has already achieved and projected towards what tomorrow might bring.

VINEYARDS - The vineyards are situated in three districts: Arcuria and the recently acquired Feudo di Mezzo at an altitude of 600 meters at the heart of the DOC, and the highest, Barbabecchi, at an altitude of 1,000 meters in the Solicchiata area. The difficulties in getting to the latter are set off by the view once you get there, not to mention the unique fragrance of its wine. Alberto has chosen to plant his new vineyards with bush-trained vines on their own roots.

WINES - **Etna Rosso Quota 600 Contrada Arcuria 2011** (● 9,000 bt) is the wine that marked the turnaround. Longer maceration has given structure and massive aromatic complexity. Hence great prospects for the future and the conceptual lightness that ought to distinguish all Etna Rossos. **Etna Bianco 2012** (○ 11,000 bt) is enjoyable. **Etna Rosso 2011** (● 29,000 bt) is characterized by minerality.

> **vino slow** **ETNA BIANCO ARCURIA 2011** (○ 2,000 bt) Intense and solidly built, packed with enfolding saltiness accompanied by welcome freshness and assertive acidity — the volcano in the glass.

FERTILIZERS natural manure
PLANT PROTECTION copper and sulphur
WEED CONTROL mechanical
YEASTS native
GRAPES 100% estate-grown
CERTIFICATION organic

FERTILIZERS natural manure
PLANT PROTECTION copper and sulphur
WEED CONTROL mechanical
YEASTS native
GRAPES 100% estate-grown
CERTIFICATION converting to organics

CASTIGLIONE DI SICILIA (CT)

I Custodi delle vigne dell'Etna

Contrada Moganazzi
tel. 393 1898430
www.icustodi.it
info@icustodi.it

13.5 ha - 35,000 bt

PEOPLE - The volcanic (sic!) Mario Paoluzi is a man with business in his blood. He has now taken over the company that belonged to Mick Hucknall, in which he used to be a partner. With his I Custodi delle vigne dell'Etna project Mario wants to carve out a niche for himself in the Etna wine world, where he is also a member of the I Vigneri consortium. The contribution of enologist Salvo Foti is fundamental.

VINEYARDS - The recipe is the same one that relaunched Etna on the world wine scene: namely high-density bush-trained vines, hand-worked without the use of chemicals, plus plenty of hard work in the vineyard to reduce interventions in the cellar to a bare minimum. The heart of the company is in the Moganazzi district, where a wine new cellar and tasting rooms are to be built. The size of the vines in the ancient Caderara vineyard is amazing.

WINES - This year's new entry is the refreshing cherry-red **Etna Rosato Alnus 2012** (☉ nerello mascalese; 7,000 bt), redolent of fresh cherries with a lingering, sweetish palate. **Etna Rosso Aetneus 2008** (● nerello mascalese, alicante; 17,000 bt), which hails from the oldest vineyards on the north slope of Etna, is the symbol of the terroir. It's an ethereal, warm-toned, deep wine with polished tannins and up-to-the mark harmony.

> **vino slow** ANTE 2011 (○ carricante, grecanico, minnella; 5,500 bt) A wine of stunningly complex aroma and flavor. Understated on the nose it invades the palate with all its force. Freshness and richness move hand-in-hand into a long, long finish. Pleasant surprises are in store for this wine in the future.

CASTIGLIONE DI SICILIA (CT)

Passopisciaro

Frazione Passopisciaro
Contrada Guardiola
tel. 0578 267110
www.passopisciaro.com
info@passopisciaro.com

26 ha - 70,000 bt

PEOPLE - Andrea Franchetti showed great farsightedness when, looking for terroirs to interpret in 2000, he bought a set of vineyards in which, with the experience acquired in Tuscany, he has since achieved amazing results with grapes uncommon in the area. Out of respect for the terroir he has continued to invest in nerello mascalese, selecting it among his various vineyards and entrusting it to the care of the people who have been working there for decades.

VINEYARDS - Properties spread out over five different districts, from the calcareous-volcanic Chiappe Macine at 500 meters of altitude, through Guardiola at 800-1,000 meters, to Rampante, over 1,000 meters high, where the soil is composed exclusively of volcanic sand from ancient lava flows. Each of the districts regale us with wines of varying degrees but always stylish acidity.

WINES - Our favorite cru was **Contrada P 2011** (● 2,700 bt), all pepper, spices, wild strawberries, acidity and harmony. One of this year's finest Italian reds, it is a Great Wine. **Contrada C 2011** (● 2,900 bt), made with grapes from the Chiappe Macine vineyard, releases clear-cut fruity aromas and has an imposing full body. Made with grapes from the 100-year-old vines of the Guardiola vineyard, **Contrada G 2011** (● 2,900 bt) is an intense wine of noteworthy finesse and balance. **Contrada R 2011** (● 2,900 bt), from the highest vineyard in the Rampante district, has terrific acidity and close-knit tannins, and is sure to age well. The first-rate **Franchetti 2011** (● petit verdot, cesanese; 3,400 bt) smacks of cherries just plucked from the tree and has a sweet, flavorsome attack.

FERTILIZERS natural manure	FERTILIZERS natural manure
PLANT PROTECTION copper and sulphur	PLANT PROTECTION copper and sulphur
WEED CONTROL mechanical	WEED CONTROL mechanical
YEASTS native	YEASTS selected
GRAPES 100% estate-grown	GRAPES 100% estate-grown
CERTIFICATION converting to organics	CERTIFICATION none

CASTIGLIONE DI SICILIA (CT)

Girolamo Russo

Frazione Passopisciaro
Via Regina Margherita, 78
tel. 328 3840247
www.girolamorusso.it
info@girolamorusso.it

15 ha - 35,000 bt | **10% discount**

66 Giuseppe Russo is a mild-mannered man of old-style cordiality. A humanist by instinct and a musician at heart, since 2004 he has taken over his father's dedicated work in the vineyard, tending them and launching a hugely successful vinification project. 99

PEOPLE - Giuseppe produces over-the-top but excellent wines which he produces with critical spirit and an open mind.

VINEYARDS - The company, named for Giuseppe's father, owns 15 hectares of vineyards in three districts: San Lorenzo, Feudo and Feudo di Mezzo. It adopts organic methods and deviates from the local conception of vine growing with mostly high-trained plantings. Restructuring work is under way on the cellar to permit greater characterization of the wines.

WINES - **Etna Rosso A'Rina 2011** (● 22,500 bt) offers outstanding value for money. Beautifully textured and enjoyable, it's the most approachable of Giuseppe's wines, which take time to be interpreted. **Etna Rosso Feudo 2011** (● 3,300 bt), a warm wine with conspicuous tannins, has lots of ripe fruit. **Etna Rosso Feudo di Mezzo 2011** (● 2,200 bt) entered the scene with all its force this year: on the nose it has inebriating balsamic notes and proceeds through a palate of great flesh and never-ending tannins into a very long finish. The austere **Etna Rosso San Lorenzo 2011** (● 4,400 bt) begins with placid notes of aromatic herbs and quinine, which are followed by well-shaped tannins — a wine that hits its target without digressions. **Etna Bianco Nerina 2012** (○ 3,000 bt) is well-rounded and fresh.

CASTIGLIONE DI SICILIA (CT)

Tenuta di Fessina

Località Contrada Rovittello
Via Nazionale
tel. 335 7220021
silviamaestrelli@tenutadifessina.com

16 ha - 60,000 bt | **10% discount**

PEOPLE - "Wines of the highest quality come from the frontiers of viticulture. From this difficult terroir we want to get the best wine possible." The words with which agronomist-enologist Federico Curtaz welcomes us to his Rovittello estate. Here an ancient wine pressing building is surrounded by vineyards so magical as to have convinced Federico and Silvia Maestrelli, the well-known Tuscan producer, to buy the whole property in 2007.

VINEYARDS - Most of the estate's vineyards are in the Rovittello district, hugged between two lava flows of different eras. The terroir is one of the coldest and dampest in the area and is home to vines 50 to 90 years old, planted and scrupulously tended by the former owner. He deserves credit for the marvelous wine heritage he has left behind, which is why the Musumeci wine is named for him.

WINES - The owners still reckon they have a lot to learn about the terroir. They thus intend to maintain a basic continuity, evidencing the family ties between wines of different vintages. This year **Etna Rosso Erse 2011** (●12,000 bt) also comes in a white version, **Etna Bianco Erse 2012** (○ carricante; 6,000 bt). Both wines are clean and approachable and reflect the terroir. The first brings out all the scents typical of nerello, infusing them into a supple structure with well-polished tannins, the second is characterized by an austere nose and very pleasing flavor indeed. **Etna Bianco A Puddara 2011** (○ 6,000 bt) is substantial, notably complex and long, a white up there with the best labels in Italy and a Great Wine. The captivating **Sicilia Ero 2012** (● nero d'Avola; 6,000 bt), is an interesting rendering of the grape. We'll wait until next year to taste Etna Rosso Musmeci 2010.

FERTILIZERS manure pellets, natural manure	FERTILIZERS none
PLANT PROTECTION copper and sulphur	PLANT PROTECTION copper and sulphur
WEED CONTROL mechanical	WEED CONTROL mechanical
YEASTS native	YEASTS selected
GRAPES 100% estate-grown	GRAPES 5% bought in
CERTIFICATION organic	CERTIFICATION none

LIPARI (ME)

Tenuta di Castellaro

Via Caolino
tel. 035 233337
www.tenutadicastellaro.it
info@comarkspa.it

RANDAZZO (CT)

I Vigneri

Largo Signore Pietà, 17
tel. 0933 982942
www.ivigneri.it
info@ivigneri.it

7.5 ha - 20,000 bt   **10% discount**

2 ha - 7,000 bt

PEOPLE - The big news this year was the inauguration, on June 23, of a new production cellar. This huge project was the brainchild of the Bergamo-born businessman Massimo Lentsch, struck down on the road to the Aeolian Islands. The facility is a big one for the islands, but has been built with the utmost respect for the environment and equipped with all the most advanced energy-saving technologies.

VINEYARDS - The company's real strength lies in its spectacular vineyards designed and developed by Salvo Foti's I Vigneri consortium. All the vines are bush-trained and very densely planted — quite a sight for lucky visitors. The names of the plots are Cappero, Castellaro, Maggiore, Lisca, Caolino and Gelso, and each is a veritable cru. The viticulture is artisan and involves extremely limited use of chemicals.

WINES - The cellar produces only two wines but they take us aback every time we find them under our noses and on our palates. They are both enological gems and we fail to understand why they haven't forced their way onto the majority of Italian wine lists. The super-scented **Nero Ossidiana 2011** (● corinto, nero d'Avola; 6,500 bt) offers capers and mulberry on the nose and raciness and body on the palate. The warm growing year comes through in a sweetish finish.

vino slow **Bianco Pomice 2011** (● malvasia, carricante; 11,000 bt) A wine with nuances of freshly mown grass and nettles, very pure and intense with a finish of hazelnuts and moss. The definition "minerally" is overused in the wine world these days and should be reserved to wines that really possess the quality. This is one of them!

66 A winery that has salvaged an old winemaking tradition, that safeguards a unique cultural landscape, that heralds the return to the land of a new generation of artisans. 99

PEOPLE - La Maestranza dei Vigneri was the name of an old guild of expert vine dressers. Today I Vigneri is the name of the winery run by Salvo Foti, a well-known Sicilian agronomist-enologist, who has revived and restored dignity to the ancient skill of vine dressing. I Vigneri is also a consortium of companies that still adopt the old methods under Foti's guidance.

VINEYARDS - I Vigneri works according to precise criteria: bush-training, a minimum of 7,000 vines per hectare, preservation of the old vineyards and clonal biodiversity. Every vine is treated individually according to capacity, age and needs. All operations are performed by hand or using rototillers or mules. Chemicals are banned as is irrigation. Worthy of a mention is Maurizio Pagano who, with 40 years' experience under his belt, leads the team that manages the vineyards of all the consortium's members.

WINES - Salvo Foti applies his enological knowledge to reduce interventions in the cellar to a bare minimum, hence to be able to use traditional methods without fear of flawed wines: no refrigeration, selected yeasts or filtrations. **Vinudilice 2012** (☉ alicante, grecanico, minnella; 1,500 bt) is made with grapes from a 100-year-old vineyard at an altitude of 1,300 meters: hyperfloral with fruity, vegetal and sulphurous notes, it impresses for a confident, very long palate of aerial lightness. **Vinupetra 2010** (● 1,200 bt) is made with nerello mascalese grapes and has aromas of ripe cherry and great tangy verve. **Vigneri 2011** (● 1,000 bt), also made with nerello mascalese is a simpler quaffing wine.

FERTILIZERS natural manure
PLANT PROTECTION copper and sulphur
WEED CONTROL mechanical
YEASTS native
GRAPES 100% estate-grown
CERTIFICATION none

FERTILIZERS natural manure
PLANT PROTECTION copper and sulphur
WEED CONTROL mechanical
YEASTS native
GRAPES 100% estate-grown
CERTIFICATION none

RANDAZZO (CT)

Tenuta delle Terre Nere

Contrada Calderara
tel. 095 924002
www.tenutaterrenere.com
info@tenutaterrenere.com

SOLICCHIATA (CT)

Frank Cornelissen

Via Nazionale, 297
tel. 0942 986315
www.frankcornelissen.it
info@frankcornelissen.it

28 ha - 180,000 bt   **10% discount**

12 ha - 35,000 bt

66 Marco De Grazia, a Tuscan businessman who's been in the wine world for over 30 years, speaks to us about Etna as if he'd been born there. In 13 years of passionate, painstaking research he has traveled round the various rural districts, cataloguing them, uncovering their secrets and their distinctive features, coaxing the best out of them. 99

PEOPLE - Marco's love of wine translates into limited production — 5,000 bottles — dedicated to his daughter: Le Vigne di Eli. Profits are donated to the Meyer pediatric institute in Florence.

VINEYARDS - The company owns vineyards in the most representative districts of Etna: Calderara, Guardiola, Santo Spirito and Feudo di Mezzo. In an effort to express the virtues of each parcel and understand its potential, the grapes have always been vinified and bottle separately. All the company's vineyards are on the north face of Etna at altitudes which vary from 600 to 900 meters.

WINES - Every Tenuta delle Terre Nere wine speaks for the terroir it comes from. **Etna Rosso Feudo di Mezzo 2011** (● 7,000 bt) is an energetic, muscular youth, raring to go and conquer all before it. It's a wine that will transform impressive texture into stylish structure in the course of time. The beautifully deft **Etna Rosso Santo Spirito 2011** (● 7,000 bt) enchants with its class, harmony and elegance, which is why it's a Great Wine. Marco's top wine, the earthy, deep-reaching and evocative **Etna Rosso Pre-fillossera Vigna Don Peppino 2011** (● 3,000 bt) is dedicated to the man who has always tended the historical vineyard which grows the grapes for it. **Etna Rosato 2012** (◉ 13,000 bt) is captivating, **Etna Rosso 2011** (● 95,000 bt) and **Etna Bianco 2012** (○ 40,000 bt) are good value.

66 Frank Cornelissen came to Etna from Belgium in 2000. Sensing the potential of the terroir, he bought his first vineyards and began harvesting immediately. He subsequently set the trend in winemaking by using natural methods that recall old practices and conjure up memories. 99

PEOPLE - In 13 years, Frank has reached such a degree of local awareness that he's prepared to predict excellent results from the "next 25 harvests" he intends to make happen.

VINEYARDS - Most of Frank's vineyards are more than 50 years old. They are scattered over the upper reaches of the northern slopes of Etna and are tended with total respect for nature and without the use of synthetic products. Save for the odd exception, the grapes grown are typical local varieties. The ungrafted youngest wines were born of a pre-phylloxera vine in the most prestigious vineyard.

WINES - Prudent use of technology and absolute attention to detail are basic tenets of Frank's philosophy. We'd like to have more time to taste these wines because when they're young the tannins are very stiff. Unfortunately, it's hard to have that time as Cornellissen sells all his bottles the year after the harvest. This is why we tasted **Munjebel 8** (● 6,000 bt) a blend of the 2010 and 2011 vintages. We enjoyed it a lot, proof that the time factor is fundamental. We have thus decided that we'll taste again and review all the crus from the 2012 vintage next year. We're expecting fireworks! **Contadino 2012** (● 9,000 bt) is a non-nonsense wine, seemingly simple on the nose but beautifully deep on the palate. **Magma 2011** (● 1,100 bt) is the summa of all Frank's wines, a synthesis of excellence!

FERTILIZERS natural manure, green manure
PLANT PROTECTION copper and sulphur
WEED CONTROL mechanical
YEASTS selected
GRAPES 30% bought in
CERTIFICATION organic

FERTILIZERS none
PLANT PROTECTION copper and sulphur
WEED CONTROL mechanical
YEASTS native
GRAPES 100% estate-grown
CERTIFICATION organic

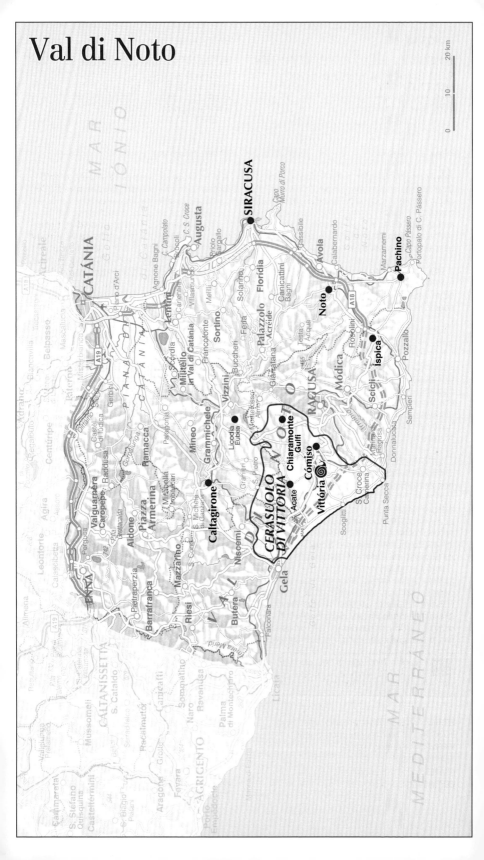

Val di Noto

Cos

S.P. 3 Acate-Chiaramonte, Km. 14,500
tel. 0932 876145
www.cosvittoria.it
info@cosvittoria.it

30 ha - 190,000 bt

66 From the introduction of amphorae to biodynamics, at Cos they've never been afraid of challenging convention to pursue their idea: a wine that speaks of the land, of the vineyard and of local culture. They have grown apace with the rebirth of Cerasuolo, in which they have been the leading players. 99

PEOPLE - Giusto Occhipinti and Giambattista Cilia have come a long way since 1980 when, as mere 20-year-olds, they established Cos.

VINEYARDS - The Cos vineyards are at Vittoria, in the Bastonaca and Fontane districts, where they sit on a plateau at an altitude of 250 meters. The lean, deep limestone soil, the influence of the sea, constant air circulation and sharp temperature swings give the grapes perfect ripe phenolics and contained alcohol proof (incidentally, Cos is fighting to have Cerasuolo's alcohol content reduced in the production disciplinary).

WINES - Elegant, expressive and engaging: these are the three distinctive traits of the wines from Cos. Amphorae and concrete vats are used in the cellar, along with large barrels for some wines. The iconic wine continues to be **Cerasuolo di Vittoria Cl. 2010** (● nero d'Avola, frappato; 70,000 bt), which is aged in concrete vats and large barrels. **Nero di Lupo 2012** (● nero d'Avola; 16.000 bt) is complex and racy. The two wines produced in jars stay on the skins for seven months: the earthy, minerally **Pithos Rosso 2011** (● nero d'Avola, frappato; 25,000 bt) has depth and character, while **Pithos Bianco 2011** (○ grecanico; 8,000 bt) has complex aromas of flower petals and spices with a dry, tangy palate.

> **vino slow FRAPPATO 2012** (● 38,000 bt) A phenomenal wine, fresh, pure, intensely scented. Incredible, unadulterated goût de terroir at an unbeatable price.

FERTILIZERS biodynamic preparations
PLANT PROTECTION copper and sulphur
WEED CONTROL mechanical
YEASTS native
GRAPES 100% estate-grown
CERTIFICATION organic

Arianna Occhipinti

Contrada Fossa di Lupo
SP68 Vittoria-Pedalino km 5,4
tel. 339 7383580
www.agricolaocchipinti.it
info@agricolaocchipinti.it

18 ha - 110,000 bt

66 For Arianna, the natural approach isn't an end but a means, the only one possible for producing a vin de terroir. 99

PEOPLE - In 2004, after graduating in enology, Arianna returned to Vittoria where she quickly showed herself to be one of the ablest, most sensitive interpreters of the terroir. Now, at 31, she's a star in the natural wine firmament. She featured in a documentary, she has written a book, she has received numerous awards — but none of this has come out of the blue. On the contrary, it's the fruit of this intelligent young lady's great dedication.

VINEYARDS - The historic nucleus of the company's vineyard is in the Fossa di Lupo district. Arianna has recently bought land in the adjacent Bombolieri district and also rents two hectares of old frappato vines in the Pettineo district. Prevalently limestone soil, constant ventilation and sharp day-to-night temperature swings produce stylish wines with a strong sense of place. The rest comes from eco-friendly organically certified agriculture, interpreted practically with elements of biodyamics here and there.

WINES - Pure and expressive, Arianna's impress with their naturalness in the glass. **SP 68 Rosso 2012** (● frappato, nero d'Avola; 75,000 bt), aged in steel vats, is fruity and earthy, while **Cerasuolo di Vittoria Cl. Grotte Alte 2008** (● 4,500 bt) is floral, tangy and inviting. Also excellent is **SP 68 Bianco 2012** (○ moscato di Alessandria, albanello; 27,000 bt), which is macerated for ten days on the skins; underscored by the aromas of the moscato grapes, it is refreshing and supple on the palate.

> **vino slow FRAPPATO 2011** (● 27,000 bt) Racy, assertive wine with somewhat eccentric aromas as always. Curious fruity, lip-smacking notes are followed up by a palate redolent of fruit juice — organic, naturally!

FERTILIZERS biodynamic preparations, green manure
PLANT PROTECTION copper and sulphur
WEED CONTROL mechanical
YEASTS native
GRAPES 100% estate-grown
CERTIFICATION organic

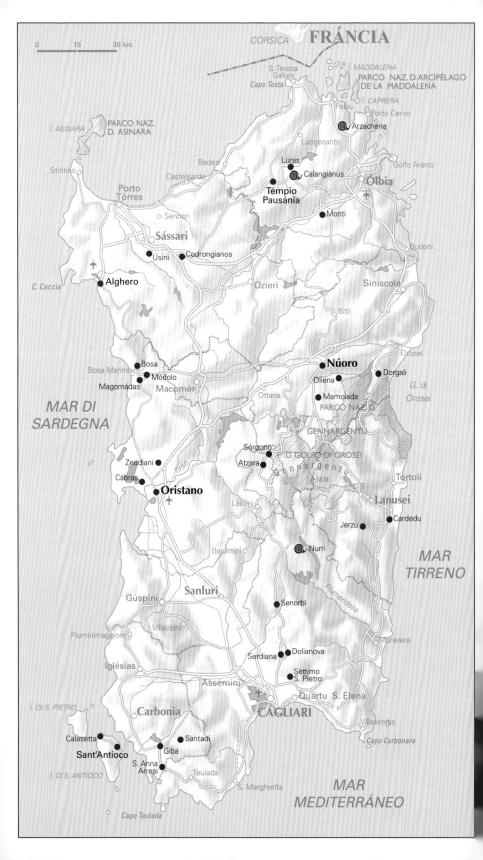

SARDINIA

Sardinia, a region of breathtaking beauty and a "melting pot" of the most diverse farming crops. A very large island which, precisely on account of its size, comprises a variety of landscapes and microclimates almost without compare in Italy, a variety that has fostered the birth and spread of a huge number of native grapes, not to mention vine-training systems that vary greatly from one place to another. Summing up our tastings, we came to the conclusion that in some areas commendable results have been achieved, whereas in others, alas, the 2012 vintage was adversely affected by strictly climatic factors.

First the bad news. This time round Gallura fails to stand out as it did in the past. In 2012 extreme rainfall in late August and early September jeopardized the quality of the grape harvest. Nonetheless, the winemakers cited in *Slow Wine* did a great job not only in saving the savable, but also in coming up with well-crafted wines, in some cases, as we acknowledge with our symbols, of the highest standard. True, the number of labels of excellence is inevitably lower than in the recent past, but, in view of the events of the year, things could have been worse. Another sore point is Vernaccia: never as this year have we tasted so few wines from this fascinating typology. Which is a great pity since, well vinified, it can be one of the most intriguing sipping wines in the world.

Now the good news, of which there's plenty. The two principal red grapes, carignano and cannonau, performed brilliantly. More specifically, the cannonau from the island's most important winegrowing area, the Jerzu-Nuoro-Dorgali triangle, filled us with emotion. Between cooperatives and private cellars, many producers are now making excellent wines, very typical in their aromas and flavors. The Sulcis lived up to expectations. At least enologically speaking, the latest news in from Sant'Antioco seems very good indeed.

We'd like to end with an appeal to launch an international campaign to raise the profile of this latter area's stupendous ungrafted bush-trained carignano vineyards. Considering the high average age of local winemakers, they risk being abandoned. Which would be a huge pity.

snails

238 ORLANDO TONDINI

238 GIUSEPPE SEDILESU

239 PANEVINO

bottles

239 FERRUCCIO DEIANA

Orlando Tondini

Località San Leonardo
tel. 079 661359
www.cantinatondini.it
cantinatondini@tiscali.it

22 ha - 80,000 bt · **10% discount**

66 Orlando Tondini has always believed in this life and professional project of his, centered round professionalism and commitment in the field. His style his sober and respectful of human and natural rhythms, a perfect synthesis of "good, clean and fair". 99

PEOPLE - Orlando's four children are accompanying him on his adventure. One of them, Antonio, is an enthusiastic and able enologist and it is he who gives life to the cellar's splendid wines.

VINEYARDS - The vineyards are situated on the granitic sandy soil of the valley between Luras and Calangianus. The climate is well-ventilated, characterized by day-to-night temperature swings, perfect for the production of rich, scented, stylish wines. Great attention is paid to work in the vineyard, where thinning and topping are carried out according to changes in the weather. Yields never exceed 50 quintals per hectare.

WINES - Antonio is working to turn his clear idea of precise, deep, drinkable wines into reality. Tasting for a second time the marvelous Laicheddu 2009 (a vintage we reviewed in the 2013 guide), we were more than impressed by its aromatic complexity and nose-palate finesse. The taut, mineral **Vermentino di Gallura Sup.** Karagnanj 2012 (O 65,000 bt) is endowed with excellent freshness and treats the nose to marvelous aromas of small spring flowers and aromatic herbs with lemony notes. **Taroni 2011** (● cannonau, nebbiolo, sangiovese; 5,000 bt) has luscious fruit with a hint of rosemary on the nose and clear-cut, nicely fresh flavor. **Siddaju 2010** (● nebbiolo, cannonau, cagnulari, sangiovese; 3,000 bt) suggests red-currant jelly over a structure buttressed by the exact dose of acidity.

FERTILIZERS none
PLANT PROTECTION chemical, copper and sulphur
WEED CONTROL mechanical
YEASTS selected
GRAPES 100% estate-grown
CERTIFICATION none

Giuseppe Sedilesu

Via Vittorio Emanuele II, 64
tel. 0784 56791
www.giuseppesedilesu.com
giuseppesedilesu@tiscali.it

15 ha - 130,000 bt · **10% discount**

66 Investment in old vineyards, manual vineyard operations (some of the plowing is carried out by oxen), organic cultivation, natural vinification without recourse to chemicals, superb wines — a model winery. 99

PEOPLE - Giuseppe Sedilesu and his wife Grazia established the winery in the 1970s when Giuseppe lost his factory job. The first bottle was commercialized in 2000. Now 13 family members contribute to its fortunes.

VINEYARDS - The vineyards sit at an altitude of 600 meters, where the soil is composed of a breakdown of granitic rock. The vines are very old, most of them having been planted more than 30 years ago, some a hundred. They are cultivated with classic bush pruning and the vineyards are plowed twice a year, by oxen on the steepest slopes. Biodynamic techniques are now being tested too.

WINES - The range submitted this year was very impressive indeed. We were particularly fond of **Cannonau di Sardegna Mamuthone 2011** (● 70,000 bt), aged for 12 years in 40-hectoliter barrels. The nose is blossomy and fruity, while the entry into the palate is classical, grapey and natural, followed up by long, juicy progression and a splendid sweet tannic finish. **Cannonau di Sardegna S'Annada 2011** (● 15,000 bt) is simpler. The somewhat rough Cannonau di **Sardegna Carnevale Ris. 2010** (● 7,500 bt) has a stiff finish, likely the result of barrique-aging.

vino slow CANNONAU DI SARDEGNA BALLU TUNDU RIS. 2010 (● 8000 bt) A true masterpiece, vinified with grapes from the over-100-year-old grapes in the highest vineyards. Full-flavored, savory, rich and deep with fine, noble tannins, it is a faithful mirror of a great terroir.

FERTILIZERS biodynamic preparations, green manure
PLANT PROTECTION copper and sulphur
WEED CONTROL mechanical
YEASTS native
GRAPES 30% bought in
CERTIFICATION organic

NURRI (CA)

Panevino

Via Trento, 61
tel. 348 8241060
mancagfranco@tiscali.it

6 ha - 12,500 bt

66 Ancestral agriculture carried forward with insight and great sensibility combined with extraordinary skill — these are the qualities embodied by Gianfranco Manca, the last winemaker left in Nurri. Downy mildew, extreme fatigue, gratuitous red-tape — he has survived all this and more! 99

PEOPLE - Gianfranco runs the winery with the indispensable help of his wife Elena Gallo. Gianfranco exports almost all his output and bottles are hard to come by in Italy. Lucky him, poor us!

VINEYARDS - It's as if Gianfranco knew the vines he cultivates one by one. Speaking with him, one has the impression he sees them as living creatures, not mere fruit trees. He owns a vast number of plots, some with ultra-centenary vines, twisted and gnarled like open-air sculptures. Interventions are reduced to a bare minimum. Gianfranco is effectively at the mercy of nature, but the fact doesn't appear to bother him overmuch!

WINES - Forget all about neat, tidy wines; this isn't a place obsessed with perfect style. Nor with brett or unchecked volatiles. Here it is the rough terrain that gives life to unique labels, masterpieces that are inimitable and very different one from another. Though no sulphur whatsoever is added, the wines, albeit fragile, conserve great integrity. We were bowled over by **CiCiPi 2011** (● cannonau; 2,000 bt), its intriguing spiciness, its hints of myrtle, its racy palate, its sweet tannins. The immense **U.V.A. 2011** (● cannonau, local grapes; 4,000 bt) has a delicately astringent suite of red berry aromas. **Piccadè 2012** (● carignano, monica; 4,000 bt) is warmer and more mature with copious alcohol.

SETTIMO SAN PIETRO (CA)

Ferruccio Deiana

Via Gialeto, 7
tel. 070 767960
www.ferrucciodeiana.it
deiana.ferruccio@tiscali.it

74 ha - 400,000 bt

PEOPLE - After studying enology in Conegliano, Ferruccio Deiana became a wholesale wine merchant. In the 1990s he decided to go back to the land and the family tradition of farming. The first part of the cellar was built in 1995. Ferruccio's collaborators are his son Dario, his wife Maria Grazia Perra, and consultant enologist Riccardo Cotarella.

VINEYARDS - The extensive vineyards are mainly situated in the zone denominated Parteolla and most of the vine rows run round the cellar. Throughout the winter, the spectacular Staini Saliu, a small freshwater lake among the vineyards, is home to a colony of flamingoes. The agricultural methods are impeccable and serious attempts have already been made to go organic.

WINES - The range of wines submitted was excellent. The magnificent Everyday Wine, Cannonau di Sardegna Sileno 2011 (● 90,000 bt), is matured in large barrels and stands out for aging potential and drinkability. It's fleshy, full-flavored and perfectly varietal. Its "elder brother" **Cannonau di Sardegna Sileno Ris. 2011** (● 10,000 bt) doesn't disappoint either. It has a darker, more austere mood with a precise finish of leather and tobacco. **Ajana 2010** (● cannonau, carignano, bovale; 14,000 bt), which ages 18 months in barriques, has tones of Mediterranean maquis and sweet spices. The two whites, **Vermentino di Sardegna Donnikalia 2012** (O 90,000 bt) and **Vermentino di Sardegna Arvali 2012** (O 55,000 bt) are both pleasant and refreshing. **Oirad 2011** (O nasco, malvasia, moscato; 7,000 bt) is all honey, apricots and butter.

FERTILIZERS none
PLANT PROTECTION copper and sulphur
WEED CONTROL mechanical
YEASTS native
GRAPES 100% estate-grown
CERTIFICATION none

FERTILIZERS none
PLANT PROTECTION chemical, copper and sulphur
WEED CONTROL mechanical
YEASTS selected
GRAPES 100% estate-grown
CERTIFICATION none

INDEX of wineries

INDEX of places

TASTING notes

GIVE THIS GUIDE ANOTHER CHANCE.
WASTE SORTING MEANS THAT PAPER CAN BE RECYCLED AND REBORN.
COMIECO MAKES SURE IT IS

comieco
Consorzio Nazionale Recupero e Riciclo
degli Imballaggi a base Cellulosica